# HEGEL'S CENTURY

The remarkable lectures that Hegel gave in Berlin in the 1820s generated an exciting and stimulating intellectual atmosphere that lasted for decades. From the 1830s, many students flocked to Berlin to study with people who had studied with Hegel, and both his original students, such as Feuerbach and Bauer, and later arrivals including Kierkegaard, Engels, Bakunin and Marx, evolved into leading nineteenth-century thinkers. Jon Stewart's panoramic study of Hegel's deep influence upon the nineteenth century in turn reveals what that century contributed to the wider history of philosophy. It shows how Hegel's notions of "alienation" and "recognition" became the central motifs for the era's thinking; how these concepts spilled over into other fields – like religion, politics, literature, and drama; and how they created a cultural phenomenon so rich and pervasive that it can truly be called "Hegel's century." This book is required reading for historians of ideas as well as of philosophy.

JON STEWART is a fellow of the Institute of Philosophy at the Slovak Academy of Sciences.

# HEGEL'S CENTURY

## Alienation and Recognition in a Time of Revolution

### JON STEWART

*Institute of Philosophy, Slovak Academy of Sciences*

CAMBRIDGE
UNIVERSITY PRESS

# CAMBRIDGE
## UNIVERSITY PRESS

University Printing House, Cambridge CB2 8BS, United Kingdom

One Liberty Plaza, 20th Floor, New York, NY 10006, USA

477 Williamstown Road, Port Melbourne, VIC 3207, Australia

314–321, 3rd Floor, Plot 3, Splendor Forum, Jasola District Centre,
New Delhi – 110025, India

103 Penang Road, #05–06/07, Visioncrest Commercial, Singapore 238467

Cambridge University Press is part of the University of Cambridge.

It furthers the University's mission by disseminating knowledge in the pursuit of
education, learning, and research at the highest international levels of excellence.

www.cambridge.org
Information on this title: www.cambridge.org/9781316519981
DOI: 10.1017/9781009019828

© Jon Stewart 2021

First published 2021

Printed in the United Kingdom by TJ Books Limited, Padstow Cornwall

*A catalogue record for this publication is available from the British Library.*

ISBN 978-1-316-51998-1 Hardback

For Katalin

# CONTENTS

vii

# ACKNOWLEDGMENTS

The present work represents the culmination of a long period of study and research. Along the way I have benefited from the generous help of a number of people. The manuscript profited significantly from discussions with students in my classes on nineteenth-century philosophy at the Bratislava International School of Liberal Arts (Slovakia) in the spring of 2019 and the University of Szeged (Hungary) in the fall of 2019. I am grateful to Samuel Abraham and Zoltán Gyenge for their kind invitations to offer these courses at their respective institutions.

An earlier version of a part of Chapter 8 was presented as the keynote speech at the conference "The Registers of Philosophy II" on May 14, 2016, in Budapest. This conference was organized by the Hungarian Academy of Sciences and the Pázmány Péter Catholic University. An earlier version of a part of Chapter 4 was presented as a lecture entitled "Feuerbach's Conception of Theology or Philosophy of Religion as Anthropology" at the conference "Memory and Anticipation as Anthropological Phenomena" in Modra-Harmonia, Slovakia, on May 14, 2019. This lecture was published as "Feuerbach's Conception of Theology or Philosophy of Religion as Anthropology," in *Modern and Postmodern Crises of Symbolic Structures: Essays in Philosophical Anthropology*, edited by Peter Šajda, Leiden and Boston: Brill Rodopi, 2021 (*Studies in the History of Western Philosophy*, vol. 356), pp. 79–92. I thank the organizers of these conferences for the opportunity to present my work on these occasions. A part of Chapter 7 appeared as "Kierkegaard as a Thinker of Alienation," in the *Kierkegaard Studies Yearbook*, 2019, pp. 193–216.

I am grateful to my colleagues at the Institute of Philosophy at the Slovak Academy of Sciences, from whom I have learned so much: František Novosád, Peter Šajda, Róbert Karul, and Jaroslava Vydrová. I humbly stand in their debt. I am also thankful to Jana Hutárová and Gerhard Schreiber for kindly helping me gain access to some of the materials needed for this study.

This work was produced at the Institute of Philosophy, Slovak Academy of Sciences. It was supported by the Agency VEGA as part of the project Synergy and Conflict as Sources of Cultural Identity, No. 2/0025/20.

# PREFACE

The target audience of this work is advanced students and general readers. The hope is that it can be used as a kind of a companion or textbook in classes on philosophy or the history of ideas. Each chapter begins with a brief account of the life and work of the figure in question. The analyses are focused on close readings of central texts from these figures. In keeping with the goal of readability and accessibility for nonspecialists, I have, in the footnotes, provided references to both the original texts and easily accessible English translations and editions. While I have generally used the most recent editions and translations of the relevant works in line with modern scholarship, in some cases I have made use of earlier editions (and the corresponding earlier translations based on them) since these were the editions that the authors under examination were working with. In the same spirit, I have generally avoided quoting in foreign languages and have attempted to clarify the technical terms as they arise.

Given the nature of the work as a general overview, I have refrained from entering into arguments and debates with other scholars and their interpretations. The use of secondary literature has been generally limited to simple recommendations for further reading on the specific topics treated. I have tried instead to present a readable and informative account of what I take to be the key thinkers and issues, all the while following the thread of the topics outlined in the Introduction.

~

# Introduction

When G. W. F. Hegel came to Berlin in 1818 to assume a professorship at the recently founded Royal Friedrich Wilhelm's University, he was already a well-known philosopher in the Germanophone world. The author of *The Phenomenology of Spirit*, the *Encyclopedia of the Philosophical Sciences*, and the *Science of Logic*, he was regarded by the Prussian authorities as a suitable successor to the celebrated and controversial Johann Gottlieb Fichte, who had died in 1814. During Hegel's tenure in Berlin, which lasted until his death in 1831, he gave a series of increasingly popular lecture courses that attracted students from all over Europe.[1] A remarkable generation came to learn from him, which included figures such as the philosophers Ludwig Feuerbach, Bruno Bauer, and Max Stirner, the theologian David Friedrich Strauss, and the poet Heinrich Heine. These men found inspiration in his ideas and made use of them in different ways as their own thought developed.

After Hegel's death in 1831, a group of his students set to work to create the first collected edition of his writings.[2] Over the next decade or so, they republished the four major monographs that Hegel had produced during his lifetime, along with his various articles and reviews. Aware of the importance of his lectures, they included these in their edition based on the redacted transcriptions of Hegel's notes, when available, and those of his students. These notes were then collated and printed for the first time as the *Lectures*

---

[1] See the useful "Übersicht über Hegels Berliner Vorlesungen," in the edition of Hegel's *Berliner Schriften: 1818-1831*, ed. by Johannes Hoffmeister (Hamburg: Felix Meiner, 1956), pp. 743-749. This overview testifies, for example, that Hegel had 116 students on his course "The History of Philosophy" in the winter semester of 1825-1826, 124 students on his course "The Philosophy of World History" in the winter semester of 1826-1827, 119 students on his course "The Philosophy of Religion" in the summer semester of 1827, and 200 students on his course "On the Proofs of God's Existence" in the summer semester of 1829.

[2] *Georg Wilhelm Friedrich Hegel's Werke. Vollständige Ausgabe*, vols. 1-18, ed. by Ludwig Boumann, Friedrich Förster, Eduard Gans, Karl Hegel, Leopold von Henning, Heinrich Gustav Hotho, Philipp Marheineke, Karl Ludwig Michelet, Karl Rosenkranz, and Johannes Schulze (Berlin: Duncker und Humblot, 1832-1845).

1

on the *Philosophy of History*,[3] the *Lectures on the History of Philosophy*,[4] the *Lectures on Aesthetics*,[5] and the *Lectures on the Philosophy of Religion*.[6] These lectures did much to increase Hegel's fame and importance, and many of the things that we today associate with his philosophy appear only in these lectures and not in the published works. In their edition the editors also supplemented two of the works that Hegel published in his lifetime, the *Philosophy of Right* and the *Encyclopedia of the Philosophical Sciences*, with "additions" to the individual paragraphs, which were again taken from student notes.

This edition was published from 1832 until 1845, and with each new volume, new discussions and controversies about Hegel's philosophy erupted. At this time students continued to flock to Berlin in the hope of studying with those who had been Hegel's students. There thus arose a second generation of what might be regarded as Hegel students at a second remove, that is, those who never attended his lectures since they only arrived in Berlin after his death, but who studied under Hegel's followers and were caught up in the buzz surrounding his philosophy. Many of those who came to Berlin during this time spoke of a kind of magical intellectual atmosphere that spread from the lecture hall to the coffee houses and beer halls. Among this talented second generation were thinkers and writers such as Karl Marx, Friedrich Engels, Søren Kierkegaard, and Ivan Turgenev. The Russian revolutionary anarchist Mikhail Bakunin reflects on his experience with Hegel's philosophy during his time in Berlin:

> Hegel . . . died at the end of 1831. But he left behind him at the Universities of Berlin, Königsberg, and Halle a whole school of young professors, editors of his works, and ardent adherents and interpreters of his

---

[3] G. W. F. Hegel, *Vorlesungen über die Philosophie der Geschichte*, ed. by Eduard Gans, vol. 9 (1837), in *Hegel's Werke*. (English translation: *The Philosophy of History*, trans. by J. Sibree [New York: Willey Book Co., 1944]. *Lectures on the Philosophy of World History*, vols. 1-3, ed. and trans. by Robert F. Brown and Peter C. Hodgson, with the assistance of William G. Geuss [Oxford: Clarendon Press, 2011ff].)

[4] G. W. F. Hegel, *Vorlesungen über die Geschichte der Philosophie*, vols. 1-3, ed. by Karl Ludwig Michelet, vols. 13-15 (1833-1836), in *Hegel's Werke*. (English translation: *Lectures on the History of Philosophy*, vols. 1-3, trans. by E. S. Haldane [London: K. Paul, Trench, Trübner, 1892-1896; Lincoln and London: University of Nebraska Press, 1995].)

[5] G. W. F. Hegel, *Vorlesungen über die Aesthetik*, vols. 1-3, ed. by Heinrich Gustav Hotho, vols. 10.1-3 (1835-1838), in *Hegel's Werke*. (English translation: *Hegel's Aesthetics. Lectures on Fine Art*, vols. 1-2, trans. by T. M. Knox [Oxford: Clarendon Press, 1975, 1998].)

[6] G. W. F. Hegel, *Vorlesungen über die Philosophie der Religion*, vols. 1-2, ed. by Philipp Marheineke, vols. 11-12 (1832), in *Hegel's Werke*. (English translation: *Lectures on the Philosophy of Religion*, vols. 1-3, trans. by E. B. Speirs and J. Burdon Sanderson [London: Routledge and Kegan Paul; New York: Humanities Press, 1962, 1968, 1972]; *Lectures on the Philosophy of Religion*, vols. 1-3, ed. by Peter C. Hodgson, trans. by Robert F. Brown, P. C. Hodgson, and J. M. Stewart with the assistance of H. S. Harris [Berkeley: University of California Press, 1984-1987].)

doctrines. Thanks to their tireless efforts, those doctrines were rapidly disseminated not only throughout Germany but in many other European countries . . . . They attracted a multitude of German and non-German intellects to Berlin as to a vital source of new light, not to say a new revelation. Unless you lived in those times, you will never understand how powerful the fascination of this philosophical system was in the 1830s and 1840s. It was believed that the eternally sought Absolute had finally been found and understood, and that it could be bought wholesale or retail in Berlin.[7]

Looking back many decades after the fact, Friedrich Engels speaks with the same tone of excitement, describing the infectious nature of Hegel's philosophy during this time:

One can imagine what a tremendous effect this Hegelian system must have produced in the philosophy-tinged atmosphere of Germany. It was a triumphal procession which lasted for decades and which by no means came to a standstill on the death of Hegel. On the contrary, from 1830 to 1840 Hegelianism reigned most exclusively, and to a greater or lesser extent infected even its opponents. It was precisely in this period that Hegelian views, consciously or unconsciously, most extensively permeated the most diversified sciences.[8]

While Engels and Bakunin describe the period that they experienced in Berlin immediately after Hegel's death, this same nostalgic view is taken by Karl Rosenkranz, who describes the earlier period when Hegel was delivering his famous lectures in the 1820s:

Men from every class attended his lectures. Students from all parts of Germany, from every European nation, especially Poland, but also Greeks and Scandinavians sat at his feet and listened to his magic words . . . . for the most part the enthusiasm of his auditors was genuine, and in this enthusiasm the University of Berlin experienced one of its most beautiful epochs.[9]

All of these thinkers testify to the special intellectual atmosphere in Berlin that arose in connection with Hegel's philosophy both during his lifetime and in the decades after his death. They were caught up by this in their youth, and the

[7] Mikhail Bakunin, *Statism and Anarchy*, trans. by Marshall S. Shatz (Cambridge: Cambridge University Press, 2005), p. 130.
[8] Friedrich Engels, "Ludwig Feuerbach und der Ausgang der klassischen deutschen Philosophie," in *Marx-Engels-Werke*, vols. 1–46, ed. by the Institut für Marxismus-Leninismus (Berlin: Dietz, 1956–2018), vol. 21, p. 270. (English translation: *Ludwig Feuerbach and the Outcome of Classical German Philosophy*, ed. by C. P. Dutt [New York: International Publishers, 1941], p. 15.)
[9] Karl Rosenkranz, *Georg Wilhelm Friedrich Hegel's Leben* (Berlin: Duncker und Humblot, 1844), p. 379f.

excitement and enthusiasm for Hegel's ideas haunted them throughout their lives.

This special atmosphere also spilled over into other countries, where Hegel's ideas were presented by his international students as they returned home. The Dane Søren Kierkegaard recalls the great sensation that was caused at the University of Copenhagen when Hegel's philosophy was introduced there in 1837.[10] Somewhat suspicious of the new trend, he recalls, "Indeed, there was a matchless movement and excitement over the system then, and . . . there was hardly anyone in the whole kingdom, or at least in the whole capital, who in one way or another was not related to the system in suspenseful expectation."[11] Another eyewitness to the reception of Hegel's thought in the Kingdom of Denmark writes:

> One had to have lived at that time to be able to conceive of the strange being [of Hegelian philosophy], indeed, even to be able to believe in the possibility of it. Under the absolutism of German philosophy, every thinker was zealous to work on the Tower of Babel of fantasy; what we heard all around us was nothing less than that every grandiloquent speaker made it virtually his goal in life to build a tower even higher. We were told that the universe with all of its large and small secret niches had been investigated and explained in the Concept; all riddles were solved; Hegel and his host of disciples in Berlin had finished the job . . . . After a short time this was the only air we inhaled.[12]

All of these excited authors describe a unique moment in the history of philosophy, which they were witness to. They concede that their powers as writers fail them when they try to convey adequately the electric and energizing mood that they experienced as young men.

What was it about Hegel's thought that was able to cause such a stir among so many highly talented thinkers coming from different countries and academic backgrounds? The present work represents an attempt to address this question. This is a selective history of European philosophy in the nineteenth century. The guiding idea is that the story of Continental philosophy in this period can be understood as the story of Hegel's philosophy, which was

---

[10] *Søren Kierkegaards Papirer*, vols. I to XI–3, ed. by Peter Andreas Heiberg, Victor Kuhr, and Einer Torsting (Copenhagen: Gyldendal, 1909–1948), vol. X–6, B 171, p. 262; *Søren Kierkegaard's Journals and Papers*, vols. 1–6, ed. and trans. by Howard V. Hong and Edna H. Hong (Bloomington and London: Indiana University Press, 1967–1978), vol. 6, 6748, p. 395. See Jon Stewart, *A History of Hegelianism in Golden Age Denmark*, Tome II, *The Martensen Period: 1837–1842* (Copenhagen: C. A. Reitzel, 2007) (*Danish Golden Age Studies*, vol. 3), pp. 1–11.

[11] *Søren Kierkegaards Papirer*, vol. X–6, B 137; *Søren Kierkegaard's Journals and Papers*, vol. 6, 6636.

[12] Johannes Fibiger, *Mit Liv og Levned, som jeg selv har forstaaet det*, ed. by Karl Gjellerup (Copenhagen: Gyldendal, 1898), p. 73.

disseminated and modified in different ways by later thinkers. The present work takes as its point of departure the intellectual milieu at the University of Berlin, which was the fountain of inspiration that nourished the leading figures of the age over a period of several decades.

The large number of interesting figures and philosophical writers that run through this period renders it impossible to aim at systematic or exhaustive coverage. For this work I have tried to isolate certain themes that I take to be defining and characteristic of this dynamic time. The text begins with Hegel's *Phenomenology of Spirit* in 1807 and ends with the death of Friedrich Engels in 1895. It tries to follow a more or less continuous line of thought that connects these thinkers and other intermediary ones. The goal is to try to see the texts and ideas as figuring in an ongoing dialogue with one another.

## Alienation and Recognition as the Guiding Thread

The history of philosophy in the nineteenth century is a complex labyrinth of crisscrossing thinkers, texts, topics, and arguments. As a result, works on this period are often difficult to read for nonspecialists, who quickly get overwhelmed, finding themselves lost in the details. This makes it hard to appreciate the richness and originality of this period and its contribution to the history of philosophy generally. The goal of this work is to present an introduction to this period for students and more general readers that avoids this problem. In order to achieve this goal, I have selected a handful of themes that run throughout the period. These have been used to organize the text. This strategy has the advantage that it allows for a single continuous narrative to be followed, and this in turn facilitates an understanding of the individual figures since it allows the reader to place them in a concrete context and to compare and contrast them with other thinkers on specific issues. The obvious disadvantage, however, is that this is only a selection of themes, which, despite their centrality and importance, in no way exhaust the period under examination. This is a natural shortcoming of the genre of the history of philosophy – and indeed the history of anything – and is not specific to the present work. It lies in the nature of interpretation itself that certain things are focused on, while others are relegated to a secondary role or neglected altogether. The success of the interpretation offered by this work can only be evaluated by an examination of whether the selected themes have an explanatory power and whether the story told is insightful and meaningful. The interpretive strategy presented here, I believe, makes possible a wide overview of the tradition of Continental philosophy from the period and helps us to make sense of a great many of its major figures and key texts. Moreover, it helps us appreciate the specific or characteristic contributions of the nineteenth century to the history of philosophy in general. Of course, I readily recognize that other researchers might well select different themes and come to very different conclusions, thereby presenting a very different picture of the period in question.

Thematically the focus in this investigation is on a number of key concepts, such as freedom, human nature, self-consciousness, rebellion, history, subjectivity, crisis, and God, but there are two related concepts that connect all of these: alienation and recognition. Alienation is a notion that arises with Hegel's philosophy and resonates throughout the rest of the century in the work of several other thinkers. It can arguably be regarded as *a defining*, if not *the defining*, feature of the history of nineteenth-century philosophy, at least in the German tradition, broadly construed. The phenomenon of alienation, of course, existed long before this, but it only became an issue of explicit philosophical consideration in this period. This was the first time that alienation was examined as a concept in its own right.

What is alienation, and why is this such an important idea? This is not an easy question since there are many different definitions of it. At its most basic level, alienation means some kind of separation or division. We are alienated from something when we are separated from it. This basic idea is reflected in the original meaning of the word, which was used to refer to the transfer of property by means of sale or gift. For example, instead of saying that someone sold a piece of land, one could say that someone *alienated* it; that is, someone, so to speak, separated themselves from the land that they had previously owned. Today this linguistic usage is antiquated. Nowadays we are more accustomed to using the word "alienation" to describe the sense of estrangement that we might feel, for example, from our community, society, or the world in general. We sometimes hear people say that they feel alienated from some person or institution. Here again the sense of separation is implicit since the idea is that one feels separated from something to which one should, under different circumstances, have a positive relation.

The sense of separation is evident in the two German words for this term, which can be found in Hegel and later thinkers. The term *Entäusserung* means literally "externalization" in the sense that something that was inner becomes outward or comes to visible expression.[13] The other term, *Entfremdung*, means literally "being foreign *(fremd)*" to something. This second term corresponds best to our usual usage of feeling alienated. English translators have sometimes attempted to capture this linguistic distinction by rendering *Entfremdung* as "estrangement" and *Entäusserung* as "alienation."

If alienation means a kind of separation, then its opposite would be *reconciliation* or *identification*. When I identify with, for example, my family, community, or society, then I am not alienated from them. I am not uncertain about who I am but rather feel confirmed and, so to speak, at home there. What this means is that I can see my role in these contexts and am happy and satisfied

---

[13] See Richard Schacht, *Alienation* (London: George Allen & Unwin, 1971), pp. 1–7.

with it. I feel my own sense of self-identity affirmed by these larger instances. I can recognize a part of myself in them. For example, I see my own will and rationality reflected in rational laws that prohibit murder or theft. Although I did not personally create these laws, I can immediately affirm them as an extension of my own rationality. If I myself were to create a new set of laws, I would be sure to include these. By contrast, when I am alienated, I am dissatisfied with my role in these different contexts and thus can refuse to play it. When I have the feeling of alienation, I cannot identify with the larger context and feel more comfortable outside it. I do not feel at home there but more like a stranger or intruder. I cannot see myself in this other, and there is a fundamental separation or division between me and it.

The second important concept that will be used as a guiding thread is that of recognition (*Anerkennung*). Although it only appears in a limited way in Hegel's texts, recognition has played an important role in the reception of his thought, especially in the twentieth and twenty-first centuries. This concept has to do with the way in which we regard each other as human beings, political agents, or members of a community.

Like alienation, recognition has a number of different meanings that can be applied in different contexts. Perhaps at its most basic level, we can talk about recognition as a kind of perception, for example, when we say that someone *recognizes* a danger. This means that one is able to look at the multitude of sensory information that we receive from the world and to identify in it something that might potentially be dangerous. This presupposes that we have ahead of time a certain idea or concept of danger in our minds, and then when we look at certain situations in the world, we are able to put them into this category. We are able to distinguish these situations from those that are not dangerous.

We can also talk about recognizing other people. This is important for issues of philosophical anthropology and ethics. When we look at the many things that are found in the world, we can immediately distinguish between human beings and other things or other living creatures. Again, at the perceptual level we have a concept of a human being that we use to identify those things in our perceptual field that fall under this rubric. In this sense I can recognize someone as human. This seems entirely obvious, but in fact it can become a complex issue. In hierarchical societies, it is necessary to recognize other people in their particular role vis-à-vis each other. We need to know if someone stands above us in the hierarchy or below us. This determines our behavior toward others and the nature of our interaction with them. This is important for our ethical relations with others and our self-image. Our understanding of ourselves is largely shaped by the recognition that we receive from others. If we are constantly subject to negative recognition, we are likely to develop a negative understanding of ourselves, our abilities, and our possibilities.

As an extension of this usage, the concept of recognition is also important for social-political philosophy. We recognize our fellow community members as human beings who have certain rights and who are protected by certain laws. This recognition is important for social life to exist at all. If we did not recognize that other people had rights, then we would be subject to constant struggles to assert our claims. If we did not recognize that a certain object is the property of someone else, then we might be inclined to take it ourselves. Thus social life itself requires us to recognize each other in many different ways. When we fail to do so, the social fabric breaks down and often violence occurs. Phenomena such as racism and sexism demonstrate a failure to fully recognize a certain group of people as being fully human and being owed the same rights and degree of respect as others. Hegel was among the first philosophers to have a glimmering of the sweeping importance of this concept.

Like recognition, alienation is a very broad concept since one can be alienated from a number of different things. It can be a question of psychology, when one feels alienated from oneself in the form of either one's individual character or human nature in general. It can be a question of ethics or personal relations, when one feels alienated from one's family, friends, or colleagues. It can be a question of social theory or politics, when one feels alienated from one's community or state. It can be a question of economics, when one feels alienated from one's labor and workplace. It can be a question of religion, when one feels alienated from the religious community, religious ceremonies, and practices. It is thus a rich concept that has a broad range of applications in several different spheres.

In this work we will look at a number of different philosophers who examined different aspects of the concepts of alienation and recognition in various contexts. As we will see, these are important ideas that shaped the direction of philosophy in the nineteenth century. This is especially true of the tradition of German philosophy, which will be the main focus here. Moreover, these concepts played an important role in the development of philosophy in the twentieth century in movements such as existentialism and Critical Theory. In the twentieth and twenty-first centuries, the application of these concepts has been extended beyond the field of philosophy. Today they are regularly used by social scientists, especially psychologists and sociologists.

Given that alienation and recognition are the guiding threads of this select-ive reading of nineteenth-century philosophy, a number of otherwise import-ant philosophers from the period have unfortunately been omitted from the present study since these concepts were not central to their thinking. These include thinkers such as August Comte and John Stuart Mill, who stand outside the tradition of German philosophy, but it also includes philosophers in this tradition, such as Schelling and Schopenhauer. The omission of any extended account of these thinkers here should not be taken to imply that they were not important for the development of the history of philosophy in the nineteenth century. Their absence is merely the result of the selection of the interpretative focus chosen. With a different focus, they could easily be regarded as central figures. It might also be pointed out that the present work contains no chapter on Max Stirner or David Friedrich Strauss, who are often discussed in the context of German philosophy in the wake of Hegel. While I readily acknowledge this shortcoming, I can only point to the normal length requirements demanded by academic publishers today. It would have been desirable to have included chapters on these figures and others if space had allowed for this, but this would have resulted in either a superficial analysis or a manuscript that was unpublishable due to its excessive length. For these reasons, the present work should be regarded not as an attempt to give an exhaustive survey of nineteenth-century Continental philosophy but rather as tracing a handful of ideas emerging from Hegel's philosophy.

## Critical Theses

There are, of course, a number of outstanding works that treat the central figures in nineteenth-century philosophy, and I have made use of them fruitfully.[14] The present study is designed as a historical overview and is not primarily polemical in nature, so I have generally refrained from discussing these works critically. However, this is not to say that it contains no critical element. I have, indeed, tried to show what I take to be the weaknesses of some

---

[14] For example, Karl Löwith, *From Hegel to Nietzsche: The Revolution in Nineteenth-Century Thought*, trans. by David E. Green (New York: Holt, Rinehart and Winston, 1964; London: Constable, 1965); William J. Brazill, *The Young Hegelians* (New Haven: Yale University Press, 1970); John Edward Toews, *Hegelianism: The Path toward Dialectical Humanism, 1805-1841* (Cambridge: Cambridge University Press, 1980); Herbert Marcuse, *Reason and Revolution: Hegel and the Rise of Social Theory*, 2nd ed. (Oxford: Oxford University Press, 1941; London: Routledge, 1955; Boston: Beacon Press, 1970); Sidney Hook, *From Hegel to Marx: Studies in the Intellectual Development of Karl Marx* (New York: Humanities Press, 1958); David McLellan, *The Young Hegelians and Karl Marx* (New York: F. A. Praeger, 1969); Warren Breckman, *Marx, the Young Hegelians, and the Origins of Radical Social Theory* (Cambridge: Cambridge University Press, 1999); Herbert Schnädelbach, *Philosophy in Germany 1831-1933*, trans. by Eric Matthews (Cambridge: Cambridge University Press, 1984); J. W. Burrow, *The Crisis of Reason: European Thought, 1848-1914* (New Haven and London: Yale University Press, 2000); Terry Pinkard, *German Philosophy 1760-1860: The Legacy of Idealism* (Cambridge: Cambridge University Press, 2002); Frederick C. Beiser, *After Hegel: German Philosophy 1840-1900* (Princeton and Oxford: Princeton University Press, 2014); C. L. Ten (ed.), *The Nineteenth Century* (London and New York: Routledge, 1994) (*Routledge History of Philosophy*, vol. 7); Dean Moyar (ed.), *The Routledge Companion of Nineteenth-Century Philosophy* (London and New York: Routledge, 2010); Alison Stone (ed.), *The Edinburgh Critical History of Nineteenth-Century Philosophy* (Edinburgh: Edinburgh University Press, 2011); Allen W. Wood and Songsuk Susan Hahn (eds.), *The Cambridge History of Philosophy in the Nineteenth Century (1790-1870)* (Cambridge: Cambridge University Press, 2012).

of the individual philosophical views discussed and to demonstrate how these prodded later thinkers to set out in new directions. Moreover, at the broad level, the present work offers a handful of perspectives or theses that are more or less new or original vis-à-vis earlier works on philosophy in the nineteenth century.

First, I want to show that religion plays an absolutely central and constitutive role in the development of philosophy during this period. In fact, the history of theology and even biblical studies cannot be separated from the history of philosophy in the nineteenth century. For many modern commentators it is surprising that the philosophy of this period was so closely tied to religion and theology; indeed, sometimes to the point that they were indistinguishable. There was much overlap between the two fields, and religious questions were key issues in the philosophical systems of the day. Likewise, philosophical questions plagued discussions of theology. It is no accident that during this period people talked about rationalism as both a philosophical and a theological school. It is thus a mistake when philosophers today reject this side of the history of philosophy since such a rejection distorts the nature of philosophy during this period. This is a modern prejudice that presupposes a clear demarcation of academic fields. But we cannot assume this of previous periods in the history of science and scholarship, when the fields had not attained the same level of specialization as today and where there was much greater tolerance for what we would nowadays regard as interdisciplinary work. As we will see, the concept of alienation is one that connects philosophy and religion in this period.

The connection between religious thinking and philosophy is often overlooked when people think of the important political dimension of nineteenth-century thought in connection with, for example, Marx, Bakunin, and the Revolutions of 1848. But, as we will see, these political trends were closely connected to the developments in religious thinking at the time. Thinkers traditionally defined by their social-political theories, such as Marx and Bakunin, were also deeply interested in the contemporary discussions concerning religion and self-consciously built on them. Indeed, Marx's famous theory of alienation in the social-economic sphere began with an interest in alienation in the context of religious belief.

Second, there is also an important and rarely recognized literary dimension to philosophy in the nineteenth century. It has been known for some time that Hegel made fairly extensive use of literary sources in his own work,[15] but the influence of his philosophy on important novelists and poets of the period has been less explored. The poet Heinrich Heine and the Danish poet-playwright Johan Ludvig Heiberg attended his lectures in Berlin and were clearly marked

---

[15] See Allen Speight, *Hegel, Literature and the Problem of Agency* (Cambridge: Cambridge University Press, 2004).

by the experience. The Russian novelist Ivan Turgenev, who belongs to the second generation of students who were in Berlin after Hegel's death, also made a close study of the germination of philosophical ideas surrounding Hegel's thought. While Dostoevsky was never a student in Berlin, he too studied Hegel's philosophy and made use of some of its key ideas. Among others, the concepts of alienation and recognition, which began in Hegel, were appropriated by these literary writers. The present work tries to sketch this literary side of philosophy in the nineteenth century, which was an organic outgrowth of the reception of Hegel's thought. This has traditionally been overlooked in studies of philosophy in the nineteenth century. Once again, much more could be done to explore the literary reception of German philosophy if space would allow for it. Here I have simply chosen a few of the most important writers for closer analysis. These choices were again dictated by their suitability vis-à-vis the guiding themes of the present work.

Third, previous works on European philosophy in the nineteenth century have tended to be almost exclusively overviews of *German* philosophy. There is a more or less standard sequence of figures from Hegel to Feuerbach to Marx that is generally followed. In this study I wish to take a more generally pan-European approach in order to better understand how key ideas migrated across borders and were born anew in different contexts. While German philosophy was the source of some of the main ideas, these were taken up again in France, Denmark, and Russia as well. Thinkers in these other countries appropriated key concepts from Hegel and developed them in their own cultural contexts. Hegel's philosophy was thus not an exclusively German phenomenon; instead, his ideas were transplanted by his students to foreign soil, where they took root and blossomed. Much more could be made of this point since there was also an important reception of Hegel's philosophy in many other countries as well, but space constraints have compelled me to stick to a few of the most salient examples that fit with the thematic focus of the present work.

It is sometimes thought that philosophy in Great Britain represents an exception to the general tendency on the Continent that came from German Idealism. According to this view, there were independent schools of philosophy such as utilitarianism and naturalism that had no real contact with German philosophy. While this is true, it would be a mistake to infer from this that German Idealism and Hegel's philosophy played no role in Britain in the nineteenth century. In fact, his thought and that of his students were taken up with excitement by some sectors of British intellectual life. The writer Mary Ann Evans (known under the *nom de plume* of George Eliot) translated Feuerbach's *The Essence of Christianity* and Strauss' *The Life of Jesus* into English. The novelist Thomas Carlyle studied in Germany and made use of German philosophy in his works. During the second half of the century, when philosophical materialism in Britain grew quickly in step with the advances of the natural sciences, there arose in opposition to this a school of idealism that was inspired by Hegel. This included figures such as James Hutchison Stirling, Thomas Hill Green, Francis Herbert Bradley, Bernard Bosanquet, Edward Caird, J. M. E. McTaggart, and Andrew Seth Pringle-Pattison. These were important figures of the day, many of whom occupied distinguished professorships. Unfortunately, it is impossible to sketch all of this in the context of the present study, but this should be enough to suggest a revision of our understanding of the philosophical tradition in Britain as something radically different and separate from what was happening in Germany and on the Continent in the nineteenth century.

Fourth, Hegel has often been portrayed as the ambitious yet naive philosopher of the system. He is caricatured as a dogmatic thinker who *ex cathedra* handed down static final truths and absolutes. In this book, I wish to demonstrate the absurdity of this still oft-heard view. I wish to show that what excited people about Hegel in the nineteenth century was not the dogmatic Hegel of the system but rather the dynamic Hegel of the dialectical method. This was the element in Hegel's thought that inspired many of his most influential followers, who appropriated this tool in their criticism of religion, politics, and culture in general. Instead of simply parroting purported fixed truths received from Hegel, they took from him a method that could be fruitfully applied in different contexts.

Fifth, along the same lines, Hegel has been traditionally portrayed as the thinker who congratulated himself for having arrived at the culmination of world history with his philosophical system. This view presents Hegel as a highly confident thinker who defended the religious and political institutions of the day as having reached a finished and just form. It is from this picture that he has sometimes been cast in the role of a political conservative. He is often thought of as a thinker who justifies the ills of the present age by celebrating its triumphs. By contrast, this study wants to present a different picture. Instead of being satisfied and even happy about the status quo, Hegel perceived his own age to be in a state of crisis. He recognized that there was a widespread feeling of alienation in the modern world. This aspect of his thought was taken up by all of the figures treated in this book. They all, to a greater or lesser degree, saw a crisis in their age, and they all developed their own diagnosis of it. Most of the thinkers treated here also had some kind of theory of alienation in order to explain this crisis. Finally, they all tried to develop ideas about what was needed to emerge from the crisis. This topic is rarely recognized as central to Hegel's thought and its reception.

Sixth, with regard to the periodization of philosophy in the nineteenth century, it is usually believed that there was a radical break between the first and the second half of the century. According to the common story, the first half of the century was still dominated by the iconic figures of German Idealism: Fichte, Hegel, and Schelling. With the rise of the natural sciences, the appeal of this tradition gradually wore off and died out in the 1840s. The second half of the century, it is argued, was dominated by materialism and naturalism, which seemed more in line with current scientific thinking. In the present study, I wish to argue that in fact the tradition of German Idealism did not die out in the first half of the century. Instead, its influence continued to be felt in the second half of the century as well.[16] This is due largely to the fact that Hegel's students of the first and the second generation did their most important work in the second half of the century. Thus Hegel's influence continued to be felt well after the school of German Idealism was thought to be dead. This point is often overlooked, perhaps due to the fact that the mainstream university philosophy in Central Europe turned toward neo-Kantianism, which was decidedly critical of Hegel. This forced out of academic life those who had sympathies with Hegel's philosophy; they were left to make a living as journalists and literary writers, and their influence was felt in fields such as politics, religion, and literature. But in the long run their work exerted an influence that was as great as, if not greater than, those who enjoyed comfortable professorships at leading universities.

Finally, there are a number of standard clichés about the key figures of this period: Hegel as a Prussian apologist, Kierkegaard as a rabid anti-Hegelian, Marx as a dogmatic communist, etc. These clichés are in the best case uninformative and in the worst outright distorting. Likewise, there are a number of traditional labels, such as right and left Hegelians, old and young Hegelians, that are usually employed to divide the material about philosophical thinking in the nineteenth century. These labels are also misleading since they assume that the individual thinkers can be cleanly assigned to one category or another. I submit that it makes more sense to understand the period as a grand debate about the importance and value of Hegel's thought. This means that thinkers in some cases coopted his ideas and methodology and in others criticized certain aspects of his thought. This is a highly complex matter since these later thinkers tended to revise their assessments in step with the developments of their own thought. These kinds of fluid developments defy any straightforward or pre-established categorization.

The present work will thus try to present a line of interpretation that tells a continuous narrative while avoiding, as much as possible, these clichéd readings and categorizations. Instead, I take a more historical approach to the organization of the present work. While focused on the themes mentioned, this work follows a chronological pattern. In the two chapters of Part I, I explore the thought of Hegel, the key source of inspiration that determines the subsequent history of nineteenth-century Continental philosophy. Part II

---

[16] See Frederick C. Beiser, *Late German Idealism: Trendelenburg and Lotze* (Oxford: Oxford University Press, 2013). This work by Beiser argues for this thesis by means of a close reading of the two figures mentioned in the title.

contains three chapters treating some of the main thinkers belonging to what I refer to as *the first generation* of Hegel students, which includes those figures, such as Heine, Feuerbach, Strauss, Stirner, and Bauer, who attended Hegel's lectures in Berlin and thus learned from him first-hand. Part III is dedicated to *the second generation*, which is comprised of figures, such as Kierkegaard, Marx, Engels, Turgenev, and Bakunin, who came to Berlin after Hegel's death in 1831 and learned about his philosophy second-hand from his students. For reasons that will become clear in due course, I have included Dostoevsky in this category, although he never studied in Berlin with the Hegelians. The concluding chapter offers some reflections on the ultimate character and significance of Continental philosophy in the nineteenth century with regard to the subsequent development of the concepts of alienation and recognition.

This work also wishes to emphasize the radicalism of philosophy in this period and the difficult conditions in which the various thinkers had to work. Many of the philosophers examined here suffered persecution for their political or religious views. Many were prevented from obtaining or maintaining academic employment. Many had their works banned or burned by the censors. Many were forced into exile from their home countries. All of this bespeaks an age in which certain ideas were emerging that were far ahead of the general cultural *ethos* and the views of the vested authorities of the day. This suggests that the fermentation of thought during this period, although perceived as a threat at the time, might potentially contain something of value for later ages. In the following pages we wish to explore, specially, the contribution of the nineteenth century to the history of philosophy. An important part of this exploration concerns how the key ideas from this period might still be relevant for us today.

# PART I

## The Beginning

# 1

# Hegel's Account of Alienation
# in *The Phenomenology of Spirit*

While Hegel enjoyed great success in the last decade of his life as a professor in Berlin, things were not always so easy for him. He spent some trying journeyman years where he struggled even to begin an academic career. Hegel was born in Stuttgart in the Duchy of Württemberg in 1770.[1] He attended the University of Tübingen from 1788 to 1793, where he studied theology at a famous Lutheran theological seminary. Among his fellow students were the philosopher Schelling and the poet Hölderlin. After completing his degree, Hegel was reluctant to enter the clergy, as was expected of him, and instead chose to work as a house tutor for noble families, first in Bern in Switzerland (from 1793 to 1797) and then in Frankfurt am Main (from 1797 to 1800). These were difficult and lonely years for Hegel, who desired to begin a university career but lacked the means to do so. At the time, the entry level positions were unsalaried, so they required one to be independently wealthy, which Hegel was not. He finally received his chance when his father died in 1799. Hegel received an inheritance from his father, which allowed him at last to embark on an academic career.

He began his academic career at the University of Jena in 1801, where he arrived after the departure of Fichte. This university belonged to the court of Weimar, and its benefactor was the Duke of Weimar, Karl August (1757–1828). This was the leading institution of higher learning in the German-speaking world, due largely to the influence of the famous writer Johann Wolfgang von Goethe, who was a diplomat and close advisor to the duke.

---

[1] For Hegel's biography, see Terry Pinkard, *Hegel: A Biography* (Cambridge: Cambridge University Press, 2000); Horst Althaus, *Hegel: An Intellectual Biography*, trans. by Michael Tarsh (Cambridge: Polity Press, 2000); Jacques D'Hondt, *Hegel in His Time*, trans. by John Burbidge (New York: Broadview Press, 1988); Kuno Fischer, *Hegels Leben, Werke und Lehre* (Heidelberg: C. Winter, 1901); Karl Rosenkranz, *Georg Wilhelm Friedrich Hegel's Leben* (Berlin: Duncker und Humblot, 1844); Franz Widmann, *Hegel: An Illustrated Biography*, trans. by Joachim Neugroschel (New York: Pegasus, 1968). A useful source of primary materials can be found in Günter Nicolin (ed.), *Hegel in Berichten seiner Zeitgenossen* (Hamburg: Felix Meiner, 1970). For a useful introduction to Hegel's thought, see Allen Speight, *The Philosophy of Hegel* (Stocksfield: Acumen, 2008).

Goethe worked to bring to Jena some of the leading scholars of the day, such as Fichte, Schelling, and Schiller.

Hegel's period in Jena was largely one of struggle. A few years before his arrival, his old friend Schelling had been appointed a professor at the university at a very early age. While Hegel was happy to be reunited with his friend, he struggled to establish his own academic identity, while Schelling received all of the attention. Ultimately Schelling left Jena in 1803, providing Hegel with the opportunity to come out of his shadow. Hegel was aware that he needed to produce an important book if he were ever to entertain seriously the idea of receiving a salaried professorship. During these years he wrote a number of drafts of a philosophical system that he did not publish. As time passed, Hegel's financial situation became increasingly precarious. The money he received from his inheritance was running out, and he urgently needed to receive a paying position. He appealed to his friend Friedrich Immanuel Niethammer (1766--1848), whom he met at the seminary in Tübingen and who was his colleague in Jena until 1804. After Niethammer's departure, Hegel wrote several letters to him asking him for financial assistance and for help in finding fixed academic employment. With his future very unclear, Hegel lapsed into bouts of depression.

It was under these difficult circumstances that Hegel wrote *The Phenomenology of Spirit*.[2] He urgently needed to finish the work but struggled to do so. As he worked, his original conception changed, and soon he seems to have lost control over the manuscript. Hegel initially reached an agreement with a publisher in Bamberg named Joseph Anton Goebhardt to publish the work with an advance when Hegel delivered the first half of the manuscript.[3] When Hegel delayed in sending the manuscript, Goebhardt changed the agreement and said that Hegel would only receive his money when the entire text was received. By now Hegel was on the verge of desperation. He was obliged to meet a strict deadline, or else his friend Niethammer would be obliged to pay the publisher. He was sending off parts of his manuscript piecemeal as French troops under Napoleon were descending on Jena. From his letters it is clear that he was vexed at the thought of some of these possibly being lost in the mail in the midst of the chaos of war. Napoleon led his army against Prussia, and they met at the Battle of Jena on October 14, 1806. The day before the battle, Napoleon occupied the city, and Hegel saw him in person and was clearly moved by the experience. Some years later he recounts that he finished the final pages of the *Phenomenology* "the night before the Battle of Jena."[4] In a letter to Niethammer, Hegel explains the tense

---

[2] G. W. F. Hegel, *System der Wissenschaft. Erster Theil, die Phänomenologie des Geistes* (Bamberg and Würzburg: Joseph Anton Goebhardt, 1807). (English translation: *Hegel's Phenomenology of Spirit*, trans. by A. V. Miller [Oxford: Clarendon Press, 1977].)

[3] See Pinkard, *Hegel: A Biography*, p. 227.

[4] Letter 233, "Hegel an Niethammer," in Johannes Hoffmeister (ed.), *Briefe von und an Hegel*, 3rd ed., 4 vols. (vols. 4.1 and 4.2 ed. by Friedhelm Nicolin) (Hamburg: Felix Meiner,

situation of the occupation and the uncertainty about how the population would be treated by the French.[5] Hegel took refuge with friends, but when he returned to his apartment, he found it occupied by boisterous French troops who had ransacked it. He claims to have carried around with him the last pages of his manuscript in his pockets. Napoleon's victory meant that the University of Jena now had far fewer students, and the instructors were also leaving in droves. With the help of Niethammer, Hegel, now destitute, received a position as a newspaper editor in Bamberg. These are the dramatic circumstances that led to the publication of *The Phenomenology of Spirit*.

## 1.1   Introduction to Hegel's *Phenomenology of Spirit*

*The Phenomenology of Spirit* appeared in 1807, and, although it did not immediately meet with a great reception, it eventually established itself as a classic in Western philosophy.[6] The tortured story of the work's composition is evident. The last few chapters of the work have an almost perfunctory look about them, and there can be little doubt that Hegel would have liked to have had the opportunity to develop them in more detail.[7]

The book is intended to be a kind of introduction to a philosophical system or what Hegel calls "science" in general. He does not mean by this what we understand by the term today. The idea is that we all begin with our notions

1961–1981), vol. 2, p. 28 (*Hegel: The Letters*, trans. by Clark Butler and Christiane Seiler [Bloomington: Indiana University Press, 1984], p. 307).

[5] Letter 74, "Hegel an Niethammer," in Hoffmeister (ed.), *Briefe von und an Hegel*, vol. 1, pp. 119–121 (*Hegel: The Letters*, pp. 114f).

[6] For works on *The Phenomenology of Spirit*, see Jean Hyppolite, *Genesis and Structure of Hegel's Phenomenology of Spirit*, trans. by Samuel Cherniak and John Heckman (Evanston: Northwestern University Press, 1974); Robert C. Solomon, *In the Spirit of Hegel: A Study of G. W. F. Hegel's Phenomenology of Spirit* (New York and Oxford: Oxford University Press, 1983); Jon Stewart, *The Unity of Hegel's Phenomenology of Spirit: A Systematic Interpretation* (Evanston: Northwestern University Press, 2000); H. S. Harris, *Hegel's Ladder*, vol. 1, *The Pilgrimage of Reason* and vol. 2, *The Odyssey of Spirit* (Indianapolis: Hackett, 1997); Howard P. Kainz, *Hegel's Phenomenology*, Part 1: *Analysis and Commentary* (Alabama: University of Alabama Press, 1976; Athens, OH: Ohio University Press, 1988); Part 2: *The Evolution of Ethical and Religious Consciousness to the Absolute Standpoint* (Athens, OH: Ohio University Press, 1983); Terry Pinkard, *Hegel's Phenomenology: The Sociality of Reason* (Cambridge: Cambridge University Press, 1994); Donald P. Verene, *Hegel's Recollection: A Study of Images in the Phenomenology of Spirit* (Albany: State University of New York Press, 1985); Merold Westphal, *History and Truth in Hegel's Phenomenology* (Atlantic Highlands: Humanities Press, 1979); Allen Speight, *Hegel, Literature and the Problem of Agency* (Cambridge: Cambridge University Press, 2004).

[7] See Jon Stewart, "Hegel's *Phenomenology* as a Systematic Fragment," in Frederick C. Beiser (ed.), *The Cambridge Companion to Hegel and Nineteenth-Century Philosophy* (Cambridge and New York: Cambridge University Press, 2008), pp. 74–93.

of common sense, which tell us that the world consists of a variety of different things that exist outside us and separately from us. I know that I am different from the objects around me in fundamental ways, just as I know that who I am is fundamentally different from other people in the world. Common sense thus tends to see things as distinct and separate since this is the way that they are presented to our perception. I am different from and independent of this pen or that person. Common sense likes to set up dualistic structures that juxtapose different kinds of things. According to Hegel's view, the idea of a true "science" is the exact opposite of this. Science understands the complex interconnections in the world. It shows how things that we might conceive as individual or atomic are in fact closely, and indeed necessarily, related to one another. The slogan that Hegel uses in the long and famous preface to the *Phenomenology* is "The true is the whole."[8] In some ways this is not so hard to understand since today we are used to different fields of science making connections and showing the complex relations of things, often uncovering hidden relations that were not known previously. Given this, we are used to seeing things not as isolated phenomena but rather as complex systems with many interconnected elements. Hegel's goal in the *Phenomenology* is to start from the ground up with our most basic intuitions about the world and to show that in fact they are all wrong. Instead of things being separate and individual, they are connected.

He organizes the work in an ascending fashion, starting with our most basic intuitions about things in the world and moving to our relations with other people and then to more complex phenomena such as history and religion. The work is divided into six chapters: "Consciousness," "Self-Consciousness," "Reason," "Spirit," "Religion," and "Absolute Knowing." These chapters are of very different lengths, with some being very short and others very long. Moreover, their internal organization becomes more and more complex as the book progresses. It seems that Hegel initially conceived of the work as containing only the first three chapters – that is, "Consciousness," "Self-Consciousness," and "Reason" – and then he realized that a fuller account had to be given, so he added the chapters on "Spirit" and "Religion."

In the "Consciousness" chapter Hegel tries to refute our common-sense models of what things are. Indeed, consciousness is by definition an awareness of things. While our common sense says that objects in the external world are radically separate from us, Hegel demonstrates that whatever model we have of a thing, it in fact always contains some element of human thought. In other words, the object does not reach us directly, but instead we play some role in determining what it is. Hegel is, of course, known as an advocate of *idealism*, a believer that what is most real is ideas and that the faculties of the human mind fundamentally shape the objects that we perceive around us. This view

---

[8] Hegel, *Phänomenologie des Geistes*, p. xxiii; *Hegel's Phenomenology of Spirit*, p. 11. (Note that all quotations are from the first edition from 1807 referenced earlier.)

stands in contrast to the doctrine of *realism*, which claims that what is most true and real are physical things outside us in the world. While our common sense immediately assumes that realism must be true, Hegel's analysis demonstrates that there is always an element of thought or ideas in how we think of or describe things in the world. Thus things do not reach us directly but are ultimately determined by our ways of thinking.

This leads Hegel to the "Self-Consciousness" chapter.[9] Self-consciousness is, of course, our awareness of ourselves in contrast to our awareness of objects. We like to think of ourselves as independent individuals. We know who we are, regardless of what the circumstances are or what others might think of us. But Hegel goes through a series of arguments to refute this view of common sense. He demonstrates that our awareness of ourselves is in fact dependent on other people. To be aware of ourselves we must be able to see ourselves from the perspective of another self-conscious agent. When we look at another person, we immediately imagine that person looking back at us, and we are concerned with what they are seeing. This interaction with the other fundamentally shapes our behavior and self-conception. We could not be fully human in isolation. Hegel thus demonstrates that our common-sense view is mistaken and in fact human beings stand in necessary relation to one another. We could not be who we are as individuals without other people.

Hegel continues in this fashion through the rest of the work. In the "Reason" chapter he explores how our ways of thinking are shaped by different social relations. Here he treats topics as diverse as the natural sciences and ethics, which represent complex conceptions that are developed and shared by groups of people. The "Spirit" chapter is dedicated to history. Here he gives an overview of world history in an attempt to show how different institutions and ways of thinking have developed through the course of time. This chapter demonstrates how history is a key element of how we think and perceive the world. In the "Religion" chapter Hegel does much the same thing by giving an overview not of the different periods of world history but of the different religions of the world.[10] He tries to show how the various conceptions of the divine develop through time. This development thus determines how we conceive of God. Finally, in the chapter "Absolute Knowing," Hegel concludes

---

[9] For this chapter, see Gwendoline Jarczyk and Pierre-Jean Labarrière, *Les premiers combats de la reconnaissance. Maîtrise et servitude dans la Phénoménologie de l'esprit de Hegel* (Paris: Aubier, 1987); Werner Marx, *Das Selbstbewußtsein in Hegels Phänomenologie des Geistes* (Frankfurt am Main: Klosterman, 1986); Otto Pöggeler, "Hegels Phänomenologie des Selbstbewußtseins," in his *Hegels Idee einer Phänomenologie des Geistes* (Freiburg and Munich: Karl Alber, 1973), pp. 231–298; Hans-Georg Gadamer, "Hegel's Dialectic of Self-Consciousness," in his *Hegel's Dialectic: Five Hermeneutical Essays*, trans. by P. Christopher Smith (New Haven: Yale University Press, 1976), pp. 54–74.

[10] See Jon Stewart, *Hegel's Interpretation of the Religions of the World: The Logic of the Gods* (Oxford: Oxford University Press, 2018).

that the sphere of philosophy or what he calls "science" has finally been reached and the different forms of common-sense dualism have been refuted and dispensed with. Now the connection of everything with everything else in all the different spheres has been demonstrated. With this refutation of common sense, the real work of science can begin with the construction of the actual philosophical system itself.

## 1.2    The Struggle for Recognition

Hegel's analysis of the lord and the bondsman from the "Self-Consciousness" chapter of *The Phenomenology of Spirit* is one of the most celebrated texts in the entire history of philosophy.[11] This discussion was in many ways the point

---

[11]  Hegel, *Phänomenologie des Geistes*, pp. 114–128; *Hegel's Phenomenology of Spirit*, pp. 111–119. Note that Hegel gives a very similar analysis in the *Encyclopedia of the Philosophical Sciences*. See G.W.F.Hegel, *Encyklopädie der philosophischen Wissenschaften im Grundrisse*, 3rd ed. (1830) (Heidelberg: August Oßwald's Universitätsbuchhandlung), pp. 445–448, §§ 430–437. (*Hegel's Philosophy of Mind: Being Part Three of the Encyclopaedia of the Philosophical Sciences*, trans. by William Wallace and A. V. Miller [Oxford: Clarendon Press, 1971], pp. 170–178.) For analyses of the lordship and bondage dialectic, see Howard Adelman, "Of Human Bondage: Labor, Bondage and Freedom in the *Phenomenology*," in Donald Phillip Verene (ed.), *Hegel's Social and Political Thought* (Atlantic Highlands: Humanities Press, 1980), pp. 119–135; J. M. Bernstein, "From Self-Consciousness to Community: Act and Recognition in the Master-Slave Relationship," in Z. A. Pelczynski (ed.), *The State and Civil Society: Studies in Hegel's Political Philosophy* (Cambridge: Cambridge University Press, 1984), pp. 14–39; Daniel Duquette, "The Political Significance of Hegel's Concept of Recognition in the *Phenomenology*," *Bulletin of the Hegel Society of Great Britain*, 29 (1994), 38–54; Karen Gloy, "Bemerkungen zum Kapitel 'Herrschaft und Knechtschaft' in Hegels *Phänomenologie des Geistes*," *Zeitschrift für Philosophische Forschung*, 39 (1985), 187–213; Eliot Jurist, "Hegel's Concept of Recognition," *The Owl of Minerva*, 19 (1987), 5–22; Eliot Jurist, "Recognition and Self-Knowledge," *Hegel-Studien*, 21 (1986), 143–150; George A. Kelly, "Notes on Hegel's Lordship and Bondage," *Review of Metaphysics*, 19 (1965), 780–802; Henning Ottmann, "Herr und Knecht bei Hegel: Bemerkungen zu einer misverstandenen Dialektik," *Zeitschrift für Philosophische Forschung*, 35 (1981), 365–384; Steven B. Smith, "Hegel on Slavery and Domination," *Review of Metaphysics*, 46 (1992), 197–124; Costas Douzinas, "Identity, Recognition, Rights or What Can Hegel Teach Us about Human Rights?," *Journal of Law and Society*, 29(3) (2002), 379–405; Robert R. Williams, *Hegel's Ethics of Recognition* (Berkeley: University of California Press, 1997); Axel Honneth, *The Pathologies of Individual Freedom: Hegel's Social Theory*, trans. by L. Löb (Princeton and Oxford: Princeton University Press, 2001); Robert B. Pippin, *Hegel's Practical Philosophy: Rational Agency as Ethical Life* (Cambridge: Cambridge University Press, 2008); Robert B. Pippin, *Hegel on Self-Consciousness: Desire and Death in the Phenomenology of Spirit* (Princeton and Oxford: Princeton University Press, 2011); Frederick Neuhouser, *Foundations of Hegel's Social Theory: Actualizing Freedom* (Cambridge, MA: Harvard University Press, 2003). See also Italo Testa and Luigi Ruggiu (eds.), *"I That Is We, We That Is I." Perspectives on Contemporary Hegel Social Ontology, Recognition, Naturalism, and the Critique of Kantian Constructivism* (Leiden and Boston: Brill, 2016); Heikki Ikäheimo and

of departure for thinkers such as Feuerbach and Marx, whom we will examine in due course. Moreover, the Russian-born philosopher Alexandre Kojève (1902–1968) gave a series of lectures in Paris in the 1930s that focused explicitly on this part of the *Phenomenology*.[12] Hegel's analysis proved to be instrumental in the development of French existentialism,[13] where it appears perhaps most prominently in the work of Jean-Paul Sartre and Simone de Beauvoir. It has also been important in post-structuralism, not to mention Jacques Lacan's psychology. More recently, this analysis has also been significant in fields such as gender studies and post-colonial studies, in the work of authors such as Nancy Fraser, Seyla Benhabib, and Judith Butler. If ever there was an influential text in the history of philosophy, this short eight-page snippet is it.

The "Self-Consciousness" chapter begins by exploring our basic relation to other things around us in the world. Hegel claims that this relation is fundamentally one of desire.[14] We have natural needs for food, drink, and shelter, and we freely make use of the objects of nature to fulfill these needs. Early hunter-gatherers took from nature what they could find to sustain themselves. By doing so, they asserted their superiority over nature and demonstrated their freedom. By killing and eating plants and animals, they confirmed their own sense of themselves as free and independent. They were generally stronger than most of the objects of nature, which were in large part at their mercy. But despite this superiority, the freedom that is demonstrated by the appropriation of nature is undermined by the fact that our natural needs are never satiated for long and soon return again. It is thus a never-ending struggle, as humans must continually go out again to gather food and obtain the basics needed for their survival.

The next step in the analysis concerns the relation of an individual not to an object of nature but rather to another person or, in Hegel's language, another

---

Arto Laitinen (eds.), *Recognition and Social Ontology* (Leiden and Boston: Brill, 2011) (*Social and Critical Theory*, vol. 11).

[12] See Alexandre Kojève, *Introduction à la lecture de Hegel. Leçons sur la Phénoménologie de l'esprit professées de 1933 à 1939 à l'École des Hautes Études*, ed. by Raymond Queneau (Paris: Gallimard, 1947). (English translation: *Introduction to the Reading of Hegel: Lectures on the Phenomenology of Spirit*, trans. by Allan Bloom [Ithaca: Cornell University Press, 1980].)

[13] See Jean Hyppolite, "La *Phénoménologie* de Hegel et la pensée française contemporaine," in his *Figures de la pensée philosophique. Écrits (1931–1968)*, vol. 1 (Paris: Presses Universitaires de France, 1971), pp. 231–241; Marcel Régnier, "Hegel in France," *Bulletin of the Hegel Society of Great Britain*, 8 (1983), 10–20; Judith P. Butler, *Subjects of Desire: Hegelian Reflections in Twentieth-Century France* (New York: Columbia University Press, 1987).

[14] See Leo Rauch, "Desire, An Elemental Passion in Hegel's *Phenomenology*," *Analecta Husserliana*, 28 (1990), 193–207; Frederick Neuhouser, "Deducing Desire and Recognition in the *Phenomenology of Spirit*," *Journal of the History of Philosophy*, 24 (1986), 243–262.

self-consciousness. He begins with a kind of thought experiment and imagines two people in a kind of state of nature seeing one another for the first time. There is no further contextualization or determination. What is the most basic kind of human interaction? How does one person relate to another, a stranger? Hegel's thesis here is that although our common sense tells us that we are separate, distinct, independent individuals, in fact, to be self-conscious at all implies that we are in interaction with other self-conscious agents. Specifically, to be self-conscious means that we are *recognized* by another person. Hegel seizes on *recognition* as the key term for his analysis. Once again, what we thought was individual and separate is in fact necessarily related to something else.

With his use of the concept of recognition, Hegel draws on the work of Fichte,[15] who explored this in connection with social-political philosophy, specifically in his book *The Foundations of Natural Right*. The question for Fichte is how to establish our basic relation to others in society as one concerning justice, based on rights and duties. As free individuals, we pursue different activities, mutually determining and conditioning one another. My individuality results from its contrast with my fellow members of society. By the same token others define themselves in contrast to me. I regard other people as free in their spheres of activity. Their freedom implies that they can potentially interfere with my sphere of activity and limit my freedom, but for our society to function properly, we must exercise control and respect others. This is a kind of self-limitation.[16] I limit myself so that others can act freely in

[15] James Alexander Clarke, "Fichte and Hegel on Recognition," *British Journal for the History of Philosophy*, 17(2) (2009), 365–385; Robert R. Williams, *Recognition: Fichte and Hegel on the Other* (Albany: State University of New York Press, 1992); Allen W. Wood, *Hegel's Ethical Thought* (Cambridge: Cambridge University Press, 1990), pp. 77–93; Ludwig Siep, *Anerkennung als Prinzip der praktischen Philosophie. Untersuchungen zu Hegels Jenaer Philosophie des Geistes* (Freiburg: Karl Alber, 1979); Wolfgang Janke, "Anerkennung. Fichtes Grundlegung des Rechtsgrundes," *Kant-Studien*, 82(2) (1991), 197–218; Gabriel Gottlieb, "A Family Quarrel: Fichte's Deduction of Right and Recognition," in *Kant and His German Contemporaries*, vol. 2, *Aesthetics, History, Politics, and Religion*, ed. by Daniel Dahlstrom (Cambridge: Cambridge University Press, 2018), pp. 170–192; Dean Moyar, "Fichte's Organic Unification: Recognition and the Self-Overcoming of Social Contract Theory," in Gabriel Gottlieb (ed.), *Fichte's Foundations of Natural Right: A Critical Guide* (Cambridge: Cambridge University Press, 2016), pp. 218–238; Douglas Moggach, "Fichte's Theories of Intersubjectivity," *The European Legacy*, 1(6) (1996), 1934–1948; Thomas P. Hohler, *Imagination and Reflection: Intersubjectivity. Fichte's Grundlage of 1794* (The Hague: Martinus Nijhoff, 1982). See also the useful articles on Fichte's relation to Hegel in Daniel Breazeale and Tom Rockmore (eds.), *Fichte, German Idealism, and Early Romanticism* (Amsterdam and New York: Rodopi, 2010) (*Fichte-Studien-Supplementa*, vol. 24).

[16] Johann Gottlieb Fichte, *Grundlage des Naturrechts nach Principen der Wissenschaftslehre* (Jena and Leipzig: Christian Ernst Gabler, 1796), p. 37. (Note that Fichte published

their spheres of activity, just as they limit themselves so that I can pursue my own projects.

Our rationality enables us to see the freedom of others and limit ourselves so as not to interfere with it. The key element is our mutual recognition of each other as free rational beings: "Thus the relation of free beings to one another is a relation of reciprocal interaction through intelligence and freedom. One cannot recognize the other if both do not mutually recognize each other; and one cannot treat the other as a free being, if both do not mutually treat each other as free."[17] This reciprocity is necessary for the development of both individuals and the society they comprise. Fichte emphasizes that his "entire theory of right rests upon it."[18] For another person, with their own rationality, to recognize me as rational is for them to agree with my own self-conception. This agreement is possible because we are both rational agents who can recognize each other as such based on our actions. I must treat other people in a way that is consistent with my view of them as rational by respecting their freedom and rationality and, by doing so, encourage them to reciprocate. This analysis by Fichte is the point of departure for Hegel in the *Phenomenology*.

In the scenario Hegel sketches, one person meets another and looks at them. The person can immediately see that what is standing opposite them is a person and not a thing or object of nature as before. When one looks at a thing, there is nothing that looks back, so the thing is not regarded as a threat. However, when I look at another person, I see their eyes looking at me. I thus become self-conscious and aware of myself. I see myself from the outside, from the perspective of the other. Hegel describes this as a kind of coming out of oneself (when one sees the other) and then returning to oneself (when one sees oneself through the eyes of the other). The eyes of the other function as a kind of mirror that one's glance bounces off before returning to the viewer.

But there is something uncomfortable about being looked at by the other person. I have my own conception of who I am, but when I look at another person looking at me, even without exchanging a word, I clearly sense that the other person's picture of me is different from my picture of myself. I can feel the other person judging me, condemning me, laughing at me, and denigrating me. In a parallel fashion, I, in turn, can give a hostile and disapproving look to the other person as well, making them feel uncertain. So the natural result of this situation is aggression and hostility. I wish to eliminate the other person's negative picture of me and thus confirm my own self-image.

---

the second part of this work the following year: *Grundlage des Naturrechts nach Principen der Wissenschaftslehre. Zweiter Theil oder Angewandtes Naturrecht* [Jena and Leipzig: Christian Ernst Gabler, 1797].) (English translation: *Foundations of Natural Right*, trans. by Michael Baur, ed. by Frederick Neuhouser [Cambridge: Cambridge University Press, 2000], p. 41.)

[17] Fichte, *Grundlage des Naturrechts* (1796), p. 38. *Foundations of Natural Right*, p. 42.
[18] Fichte, *Grundlage des Naturrechts* (1796), p. 38. *Foundations of Natural Right*, p. 42.

We can understand Hegel's idea here at a common-sense level. We all have views about ourselves and the world that we take to be true. But other people also have their views, and some of these stand in contradiction to ours. This makes us uncertain. We want to believe that our views are correct, but they seem to be called into question if we are alone in holding them to be true. But if our views are also held to be true by others – for example, our friends or family – then this seems to serve as a kind of confirmation of their truth. A given opinion is thus not just my personal view but is really true since everyone else thinks the same thing. This makes us feel more certain and confident about both ourselves and the world. We thus spend much time and energy negotiating truth claims, large and small, with other people. We usually do this with arguments and persuasion. In the scenario that Hegel wants to describe, the people involved do not yet have at their disposal the tools to mediate their truth claims by means of logical argument. Instead, their only resort is to try to intimidate or physically force the other person into agreement.

I need to prove to the other that I am better than they think I am. In their eyes I can see that they regard me as nothing other than an object of nature, like an animal. In other words, they see that I have natural drives and desires and that these are what rule my life; the other person does not recognize me for who I really am – as someone who is higher than just this creature of nature. The lives of animals are dictated by their natural drives, which they immediately try to satisfy. They seem generally incapable of doing anything else. Humans, by contrast, can defer the satisfaction of their natural drives and prioritize them as lower than other things. In this way we are able to master the element of nature in ourselves and demonstrate that we are free, that is, that we have a higher faculty than the natural drives. One of the most basic instincts or drives is that of self-preservation. So, in the scenario that Hegel presents, in order to show the other the truth of who I am, I must risk everything, even my own life. I must show the other that I am completely independent and not attached to anything by overcoming my drive to preserve my own life. Only in this way can I prove that I am in fact free from the limitations of nature, and only in this way can I show that I am what Hegel calls "spirit," that is, a self-conscious person.

This development happens on both sides since just as I feel threatened by the other, so also the other person feels threatened by my disapproving look. The result of this is a violent struggle during which each person attempts to assert their own independence from nature and demonstrate to the other that they are not weighed down by the natural aspect of their being. Each side must thus risk death as a way of proving their true self.

One outcome of this violent struggle is that one of the contenders is defeated and dies. The defeated party demonstrated their independence from nature and risked their life, but if they die, they have gained nothing from this. The victorious party is in much the same position. The victor's goal was to compel the other person to recognize them for who they are, but with the other person dead, no such recognition is forthcoming. The immediate threat to one's own conception of oneself is eliminated, but no confirmation of one's own view has been achieved.

The other possible outcome is that one of the two combatants eventually surrenders for fear of losing their life. At this moment, that person shows that in fact they are still dependent on nature; by capitulating, they still hold their natural self to be of value and do not want to lose it. This inferior relation to nature is exactly what the other person wanted to see. Thus the victorious party is confirmed in their negative and disapproving view of the defeated person. This outcome means that the two people now emerge into two different roles: one is dominant, the master, and the other submissive, the bondsman or servant.

A key point in Hegel's account is that the very nature of self-consciousness depends on our interaction with others. To know who we are, we must have the other as the vehicle by means of which we see ourselves. An important implication of this is that self-consciousness is not something fixed and static; instead, it is a process. Just as our relations to others are always changing, so also is our self-conscious understanding of ourselves. We develop a sense of self-consciousness as small children, and this basic self-awareness is always present to us throughout our lives. But the details of our self-conception are always being negotiated in our various interactions with other people. As individuals, we do not appear as finished and forever fixed. Rather we are fluid, constantly changing and developing.

## 1.3    Hegel's Analysis of the Lord and the Bondsman

In this new situation the master receives from the bondsman the recognition for being the master. The bondsman, by contrast, receives only the negative recognition of being the servant and the one who lost the struggle. He is accordingly disdained and treated with contempt by the master. The master's negative view of him is reflected back to the bondsman, who is compelled to accept it as his own self-image. He regards himself as weak, unimportant, and inessential. As a consequence of his condition, the bondsman is compelled to work for the master in order to produce what is needed to meet the master's needs. The bondsman must labor in terror every day, while the lord simply enjoys the fruits of the bondsman's labor without having to work for them.

So it looks as if the master has created a good situation that he can exploit for a long time. But then in the course of things his situation proves to be not as favorable as one might think. The lord gains his recognition and the confirmation of his self-image from the slave. He knows that he is the master because the bondsman recognizes him as such. But when he sees the fear in the eyes of the bondsman, he realizes that the bondsman's recognition is not freely given but rather coerced. The master is in effect forcing the bondsman to recognize him with the constant threat of renewed violence. The bondsman will say or do almost anything to avoid this, so he is willing to pretend to recognize the master, but deep down he despises him and resents his own position of servitude. So the recognition that the master receives from the bondsman is not real or meaningful.

This is the same kind of recognition that dictators and tyrants receive from their terrified subjects. Afraid of losing their property, their jobs, their freedom, or even their lives, people in a tyrannical regime will go to great lengths to assure the dictator of their goodwill and loyal support. But in the privacy of their minds, everyone resents the dictator. Since no one can do anything about the situation, everyone fears speaking openly about it, and this only causes the resentment toward the dictator to grow. In this kind of social condition, it is clear that the recognition ostensibly given is in fact false since it is coerced. One cannot force love or respect. These are things that must be freely given in order to be meaningful. Coerced recognition from a terrified subject or a slave means nothing. Recognition only makes sense if it comes freely and spontaneously from an equal. This undermines the lord's sense of recognition and makes him forever uncertain about what the bondsman really thinks.

Further, the master does not have to work but can simply enjoy the fruits of the slave's labor. In the course of time this means that the master begins to lose his independence from nature and becomes dependent on the slave. This is paradoxical since the initial struggle was all about both parties demonstrating their independence from nature and each other. Thus another inversion of roles takes place. The initial situation is now strangely reversed, with the master being dependent on the slave and recognizing him.

The situation of the bondsman is also transformed in the course of time. Initially the bondsman was the one who capitulated since he was unable to overcome his fear and risk everything. Now in his position as a slave, he lives in daily fear and is subject to hard work. In time this allows him to develop discipline and to overcome his anxiety. He is exposed to many hardships, which he gradually gets used to, and this makes it easier for him to endure the difficulties of doing without things that are necessary for him to meet his natural needs. He thus becomes stronger and more self-sufficient as he develops and works. Moreover, although he is deprived of the enjoyment of the product of his labor, which he must immediately surrender to the master, nonetheless he gains recognition from the master for it. By making use of the servant's product, the master, without even saying a word, is conceding that the servant has done something well and has produced something valuable. The master thus recognizes his work and ability. The servant, therefore, oddly receives the more meaningful form of recognition of the two. Now he finds a sense of gratification from his work. He feels fulfilled by being able to work and create something valuable.

At the conclusion of this analysis, Hegel talks about the relationship of the lord and the bondsman as one of alienation.[19] Each person regards the other as something fundamentally different and separate – a foreign threat. Initially, the two individuals feel alienated from one another since each sees in the eyes of the other a negative view of themselves. They have a self-image that is contradicted by the picture of themselves that the other person has. They cannot identify with the negative image that the other person is projecting of them, and this is the cause of the conflict. Then, when the roles of lord and bondsman are established, the bondsman continues to feel alienated from the lord since the lord has a negative and demeaning conception of the bondsman that the bondsman cannot identify with. But through labor, the bondsman creates a product, which is recognized by the lord as important and valuable. The bondsman can thus identify with the product; it is an object in the external world that is a reflection of his own personality. As an object, the product acts as a sign representing him in the world even when he is not around. It is recognized and appreciated by the lord, and in this way the positive estimation of its value is not just postulated by the personal opinion of the bondsman but is validated by the other. Thus through his labor the bondsman's initial alienation is overcome. By seeing his product in the world as something valued by others, the bondsman is reconciled with the condition of the world and sees a part of himself in it.

Hegel also talks about alienation in terms of overcoming fear. At first, the individual is confronted by another, whom he fears. This fear is what makes him a bondsman. In a sense this is the relation that children have to their parents or teachers. When we are young, we wish to act immediately on our desires and inclinations, and we are prevented from doing so by, for example, our parents. They set the rules and tell us what we can and cannot do. Children *fear* the anger and punishment of their parents, so they try to adhere to the rules. But in the course of time, as children grow and develop, this kind of parental control is gradually phased out. As the child grows into adulthood, they no longer need this kind of check since they have learned how to manage their own desires and inclinations in an appropriate manner. One can say that the child has internalized the voice of the parent or the teacher in their own conscience, good judgment, or, if one will, superego. What was at first outside or external is now internal. So at first the child was confronted by what Hegel calls an "alien being,"[20] that is, another person, but then this alien entity is overcome and becomes a part of oneself. In this way the individual becomes

---

[19] Hegel, *Phänomenologie des Geistes*, pp. 126f.; *Hegel's Phenomenology of Spirit*, pp. 118f.
[20] Hegel, *Phänomenologie des Geistes*, p. 126; *Hegel's Phenomenology of Spirit*, p. 118.

independent since they no longer depend on others or external forces to
determine their behavior. Instead, they can regulate it themselves.

The lordship and bondage analysis represents an interesting reversal of roles
in the relation of recognition. The master, who initially demonstrated his
independence from nature, in fact proves to be dependent on the slave.
Although the master, as the dominant figure, initially enjoyed the recognition
of the slave, ultimately he receives no meaningful recognition at all. Likewise,
the slave, who initially was overly dependent on nature, through work and
discipline is able to overcome and master it and in the end show his independence over it.[21] The slave, who at the outset was regarded as nothing, in fact,
through his labor, comes to receive recognition from the master. This is
a complex analysis that is insightful for issues of interpersonal relations. It
can be read as an account of class conflict between groups of people. Hegel's
analysis was decisively influential for the theory of alienated labor that Marx
and Engels later developed.[22]

An important point that Hegel wants to make, again in an extension of
Fichte's analysis, is that as individuals we are fundamentally determined by our
interactions with others. Our common sense tells us that we are who we are on
our own and separate from other people. We do not need them in any way for
the creation of our own self-image or self-conception. We are all familiar with
the idea of the self-made man, who came from impoverished circumstances to
achieve a position of great wealth and power. The idea behind this is that the
self-made man's success was accomplished solely due to his own industry,
diligence, and ability and that he received no assistance from his family,
community, state, or anything else. As sociologists like to point out, this idea
is a myth. Hegel's analysis of the lordship-bondage dialectic shows that who we
are is dependent on the kind of recognition that we receive from others. Our
self-conception is never something that is created and developed in isolation.
Rather, it is in constant interaction with other people, from whom we are
always receiving feedback that we take into consideration. In this constant
negotiation of our views with those of others, we come to constitute our ideas
of ourselves. So one of the goals of Hegel's analysis is to refute the view that we
all exist as isolated, atomic individuals who have nothing to do with one
another. Instead, he argues, our very self-conception and our very freedom
are dependent on other people.

Hegel's analysis of the lord and the bondsman is also relevant for social-
political philosophy. His account has been compared to a kind of state-of-
nature situation that the contract theorists, such as Hobbes and Locke, posit as

---

[21] See Rudolf Gumppenberg, "Bewußtsein und Arbeit. Zu G. W. F. Hegels *Phänomenologie
des Geistes*," *Zeitschrift für Philosophische Forschung*, 26 (1972), 372–388.

[22] See Werner Becker, *Idealistische und materialistische Dialektik. Das Verhältnis von
Herrschaft und Knechtschaft bei Hegel und Marx* (Stuttgart: Kohlhammer, 1970).

existing prior to the creation of the state.[23] According to contract theory, the state comes into being when individuals jointly come to an agreement to enter into a cooperative community ruled by a designated leader for the sake of mutual protection. This view presents individuals as fully free and developed in the state of nature. The political state is then conceived as something artificial in contrast to the original human condition in the state of nature. The state is in a sense conceived as a necessary evil since individuals are required to limit their freedom in order to live in a community. For Hegel, this view is fundamentally wrong. Our relation to other human beings is not simply something accidental or arbitrary. It is not just that we simply happen to prefer to live together with other human beings. Rather, there is something necessary about this relation and order of things. To be who we are, we necessarily need the other. Our very self-consciousness and identity are created in interaction with others. Therefore, the state and social life in general are necessary expressions of the individual. Similarly, the freedom that the contract theorists claim humanity enjoyed in the state of nature is meaningless. True freedom is not simply the ability to do whatever one wants whenever one wants, free from any external constraint. Rather, it means rationally choosing to limit oneself in different ways. Thus we enjoy true freedom when we live with others in a community and when we freely choose to submit to laws that permit us to develop ourselves as individuals. A child is not free who is allowed to do anything they want. Instead, they can only be said to be genuinely free when, through education and upbringing, they learn right and wrong and act according to their own rational choice. Hegel's account here can be regarded as a refutation of the myth that we are all ultimately atomic and isolated individuals who could just as well live without civic or social life. On the contrary, our personality, self-identity, and indeed our very freedom are all necessarily bound up with this social sphere. To be who we are, we must live with others in social relations.

## 1.4   Hegel's Analysis of the Unhappy Consciousness

Hegel's discussion of the so-called unhappy consciousness follows the account of the lord and the bondsman in the "Self-Consciousness" chapter of *The Phenomenology of Spirit*.[24] Specifically, it appears as the third part of a section called "Stoicism, Skepticism and the Unhappy Consciousness." While not as influential as the lordship and bondage section, the unhappy consciousness has nonetheless played an important role in the reception of Hegel's philosophy in

---

[23] See Ludwig Siep, "Der Kampf um Anerkennung zu Hegels Auseinandersetzung mit Hobbes in den Jenaer Schriften," *Hegel-Studien*, 9 (1974), 155–207.

[24] Hegel, *Phänomenologie des Geistes*, pp. 141–161; *Hegel's Phenomenology of Spirit*, pp. 126–138.

the thought of figures such as the French philosopher Jean Wahl (1888–1974).[25] Perhaps one of the reasons why this analysis has not caught on in the same way as the lordship and bondage discussion is that there is less agreement about its content and meaning.

The unhappy consciousness can be understood as an analysis of a form of religious thinking. Hegel explores different ways in which the pious religious believer understands themselves and their relation to the divine. It might strike one as strange that this kind of analysis would follow the account of the lordship and bondage discussion that we just explored. But these discussions are in fact related in an important way. While the lordship and bondage analysis featured two individuals and the different forms of alienation that took place between them, the unhappy consciousness moves this relation to the inwardness of a single individual. In other words, the split between two separate individuals can be seen as occurring in the mind of a single person.[26] Thus the form of alienation is not one between two separate people but rather is a kind of self-alienation. Hegel refers to this as the "unhappy" consciousness for precisely this reason: the individual is split or divided within themselves. The different aspects of this relation that Hegel traces can be understood as different attempts by the individual to overcome this split or division and to reach a form of reconciliation.

The basic terms of the dual consciousness are simply the pious believer and God. On the one hand, the believer is aware of themselves, and on the other, they have an idea of God. But insofar as the idea of God is just that, *an idea* in the mind of the believer, both elements – that is, their awareness of themselves and their awareness of God – are in their own mind. It lies in the nature of self-consciousness that we can imagine other people without them being physically present. From this ability we can always imagine the eye of God upon us, even when there is no perceptible evidence of this. But the believer does not realize this, and when they think of God, they imagine an externally existing being.

Hegel uses his own jargon to refer to this relationship. God is conceived of as "the Unchangeable," that is, as an eternal, substantial, transcendent entity. God creates the universe, which is always changing, but God himself, who is beyond

---

[25] See Jean Wahl, *La conscience malheureuse* (Paris: Denoël et Steele, 1936). See also Bruce Baugh, "Hegel in Modern French Philosophy: The Unhappy Consciousness," *Laval théologique et philosophique*, 49(3) (1993), 423–438; Murray Greene, "Hegel's 'Unhappy Consciousness' and Nietzsche's 'Slave Morality,'" in Darrel E. Christensen (ed.), *Hegel and the Philosophy of Religion* (The Hague: Martinus Nijhoff, 1970), pp. 125–141; Gwendoline Jarczyk and Pierre-Jean Labarrière, *Le malheur de la conscience ou l'accès à la raison. Liberté de l'autoconscience: stoïcisme, scepticisme et la conscience malheureuse. Texte et commentaire* (Paris: Aubier, 1989); Jon Stewart, "Die Rolle des unglücklichen Bewußtseins in Hegels *Phänomenologie des Geistes*," *Deutsche Zeitschrift für Philosophie*, 39 (1991), 12–21.

[26] Hegel, *Phänomenologie des Geistes*, p. 141; *Hegel's Phenomenology of Spirit*, p. 126.

nature, never changes. By contrast, the individual conceives of the world and everything in it, including themselves, as "the Changeable." The world consists of finite, empirically perceivable things, which are forever coming into being, decaying, and passing away. In theological language, this is the distinction between the Creator and Creation.

The basic feature of the world of nature is change. The believer is aware of this, and the basic changes that characterize their own being separate them radically from God as an eternal being. The believer thus has a negative conception of themselves as finite, transitory, and sinful, in absolute contrast to the conception of God as infinite, eternal, and perfect. The individual thus conceives of the divine as, in Hegel's words, an "alien being"[27] or an "alien reality."[28] The individual and the divine are radically separated and thus "alien to one another."[29]

Hegel outlines three ways in which the believer tries to overcome this radical difference and become one with God. The first attempt concerns the Incarnation of God in Christ. Initially, God as the creator of the universe is thought of as transcendent and beyond the world that is known to the believer. In this relation, the believer can try to think of or imagine God, but it is impossible for them to get any closer than their own imagination. According to Hegel, the religious believer relates to this conception of God not in terms of concepts but rather feelings. He calls this "devotion," "the pure heart," or "musical thinking" and refers to different aspects of the church service, such as the use of bells, incense, and the singing of hymns.[30] This feeling serves only to underscore the painful separation from the transcendent God. This is the form of religious belief of unreflective or uneducated believers.

With the Incarnation, God is incarnated in human form and enters into the world of actuality. One important aspect of the doctrine of the Incarnation is that of reconciliation. With the figure of Christ, humans are reconciled with God and the burden of original sin is overcome. The figure of Christ plays an important role in the relation of recognition since the believer can now see themselves through the eyes of the divine by seeing Christ. A concrete relation of self-conscious recognition arises when one sees that the divine is in fact a human being and then realizes that, as a human being, one has something of the divine in oneself. (Humans are made in the image of God.) This realization helps the individual to overcome what seemed to be a radical split or opposition between the divine and the human.

---

[27] Hegel, *Phänomenologie des Geistes*, p. 142 (*ein Fremdes*); *Hegel's Phenomenology of Spirit*, p. 127. *Phänomenologie des Geistes*, p. 143 (*das fremde . . . Wesen*); *Hegel's Phenomenology of Spirit*, p. 128.

[28] Hegel, *Phänomenologie des Geistes*, p. 146; *Hegel's Phenomenology of Spirit*, p. 130.

[29] Hegel, *Phänomenologie des Geistes*, p. 141; *Hegel's Phenomenology of Spirit*, p. 127.

[30] Hegel, *Phänomenologie des Geistes*, p. 148; *Hegel's Phenomenology of Spirit*, p. 131.

But Hegel points out that this form of reconciliation or recognition has limitations. Christ is a human being in the world of actuality, and, like everything else in the world of actuality, he too must change and ultimately perish. This means that after his death he is no longer physically present to offer the kind of immediate recognition that the religious believer yearns for. Christians born after the death of Christ attempt to recover some vestige of the physical remains of the divine and to hold on to them firmly. The result of this is the desire to collect holy relics, such as splinters from the cross or the funeral shroud of Jesus. Hegel also mentions the desire to locate and preserve the grave of Jesus. (These can be taken as references to different practices of medieval Christianity and to the discovery of the purported site of the crucifixion and the tomb of Christ by St. Helena, the mother of Constantine the Great.)[31]

According to Hegel, these attempts all end in failure. Whenever one tries to get hold of Christ as an object of sense perception, he disappears, and all that is left is the physical remains. This demonstrates that the divine has again become a transcendent entity that is "beyond" the world and again radically separated from the religious believer. Moreover, it is a misunderstanding to think of the importance of God or Christ as something physical. What is physical changes, decays, and perishes; by contrast, a thought or a concept – the Christian message – is eternal. Thus the approach to religious faith that is focused primarily on emotion, feeling, or the senses is misguided since it leads to a constant struggle in the face of the transitory and ever-changing nature of the subject of faith when it is regarded as the object of sense perception.

The second attempt at reconciliation concerns what Hegel refers to with the terms *desire* and *work*.[32] Hegel seems to have in mind the kind of work that religious penitents do in order to atone for sins, deprecate themselves, and thereby get closer to God. The believer puts aside their own private interests and focuses on work, dedicating their labor and its fruits to God. They denigrate themselves, regarding themselves as nothing and selflessly working for the divine. Hegel points out a contradiction in this attempt to renounce oneself entirely and to unite with the divine through work. In their self-deprecation, the individual must claim that their own efforts with all of their labor are meaningless. But this then undermines the idea that their work is for God, for whom the work is supposed to be meaningful in some way. The work that the believer does, they ascribe not to themselves but to God, who gave them the ability to perform it. Moreover, the believer renounces all personal interests and enjoyment in the products of their labor, which are all dedicated to God. But this is not entirely true either since in fact the individual also lives from the products of this work, consuming the bread and the wine that they

---

[31] See John W. Burbidge, "'Unhappy Consciousness' in Hegel: An Analysis of Medieval Catholicism?," *Mosaic*, 11 (1978), 67–80.

[32] Hegel, *Phänomenologie des Geistes*, p. 150; *Hegel's Phenomenology of Spirit*, p. 132.

and others like them have made. Further, the individual cannot deny the fact that they indeed did perform the work and derive satisfaction from this. (Here we see an echo of the bondsman's relation to the master in the previous analysis.) This undermines the idea that the work represents an entirely selfless devotion to God since it contains a clear element of self-interest.

The third attempt at reconciliation comes through the idea of a mediator, that is, a priest who stands between God and the believer. Here Hegel seems to have in mind a model such as that of a monastery or a nunnery. When a monk enters a monastery, he is obliged to give up his possessions and property. He thus abandons life in the world, where one works in order to accumulate private wealth. Instead, his new goal is to do the work of God, which means putting his own will and personal interests aside. The monk is thus obliged to work and perform a number of tasks that are necessary to keep the monastery running. The religious believer or monk again works for God, but now he can transfer the product of his labor to the Church. He can thus renounce his own agency and refer everything to the Church. The abbot or prior is responsible for the actions of the monks and makes all decisions for them. So the work of the monk is no longer his own but rather belongs to the abbot or the Church, as do the products of his labor. But here ultimate reconciliation still eludes the believer. While one renounces one's own will and transfers it to the Church, the believer does not see their will reflected in the Church again, and thus their alienation from God is merely replaced by an alienation from the Church. The promise of salvation in the Church is not something that the believer can redeem in this life. It is a promise for the future, and thus the believer remains separated from it. The believer finds themselves confronted by yet another transcendent entity, and the division of consciousness remains.

The point of the unhappy consciousness is that the efforts of the individual are closely connected with the efforts of others, and indeed with human institutions such as the Church. When people work in the context of these institutions, their actions take on an importance that is greater than merely the subjective, arbitrary actions of individuals. Instead, their actions become a part of a broader project. This opens up the possibility of greater fulfillment and recognition for one's work. This then leads Hegel, later in the *Phenomenology*, to explore in more detail the different kinds of human institutions and ways of thinking that involve groups of people instead of more or less isolated individuals. While we started with two people in the lordship and bondage scenario, we have now reached a considerably more complex situation with groups of people and social institutions.

The unhappy consciousness illustrates different forms of alienation. Most obviously, the unhappy consciousness conceives of God as a separate and radically different entity from itself. The unhappy consciousness is alienated from God in the sense that it cannot overcome the split between itself and God. Despite many attempts to resolve the dualism, God always remains separate and other. This idea also leads to a sense of alienation from one's own self-conception. The unhappy consciousness conceives of itself both as a believer strenuously trying to get closer to God and as a hopeless sinner. In this way the unhappy consciousness is also unhappy because it has a contradictory view of itself that it cannot overcome. The unhappy consciousness believes it has a human nature that was created by God, but, due to sin, it cannot live up to this, and this causes it to be alienated from itself.

### 1.5  *The Phenomenology of Spirit* as a Book about Alienation

One of the main issues in *The Phenomenology of Spirit* is the overcoming of alienation. This lies in the nature of the work as a whole.[33] Hegel's goal is, as noted, to refute and thus overcome different forms of common-sense dualism, that is, different conceptions of the split between subject and object, and subjects and other subjects. It was also noted that the idea of alienation always concerns some conception of separation or difference. In this sense, all of Hegel's analyses here can be seen as treating different forms of alienation since they all examine forms of dualism, which are characteristic of this concept. With alienation there is always, so to speak, *an other*.

In the "Consciousness" chapter, an attempt is made to overcome the alienation with objects that appear as independent, self-subsisting others. Hegel shows that in fact they are necessarily bound up with the conscious subject. We cannot even begin to describe an object without having recourse to forms of human thought. As we saw in the "Self-Consciousness" chapter, an attempt is made to overcome the alienation with *the other* as a self-conscious subject, which appears as independent and foreign. Who we are as individuals is necessarily determined by the recognition that we receive from others. In the "Reason" chapter, *the other* is different groups of people and their ways of thinking. In other words, I have my own way of viewing the world, and this may be at variance from the ways in which other people view it. So, in a sense, the relation of one person vis-à-vis another that we saw in the lordship and bondage dialectic is replaced here by a relation of one person vis-à-vis a group of people and their collective ways of thinking. The goal is to overcome the

---

[33] See Timothy L. Brownlee, "Alienation and Recognition in Hegel's *Phenomenology of Spirit*," *Philosophical Forum*, 46(4) (2015), 377–396; Gavin Rae, "Hegel, Alienation, and the Phenomenological Development of Consciousness," *International Journal of Philosophical Studies*, 20(1) (2012), 23–42; Gavin Rae, "Alienation and the *Phenomenology of Spirit*," chapter 6 in his *Realizing Freedom: Hegel, Sartre, and the Alienation of Human Being* (London: Palgrave MacMillan, 2011), pp. 143–164; Helmut Nicolaus, "Entfremdung nach der *Phänomenologie*," chapter 5 of his *Hegels Theorie der Entfremdung* (Heidelberg: Manutius, 1995), pp. 247–329; Conrad Boey, *L'aliénation dans la Phénoménologie de l'esprit de G. W. F. Hegel* (Paris and Bruges: Desclée, De Brouwer, 1970).

alienation of the individual from the group and to bring into alignment the view of the particular person with that of the whole.

In the "Spirit" chapter, *the other* is represented by different kinds of customs and institutions that the individual finds in the world, seen from a historical perspective. In fact, it is here, where Hegel uses the term "alienation" most frequently, specifically, in the section entitled "Self-Alienated Spirit: Culture"[34] and its first part, "The World of Self-Alienated Spirit."[35] In Hegel's grand scheme, this section corresponds to the "Self-Consciousness" chapter but at a higher level of development.[36] Here he treats different concrete historical institutions, ways of thinking and interacting that appeared in medieval European culture. Individuals are confronted by seemingly arbitrary practices and customs that they did not create. They thus feel alienated from them as something that is external and imposed on them from the outside. Yet people are obliged to go along with them if they are to participate in social life at all. In this context Hegel explores the relations between a king or sovereign and their vassals. This analysis is an echo of the lordship and bondage dialectic. The nobles or vassals disdain the king, and only by compulsion do they *recognize* the royal power. They must overcome this by their noble actions in the service of the court and the accumulation of private wealth. The different roles in society are established by a complex network of recognition, with some people standing above one's given station and others standing below it. The individual's self-understanding is bound up with their placement in this social hierarchy, which is determined by the recognition and acceptance of it by others.

In the next chapter, "Religion," *the other* is represented by different conceptions of the divine. The gods appear as independent and foreign entities. According to Hegel, human beings are what he calls "spirit," but this is not something that is simply given but rather takes some time to develop. As humans evolve from nature, they are initially not aware of this element of their character. It remains as unfulfilled potential. Instead, they see themselves as continuous with nature. This is reflected in their religious beliefs and specifically their conceptions of the divine. Early human beings have ideas of the gods as entities closely associated with natural objects: the sun, the moon, a river, water, or other natural elements. In Zoroastrianism, fire is worshiped as sacred, and in Hinduism and the Egyptian religion, there are sacred bulls and cows. For Hegel, this is not surprising since these peoples, he claims, had not yet developed to the point where they could understand the divine as

---

[34] Hegel, *Phänomenologie des Geistes*, pp. 429–547; *Hegel's Phenomenology of Spirit*, pp. 294–363.

[35] Hegel, *Phänomenologie des Geistes*, pp. 434–485; *Hegel's Phenomenology of Spirit*, pp. 296–328.

[36] See Jon Stewart, "The Architectonic of Hegel's *Phenomenology of Spirit*," *Philosophy and Phenomenological Research*, 55(4) (1995), 747–776.

something higher – as spirit. Only in later religions, such as Greek and Roman polytheism, do the gods take on an anthropomorphic character. According to the story that Hegel wants to tell, human beings feel a sense of alienation from their gods until they reach the point where they can conceive of God as spirit. This has to do with the concept of recognition. When we see a god as a terrifying force of nature, an animal, or a creature such as the Egyptian god Anubis, who has the head of a jackal, we feel alienated. We cannot recognize ourselves in these forms of the divine. Only when we see the divine as human can we recognize ourselves in it.

At each level in *The Phenomenology of Spirit*, there is some kind of *other* that confronts the human mind. The goal is to work through these different conceptions and to overcome them by showing the deeper, hidden unity. Thus the goal of overcoming alienation is present throughout. Indeed, it can be said that alienation is the motor that drives Hegel's dialectical analysis forward. Since there is a separation or division at each stage, there is a need to overcome it with a new conception. Given the centrality of this motif and even Hegel's explicit use of the term, it is odd that it was only in the twentieth century that the concept of alienation was fully recognized as an important topic in his philosophy.[37] But in many ways it can be said that this work and this motif played a significant role in setting the philosophical agenda for the nineteenth century.

[37] See Walter Kaufmann, "The Inevitability of Alienation," introductory essay in Richard Schacht, *Alienation* (London: George Allen & Unwin, 1971), pp. xvff.

## 2

# Hegel's Account of Christianity and Its Origins in the *Lectures on the Philosophy of Religion* and *Lectures on the Philosophy of History*

Hegel's *Lectures on the Philosophy of Religion* were published in 1832, after his death, by one of his followers, the theologian Philipp Marheineke (1780–1846).[1] This is a profoundly rich work that attempts to give a defense of Christianity. The text is divided into three large parts: "The Concept of Religion," "The Determinate Religion," and "The Absolute Religion." The first part examines the abstract conception of the divine. It asks simply what is God in general, without any specific analysis of any given religion. By contrast, the second section, "The Determinate Religion," gives an overview of the religions of the

---

[1] G. W. F. Hegel, *Vorlesungen über die Philosophie der Religion*, vols. 1–2, ed. by Philipp Marheineke, vols. 11–12 (1832), in *Georg Wilhelm Friedrich Hegel's Werke. Vollständige Ausgabe*, vols. 1–18, ed. by Ludwig Boumann, Friedrich Förster, Eduard Gans, Karl Hegel, Leopold von Henning, Heinrich Gustav Hotho, Philipp Marheineke, Karl Ludwig Michelet, Karl Rosenkranz, and Johannes Schulze (Berlin: Duncker und Humblot, 1832–1845). (English translation: G. W. F. Hegel, *Lectures on the Philosophy of Religion*, vols. 1–3, trans. by E. B. Speirs and J. Burdon Sanderson [London: Routledge and Kegan Paul; New York: Humanities Press, 1962].) For works on Hegel's philosophy of religion, see John W. Burbidge, *Hegel on Logic and Religion: The Reasonableness of Christianity* (Albany: State University of New York Press, 1992); Martin J. De Nys, *Hegel and Theology* (London and New York: T. & T. Clark, 2009); William Desmond, *Hegel's God: A Counterfeit Double?* (Aldershot: Ashgate, 2003); Emil L. Fackenheim, *The Religious Dimension in Hegel's Thought* (Bloomington: Indiana University Press, 1967); Peter C. Hodgson, *Hegel and Christian Theology: A Reading of the Lectures on the Philosophy of Religion* (Oxford: Oxford University Press, 2005); Walter Jaeschke, *Die Religionsphilosophie Hegels* (Darmstadt: Wissenschaftliche Buchgesellschaft, 1983); Walter Jaeschke, *Die Vernunft in der Religion: Studien zur Grundlegung der Religionsphilosophie Hegels* (Stuttgart-Bad Cannstatt: Frommann-Holzboog, 1986) (English translation: *Reason in Religion: The Foundations of Hegel's Philosophy of Religion*, trans. by J. Michael Stewart and Peter C. Hodgson [Berkeley and Los Angeles: University of California Press, 1990]); Philip M. Merklinger, *Philosophy, Theology, and Hegel's Berlin Philosophy of Religion, 1821–1827* (Albany: State University of New York Press, 1993); Cyril O'Regan, *The Heterodox Hegel* (Albany: State University of New York Press, 1994); Dale M. Schlitt, *Divine Subjectivity: Understanding Hegel's Philosophy of Religion* (London and Toronto: Associated University Presses, 1990); Jon Stewart, *Hegel's Interpretation of the Religions of the World: The Logic of the Gods* (Oxford: Oxford University Press, 2018).

world and examines their various conceptions of the divine. The goal is to compare these different views with the concept of the divine in general, which was established in the first part. Part I can thus be regarded as a *universal*, an abstract definition or idea, whereas Part II represents an account of a diversity of concrete *particulars* that are then compared to this definition. Finally, in Part III, "The Absolute Religion," these two things come together. This third part is Hegel's account of Christianity, which, he believes, is the one religion that actually corresponds to the adequate and correct conception of the divine that was set out in Part I. This is where the universal and the particular are unified or, put differently, where the particular corresponds to the universal.

In the second part of the lectures, Hegel gives an account of Judaism in his overview of the world religions. This analysis is relevant for his treatment of both the lord-bondsman relation and the unhappy consciousness since he seems to take certain aspects of Judaism to be the model for these famous discussions from *The Phenomenology of Spirit*. He sees in Judaism key elements that are relevant for the topics of alienation, the struggle for recognition, and human freedom.

## 2.1   Hegel's Analysis of the Fall

As a part of his analysis of Judaism, Hegel gives a provocative reading of the famous myth of the Fall at the beginning of Genesis.[2] As is well known, this story is intended to explain certain aspects of the human condition and not least of all the origin of evil in the world. Hegel points out that in earlier religions the issue of evil was not a problem since these religions were polytheistic. In polytheism there are many different gods and goddesses who have responsibility for certain spheres of the universe. There are, for example, rain gods, fire gods, harvest gods, sea gods, and so forth. These deities are limited in their power to the specific natural force that they govern. They have no power or authority over other forces that lie outside their spheres. This is not to say that their powers are equal since there are, of course, some gods or goddesses who are stronger than others depending on what natural force they represent

---

[2]  G. W. F. Hegel, *Vorlesungen über die Philosophie der Religion*, Parts I–III, ed. by Walter Jaeschke (Hamburg: Felix Meiner, 1983–1985, 1993–1995), Part II, vol. 4a, pp. 338n–343n. (This constitutes volumes 3–5 in the edition: G. W. F. Hegel, *Vorlesungen. Ausgewählte Nachschriften und Manuskripte*, vols. 1–17 [Hamburg: Felix Meiner, 1983–2008]. Part I, *Einleitung. Der Begriff der Religion* = vol. 3. Part II, *Die Bestimmte Religion. a: Text* = vol. 4a. Part II, *Die Bestimmte Religion. b: Anhang* = vol. 4b. Part III, *Die vollendete Religion* = vol. 5.) *Lectures on the Philosophy of Religion*, vols. 1–3, ed. by Peter C. Hodgson, trans. by Robert F. Brown, P. C. Hodgson, and J. M. Stewart with the assistance of H. S. Harris (Berkeley: University of California Press, 1984–1987), vol. 2, *Determinate Religion*, pp. 438n–442n. In what follows, all references will be to this new edition of Hegel's lectures, which does not use Marheineke's edition as its textual basis.

and what their area of influence is. For example, Zeus and Jupiter are powerful gods who rule over the others, but their power is not absolute by any means. Instead, they are also limited and need to negotiate with the other gods in order to execute their plans. In this sort of world, the origin of evil is not a problem since it can always be ascribed to malevolent deities. There are some good gods and goddesses who aid and assist human beings, and there are evil ones who vex them. This can be seen most clearly in the two main gods of Zoroastrianism, the god of Light and the Good, Ormuzd, and the god of Darkness and Evil, Ahriman. In this dualistic religion the origin of evil in the world is entirely straightforward – it comes from the evil god, Ahriman.

The problem of evil arises in Judaism since it is a monotheistic religion. There is only one God, Jehovah or Yahweh, and he is supposed to be all-powerful and good. If this is the case, then some explanation must be given for how evil arose in the world since this God could not have created it since he is good. Moreover, if he is all-powerful, he could have prevented it from arising. So the story of the Fall is presented as a way to understand the origin of evil in the universe. In addition, it gives etiologies or explanations for other fundamental facts of human existence.

According to the story in Genesis, the first human beings, Adam and Eve, lived in a paradise, a garden, where all of their needs were met. They were in complete harmony with God and the natural world around them. They had a specific nature as created beings just like the animals and other natural objects. There was in the garden a tree with the knowledge of good and evil, and God forbade Adam and Eve to eat from it. Seduced by the serpent, they defied this prohibition and took fruit from the tree. This then caused a change in their nature, and they suddenly realized that they were different from the animals and for the first time were ashamed of their nakedness. Angered by this defiance, God issued punishments for both Adam and Eve, which their descendants also had to bear. God further exiled them from the garden, and they then had to find what they needed to survive for themselves. Humans have mourned this lost paradise ever since.

Hegel thinks that this familiar story contains certain hidden philosophical truths, although they are expressed in a mythological and pictorial form. At first, humans are natural beings. They live like animals in nature. But then a change occurs, and humans develop what Hegel calls "spirit," that is, a rational or reflective side that animals do not have. In this sense humans step out of nature. Spirit is what makes it possible for humans to develop culture in all of its many forms: science, history, art, religion, philosophy, and so forth. Humans are thus different from nature.

An important part of this difference is the awareness of good and evil. We do not think of animals or small children as either good or evil. They do not have the capacity for reflective thought, so these categories simply do not apply to them. They act on their immediate natural impulses. In Hegel's language, they have not yet separated themselves from nature. Truly human action means that we are aware of good and evil and that we freely choose one or the other. This is what it is to exercise free will. Therefore, Hegel claims that evil consists not in leaving the natural state as represented by the garden but rather in remaining in it. In this state we are the victims of our natural drives, which dictate our actions. But it is only when we have the freedom to overcome these natural impulses that we step out of nature and enter the human sphere.

The idea in the story of the Fall is that this notion of freedom is precisely what Adam and Eve were lacking in the garden. They were like the animals, not knowing good and evil. They did not know that they were naked and felt no shame. It was precisely the knowledge of good and evil that was forbidden to them. God issued this prohibition because this knowledge was reserved for him. Indeed, the serpent points this out when he tempts Adam and Eve by saying that if they eat of the tree, then they will become like God. After they do so, God himself confirms this by recognizing the change that has taken place in them and saying, "See, the man has become like one of us, knowing good and evil."[3] The idea here is that this knowledge is something divine, and humans are not supposed to have it. God knew that humans would be unable to manage the temptations of evil and were thus better off without this knowledge of good and evil, and this is one of the reasons why he issued the prohibition in the first place. When Adam and Eve become aware of their nakedness, they become self-conscious for the first time. Only then can they see themselves from the perspective of the other and feel a sense of shame. The very idea of self-consciousness is thus closely related to what, in biblical language, is described as the knowledge of good and evil. This recalls Hegel's analysis of self-consciousness in *The Phenomenology of Spirit*.

Hegel is, however, critical of the moral interpretation of the story as it appears in the Hebrew Bible. He argues that it lies in the very nature of human beings to be free. Thus as long as one lives in the garden with the animals, one will never lead a fully human life. Once again, to be human means to have free will, and this means to have the possibility of choosing both good and evil. This, however, implies that the possibility of evil is part and parcel of what it is to be human. This possibility must exist for freedom to be meaningful. But there is one unfortunate result of this: There will always be some people who choose evil over good. This is the price that we pay for freedom. For this reason, freedom is always a two-edged sword.[4] But, for Hegel, the loss of the

---

[3] Genesis 3:22. All translations are from *Holy Bible: New Revised Standard Version* (New York and Oxford: Oxford University Press, 1989). See Hegel, *Vorlesungen über die Philosophie der Religion*, Part II, *Die Bestimmte Religion*, vol. 4a, *Vorlesungen. Ausgewählte Nachschriften und Manuskripte*, p. 338n; *Lectures on the Philosophy of Religion*, vol. 2, *Determinate Religion*, p. 439n.

[4] Hegel, *Vorlesungen über die Philosophie der Religion*, Part II, *Die Bestimmte Religion*, vol. 4a, p. 339n; *Lectures on the Philosophy of Religion*, vol. 2, *Determinate Religion*, p. 439n: "Cognition or knowledge is this two-sided, dangerous gift."

paradise of Eden is not something to be lamented but rather a natural part of human development. We have to leave paradise behind us to become fully human.

Hegel is also attentive to the important role played by work, which is later developed by Marx. One of the punishments that God issues to Adam and Eve is that human beings will have to work hard in order to earn a living, or as it is put in Genesis, "cursed is the ground because of you; in toil you shall eat of it all the days of your life; thorns and thistles it shall bring forth for you .... By the sweat of your face you shall eat bread."[5] In the garden, Adam and Eve could readily find whatever they needed to satisfy their natural needs. They had immediate access to the food and water that they needed to sustain themselves since this was provided directly by God, just as he provides it to the other animals. But after the Fall, this changed. Now humans must work for this themselves and cannot expect to receive it as a free gift. In the story in Genesis, this is portrayed as a terrible punishment, but Hegel argues that this misrepresents the situation. To work and to make one's living by means of one's own skills, abilities, and intelligence is exactly what it is to be a human being. This is what makes us higher than the animals that are unable to do this. For this reason, we naturally take pride in things that we have created or in jobs that we have done well. With this we can see an echo of the slave's relation to their product as portrayed in the lordship-bondage dialectic. This sense of pride in our work constitutes a part of the truly human side of our nature. Therefore, to conceive of the need to work as a punishment, a terrible curse, and something to be lamented, as in Genesis, is a misunderstanding, according to Hegel.

## 2.2   The Fall as a Story of Alienation

The story of the Fall is a story of alienation. Hegel explains that it is a mistake to think of the narrative of Adam and Eve and the apple as some contingent, accidental event that might just as well have happened or not have happened. Rather, he claims, this represents the "eternal history and nature of humanity" in general.[6] In other words, all humans are like Adam and Eve. When we are small children, we are like the animals, acting on our immediate natural drives and instincts. Then as we grow, we develop out of this condition and learn how to control our natural side with the mind. We learn the difference between right and wrong, good and evil. So in a sense the story of Adam and Eve is repeated in every human being.

[5] Genesis 3:17–18. See Hegel, *Vorlesungen über die Philosophie der Religion*, Part II, *Die Bestimmte Religion*, vol. 4a, p. 340n; *Lectures on the Philosophy of Religion*, vol. 2, *Determinate Religion*, pp. 439n–440n.
[6] Hegel, *Vorlesungen über die Philosophie der Religion*, Part II, *Die Bestimmte Religion*, vol. 4a, p. 339n; *Lectures on the Philosophy of Religion*, vol. 2, *Determinate Religion*, p. 439n.

According to the biblical story, humans are created with a specific nature in the same way as the animals are. Human nature was initially in some ways similar to the nature of the animals, and for this reason Adam and Eve lived in harmony with nature. But with the Fall and the original sin, a split or rupture appeared. Now the first humans were suddenly separated from their original nature. They no longer felt at home in their world, and a sign of this is that they realized for the first time that they were naked. Human nature had become divided. Humans continued to have a natural side, but now they also had another side, a rational side, that, as noted, Hegel refers to as "spirit." This is the side that they share with God. Humans are thus thought to occupy a special place in the universe. They are not wholly like the animals, although they share a natural element with them. Nor are they wholly like God, although they share a rational element with him. Instead, humans are alone in having a divided being. The Fall is thus the story of how humans became separated or alienated from their own nature. But, as Hegel critically points out, this mistakenly implies that the true, but now lost, nature of humankind is to be like the animals.

The story also describes another form of alienation. Initially, Adam and Eve were the special creations of God. Just as they were in harmony with nature, so also they were in harmony with the divine. God created them and their essence, and so long as they lived in accordance with this, there was no problem. But by defying God's prohibition, they committed a grave crime that forever separated or alienated them from God. God then punished them and banished them from the garden. From that moment on, human beings were on their own and had to make a living for themselves.

As a result of this division, the notion of sin plays an important role in Judaism. One is eternally vexed by one's own moral unworthiness. This is an important element that Hegel sketches in his analysis of the unhappy consciousness in *The Phenomenology*. One forever dwells on the seemingly infinite separation from God. The Hebrew Bible is full of stories that depict the Jews falling away from the correct faith and subsequently being punished by God. Hegel points out that the Psalms contain many laments about the human condition of sinfulness and the great distance to God.[7]

While it is true that some forms of reconciliation do take place when God makes a covenant with the Jews and gives them laws, Hegel emphasizes that these are never fully adequate forms of reconciliation, and the obsession with sinfulness and the separation from God are constant features of Judaism that are not fundamentally changed by this. So, for Hegel, Judaism represents a religion of alienation. According to him, there was a movement from an initial harmony – that is, in the time before the Fall – to a separation or

---

[7] Hegel, *Vorlesungen über die Philosophie der Religion*, Part II, *Die Bestimmte Religion*, vol. 4a, p. 341n; *Lectures on the Philosophy of Religion*, vol. 2, *Determinate Religion*, p. 441n.

alienation – that is, in the time after the Fall. These can be regarded as two steps in a developmental process, which, however, is not yet complete.

His positive view is that the condition of alienation is not permanent and irresolvable; instead, a new and higher harmony can be achieved.[8] Here he anticipates his analysis of Christianity. He argues that Christianity represents the third step of reestablishing a harmony with God. But this harmony is, of course, different from the initial harmony. The third step is not simply a reversion to the first one. We cannot go back and become like animals again, and even if we could, this would hardly be desirable. Rather, we can enter into a harmony with God by means of what we have in common with him: spirit. With the rational faculty of the human mind, we can choose good. We can embrace the higher part of our nature and exercise our freedom fully by rejecting evil and the temptations of our natural or selfish side.

Today we tend to think of alienation as a contingent fact of modern culture. We feel alienated from modern society due to, for example, the ways in which certain goods are produced or certain administrative structures function. But it is often thought that this is just an unfortunate result of modern life that could certainly be different if society were organized in a different manner. In contrast to this view, Hegel's analysis of the Fall shows that he believes that alienation is a necessary and fundamental fact of human existence. It is not something that is accidental or contingent. It is a basic truth of human nature that we are self-divided and therefore self-alienated. We have one part nature and one part spirit, and this is what it is to be human. The conflict between these two elements is what it means to be free. Throughout their lives, humans must forever struggle with the natural or irrational side of their nature, which leaves them no rest. For this reason, the idea of an original harmony sounds initially attractive. But the fact that we have this inner struggle is an indication that we have the ability to make the choice to control our natural side and act in accordance with reason. This is a higher form of life than the original harmony of animals, who act immediately on natural desire.

## 2.3   Judaism as a Lordship-Bondage Relation

Hegel characterizes the God Jehovah as a master who rules over the Jewish people tyrannically.[9] The basic relation of the Jews to their God, he claims, is one of fear. God is the absolute, infinite power over the universe and human

---

[8] Hegel, *Vorlesungen über die Philosophie der Religion*, Part II, *Die Bestimmte Religion*, vol. 4a, p. 339n; *Lectures on the Philosophy of Religion*, vol. 2, *Determinate Religion*, p. 439n: "This original natural state must be the starting point, but the separation that then occurs must also in turn be reconciled."

[9] Hegel, *Vorlesungen über die Philosophie der Religion*, Part II, *Die Bestimmte Religion*, vol. 4a, pp. 339–345; *Lectures on the Philosophy of Religion*, vol. 2, *Determinate Religion*, pp. 441–445.

beings. He regularly punishes the people for their sinfulness and even wipes out other peoples, such as the inhabitants of Sodom and Gomorrah.[10] Given this, it makes sense that the Jews live in terror of his wrath.

Hegel quotes from Psalm 111:10, as he did in *The Phenomenology of Spirit*: "The fear of the Lord is the beginning of wisdom."[11] But unlike in the *Phenomenology*, Hegel now explains what he means by this reference. He refers to this as a "wise fear" and argues that this is the *beginning* of freedom.[12] His claim here is that the fear of the slave or bondsman is an important stepping-stone on the way to freedom. A child fears punishment from their parents, and this fear motivates them to control the natural desires that they would otherwise immediately act on. Over time in the course of their upbringing, the child learns to regulate these inner desires themselves, and later it is no longer a great struggle to overcome them. Thus the child surpasses the immediate natural state and becomes fully human. Fear makes this possible. Similarly, the slave must live with fear daily, and in so doing, they come to develop an inward discipline. This allows them to master their natural desires and drives and to come to regard their natural side as nothing. In this way, the slave gradually overcomes their fear and becomes independent of the things of nature. When the master threatens to deprive the slave of these things or the satisfaction of their needs, the slave no longer thinks of this as a serious or threatening matter. Hegel explains that the wise fear "is not a particular fear of the particular but just the positing of this particular fear as null, emancipating oneself from fear."[13] So, just as with the lordship and bondage relation, this fear is in fact a reversal. In any case, in the psalm that Hegel quotes, the emphasis is on the "beginning" of freedom. The fear is not the freedom itself, but in order to reach a state of freedom, one must experience a stage of fear and overcome it.

Hegel thus describes the ancient Jews as living in a condition of servitude to their God. Like the unhappy consciousness, they regard God as the infinite and the absolute, and themselves as nothing and worthless. In order to get closer to God, one must eliminate all of the negative and sinful aspects of oneself. One's only justification lies in this relation to God, but this is not a positive kind of justification since it requires one to regard oneself as sinful or having no value.

---

[10] Genesis 19.

[11] Hegel, *Vorlesungen über die Philosophie der Religion*, Part II, *Die Bestimmte Religion*, vol. 4a, p. 343n; *Lectures on the Philosophy of Religion*, vol. 2, *Determinate Religion*, p. 445n. See G. W. F. Hegel, *System der Wissenschaft. Erster Theil, die Phänomenologie des Geistes* (Bamberg and Würzburg: Joseph Anton Goebhardt, 1807), p. 125; *Hegel's Phenomenology of Spirit*, trans. by A. V. Miller (Oxford: Clarendon Press, 1977), pp. 117f.

[12] Hegel, *Vorlesungen über die Philosophie der Religion*, Part II, *Die Bestimmte Religion*, vol. 4a, p. 343n; *Lectures on the Philosophy of Religion*, vol. 2, *Determinate Religion*, p. 445n.

[13] Hegel, *Vorlesungen über die Philosophie der Religion*, Part II, *Die Bestimmte Religion*, vol. 4a, p. 343n; *Lectures on the Philosophy of Religion*, vol. 2, *Determinate Religion*, p. 445n.

According to Hegel, one can see the tyrannical nature of the God of the Hebrew Bible in his commands and the kind of obedience that he demands.[14] Today in the state or in different institutions, or even in families, there are instances where obedience is required. In these cases, there are rational laws or customs that demand our compliance. When, as rational adults, we examine these with our critical faculty, we come to see the rationality in them, and we gladly give our consent to them. In these cases we choose to act on the shared universal and not on our selfish desires, which would be in contradiction to this. In this scenario, obedience presupposes an inward sphere of human rationality and reflection. The assumption is made that we are all rational adults who are capable of this, and so we can, each on our own, reach the conclusion and find the rationality of the laws and customs in question. But this is not the kind of obedience that the God of the Hebrew Bible is asking for. Instead, he demands an absolute and immediate compliance without any consent. His demand is simply that one complies or faces the consequences of terrible punishment. He does not care if the Jews agree with him or not or if they find his laws and regulations correct or not. Their opinion on the matter is entirely irrelevant. Their duty is simply to obey and ask no questions. This is the form of command that Hegel refers to as "positive." It is not based on any deeper system of rationality but is simply an arbitrary command.

Hegel points out that this fails to recognize the sphere of inwardness and reflection that exists in mature human beings. This is close to the model of how parents discipline small children, where the assumption is that they are too young to exercise rationality and reflection and are thus incapable of giving rational consent. Likewise, this is how we tend to discipline animals, which are unable to be reasoned with. They merely understand their role as a subordinate in a hierarchy, and this role must be established and maintained by the threat of force. In such cases, the only recourse is threats, coercion, and violence. So, according to Hegel, the Jews do not follow the laws as free individuals who grant their consent but rather as "servants."[15] He illustrates this with a quotation of a long list of God's threats (from Leviticus 26:15–20), which are intended to intimidate and force compliance.[16]

By contrast, he believes, Christianity recognizes and develops the inward side of the human being. Jesus is critical of blind obedience to the law as followed by the scribes and the Pharisees. He argues that the law is not something outward but rather an inner principle that dwells in the heart of

[14] Hegel, *Vorlesungen über die Philosophie der Religion*, Part II, *Die Bestimmte Religion*, vol. 4a, pp. 348–351; *Lectures on the Philosophy of Religion*, vol. 2, *Determinate Religion*, pp. 449–451.

[15] Hegel, *Vorlesungen über die Philosophie der Religion*, Part II, *Die Bestimmte Religion*, vol. 4a, p. 350; *Lectures on the Philosophy of Religion*, vol. 2, *Determinate Religion*, p. 450.

[16] Hegel, *Vorlesungen über die Philosophie der Religion*, Part II, *Die Bestimmte Religion*, vol. 4a, pp. 350f.; *Lectures on the Philosophy of Religion*, vol. 2, *Determinate Religion*, pp. 450f.

each human being. Thus the idea of the new law in Christianity is one that is
based on the notion that humans have a rational inward side that involves
conscience and moral sentiment. Given this, there is no need for force, coercion, and violence. As a result, the relation of Christians to their God has
a different character from that of the Jews to Jehovah.

## 2.4   Hegel's Analysis of the Roman Empire

The first edition of Hegel's *Lectures on the Philosophy of History* was published
in 1837 by his student, the jurist Eduard Gans (1797–1839).[17] This is one of
Hegel's most readable and popular series of lectures. Here he sketches the
course of human development from prehistoric times to his own day. He
organizes his lectures in terms of specific peoples, each of which represents
a specific period of world history. He thus devotes individual chapters to
China, India, Persia, Egypt, Greece, and Rome. His thesis is that in history
one finds the development of human freedom. This can be discerned not just
in historical events, strictly speaking, but also and primarily in customs,

[17] G. W. F. Hegel, *Vorlesungen über die Philosophie der Geschichte*, ed. by Eduard Gans, vol.
9 (1837) (2nd ed. by Karl Hegel, 1840), in *Georg Wilhelm Friedrich Hegel's Werke.
Vollständige Ausgabe*. (English translation: *The Philosophy of History*, trans. by J. Sibree
[New York: Willey Book Co., 1944].) In what follows, I will refer to the new edition:
*Vorlesungen über die Philosophie der Weltgeschichte: Berlin 1822–1823*, ed. by Karl
Heinz Ilting, Karl Brehmer, and Hoo Nam Seelmann (Hamburg: Felix Meiner, 1996),
vol. 12 of Hegel, *Vorlesungen. Ausgewählte Nachschriften und Manuskripte*, vols. 1–17
(Hamburg: Felix Meiner, 1983–2008). (English translation: *The Philosophy of World
History*, vol. 1, *Manuscripts of the Introduction and the Lectures of 1822–3*, trans. by
Robert F. Brown and Peter C. Hodgson with the assistance with William G. Geuss
[Oxford: Oxford University Press, 2011].) For Hegel's philosophy of history, see
Timo Bautz, *Hegels Lehre von der Weltgeschichte. Zur logischen und systematischen
Grundlegung der Hegelschen Geschichtsphilosophie* (Munich: Wilhelm Fink Verlag,
1988); Oscar Daniel Brauer, *Dialektik der Zeit. Untersuchungen zu Hegels Metaphysik
der Weltgeschichte* (Stuttgart and Bad Cannstatt: Frommann-Holzboog, 1982); Eric
Michael Dale, *Hegel, the End of History, and the Future* (Cambridge: Cambridge
University Press, 2014); Will Dudley (ed.), *Hegel and History* (Albany: State University
of New York Press, 2009); Emil L. Fackenheim, *God's Presence in History* (New York:
New York University Press, 1970); Peter C. Hodgson, *Shapes of Freedom: Hegel's
Philosophy of World History in a Theological Perspective* (Oxford: Oxford University
Press, 2012); Jean Hyppolite, *Introduction to Hegel's Philosophy of History*, trans. by
Bond Harris and Jacqueline Bouchard Spurlock (Gainesville: University Press of
Florida, 1996); Joseph McCarney, *Hegel on History* (London and New York: Routledge,
2000); Robert L. Perkins (ed.), *History and System: Hegel's Philosophy of History* (Albany:
State University of New York Press, 1984); Rudolf J. Siebert, *Hegel's Philosophy of History:
Theological, Humanistic and Scientific Elements* (Washington, DC: University Press of
America, 1979); John Walker, *History, Spirit and Experience: Hegel's Conception of the
Historical Task of Philosophy in his Age* (Frankfurt am Main and New York: Peter Lang,
1995); Burleigh Taylor Wilkins, *Hegel's Philosophy of History* (Ithaca: Cornell University
Press, 1974).

institutions, practices, and, generally speaking, all forms of culture. So although he is ostensibly treating history in these lectures, Hegel also strays over into many different areas.

His treatment of ancient Rome is particularly important for our purposes since it was in the context of the early Roman Empire that Christianity arose.[18] According to Hegel's analysis, the problems of the Roman world prepared the ground for Christianity. Roman civilization was characterized by a deep-seated sense of longing and alienation. People yearned for some form of reconciliation, and this made them receptive to the message that Christianity offered. Thus in this sense Rome can be considered to be a historical pendant to Judaism, according to Hegel's analysis, in the sense that Judaism was also characterized by a deeply rooted alienation and an unanswered need for reconciliation.

Hegel begins his discussion with an account of the Roman emperors. They were the unchallenged leaders of the empire, who ruled as absolute dictators. Their power was based on the support of the army and their special bodyguards, the Praetorians. The emperors maintained some of the old democratic institutions from the Republic, such as the senate, but deprived them of any real power. The emperors themselves had the power of life and death over their subjects, and any form of opposition or resistance to their will was severely dealt with. With no external constraints, the behavior of the emperors was characterized by caprice and arbitrariness. They did not rule for the benefit of the state but rather used their office to pursue their private self-interest. Thus they had their critics and enemies routinely imprisoned, tortured, and executed. Hegel points out that, although there were occasionally virtuous and benevolent emperors, there was never any attempt to change this state of affairs by introducing democratic reforms that would restore freedom to the people.[19] The good emperors simply came and went without ever making any lasting change to the dictatorial system as such.

The relation of the emperor to his subjects is much the same as the master-slave relation that Hegel described in *The Phenomenology of Spirit*. Although, strictly speaking, the people enjoy certain rights as citizens of Rome, this has no ultimate meaning since the emperor is always above the law and can persecute anyone he likes, whenever he likes, and there is no legal recourse against this. For Hegel, this means that all Romans are put on an equal basis with each other vis-à-vis the emperor. In this sense there is no real difference between a slave and a free citizen since even the rights of the free citizen count for nothing in

[18] Hegel, *Vorlesungen über die Philosophie der Weltgeschichte: Berlin 1822–1823*, pp. 419–436; *The Philosophy of World History*, vol. 1, *Manuscripts of the Introduction and the Lectures of 1822–3*, pp. 447–459.
[19] Hegel, *Vorlesungen über die Philosophie der Weltgeschichte: Berlin 1822–1823*, p. 418; *The Philosophy of World History*, vol. 1, *Manuscripts of the Introduction and the Lectures of 1822–3*, p. 446.

the end. This sounds very similar to what he said about the God of Judaism, who rules over the Jews in a tyrannical fashion. In neither case are the people allowed to develop their own subjective freedom. They are simply frightened and intimidated into a condition of absolute obedience and submission – the condition of slaves.

Hegel also discusses the concept of a legal person that Roman law introduced.[20] This was connected with citizenship rights, which the Romans used effectively as a diplomatic tool. They granted citizenship rights to conquered people in order to stem rebellion and incorporate them into their empire. One key aspect of the status of being a Roman citizen was the right to own property. The individual expresses themselves concretely in the world by means of their property. In their property they see an external manifestation of themselves that is also recognized by others. But Hegel believes that this concept of a legal person is too abstract since it only captures one dimension. An individual is much richer as a human being than simply their property or legal rights. Hegel believes that this leads to a kind of social atomism, whereby everyone exists for themselves, separated from one another, without any meaningful conception of community or commonality that might bind them together at a deeper level. Due to the tyranny of the emperor, each individual retreats into themselves and pursues their own private interests; there is no deeper sense of common values and ethics to unite people, as was the case with the Greeks. For this to take place, more institutions are required that would create ties among people and with the state and its ruler. The abstract idea of being a legal person as a property holder is a pale shadow of a real human being.

Hegel points out that the schools of Roman philosophy – Stoicism, Epicureanism, and Skepticism – all had in common the goal of making the individual indifferent to whatever was happening in the external world.[21] This is a response to the widespread feeling of alienation in the Roman world. The individual ultimately had no control over their own life or destiny since this was in the hands of the emperor. The individual was frustrated by not being able to fulfill their goals and dreams in this world. *Stoicism* tries to offer a form of reconciliation in the realm of thought. But this remains abstract and empty since it is never realized in the real world. In *Epicureanism* one simply tried to resign oneself to the sad state of affairs and make the best of it by enjoying sensual pleasures as long as one could. But this was never a meaningful or lasting form or reconciliation in the world. *Skepticism* is the denial of any truth

---

[20] Hegel, *Vorlesungen über die Philosophie der Weltgeschichte: Berlin 1822–1823*, p. 423; *The Philosophy of World History*, vol. 1, *Manuscripts of the Introduction and the Lectures of 1822–3*, p. 450.

[21] Hegel, *Vorlesungen über die Philosophie der Weltgeschichte: Berlin 1822–1823*, p. 424; *The Philosophy of World History*, vol. 1, *Manuscripts of the Introduction and the Lectures of 1822–3*, p. 451.

or value in the world. This school prided itself on seeing this clearly, but it also left the individual with a sense of emptiness. In this context, people were keen to have some form of reconciliation with the real world. They wanted to be able to identify with the events that took place in actuality. This sentiment prepared the ground for the birth and growth of Christianity in the Roman world.

According to Hegel, the different forms of alienation both in the Roman world and in Judaism together produced Christianity. He claims that the principle of Rome is that of particularity since people were only concerned with pursuing their own private interests and making these their primary ends. Rome itself was involved in a multitude of practical tasks that needed to be accomplished to keep the empire running. This is also reflected in Roman religion, which Hegel claims is characterized by "finite purposiveness."[22] The Romans have gods and goddesses who are responsible not just for great natural forces, such as storms and volcanoes, but also for mundane human affairs, such as coining money and ensuring the function of the sewage drains.[23] Hegel takes this focus on the particular to represent the Western spirit. By contrast, the principle of the East was abstraction, as found in the Jewish conception of God as the One, with no further content or determination. There is alienation and longing for both principles. The Western spirit dwells in a kind of nihilism or skepticism that rejects any deeper truth or meaning. It thus longs for the universal. This is the world of the unhappy consciousness.[24] By contrast, the Eastern spirit has the universal, but it is empty and abstract. It longs to see this universal truth in the concrete world of everyday life. In short, it longs for the particular. The Roman Empire brings these two principles into contact, and from this arises Christianity.[25] Hegel explains, "This unification is what the times needed. Spirit, dispersed and lost in finite purposiveness, in the finitude of the Roman Empire, called for something infinite and found it in the East."[26] The Christian conception

[22] Hegel, *Vorlesungen über die Philosophie der Weltgeschichte: Berlin 1822–1823*, p. 423; *The Philosophy of World History*, vol. 1, *Manuscripts of the Introduction and the Lectures of 1822–3*, p. 450.

[23] See Jon Stewart, *Hegel's Interpretation of the Religions of the World: The Logic of the Gods* (Oxford: Oxford University Press, 2018), p. 265.

[24] Hegel, *Vorlesungen über die Philosophie der Weltgeschichte: Berlin 1822–1823*, p. 424; *The Philosophy of World History*, vol. 1, *Manuscripts of the Introduction and the Lectures of 1822–3*, p. 451: "it is the consciousness that has arrived at this understanding or, however, only at this unhappy state of abstraction, at the unhappy state of looking upon the bounds of constraint as what is ultimate."

[25] Hegel, *Vorlesungen über die Philosophie der Weltgeschichte: Berlin 1822–1823*, pp. 426f.; *The Philosophy of World History*, vol. 1, *Manuscripts of the Introduction and the Lectures of 1822–3*, pp. 452f.

[26] Hegel, *Vorlesungen über die Philosophie der Weltgeschichte: Berlin 1822–1823*, p. 426; *The Philosophy of World History*, vol. 1, *Manuscripts of the Introduction and the Lectures of 1822–3*, p. 452.

of a Trinitarian God resolves the issue by taking up the elements of both the universal and the particular, which are then united.

## 2.5  Hegel's Understanding of Christian Revelation: God as Self-Conscious

Hegel's *Lectures on the Philosophy of Religion* culminate in his analysis of Christianity, which, as noted, he refers to as "The Absolute Religion." After having given a long account of the development of the world's religions, he now presents Christianity as the final, complete, and true form of religion. One can thus see Hegel playing the role of a Christian apologist and fulfilling his stated goal at the outset of the lectures, namely to provide a firm foundation for Christianity at a time when its basic dogmas and beliefs were being called into question.

In his introductory comments about Christianity,[27] Hegel explains that it lies in the very concept of God to be a self-conscious entity. While earlier religions might have worshipped objects of nature, these physical things do not correspond with our understanding of God. For God to be God, he must be self-conscious. But we learned from the "Lordship and Bondage" section of *The Phenomenology of Spirit* that in order for one to be self-conscious, one needs to be in interaction with another self-conscious subject. Only when one can see oneself from the perspective of another can one become fully aware of oneself. This also holds true of God. If God is to be a self-conscious deity, this implies that he must be determined by other self-conscious beings, namely his worshippers.

Hegel believes that the idea of God as a self-conscious subject is seen most clearly in the Christian doctrine of the Revelation, and for this reason he refers to Christianity as "the *revelatory* religion."[28] The traditional doctrine of the Revelation states that God became incarnate in human form in the person of Jesus Christ and thus revealed himself to the world. So in Christianity there are initially two different conceptions of God: one as the all-powerful creator of the universe who is omnipresent and beyond nature, and the other as a concrete particular human being. Judaism and Islam share with Christianity the first conception of God as the creator of the universe, but they stop there and reject the Christian idea of the Revelation and the Incarnation. The God of Judaism and Islam remains abstract, and this, for Hegel, is a major defect. Since there is an absence of revelation, this God never becomes concrete and never takes on

---

[27] Hegel, *Vorlesungen über die Philosophie der Religion*, Part III, *Die vollendete Religion*, vol. 5, *Vorlesungen. Ausgewählte Nachschriften und Manuskripte*, pp. 99–105; *Lectures on the Philosophy of Religion*, vol. 3, *The Consummate Religion*, pp. 163–170.

[28] Hegel, *Vorlesungen über die Philosophie der Religion*, Part III, *Die vollendete Religion*, vol. 5, p. 177, p. 179; *Lectures on the Philosophy of Religion*, vol. 3, *The Consummate Religion*, p. 250, p. 252.

any concrete content. But with Christianity the life and teachings of Christ provide a rich particular content. Without this content, the notion of God remains an abstraction, an empty universal. For something to have content, it must come out of the realm of mere thought and become an object in actuality.[29] In Hegel's language, it must *objectify* itself.

The doctrine of the Incarnation makes it possible for God to become fully self-conscious since only when God appears as a concrete, incarnate being does he enter into contact with other human beings. Only in this way can the dialectic of recognition take place, which, according to Hegel, is essential for the development of self-consciousness. As long as God remains a transcendent being, this is impossible since God, *qua* transcendent, is not in a relation with some other. So the idea of the Incarnation is not something accidental or contingent as is often thought.[30] Instead, it lies in the very nature of God, as self-conscious, to become concrete. Thus the Incarnation is necessary for God to become a fully self-conscious entity. As Hegel puts it, "A spirit that is not revelatory is not spirit."[31]

This issue is relevant for the theme of alienation that we have been tracing. The notion that God is something fundamentally external and other to us is the point of departure for different forms of alienation. As we saw, alienation is always about a split or division between two things: in this case God and human beings. When other peoples believed that the gods were something radically different or separate from them, they had a sense of alienation. Hegel believes that even Christian theologians mistakenly follow this model in their conception of the divine:

> At first sight, what theology is about is the cognition of God as what is solely objective and absolute, what remains purely and simply separate from subjective consciousness. Therefore God is an external object – like the sun or the sky – but still a thought-object. An external object of consciousness exists where the object permanently retains the character of something other and external.[32]

This was in many ways the problem of the unhappy consciousness, which always conceived of God as being transcendent and infinitely distant from itself. But Hegel believes that, in contrast to the other religions, Christianity overcomes this problem since it suggests that there is a "unity of this object" – that is, God – "with

[29] Hegel, *Vorlesungen über die Philosophie der Religion*, Part III, *Die vollendete Religion*, vol. 5, pp. 103f.; *Lectures on the Philosophy of Religion*, vol. 3, *The Consummate Religion*, p. 168.

[30] Hegel, *Vorlesungen über die Philosophie der Religion*, Part III, *Die vollendete Religion*, vol. 5, p. 105; *Lectures on the Philosophy of Religion*, vol. 3, *The Consummate Religion*, p. 170.

[31] Hegel, *Vorlesungen über die Philosophie der Religion*, Part III, *Die vollendete Religion*, vol. 5, p. 105; *Lectures on the Philosophy of Religion*, vol. 3, *The Consummate Religion*, p. 170.

[32] Hegel, *Vorlesungen über die Philosophie der Religion*, Part III, *Die vollendete Religion*, vol. 5, p. 101; *Lectures on the Philosophy of Religion*, vol. 3, *The Consummate Religion*, pp. 165f.

the subject."[33] Reconciliation is only possible if the two terms are not conceived as radically separate and distinct from the start, and this means that human subjectivity must be understood to be a part of the nature of God.[34] This idea is what Hegel refers to as the universal idea of the human being or absolute spirit.[35]

It should also be noted that Hegel uses a special term in his description of the movement from the first to the second person of the Trinity, that is, from God the Father to God the Son, or from God as transcendent creator of the universe to God as incarnate human being. He explains that God *externalizes* himself in order to create the universe and then to create another self-conscious entity, the Son. This follows the model that Hegel used to describe self-consciousness itself, whereby one individual starts with themselves and then, when another person appears, the individual must, so to speak, go out of themselves and see themselves from the perspective of the other. Their understanding of themselves is thus necessarily bound up with the other. The word Hegel uses for this is *Entäusserung*, which means "separation" or "externalization," but, as mentioned in the Introduction, this term has also been translated as "alienation." It will be noted that this is a slightly different sense of the term "alienation" from the one we have been working with so far. The notion of alienation, understood as a feeling of estrangement from another person or a community, corresponds to the German word *Entfremdung*. But in any case, what is at issue are two things considered fundamentally separate from one another. Thus Hegel uses two different terms to capture two different senses of the English word "alienation."

For Hegel, the doctrine of the Revelation represents the idea that humans can see and recognize God in person, and with this recognition God becomes who he is as a self-conscious entity. This implies that human beings play a role in determining what God is, or, put differently, they are a part of God. This is a counterintuitive idea and has given rise to debates about the orthodoxy of Hegel's ultimate view on Christianity. We just recalled that Hegel's official position is that he wishes to defend Christianity as the one true religion. This is the side of his thought that the right Hegelians emphasize. But his claim about the self-conscious nature of God can also be interpreted in a way that points in a different direction. When he says that for God to be a self-conscious entity, God must be recognized by other self-conscious entities, this can be taken to imply that if God were not recognized in this way, then he would not exist. In other words, if self-conscious human beings did not think of God, then there

---

[33] Hegel, *Vorlesungen über die Philosophie der Religion*, Part III, *Die vollendete Religion*, vol. 5, p. 101; *Lectures on the Philosophy of Religion*, vol. 3, *The Consummate Religion*, p. 166.

[34] Hegel, *Vorlesungen über die Philosophie der Religion*, Part III, *Die vollendete Religion*, vol. 5, pp. 144f.; *Lectures on the Philosophy of Religion*, vol. 3, *The Consummate Religion*, p. 213.

[35] Hegel, *Vorlesungen über die Philosophie der Religion*, Part III, *Die vollendete Religion*, vol. 5, p. 45; *Lectures on the Philosophy of Religion*, vol. 3, *The Consummate Religion*, p. 109.

would be no God since God only exists in the minds of the religious believers. In short, God is just a figment of the collective human imagination. This is the interpretation of Hegel that some of his critics raised and that is central to the left Hegelian school.

## 2.6   The Christian Elevation of the Value of the Human Being and Overcoming Alienation

Hegel also claims that Christianity is the religion of freedom in contrast to earlier religions. What he means by this is that it is the one religion that recognizes the infinite value of each individual. This is a result of the doctrine of the Incarnation. When God is conceived merely as an abstract being in some transcendent beyond, then there is a radical split between human beings and the divine. This is the point of departure of the unhappy consciousness, which believes that God is infinite, unchangeable, and absolute and, by contrast, regards itself negatively as finite, changeable, and contingent. If God dwells beyond this world, then the implication is that this world has no deeper meaning or value. This world is thus devoid of truth, and this also holds for the inhabitants of this world. As noted, this leads to the negative, self-deprecating sense of self that one finds in the unhappy consciousness or, according to Hegel, in the Psalms.

But when, with the Incarnation, God enters the world, this shows that the divine can also exist in the finite, mundane sphere that we are familiar with. The truth and the absolute are not reserved for some *beyond* but rather dwell in the same world as we do. The world is now invested with a new importance, and so are human beings. When God comes down from the heavens and appears in the real world as a specific individual, he shows that the world itself has value and legitimacy. This in turn means that the believers who dwell in it have some importance. Now for the first time "subjectivity is absolutely essential . . . . this standpoint elevates subjectivity into the essential characteristic of the whole range of the religious relationship."[36] In the form of Christ, God is in principle able to enter into a relation with each specific human being. There is a recognition of every single believer. There is something of infinite value in every human being. This has major implications not just for one's self-image but also for social institutions, ethics, and legal relations. For example, since Christianity regarded each individual as having some special value, something divine in them, it opposed the long-standing practice of slavery in the Greco-Roman world. If God recognizes my neighbors as being free, then I must also extend my recognition to them.

---

[36]   Hegel, *Vorlesungen über die Philosophie der Religion*, Part III, *Die vollendete Religion*, vol. 5, p. 103; *Lectures on the Philosophy of Religion*, vol. 3, *The Consummate Religion*, pp. 167f.

This issue is also related to the question of our knowledge of the divine. Hegel believes that it is a characteristic view of his own day that, in the wake of the Enlightenment criticisms of religion, people deny that God can be known. The idea is that God far surpasses our finite human abilities to understand the world. He dwells in some transcendent sphere that we can never have access to. So the only recourse that we have is to look into ourselves and our own beliefs. In other words, since no objective knowledge about God is possible, the only thing left is our subjective disposition. We just need to make sure that we believe in our hearts, but the actual content of that belief is left entirely open.

Hegel has a mixed assessment of this modern view. He thinks that there is something wrong about the idea that we cannot know God. The doctrine of the Revelation is all about knowing the divine. God entered the world as an incarnate human being in order to reveal himself, that is, in order to show human beings who he was. The whole point is that God should be known and that after the Revelation we should have no excuses for saying that we do not know him. When God enters the world with the Revelation, he shows that the truth can exist in the world and can be known by human beings. It no longer exists only in some transcendent sphere from which we are cut off.

But Hegel also thinks that there is something correct about the focus on subjectivity. At the beginning of the history of human culture, the idea of subjectivity or the individual was not something that had any value or merit. The truth was considered to be something external in the world; for example, the oracle of the gods or the established custom of one's community or family. In this context, the personal ideas and wishes of the individual did not matter at all. People had to follow the directions of the oracle or the dictates of their families or communities. But in the modern world, we have come to realize the importance and legitimacy of the individual. In the course of time, the idea of human rights arose, which acknowledged the value of each person.[37] So there is something right and very important about this view.

For Hegel, there is, however, a real danger in the modern view that we cannot know God but must instead focus on our inward subjectivity. If we cannot know God, then, he claims, our subjectivity is arbitrary. One can believe in many different kinds of things in an authentic, subjective, or inward manner, but this is wholly formal and has no content. This means that in practice, the abstract, undetermined idea of God can be filled with any number of different beliefs and practices, many of which may be absurd, contradictory, or even destructive. Instead, the true form of subjectivity is one that also recognizes an objective truth and uses this as the point of departure. For Hegel, there is thus both a *subjective* and an *objective* element to truth. We have the right to use our reason and make our own judgments, and in this

---

[37] See Jon Stewart, "Hegel's Theory of the Emergence of Subjectivity and the Conditions for the Development of Human Rights," *Filozofia*, 74(6) (2019), 456–471.

sense we exercise our subjectivity. But this is not entirely satisfying unless the content of our judgments and beliefs is something shared and recognized by others. Thus the content must be something objective.

The true subjective element lies in the fact that each individual is enjoined to consent to the truth in their own conscience. People are not coerced or commanded but rather give their consent freely and willingly since they recognize the content to be rational. This is what true freedom amounts to. One can give recognition and acknowledge the truth freely based on one's own intuitions. Hegel believes that this is what the Christian religion makes possible. It uncovers the important realm of subjectivity and the value of the individual, but since the incarnate God is concrete and has a specific content, this prevents the realm of subjectivity from slipping into arbitrariness and relativism. According to his view, both the subjective and the objective get their due.

With regard to the issue of alienation, the Incarnation means that human beings no longer perceive the world around them as "something alien."[38] Christianity offers reconciliation that overcomes the deep-seated sense of alienation that humans feel. As we have seen, initially there was "God, who confronts a world that is estranged from him, and a world that is estranged from its essence."[39] This is the notion of the transcendent God or creator, which resulted in the unhappy consciousness, which was infinitely separated and thus alienated from the divine. But the unhappy consciousness also represents a form of self-alienation or self-estrangement since it regards itself as wholly worthless and without meaning or value (in contrast to the divine). According to Hegel, in Judaism there is an alienation from oneself and a deep sense of sinfulness and inner worthlessness. In Islam there is also an alienation from the world, which is believed to have no value or meaning at all. But, unlike Judaism or Islam, Christianity presents a reconciliation that overcomes the separation from the divine and the radical split between God and the world.[40]

Hegel believes that Christianity, in contrast to other religions, offers this reconciliation because it conceives of God as a concrete human being. In earlier religions where the divinities were conceived of as animals, for example, it was impossible to experience a sense of recognition in this relation. One cannot receive meaningful recognition from an animal. But when God appears as a concrete human being, it is possible for individuals to enter into a relation with him and for genuine recognition to take place. When one sees God in

---

[38] Hegel, *Vorlesungen über die Philosophie der Religion*, Part III, *Die vollendete Religion*, vol. 5, p. 106; *Lectures on the Philosophy of Religion*, vol. 3, *The Consummate Religion*, p. 171.
[39] Hegel, *Vorlesungen über die Philosophie der Religion*, Part III, *Die vollendete Religion*, vol. 5, p. 107; *Lectures on the Philosophy of Religion*, vol. 3, *The Consummate Religion*, p. 171.
[40] Hegel, *Vorlesungen über die Philosophie der Religion*, Part III, *Die vollendete Religion*, vol. 5, p. 107; *Lectures on the Philosophy of Religion*, vol. 3, *The Consummate Religion*, p. 172.

human form, one sees oneself, *qua* human, in God. One realizes that the true form of the divine is that of a human being. One sees that there is a "unity of divine and human nature,"[41] that is, spirit. This is the culmination of the development of the world religions.

Here again we stumble upon an important interpretative ambiguity in Hegel's position. What exactly is the force of the claim that Christianity is the pinnacle of the development of the world's religions because it alone reaches the idea of the unity of the divine and the human? This might be taken to mean simply that the key is the focus on the doctrine of the Incarnation and the nature of Jesus in the way that has just been outlined. In previous religions the divine was always thought to be something else, something lower; for example, an animal, a river, or a natural force. But only with Christianity does humanity reach a point where it conceives of the divine as a human being, which is the highest form of divine revelation. But this might be taken to imply that the divine is *just* the human in the sense that there is nothing higher than the human spirit, but it took humanity many centuries to realize this. Only with Christianity do humans realize that God is *nothing more* than the human. This view is that of the left Hegelians, and it, of course, undermines the traditional views of Christianity since it seems to imply that there is nothing genuinely divine apart from the human spirit itself.

One might argue that there is evidence for the left Hegelian view when Hegel refers to the idea of Christian reconciliation not as a unique event that takes place with Christ and the Incarnation but rather as a "universal process."[42] In other words, reconciliation and the overcoming of alienation are a part of the general development of each human being. Each person must come to see themselves reflected in the world and in the eyes of other people, and this is what constitutes both the human and the divine spirit. Self-consciousness is not something static or fixed, but rather a constant, ongoing activity that involves other people.

## 2.7   Christianity as the Religion of Freedom

Hegel emphasizes that Christianity is also the religion of freedom, which seems to imply that the other religions of the world do not allow their devotees to be free. He defines freedom as the spirit being at home with itself or more specifically having itself as its object. This means that when we are confronted with an external entity in the world, it does not strike us as something *other* but rather as a reflection of ourselves. In this sense, alienation or having a relation

---

[41]   Hegel, *Vorlesungen über die Philosophie der Religion*, Part III, *Die vollendete Religion*, vol. 5, p. 107; *Lectures on the Philosophy of Religion*, vol. 3, *The Consummate Religion*, p. 172.

[42]   Hegel, *Vorlesungen über die Philosophie der Religion*, Part III, *Die vollendete Religion*, vol. 5, p. 107; *Lectures on the Philosophy of Religion*, vol. 3, *The Consummate Religion*, p. 172.

to something different or foreign to oneself is connected with the ability to be free.

For Hegel, this relation is not static but always dynamic. Freedom refers to the process of overcoming the difference or alienation from the other thing.[43] In Hegel's language, this difference must be *negated*. This recalls the analysis of the lord and the bondsman, where initially the relation was one of alienation. Each party was confronted with a self-conscious other who was different from them. When one looked at the other and saw oneself reflected in the eyes of the other, the picture of oneself was something foreign. This is what needs to be negated in order for the individual to assert their own view of themselves. Only when their view is seen reflected in the eyes of the other does the individual attain self-certainty and freedom. As we saw in that discussion, for Hegel, freedom is therefore necessarily bound up with self-conscious recognition.[44]

When this is applied to the realm of religion, this means that Christianity is the religion of freedom since here the believers have overcome alienation and are at home in the world. They can see themselves recognized as free by their God. The divine is no longer something alien or separate but rather the same as the believer: spirit. So here the individual finds their self-conception mirrored in and confirmed by God. This point comes into focus when we recall the other conceptions of God that Hegel discusses. For example, the God of Judaism commands obedience but does not recognize the inward value and rationality of each individual. Thus the recognition that one receives from this deity is like the recognition that the slave receives from the master. In the eyes of the master, the slave is not fully human. By contrast, in Christianity each individual is recognized as infinitely valuable. God recognizes the rationality of all human beings and appeals to it. The God of Christianity teaches a doctrine of love and does not threaten dire punishments for disobedience. For Hegel, only the recognition that one receives in Christianity leads to a fully developed sense of human freedom.

Hegel's talk about overcoming the separation or distinction from the other might sound very strange. What does it mean really to find oneself in another? It will be recalled that in his analysis of the Roman world, Hegel criticized Roman law and its concept of abstract right, which understood individuals as legal persons with the rights of citizenship and property. His argument there was that this does not do justice to the full human being; moreover, if individuals are just reduced to citizens or property holders, this results in alienation or, as he put it, social atomization since the individuals have nothing deeper in common. In his analysis of Christianity, he outlines what he takes to be

---

[43] Hegel, *Vorlesungen über die Philosophie der Religion*, Part III, *Die vollendete Religion*, vol. 5, p. 106; *Lectures on the Philosophy of Religion*, vol. 3, *The Consummate Religion*, p. 171.

[44] Hegel, *Vorlesungen über die Philosophie der Religion*, Part III, *Die vollendete Religion*, vol. 5, p. 108; *Lectures on the Philosophy of Religion*, vol. 3, *The Consummate Religion*, p. 173.

a higher conception of personhood that he believes is absent in the Roman conception.[45] In this conception, individuals are related to one another in a more fundamental way. They have shared beliefs and ethical notions, and they can see themselves in these as a reflection of themselves. This goes far beyond a sterile legal relation between otherwise isolated individuals.

Hegel begins by recognizing the notion of common sense that claims that we all, as individuals, are separate from one another. Each of us is unique, with our own abilities, interests, and personalities. We all, as individuals, exist on our own, independent of others. According to this view, it is absurd to say that two different people can be one. Hegel argues that there is a deeper truth about human relations that this common-sense view fails to see. He points out that in our most important relations of love and friendship, we in fact willingly give up a part of ourselves. When we are in love, we freely put aside our personal wishes in order to help the one we love or in order to commit to the relation of love. When we do this, we do not feel like we are giving up a part of our freedom, and we do not regret this since we are happy to be in the love relationship. It is in this relation that I find myself again at a higher level. So also with a relation of friendship; I might be required to do something to help my friend that I might otherwise not have been inclined to do, but out of friendship, I do so willingly and gladly. Again, in this kind of case, I give up a part of myself in order to gain a higher conception of myself in the relation of friendship. Hegel claims that, in contrast to the idea of a legal person in Roman law, this constitutes the true nature of personality.[46] With examples like these it is easier to see what Hegel means by finding oneself in the world and how this can be understood as an expression of freedom. In a relation of love or friendship I feel immediately at home with the other person, and I do not have to sacrifice myself.[47] Even though I do make certain compromises or do things that I might not otherwise do, I do not regard these as painful sacrifices or something foreign to myself. So this conception of freedom means overcoming one's immediate selfish impulses and attaining a higher relation with other people. This analysis shows the complex conceptual knot that includes ideas such as alienation, self-consciousness, freedom, recognition, God, and interpersonal relations. We are used to thinking of these things as different topics, but Hegel demonstrates that in fact they are all closely and necessarily related to one another.

---

[45] Hegel, *Vorlesungen über die Philosophie der Religion*, Part III, *Die vollendete Religion*, vol. 5, pp. 127–129, pp. 209–213; *Lectures on the Philosophy of Religion*, vol. 3, *The Consummate Religion*, pp. 193–196, pp. 284–286.

[46] Hegel, *Vorlesungen über die Philosophie der Religion*, Part III, *Die vollendete Religion*, vol. 5, p. 211; *Lectures on the Philosophy of Religion*, vol. 3, *The Consummate Religion*, p. 286.

[47] Hegel, *Vorlesungen über die Philosophie der Religion*, Part III, *Die vollendete Religion*, vol. 5, p. 127; *Lectures on the Philosophy of Religion*, vol. 3, *The Consummate Religion*, p. 194.

## 2.8 The Conclusion of Hegel's *Lectures on the Philosophy of Religion*

Hegel ends his *Lectures on the Philosophy of Religion* on a somewhat surprising note.[48] His stated goal was to demonstrate the truth of Christianity in contrast to the other religions of the world. This meant demonstrating the rational content of Christian doctrine. With this demonstration, he feels a reconciliation is possible with religion in general. As we have seen, he emphasizes this element in the doctrines of the Incarnation and the Revelation. So while the other religions remain in a situation of alienation since their religious devotees cannot recognize themselves in their gods, Christianity finally overcomes this.

But at the end of his lectures, Hegel seems to qualify this conclusion somewhat. He argues that, from a philosophical standpoint, the alienation has been overcome and a reconciliation can take place, and he takes his lectures to have demonstrated this. If we are philosophers and can understand the true nature of the concepts involved in Christianity, then we can understand the reconciliation that it offers. But then he indicates that there is still a "discordant note" in actuality.[49] In other words, while we might be able to attain a reconciliation in thought, this is still not the case in the real world.

He claims that his own time in the 1820s has certain elements in common with the Roman Empire, when the world of culture had lost its meaning and people fell into a state of alienation and despair.[50] As we have seen, he argued that the Roman world had descended into a state of arbitrariness or relativism because the Romans could not realize any enduring hopes and dreams in actuality since the emperor could intervene at any time and destroy them. There was no higher, absolute principle that was respected but instead only the dangerous and unpredictable will of the emperor. As a result, people withdrew from public life and focused on themselves and their own private interests. This led to the social atomism of individuals, who felt no broader sense of affiliation or loyalty. There was no meaningful conception of truth and justice in this world, so people lapsed into relativism and nihilism. Hegel sees a similar movement in his own time. Traditional values and ideas have been eroded since the Enlightenment. As a result, people have lost their belief in external, objective truths. This means that the religious community is no longer

---

[48] Hegel, *Vorlesungen über die Philosophie der Religion*, Part III, *Die vollendete Religion*, vol. 5, p. 94n; *Lectures on the Philosophy of Religion*, vol. 3, *The Consummate Religion*, pp. 161n–162n.

[49] Hegel, *Vorlesungen über die Philosophie der Religion*, Part III, *Die vollendete Religion*, vol. 5, p. 94n; *Lectures on the Philosophy of Religion*, vol. 3, *The Consummate Religion*, p. 161n. See Jon Stewart, "La "nota discordante" de Hegel: La crisis cultural y la inspiración detrás de *Sobre la importancia de la filosofía para la época presente* de Heiberg," *Estudios Kierkegaardianos. Revista de filosofía*, 4 (2018), 25–44.

[50] Hegel, *Vorlesungen über die Philosophie der Religion*, Part III, *Die vollendete Religion*, vol. 5, p. 94n; *Lectures on the Philosophy of Religion*, vol. 3, *The Consummate Religion*, p. 161n.

regarded as having any truth or validity. This has led people to seek the truth in themselves. As a result, the age of Romanticism is often associated with an emphasis on individuality, subjectivity, and inwardness. This corresponds to the relativism and social atomism of the Roman world.

This diagnosis leads Hegel to characterize his age as one of "infinite anguish,"[51] which sounds very much like an echo of the unhappy consciousness. This means clearly that despite all of his efforts to demonstrate philosophically the reconciliation offered by Christianity, nonetheless Hegel believes that his own age is one that is wallowing in alienation. He claims that the reconciliation offered by philosophy is only partial.[52] He portrays philosophy as a sort of monastery that is set apart from society, where monks can work for and reach the truth on their own. Yet their efforts remain apart from actuality and have no effect on real life.

What is puzzling about Hegel's use of the motif of a cultural crisis is that it seems to be clearly in tension with his assessment of his age in his other works. In fact, Hegel is generally known for ending his books with a positive or even triumphant tone. For example, The Phenomenology of Spirit culminates in the concept of "Absolute Knowing," which is the sublation (Aufhebung) of all of the previous forms of knowing that the work has explored. Along the same lines, the Science of Logic concludes with "The Absolute Idea" and the Encyclopedia of the Philosophical Sciences with "Absolute Spirit," both of which are intended to represent the highest form of knowing. Perhaps most overtly, in his notorious celebratory remarks at the end of his Lectures on the Philosophy of History, Hegel states that the culmination of history and the development of subjective freedom and self-knowing have been attained in his own time.

One of the standard objections that Hegel has been subject to by thinkers such as Feuerbach, Marx, and Kierkegaard is that his philosophy is overly abstract and out of touch with the real world. This is a key point for the reception of his philosophy in the nineteenth century. One recalls Marx's famous claim: "The philosophers have only interpreted the world in various ways; the point is to change it."[53] This intuition states that all forms of

---

[51] Hegel, Vorlesungen über die Philosophie der Religion, Part III, Die vollendete Religion, vol. 5, p. 95n (more precisely "infinite pain," "dem unendlichen Schmerze"); Lectures on the Philosophy of Religion, vol. 3, The Consummate Religion, p. 161n.

[52] Hegel, Vorlesungen über die Philosophie der Religion, Part III, Die vollendete Religion, vol. 5, p. 96; Lectures on the Philosophy of Religion, vol. 3, The Consummate Religion, p. 162.

[53] Karl Marx, "Thesen über Feuerbach," in Marx-Engels-Werke, vols. 1–46, ed. by the Institut für Marxismus-Leninismus (Berlin: Dietz, 1956–2018), vol. 3, p. 7. (English translation: "Theses on Feuerbach," in The Marx-Engels Reader, ed. by Robert C. Tucker [New York and London: W. W. Norton & Company, 1978], p. 145.) It is a matter of indifference whether by "philosophers" here, reference is made to Feuerbach, Hegel, or both.

knowledge must in the end have some practical application that can be used to improve people's concrete lives. It is from this intuition that the philosophical traditions of Marxism, utilitarianism, pragmatism, and, in a sense, existentialism all proceed.

Hegel, by contrast, has a different intuition that goes back to the opening line of Aristotle's *Metaphysics*, where it is stated that all human beings by nature desire to know. According to this view, it is a part of human nature to be curious about the world around us and to try to understand it. This natural curiosity is absolutely fundamental and precedes any consideration about practical ends. This view claims that the true philosophical vocation is simply understanding on its own terms and no further justification is needed in the form of results or concrete effects in the real world.

On this issue Hegel has often been caricatured as an ivory tower academic, entirely out of touch with the real world and having a woefully naive understanding of social and political realities. However, a closer look enjoins us to call this into question. Hegel himself has a critical view of the applications of knowledge; he claims, for example, that it is absurd to think that the importance of studying history is that we can learn from it and with this knowledge can avoid repeating the mistakes of the past. According to his sober view, humans have never learned anything at all from history. Given this, he starts to look considerably less naive than his opponents, who are zealous about using new knowledge and information to improve the world.

Another part of Hegel's naiveté is thought to be found in the view that he claims to have resolved the key problems of the world with his philosophical system. In other words, as we have just seen, he takes himself to have arrived at the truth of religion by determining the correct understanding of Christianity. Scholars have thus been quick to ascribe to Hegel a form of optimism about the world or history. This means that he believes that his present age is one where everything falls into place, and truth, peace, and harmony have finally been achieved. Truth has been reached, alienation overcome, and history comes to an end. But here again we are enjoined to rethink this well-known caricature. As we have just seen, Hegel ends his *Lectures on the Philosophy of Religion* not with a triumphant tone but rather one of discord, disruption, and alienation. His analysis of his own age is not one of self-congratulation but rather of criticism and concern. Like his many critics, he believes his age is one of uncertainty, doubt, nihilism, and alienation.

The "discordant note" thus raises important questions about the standard view of Hegel's understanding of the end of history. The motif suggests a more fluid picture of historical development and a less self-congratulatory stance with regard to the present age. Despite whatever victories have been won historically, the age finds itself in a state of confusion and alienation. This appears to show a far more sensitive grasp of the problems of the day than Hegel is usually given credit for. It seems to imply that the historical process is still ongoing, and there are still conflicts and dissonances that need to be addressed and reconciled.

With these few examples we can see that Hegel is a much richer and more complex thinker than these caricatures give him credit for. Moreover, his penetrating analyses of the ills of his own day opened the door for later thinkers in the nineteenth century to develop their own theories. Especially with his introduction of key concepts such as alienation, recognition, and subjective freedom, Hegel cast a long shadow on the development of philosophy and other fields in the nineteenth and twentieth centuries.

# PART II

## The First Generation

# 3

# Heine, Alienation, and Political Revolution

Another thinker inspired by Hegel was the poet and writer Heinrich Heine (1797–1856).[1] Today Heine is perhaps best known as one of the leading figures in the Young Germany movement, which carried on a campaign for enlightened politics in the context of the Restoration. He was born in Düsseldorf into a Jewish family and felt the alienation of being a part of a minority group that was subject to special laws and restrictions. An important part of the development of Heine's political views was his experience as a youth living under French rule during the time of Napoleon's occupation. Napoleon had brought with him the ideas of the French Revolution and thus a progressive policy with regard to the Jews, who were granted civil rights on equal terms with other citizens. However, with the fall of Napoleon in 1815, Düsseldorf became a part of Prussia, which overturned these policies and reinstated the traditional anti-Semitic laws along with many other oppressive measures. Heine spent much of his life militating against the Restoration's many forms of repression.

In accordance with the wishes of his father, Heine began his university studies in law at the University of Bonn in 1819. His interests during this time drifted to literature, and he attended the lectures of the famous Romantic critic August Wilhelm Schlegel. Dissatisfied with Bonn, Heine next went to the University of Göttingen to continue his studies. However, after challenging a fellow student to a duel, he was expelled from the university. In 1821 Heine went to Berlin, where he remained until 1823. There he attended Hegel's lectures and came into contact with the growing circle of his students. Hegel's influence on Heine has been a matter of debate in the scholarship due to the fact that Heine does not say much about the matter explicitly.[2]

---

[1]  See Jeffery L. Sammons, *Heinrich Heine: A Modern Biography* (Manchester: Carcanet New Press, 1979); Philip Kossoff, *Valiant Heart: A Biography of Heinrich Heine* (New York: Cornwall Books, 1983); Eberhard Gallert, *Heinrich Heine*, 4th ed. (Stuttgart: J. B. Metzler, 1976); Anthony Phelan, *Reading Heinrich Heine* (Cambridge: Cambridge University Press, 2006), Roger F. Cook (ed.), *A Companion to the Works of Heinrich Heine* (Rochester, NY: Camden House, 2002); Rolf Hosfeld, *Heinrich Heine: Die Erfindung des europäischen Intellektuellen – Biographie* (Munich; Seidler Verlag, 2014); Christian Liedtke, *Heinrich Heine* (Reinbek bei Hamburg: Rowohlt Verlag, 1997 [2006]).
[2]  See WolfgangHeise, "Zum Verhältnis von Heine und Hegel," in his *Realistik und Utopie. Aufsätze zur deutschen Literatur zwischen Lessing und Heine* (Berlin: Akademie-Verlag,

Moreover, his views on Hegel seem to have changed over time. Given that
Heine attended Hegel's "Lectures on the Philosophy of History" in 1823,
scholars have been quick to point out connections in this sphere.[3] In his
memoirs Heine recounts an episode that seems to imply that, as a student,
he was on very good terms with Hegel personally:

> One beautiful starry evening, we stood, the two of us, at a window, and I,
> a young person of twenty-two, having just eaten well and drunken coffee,
> spoke rapturously about the stars, calling them the habitations of the
> blessed. The master, however, mumbled to himself, "The stars, ho! hum!
> the stars are just leprous spots glowing on the sky." For God's sake –
> I cried – is there no happy place up there to reward virtue after death?
> Hegel just stared at me with his pale eyes and said cuttingly, "You took
> care of your sick mother, and you didn't poison your brother. Do you
> really expect to receive a tip?" After these words, he looked around
> anxiously but seemed to grow calm soon afterwards when he saw that it
> was only Heinrich Beer approaching him to invite him to a round of
> whist.[4]

Hegel's anxiety about being overheard can be taken as evidence that he was
careful to conceal his more radical religious views. The anecdote reveals in any
case that, despite their age difference, Hegel and Heine were on close enough
terms that they could discuss such sensitive things openly with one another.

---

1982), pp. 254–287; Georgi MichailowitschFridlender, "Heinrich Heine und die Äesethetik
Hegels," in *Heinrich Heine. Streitbarer Humanist und volksverbundener Dichter.
Internationale wissenschaftliche Konferenz aus Anlaß des 175. Geburtstages von Heinrich
Heine, Weimar 1972*, ed. by Karl WolfgangBecker, HelmutBrandt, and SiegfriedScheib
(Weimar: Nationale Forschungs- und Gedenkstätten, 1973), pp. 35–48; ManfredWindfuhr,
"Heine und Hegel. Rezeption und Produktion," *Internationaler Heine-Kongreß 1972*, ed. by
ManfredWindfuhr (Hamburg: Hoffmann und Campe, 1973), pp. 261– 280; HeinzHengst,
*Idee und Ideologieverdacht, Revolutionäre Implikationen des deutschen Idealismus im
Kontext der zeitkritischen Prosa Heinrich Heines* (Munich: Wilhelm Fink, 1973);
EduardKrüger, *Heine und Hegel. Dichtung, Philosophie und Politik bei Heinrich Heine*
(Kronberg: Scriptor-Verlag, 1977); MichaelBaumgarten and WilfriedSchulz, "Topoi
Hegelscher Philosophie der Kunst in Heines *Romantischer Schule*," *Heine Jahrbuch*, 17
(1978), 55–94; Jochen Zinke, "Heine und Hegel. Stationen der Forschung," *Hegel-Studien*,
14 (1979), 295–312; Jean Pierre Lefebvre, *Der gute Trommler. Heines Beziehung zu Hegel*,
trans. by Peter Schöttler (Hamburg: Hoffmann und Campe, 1986).
[3] Terry Pinkard, "Introduction," in Heinrich Heine, *On the History of Religion and
Philosophy in Germany and Other Writings*, ed. by Terry Pinkard and trans. by Howard
Pollack-Milgate (Cambridge: Cambridge University Press, 2007), pp. xiv–xv;
Ortwin Lämke, *Heines Begriff der Geschichte. Der Journalist Heinrich Heine und die
Julimonarchie* (Stuttgart and Weimar: J. B. Metzler, 1997).
[4] Heinrich Heine, "Geständnisse," in *Vermischte Schriften*, vols. 1–3 (Hamburg: Hoffmann
und Campe, 1854), vol. 1, pp. 61f.; "From *Confessions*," in *On the History of Religion and
Philosophy in Germany*, p. 206.

In Berlin Heine became a close associate of the Hegelian jurist and fellow Jew, Eduard Gans, who was one of the leaders of the Association for the Culture and Science of Judaism, which Heine also took part in for a time. It has been suggested that the common feeling of alienation and sense of homelessness felt by being German Jews formed a bond between Gans and Heine.[5] After his studies, Heine traveled extensively in England, Italy, and the German states. These travels were the source of inspiration for a number of poetic works. In 1825 Heine had himself baptized in the hope that this would open up some career opportunities to him that would otherwise be closed to Jews.

By this time Heine had long tired of the reactionary politics in the German states and the strict censorship laws to which his works were subject. Hopeful after the French Revolution of 1830, he moved to Paris in 1831, where he resided until his death. He earned his living as a reporter for the German newspaper the *Allgemeine Zeitung*. In this capacity he explained the political and cultural events in France to the German readers. But he was also interested in conveying information about the German states to French readers. In 1834 he published *On the History of Religion and Philosophy in Germany*, in which he explains to the French reader both recent and past trends in German thought. Heine's writings were critical of the conservative politics of Prussia and the German states, and in 1835 Prussia permanently banned Heine's works.

Heine was joined in Paris by other like-minded German intellectuals in exile. One of these was his third cousin Karl Marx, who arrived in 1843. Marx and Heine became friends, sharing a similar frustration with the current political situation and thirsting for revolution. Although no communist himself, Heine was also concerned about poverty, the exploitation of the workers, and the disenfranchised and oppressed classes. It thus makes sense that he published some of his works in journals edited by Marx. In the fall of 1843, Heine returned to Germany to meet with his publisher. He describes his journey in a poem entitled *Germany: A Winter's Tale*, which satirizes, among other things, the political situation in Prussia and the German states. In 1844 an arrest warrant was issued, thus preventing him from ever returning to his homeland again. From 1848 until the end of his life in 1856, Heine was bedridden, suffering from lead poisoning. During these years, however, he continued to write despite his pain and partial paralysis.

While Heine is not known today as a philosopher, he can be rightly included in the history of philosophy in the nineteenth century.[6] Like the other figures

---

[5] Pinkard, "Introduction," in *On the History of Religion and Philosophy in Germany and Other Writings*, pp. x–xi.

[6] Although Heine is not usually included in works on the history of philosophy in the nineteenth century, a brief analysis of his contribution appears in Warren Breckman's *Marx, the Young Hegelians, and the Origins of Radical Social Theory* (Cambridge: Cambridge University Press, 1999), pp. 187–192.

treated in this work, he was inspired by certain elements in Hegel's thought, which he made use of in his own way. He felt an acute sense of alienation from German society and politics, which is in line with Hegel's assessment of the crisis of his age. On a personal level, he struggled with questions of self-identity and self-alienation as a German Jew. Moreover, he had a burning desire for political liberation, for which he made an impassioned plea in his poetry. Thus Heine disseminated philosophical ideas in more popular contexts and won a wider readership for them.

Like Hegel, Heine also believed that there was a great crisis of the day, but it was not so much in the form of culture generally as in the form of the political oppression caused by the Restoration. The crisis was a political one that stood in the way of human freedom and development. New conditions must be created in order to make true human flourishing possible. Heine believed that poetry had an important role to play in the modern crisis and was critical of the escapist tendency of Romanticism. In his view, there should be no radical break between poetry and life. Poetry should not be a fantasy or the work of pure imagination; instead, it should constitute a part of one's real life and be a source of reflection, inspiration, and renewal.

### 3.1   Introduction to *On the History of Religion and Philosophy in Germany*

In 1833 Heine's *On the History of Religion and Philosophy in Germany* was first published in a series of individual articles in French in the magazine *Revue des deux Mondes*.[7] The German version appeared in 1834, where it constituted most of the second volume of his collection *Der Salon*, which also contains some poems.[8] The text consists of three books, corresponding to the three original articles. In this work Heine seeks to correct the mistaken views about Germany that were in circulation in France due to Madame de Stael's book *De l'Allemagne*.[9] Heine rightly sees German philosophy not as a separate or an independent element of culture but rather as closely related to the

---

[7] Henrich Heine, "De L'Allemagne depuis Luther," *Revue des deux Mondes* (1834), "Première Partie," Tome 1, 473–505; "Deuxième Partie," Tome 4, 373–408; "Troisième Partie," Tome 4, 633–678.

[8] Heinrich Heine, *Zur Geschichte der Religion und Philosophie in Deutschland*, in his *Der Salon*, vols. 1–2 (Hamburg: Hoffmann und Campe, 1834), vol. 2, pp. 1–284. (English translation: *On the History of Religion and Philosophy in Germany and Other Writings*, ed. by Terry Pinkard and trans. by Howard Pollack-Milgate, Cambridge: Cambridge University Press 2007.)

[9] La Baronne de Stael Holstein, *De l'Allemagne*, vols. 1–3 (Paris: M. Nicolle; London: John Murray, 1813). The originally planned edition of 1810 was seized and destroyed by the authorities at Napoleon's order before its publication, and the work only appeared three years later.

development of religious thinking. His work is thus dedicated not just to philosophy but also to religion.

On the face of it, this does not look like a particularly radical work, although there are a number of critical remarks about religion. In the first of the three books, Heine recounts the history of German religious thinking from Catholicism to Luther and the Reformation. He portrays Luther as the hero of German culture. By claiming that he respected no authority beyond that of the Bible and human reason, Luther paved the way for German philosophy:

> In saying that his teachings could be contradicted only by the Bible itself or by means of rational argument, Luther granted human reason the right to explain the Bible, and Reason was thus acknowledged as the highest judge in all religious controversies. Thus arose in Germany what is called freedom of the spirit or, by another name, freedom of thought. Thinking became a right, and the authority of reason became legitimate.[10]

This important step led to an increased freedom of thought in the German-speaking world. With his translation of the Bible, Luther created the German language and struck a blow for freedom of speech since it made it possible for everyone to discuss religious issues. In this respect Heine follows Hegel's positive assessment of Luther's role in the development of the freedom of the individual in human history. With Luther, blind belief in authority was undermined and the value of the individual conscience arose: "The authorities have collapsed; reason remains the one lamp of humanity, and one's conscience is the only staff in the dark labyrinth of this life."[11]

Heine thus portrays Luther's Reformation as a great German revolution in thought that was an indispensable factor in the later development of German philosophy. In the second book he turns his attention to the background for German philosophy in the modern period. Attentive to his French readership, he ascribes to Descartes the title of the founder of modern philosophy. With his rejection of scholasticism, Descartes is hailed for his emancipation of philosophy from theology.[12] Heine then traces the development of philosophical thought through, among others, Leibniz, Spinoza, Wolff, Mendelssohn, and Lessing. In this context, he gives an account of pantheism and even offers a defense of it. He writes,

> God is identical with the world. He manifests himself in plants, which lead cosmic-magnetic lives devoid of consciousness. He manifests himself in animals, which in their sensuous dream-lives have more or less vague

---

[10] Heine, *Zur Geschichte der Religion und Philosophie in Deutschland*, p. 68; *On the History of Religion and Philosophy in Germany*, p. 32.

[11] Heine, *Zur Geschichte der Religion und Philosophie in Deutschland*, p. 89; *On the History of Religion and Philosophy in Germany*, p. 42.

[12] Heine, *Zur Geschichte der Religion und Philosophie in Deutschland*, pp. 95f.; *On the History of Religion and Philosophy in Germany*, p. 43.

feelings of existence. But most magnificently, he manifests himself in the human being, who feels and thinks at the same time, who knows how to differentiate himself as an individual from objective nature, and who, in his reason, already possesses the same ideas which exhibit themselves to him in the world of appearance. In the human being, divinity comes to self-consciousness, and such self-consciousness again itself reveals the divine by means of the human being.[13]

His emphasis on the relation between humans and the divine resembles Hegel's philosophy of religion. Humans share with God the quality of spirit by means of which they are separate from nature. People become aware of God by means of their self-consciousness.

In Hegel's philosophy of religion, he notes that the different religions tend to be associated with specific peoples. The Indians, Persians, Egyptians, and Greeks all have their own religions with their own gods. Religion thus constitutes group beliefs and practices and not the idiosyncratic ideas of specific individuals. Each religion has its own divine revelation, but it is only when all of the world religions are taken together that the complete picture emerges. Heine explains,

> But this revelation [i.e., of God] does not occur in and through the individual human being, but rather in and through the entirety of human-ity, so that each person only grasps and represents a part of the God-World-Universe, but all of humanity together will grasp and represent the entire God-World-Universe in idea and in reality. Every people, perhaps, has the mission to know and make known a particular part of that God-World-Universe, to comprehend a series of appearances and to bring a series of ideas to appearance, and to hand down these results to the peoples who come after, who have their own, similar missions. God is thus the true hero of world-history; it is his constant act of thinking, his constant action, his word, his deed. And one can justly say of humanity in its entirety, it is an incarnation of God![14]

Heine repeats here what Hegel says at the end of his *Lectures on the Philosophy of History*, namely that the development of history represents human beings coming to awareness of themselves as freedom and spirit.[15] Thus the idea of God as spirit and the human spirit merge.

[13] Heine, *Zur Geschichte der Religion und Philosophie in Deutschland*, pp. 130f.; *On the History of Religion and Philosophy in Germany*, p. 57.
[14] Heine, *Zur Geschichte der Religion und Philosophie in Deutschland*, p. 131; *On the History of Religion and Philosophy in Germany*, p. 57.
[15] G. W. F. Hegel, *Vorlesungen über die Philosophie der Weltgeschichte: Berlin 1822–1823*, ed. by Karl Heinz Ilting, Karl Brehmer, and Hoo Nam Seelmann (Hamburg: Felix Meiner, 1996), pp. 152–154. (*The Philosophy of World History*, vol. 1, *Manuscripts of the Introduction and the Lectures of 1822–3*, trans. by Robert F. Brown and Peter

Book 3 recounts the story of German Idealism, and Heine devotes vignettes to Kant, Fichte, Schelling, and his old teacher from Berlin, Hegel. In this chapter he develops an analogy between what he characterizes as the German revolution in thought and the actual French Revolution of 1789. In connection with the "spiritual revolution" caused by Kant's philosophy, he writes, "We [i.e., Germans] have uprisings in the world of ideas just as you [i.e., French] do in the material world, and tearing down the old dogmatism makes us as hot as storming the Bastille makes you."[16] He portrays Kant as the destroyer of the *ancien régime* of philosophy, comparing him with Robespierre, the leader of the Reign of Terror.[17] By this he seems to refer to Kant's claim that God, immortality, freedom, and things-in-themselves cannot be known by theoretical reason. Similarly, Fichte is compared with Napoleon, who attempts to reestablish order after the Kantian reign of terror.[18]

Without mentioning him by name, Friedrich Engels refers to Heine's idea of the different characters of the revolutions in France and Germany. In *The Condition of the Working Class in England*, he develops Heine's comparison further, writing, "The Industrial Revolution is of the same importance for England as the political revolution for France and the philosophical revolution for Germany; and the difference between England in 1760 and in 1844 is at least as great as that between France under the *ancien régime* and during the July Revolution."[19] The Industrial Revolution thus represents the third major movement that shapes the social-political conditions of the times. Compared with the revolutions in Germany and France, this revolution was perhaps even more transformative. Thus Engels extends Heine's insight and adds an important new dimension to his diagnosis of the Zeitgeist.

## 3.2   Heine's Assessment of Schelling and Hegel

Heine gives a critical account of Schelling's philosophy, which he takes to be largely derived from Spinoza. If Kant and Fichte are philosophers of the revolution, then Schelling is the philosopher of the Restoration. Heine had seen Schelling in Munich in 1827 and had respect for his early philosophy.

C. Hodgson with the assistance of William G. Geuss [Oxford: Oxford University Press, 2011], pp. 87–89.)

[16] Heine, *Zur Geschichte der Religion und Philosophie in Deutschland*, pp. 214f.; *On the History of Religion and Philosophy in Germany*, p. 88.

[17] Heine, *Zur Geschichte der Religion und Philosophie in Deutschland*, p. 189, p. 191.; *On the History of Religion and Philosophy in Germany*, p. 78, p. 79.

[18] Heine, *Zur Geschichte der Religion und Philosophie in Deutschland*, p. 225; *On the History of Religion and Philosophy in Germany*, p. 92.

[19] Friedrich Engels, *Die Lage der arbeitenden Klasse in England. Nach eigner Anschauung und authentischen Quellen* (Leipzig: Otto Wigand, 1845), p. 28. (English translation: *The Condition of the Working Class in England*, ed. by David McLellan [Oxford: Oxford University Press, 1993], p. 29.) (Translation slightly modified.)

Schelling's thought on the philosophy of nature is portrayed as his most important work, but Heine claims that even this, in the end, reduces to nonsense. Heine introduces Hegel in his overview at the end of his account of Schelling and the movement of philosophy of nature, which Schelling and his school represented. In this context Hegel is presented thus:

> A greater thinker now emerges who develops *Naturphilosophie* into a complete system, who explains with this synthesis the entire world of appearances, who adds even grander ideas to the grand ideas of his predecessors, and who carries out the synthesis in every discipline, thus grounding it scientifically. He is a pupil of Mr. Schelling, but a pupil who gradually assumed all of the power of his teacher in the realm of philosophy; seeking dominance, he outgrew Schelling, and finally cast him out into the darkness. It is the great Hegel, the greatest philosopher produced by Germany since Leibniz. There is no question that he towers above both Kant and Fichte.[20]

Heine recalls that while Schelling had been a child prodigy, Hegel's fame was slower to come. When the two were together at Jena and jointly published the *Kritische Journal der Philosophie*, Schelling was the better known of the two, and it was commonly assumed that Hegel was one of his students. But now in hindsight, there could, for Heine, be no doubt about Hegel's role as the culmination of the rich tradition of German philosophy.

For as much as Hegel is celebrated, Schelling is reviled. Although acknowledging that the young Schelling was a progressive mind, Heine claims that over time he turned into an agent for the Restoration: "the same man who once expressed most boldly the religion of pantheism, who proclaimed most loudly the sanctification of nature and the reinstatement of humanity to its divine rights, this man became a renegade to his own teaching."[21] We should recall that this was published in 1834, at a time when Schelling had largely disappeared from the public eye. After his early years, when Schelling had been celebrated as the successor of Kant and Fichte, he went through a long period where he published nothing. Then in 1841, alarmed by the rise of the free-thinking left Hegelians, King Friedrich Wilhelm IV of Prussia hired him to take up a high-paying professorship at the University of Berlin with the express purpose of combating Hegelian thinking. The court's representative, Karl Freiherr von Bunsen, explains the king's desire for Schelling to come to Berlin and join in the fight against "the dragon seed of Hegelian pantheism."[22] Schelling's inaugural lecture course, "The Philosophy of

---

[20] Heine, *Zur Geschichte der Religion und Philosophie in Deutschland*, pp. 272f.; *On the History of Religion and Philosophy in Germany*, p. 110.

[21] Heine, *Zur Geschichte der Religion und Philosophie in Deutschland*, pp. 274f.; *On the History of Religion and Philosophy in Germany*, p. 111.

[22] See F. W. J. Schelling, *Philosophie der Offenbarung 1841–42*, ed. by Manfred Frank (Frankfurt am Main: Suhrkamp, 1977) (3rd revised ed., 1993); Appendix II:

Revelation," took place in the fall of 1841 and was a major event.[23] Everyone at the university, students and professors alike, wanted to attend, and the crowd of auditors spilled out into the hall. Present at Schelling's lectures were a number of thinkers who would later become important in their own right, including Søren Kierkegaard, Mikhail Bakunin, and Friedrich Engels. But the general assessment at that time largely agreed with Heine's view here seven years earlier. Schelling had nothing new to say and had become an obscure thinker who had sold out to the Prussian state for money. The initial unlimited interest in Schelling's lectures gradually tapered off as his auditors grew disgusted with them.

In a later poem Heine satirizes Friedrich Wilhelm IV, casting the Prussian king in the role of the reactionary Emperor of China. In the work Schelling is referred to as "Confusius," the wise man of the court.[24] Heine subtly changes the orthography of the name of the Chinese sage from Confucius to Confusius, implying that Schelling's thinking was confused, which was a common perception among his auditors. Thus Schelling's Berlin lectures, which might have been taken as an epic episode in the history of nineteenth-century philosophy, in the end turned into a major disappointment for all parties involved. So in a sense it can be argued that Heine's negative assessment of Schelling's moral character in *On the History of Religion and Philosophy in Germany* in fact prefigures the later events. Schelling had betrayed not only himself but also philosophy: To compare Hegel with "Schelling is completely impossible; for Hegel was a man of character."[25]

If Schelling is the villain, then Hegel is the hero of the story of German philosophy that Heine wants to tell. Hegel is thus portrayed as the high point of the development of German thought. In this spirit, Heine writes, "Our philosophical revolution is over. Hegel completed its great circle."[26] Despite this, the reader is disappointed to find no detailed account of Hegel's philosophical

---

"Historische Hintergründe der Berufung Schellings; Schellings Auftreten in Berlin 1841," p. 486. See also Kuno Fischer, *Schellings Leben, Werke und Lehre* (Heidelberg: C. Winter, 1899), p. 239.

[23] For accounts of Schelling's lectures, see Helmut Pölcher, "Schellings Auftreten in Berlin (1841) nach Hörerberichten," *Zeitschrift für Religions- und Geistesgeschichte*, 6(3) (1954), 193–215; Xavier Tilliette (ed.), *Schelling im Spiegel seiner Zeitgenossen* (Turin: Bottega d'Erasmo, 1974), pp. 435–466; Schelling, *Philosophie der Offenbarung 1841-42*, pp. 495–581.

[24] Heine, "Der Kaiser von China," in *Neue Gedichte, Zeitgedichte* (Hamburg: Hoffmann und Campe; Paris, J. J. Dubochet & Cie., 1844), pp. 259–261, p. 260. (English translation: "The Emperor of China," in *The Poetry of Heinrich Heine*, ed. by Frederic Ewen [Secaucus, NJ: Citadel Press, 1969], pp. 255–256, p. 256.)

[25] Heine, *Zur Geschichte der Religion und Philosophie in Deutschland*, p. 273; *On the History of Religion and Philosophy in Germany*, p. 111.

[26] Heine, *Zur Geschichte der Religion und Philosophie in Deutschland*, p. 280; *On the History of Religion and Philosophy in Germany*, p. 113.

system or key ideas at the end of the work. Heine praises Hegel's moral
character and explains how Hegel's philosophy displaced that of Schelling,
but he does not enter into a discussion of any of Hegel's actual works. In his
memoirs many years later, Heine explains that he intended to correct this
oversight by adding a detailed account of Hegel's philosophy to a planned new
edition of On the History of Religion and Philosophy in Germany. However,
after having worked on this for over two years, he was dissatisfied with the
result and committed his manuscript to the flames.[27] The reason that he gives
for his disappointment is not that he had been unsuccessful in translating
Hegel's difficult thought and philosophical jargon into an accessible form, but
rather that he, at this later point in time, found something repellent about it. In
the intervening period Heine had seen other students of Hegel, such as Strauss,
Bauer, and Feuerbach, make use of Hegel's ideas to issue a criticism of religion.
While these thinkers became increasingly radical in their religious views,
Heine became more conservative and eventually abandoned the atheism of
his youth. Today scholars still debate about the degree to which these later
thinkers were continuing with Hegel's project or criticizing it. But for Heine,
the matter was clear. He writes, "I had to admit to myself that Hegelian
philosophy gave the most formidable support to all of these forms of
atheism."[28] He portrays Hegel as "the mother-hen" sitting "on the disastrous
eggs" of the atheistic left Hegelians.[29] Ironically, his alarm at the dangerous
implications of Hegel's philosophy squares with that of the Prussian government that hired Schelling to combat it. Thus Heine's views on Hegel clearly
changed in step with his own changing religious convictions. In his memoirs
many years later, Heine takes a considerably more critical tone toward Hegel's
philosophy than is found in the triumphant story told in On the History of
Religion and Philosophy in Germany in 1834.

### 3.3   Heine's Bold Prediction of a German Revolution

Toward the end of the work, Heine describes German philosophy as
a revolution in thought, which began with the Protestant Reformation. These
passages were apparently cut by the censors and cannot be found in the
printing of Zur Geschichte der Religion und Philosophie in Deutschland in
the second volume of Der Salon in 1834, although they appear in the original
French printing in the Revue des deux Mondes. Heine again compares this
revolution of the mind with the French Revolution of actual deeds. While

---

[27] Heinrich Heine, "Geständnisse," in Vermischte Schriften, vol. 1, pp. 62–70; "From
    Confessions," in On the History of Religion and Philosophy in Germany, pp. 206–209.
[28] Heine, "Geständnisse," pp. 63f.; "From Confessions," in On the History of Religion and
    Philosophy in Germany, p. 207.
[29] Heine, "Geständnisse," p. 59; "From Confessions," in On the History of Religion and
    Philosophy in Germany, p. 205.

France had a real political revolution, Germany had merely a revolution in philosophy:

> only our most distant descendants will be able to decide whether we should be praised or reproached for first working out our philosophy before working out our revolution. It seems to me that a methodical people like us had to begin with the Reformation, could only on that basis occupy itself with philosophy, and solely after its completion be able to pass over to political revolution.[30]

However, he claims that German philosophy has prepared the way for a real political revolution. Heine believes that the age in which he is living is suffering from a crisis of political oppression and thinks that philosophy is the solution to the problem. Philosophy will lead the revolution that will overthrow the repressive forces and liberate humanity. Only with the implementation of philosophy is human freedom and fulfillment possible. For Heine, the issue of political emancipation is one of the utmost gravity. It is intimately connected to the other spheres of culture, as is seen most obviously in the work of the censors. In order for cultural life to flourish, it must be permitted certain fundamental freedoms, which must be granted by the state. Thus to occupy oneself with politics is not a sign that one is uncultured but rather is a legitimate expression of the need of the age to free itself from oppression. Indeed, it is a precondition for the development of culture in the form of art, religion, and philosophy.

Heine uses the last few pages of *On the History of Religion and Philosophy in Germany* to describe for the French reader the coming revolution in Germany that will be inspired by philosophy. He explains, "The German revolution will not be more mild and gentle because it was preceded by Kantian criticism, Fichtean transcendental idealism, and even *Naturphilosophie*. Because of these very doctrines, revolutionary forces have developed which are simply biding their time to break out and to be able to fill the world with horror and admiration."[31] He imagines revolutionary Kantians and armed Fichteans and natural philosophers taking up the struggle in the streets.

Heine anticipates his French readers smiling at his predictions of a German revolution when there appear to be no real signs of it. But he warns them,

> Do not take my advice lightly, the advice of a dreamer who warns you about Kantians, Fichteans, and *Naturphilosophen*. Do not take lightly the fantastic poet, who expects in the realm of appearance the same revolution

---

[30] Heine, "De L'Allemagne depuis Luther," *Revue des deux Mondes* (1834), "Troisième Partie," Tome 4, 675; *On the History of Religion and Philosophy in Germany*, p. 115. (As noted, this passage and the following are omitted in *Zur Geschichte der Religion und Philosophie in Deutschland* in the second volume of *Der Salon*.)

[31] Heine, "De L'Allemagne depuis Luther," *Revue des deux Mondes* (1834), "Troisième Partie," Tome 4, 676; *On the History of Religion and Philosophy in Germany*, p. 115.

which has happened in the province of the spirit. Thought goes before deed as lightning before thunder. German thunder is certainly German; it is not very agile and begins to rumble very slowly. But it will come and when you hear crashing, as it has never crashed before in all of world history, you will know, German thunder has finally reached its goal.[32]

Heine clearly believes that Germany has a world-historical mission in the struggle for human freedom. He is brimming with excitement and enthusiasm for the great spiritual power of German philosophy that will bring about the revolution. He continues with the image; with the sound of the German thunder, "eagles will fall dead from the sky, and lions in the most distant desert in Africa will put their tails between their legs and crawl into their royal caves."[33] The eagle was a well-known symbol for Prussia and appeared on the Prussian flag. The lion, as the king of the beasts, was a symbol of kingship and royalty.

Heine then dramatically compares the coming German revolution with the actual French Revolution known to his readers: "A play will be enacted in Germany which will make the French Revolution look like a harmless idyll."[34] It is easy to miss the force and power of this claim. While many intellectuals in the German states, such as Hegel, were enthusiastic admirers of the French Revolution and the progressive ideas that motivated it, they were horrified by the Reign of Terror that it turned into. The murderous violence of the revolution was used as an argument by the forces of the Restoration for the need to curb political freedom. It was claimed that people were not able to handle their freedoms and would misuse them by committing acts of violence that would undermine society. Thus mention of the French Revolution caused anxiety in the hearts of the conservatives of the day, who were intent on keeping a lid on dangerous progressive ideas. Heine's claim is that the coming German revolution will be even more radical than the French Revolution and will make it look harmless. In its historical context, this was a provocative claim.

Heine's enthusiasm for the future is unbridled, and especially important is the power that he ascribes to philosophy in the coming conflict. Like the French Revolution of 1789, which shocked all of Europe, the coming German revolution will be a world-historical event: "And the hour will come. As on the rows of an amphitheater, nations will gather around Germany to see the great games of battle."[35] One might think that the faith

---

[32] Heine, "De L'Allemagne depuis Luther," *Revue des deux Mondes* (1834), "Troisième Partie," Tome 4, 677; *On the History of Religion and Philosophy in Germany*, p. 116.

[33] Heine, "De L'Allemagne depuis Luther," *Revue des deux Mondes* (1834), "Troisième Partie," Tome 4, 677; *On the History of Religion and Philosophy in Germany*, p. 116.

[34] Heine, "De L'Allemagne depuis Luther," *Revue des deux Mondes* (1834), "Troisième Partie," Tome 4, 677; *On the History of Religion and Philosophy in Germany*, p. 116.

[35] Heine, "De L'Allemagne depuis Luther," *Revue des deux Mondes* (1834), "Troisième Partie," Tome 4, 677; *On the History of Religion and Philosophy in Germany*, p. 117.

that Heine places in the power of German philosophy to change the world and liberate humanity is unwarranted and overly enthusiastic. However, it should be noted that in fact many of Hegel's students played important roles in the Revolution of 1848. In this sense it can be argued that his hope and zeal were not entirely misplaced.

### 3.4   The Poem "Adam the First" as a Hegelian Anthropology

Heine's poem "Adam the First" was first published in 1844 in the collection *Neue Gedichte, Zeitgedichte*.[36] The poem recounts the biblical story of the Fall. At first, one might think that this poem reflects Heine's Jewish background. But while it does, of course, demonstrate his knowledge of the Hebrew scriptures, his version of the story is highly heterodox. Unlike the theological readings that see Adam and Eve as terrible sinners, Heine's poem portrays them as heroes of humanity. The poem begins as follows, as the poet addresses God: "You sent forth, with their swords of flame, / The guards of your heavenly city, / And chased me out of Paradise / With neither justice nor pity." (Du schicktest mit dem Flammenschwert / Den himmlischen Gensd'armen, / Und jagtest mich aus dem Paradies, / Ganz ohne Recht und Erbarmen!)[37] This refers to Genesis 3:23–24, where it is said that God drove Adam and Eve from the garden and placed cherubim with flaming swords as guards in order to prevent them from returning. With the use of the first person, the poet puts himself in the role of Adam, thus implying that he represents humanity in general. Most striking about this first stanza is the implication in the final line that God is neither just nor merciful, two qualities that are always associated with the divine. Instead, God is portrayed as a tyrant who acts arbitrarily and who enforces his will with the threat of violence, here in the form of his servants the cherubim with swords.

The second stanza alludes to the knowledge gained from eating of the tree of the knowledge of good and evil. Heine continues in the first person, "I trudge along beside my wife / Towards regions far and strange; / But I have fed on wisdom's fruit, / And this you cannot change." (Ich ziehe fort mit meiner Frau / Nach and'ren Erdenländern; / Doch daß ich genossen des Wissens Frucht, / Das kannst du nicht mehr ändern.)[38] Heine portrays Adam as defiant; he taunts God, who, despite his infinite power, is unable to deprive Adam and Eve of their newly gained wisdom. The only thing that God can do is to send them away, but he cannot reverse their new nature as fully human. Although it

---

[36] Heine, "Adam der Erste," in *Neue Gedichte, Zeitgedichte*, pp. 228–229. (English translation: "Adam the First," in *The Poetry of Heinrich Heine*, pp. 257–258.)

[37] Heine, "Adam der Erste," in *Neue Gedichte, Zeitgedichte*, p. 228; "Adam the First," in *The Poetry of Heinrich Heine*, p. 257.

[38] Heine, "Adam der Erste," in *Neue Gedichte, Zeitgedichte*, p. 228; "Adam the First," in *The Poetry of Heinrich Heine*, p. 258.

is a difficult life in the hostile world outside paradise, nonetheless Adam and Eve are now free and wise, and with these qualities, they are able to take on the challenges.

The third stanza continues the defiant tone and even taunts God: "You cannot steal what I have learned: / How weak you are, and small, / Trying to prove, with thunder and death, / That you are Lord of all!" (Du kannst nicht ändern, daß ich weiß, / Wie sehr du klein und nichtig, / Und machst du dich auch noch so sehr / Durch Tod und Donnern wichtig.)[39] Heine emphasizes the violence of the God of the Hebrew Bible, who intimidates "with thunder and death." Here Heine picks up on Hegel's interpretation of Judaism that was discussed earlier.[40] It will be recalled that Hegel claimed that one of the key characteristics of Judaism was its portrayal of God as commanding and threatening human beings in a way that failed to recognize their inwardness and subjective freedom. The God of Judaism treats humans not as mature and free individuals but rather like children or even animals. God does not enjoin the ancient Hebrews to follow his laws because they can see the rationality of them with their own understanding and reason. Instead, he simply issues commands and expects them to follow them, whether they like it or not. Their consent does not matter. Heine also emphasizes this element in his portrayal of the God of Genesis. By treating humans in this way, Heine notes, God also diminishes himself. Heine portrays him like a child who, by making a lot of noise, tries to draw attention to himself. By treating others like children, God is reduced to a child himself. One might think that being a Jew, Heine would be offended at Hegel's interpretation of this important story in the Jewish tradition. However, surprisingly, he embraces it and even expands on it.

Like Hegel, Heine celebrates the fact that humans left the paradise of the garden and developed their full capacities as human beings. The garden was only suitable for animals, and once humans became free, they could no longer remain there. But instead of being something negative, as in the theological interpretations, this is something positive for both the philosopher and the poet. Heine has Adam say, "I'll never yearn for Paradise; / Your Eden wasn't much: / I found some lovely trees, whose fruit / I was not allowed to touch." (Vermissen werde ich nimmermehr / Die paradiesischen Räume; / Das war kein wahres Paradies – / Es gab dort verbotene Bäume.)[41] Here Heine calls into question the value of being in Paradise if one is treated like a child and forbidden to be who one is, namely a free and rational human being. When

---

[39] Heine, "Adam der Erste," in *Neue Gedichte, Zeitgedichte*, p. 228; "Adam the First," in *The Poetry of Heinrich Heine*, p. 258.

[40] See Chapter 2, Section 2.3.

[41] Heine, "Adam der Erste," in *Neue Gedichte, Zeitgedichte*, p. 229; "Adam the First," in *The Poetry of Heinrich Heine*, p. 258.

the story is seen from this perspective, there is no reason to regret or lament the loss of paradise. Instead, it represents the progress of human freedom. This recalls Bruno Bauer's claims, to be explored in Chapter 5, about how religion prevents humans from developing by forbidding them from using their faculty of critical reason. Religion thus keeps people in a state of unthinking ignorance and undermines all natural growth and development.

In the final stanza of the poem, Heine makes explicit the political implications of the story. He has Adam say, "My freeman's right must be complete! / If I should ever feel / The slightest limit – Heaven would be / A Hell, and a prison!" (Ich will mein volles Freiheitsrecht! / Find ich die geringste Beschränknis, / Verwandelt sich mir das Paradies / In Hölle und Gefängnis.)[42] Adam is thus transformed into a revolutionary who demands freedom. Far from being a paradise, the garden was in fact a prison. Human beings require freedom in order to be who they are. When they are kept in a condition of subordination and subject to the rule of tyrants, they can never develop their full potential.

It can be said that this work is a poetic version of Hegel's account of Judaism and philosophical anthropology. Heine appreciates Hegel's criticism of the story of the Fall and his recognition of human beings as spirit. This was a powerful message for Heine given the political situation at the time of the Restoration, when people were constantly subject to arbitrary control and the limitation of their freedoms. Heine rewrites the story of the Fall, changing it from a sad story of loss and sin to a symbol of liberation and a message of the true potential of all human beings. No longer a great sinner who passed on a great curse to the human race, Adam is now a kind of Prometheus who stole something essential from the gods (knowledge and freedom) and gave it to humans. The title of the poem can be taken at face value as referring to Adam as the first human being or the first sinner, but on Heine's interpretation he represents the first rebel or the first truly free person. This is a poem of defiance and celebration that is inspired by Hegel.

### 3.5  The Poem "Tendency" and the Role of Poetry in Politics

In the same collection, *Neue Gedichte*, Heine published a poem simply called "Tendency." In it he urges his fellow German poets to write poetry in the service of political emancipation. The first stanza runs as follows: "German singers! Sing and praise / German freedom – til your song / Takes possession of our souls, / And inspires us to goals, / As the noble *Marseillaise*." (Deutscher Sänger! sing' und preise / Deutsche Freiheit, daß dein Lied / Unsrer Seelen sich bemeistre / Und zu Thaten uns begeistre, / In

---

[42]  Heine, "Adam der Erste," in *Neue Gedichte, Zeitgedichte*, p. 229; "Adam the First," in *The Poetry of Heinrich Heine*, p. 258. (Translation modified.)

Marseillerhymnenweise.)[43] The comparison between a possible revolution in
Germany and the real one in France, which was broached in his *On the
History of Religion and Philosophy in Germany*, is now taken up again with
the reference to the French revolutionary song "La Marseillaise." Heine
clearly believes that poetry can play an important role in moving people to
action to resist the forces of oppression in his day. The poet and the revolutionary thus share the same goal.

Heine criticizes the work of the German Romantics and others, which he
regards as self-indulgent and politically irrelevant. He refers to Goethe's classic
*The Sufferings of Young Werther* as follows, "No more Werthers need be
heard – / We have cooed and wooed too long – / Be your people's guide and
rock – / Tell them that the hour has struck; / Speak the sword, the dagger
word!" (Girre nicht mehr wie ein Werther, / Welcher nur für Lotten glüht – /
Was die Glocke hat geschlagen / Sollst du deinem Volke sagen, / Rede Dolche,
rede Schwerter!)[44] One should not waste time with the self-pitying of
Werther's travails of love. Instead, poetry has a far more important role to
play by urging people to fight for their freedom.

The final stanza radically issues imperatives to the German poets: "Shatter,
thunder, night and day – / Till you've righted every wrong! / Sing to waken, to
incite!" (Blase, schmettre, don're täglich, / Bis der letzte Dränger flieht – / Singe
nur in dieser Richtung.)[45] In the final lines, he urges caution with regard to not
attracting the attention of the censors. He advises his fellow poets, "But be
careful that you write / In the vaguest sort of way." (Aber halte deine
Dichtung / Nur so allgemein als möglich.)[46]

This poem has a tone of urgency with regard to the political situation. Its call
for concrete action echoes the sentiment of many thinkers of the period. What
is particularly interesting here is the important role that Heine ascribes to the
poet. As we will see,[47] in the same year that Heine published his poem, his
friend and relative Karl Marx published his "Introduction to the Contribution
to the Critique of Hegel's *Philosophy of Right*" in the *Deutsch-Französische
Jahrbücher*.[48] At the end of this article, Marx sees the role of the philosopher as

---

[43] Heine, "Die Tendenz," in *Neue Gedichte, Zeitgedichte*, p. 252; "Tendency," in *The Poetry of Heinrich Heine*, p. 254.

[44] Heine, "Die Tendenz," in *Neue Gedichte, Zeitgedichte*, p. 252; "Tendency," in *The Poetry of Heinrich Heine*, p. 254.

[45] Heine, "Die Tendenz," in *Neue Gedichte, Zeitgedichte*, p. 253; "Tendency," in *The Poetry of Heinrich Heine*, p. 254.

[46] Heine, "Die Tendenz," in *Neue Gedichte, Zeitgedichte*, p. 253; "Tendency," in *The Poetry of Heinrich Heine*, p. 254.

[47] See Chapter 6, Section 6.2.

[48] Karl Marx, "Zur Kritik der Hegel'schen Rechts-Philosophie. Einleitung," *Deutsch-Französische Jahrbücher*, 1–2 (1844), 85. (English translation: "Contribution to the Critique of Hegel's *Philosophy of Right*: Introduction," in *The Marx-Engels Reader*, ed. by Robert C. Tucker [New York and London: W. W. Norton & Company, 1978], p. 65.)

standing side by side with the worker in campaigning for the cause of social revolution. The philosopher provides the theoretical basis, while the workers actualize these thoughts in the real world. Thus philosophy has a significant role to play in the revolution. Here Heine makes a similar claim with regard to the role of the poets. He believes that poetry can have a powerful effect on people and can inspire them to great deeds.

In this respect Heine's position resembles that of the Danish poet-philosopher Johan Ludvig Heiberg, who was also a student of Hegel in Berlin. While Heiberg was not a revolutionary in the same sense as Marx or Heine, he did believe that the age was in a great crisis for which philosophy was the solution.[49] He urged his students to go out into the world and apply their philosophical education in the different spheres of life. Heiberg also believed in the special power of poetry to convey this philosophical message inspired by Hegel. In 1838 he tried to bring Hegel's philosophy to the stage of the Copenhagen Royal Theater with a piece of dramatic poetry entitled *Fata Morgana*.[50] His most successful work, *New Poems* from 1841, contains a number of Hegelian elements.[51] For Heiberg, the solution to the crisis of the age was not just philosophy but also art and especially poetry. Heine seems to agree with this view of the important role of poetry, although he conceives it in a more radical way than Heiberg. While for Heiberg, the issue is about convincing people of the truth of Hegel's speculative philosophy, for Heine, it is a call to arms. Here we can see a gradual movement from Hegel's quietist view of philosophy as a cloister to Heiberg's plea for a revolution of the mind or the reformation of culture to Heine's and Marx's incitement to direct political revolt. Particularly important here is Heiberg's and Heine's perception of the role that poetry can play in this development. Poetry is not just a mindless bourgeois pastime, but rather it can speak to people's hearts and show them

---

[49] Johan Ludvig Heiberg, *Om Philosophiens Betydning for den nuværende Tid. Et Indbydelses-Skrift til en Række af philosophiske Forelæsninger* (Copenhagen: C. A. Reitzel, 1833), pp. 3–10. (English translation: *Heiberg's On the Significance of Philosophy for the Present Age and Other Texts*, ed. and trans. by Jon Stewart [Copenhagen: C. A. Reitzel, 2005] [*Texts from Golden Age Denmark*, vol. 1], pp. 87–91.)

[50] Johan Ludvig Heiberg, *Fata Morgana, Eventyr-Comedie* (Copenhagen: Schubothe, 1838). See Jon Stewart, *A History of Hegelianism in Golden Age Denmark*, Tome II, *The Martensen Period: 1837–1842* (Copenhagen: C. A. Reitzel, 2007) (*Danish Golden Age Studies*, vol. 3), pp. 137–154; Jon Stewart, "Heiberg's Conception of Speculative Drama and the Crisis of the Age: Martensen's Analysis of *Fata Morgana*," in *The Heibergs and the Theater: Between Vaudeville, Romantic Comedy and National Drama*, ed. by Jon Stewart (Copenhagen: Museum Tusculanum Press, 2012) (*Danish Golden Age Studies*, vol. 7), pp. 139–160.

[51] Johan Ludvig Heiberg, *Nye Digte* (Copenhagen: C. A. Reitzel, 1841). See Stewart, *A History of Hegelianism in Golden Age Denmark*, Tome II, *The Martensen Period: 1837–1842*, pp. 508–535.

a vision of the future that can motivate them to resist the forces of oppression that they find in the present. This was a powerful message at the time.

### 3.6 "The Silesian Weavers"

Heine himself embodied the image of the political poet that he sketched in "Tendency." Perhaps his most famous work in this regard is his poem "The Silesian Weavers," which originally appeared under the title "The Poor Weavers" in the journal *Vorwärts! Pariser deutsche Monatsschrift* on July 10, 1844.[52] Marx had recently become one of the editors of the journal, and through his influence it published Heine's poem as well as articles by Engels and Bakunin. Heine later added an extra stanza to the poem and published it with the new title "The Silesian Weavers" in the collection *Album. Originalpoesien* in 1847.[53]

The subject of the work is the rebellion of weavers that began in July of 1844 in Peterswaldau in Silesia in Prussia (today Pieszyce in Poland).[54] The weavers found themselves struggling to make a living because the price of their products had been severely driven down by competition from the British, who had introduced new machines to do the work and had made use of cheaper cotton instead of linen. The practice for the Silesian weavers was to buy the raw materials from a merchant and then to sell back to him the finished product. Over time the merchants gradually lowered the prices that they were willing to pay, and this brought the weavers into a desperate situation since, despite their increased work hours, they were not able to earn enough to support themselves. The weavers in a body went to the home of their employer and demanded a higher price for their labor. When their demands were not met, they destroyed the merchant's house and looted the factories. The uprising was put down by the Prussian military, which killed a number of weavers by firing indiscriminately into the crowd. This episode is often hailed as the beginning of the German workers' movement. Marx and Engels both wrote about this conflict, expressing their support for and solidarity with the weavers' cause.

---

[52] Heinrich Heine, "Die armen Weber," *Vorwärts! Pariser deutsche Zeitschrift*, 55 (July 10, 1844).

[53] Heinrich Heine, "Die schlesischen Weber" in Hermann Püttmann (ed.), *Album. Originalpoesien* (Borna [Bremen/Brussels]: Albert Reiche, 1847), pp. 145–146. (English translation: "The Silesian Weavers," in Frederic Ewen [ed.], *The Poetry of Heinrich Heine*, p. 244.)

[54] See Helga Grebing, *History of the German Labour Movement: A Survey*, trans. by Edith Körner (Leamington Spa: Berg Publishers, 1985); Hans E. Bremes (ed.), *140 Jahre Weberaufstand in Schlesien. Industriearbeit und Technik – gestern und heute. Ein Beitrag zur politischen Kulturarbeit* (Münster: Verlag Westfälisches Dampfboot, 1985); Christina von Hodenberg, *Aufstand der Weber. Die Revolte von 1844 und ihr Aufstieg zum Mythos* (Bonn: Dietz, 1997); Lutz Kroneberg and Rolf Schloesser, *Weber-Revolte 1844. Der schlesische Weberaufstand im Spiegel der zeitgenössischen Publizistik und Literatur* (Cologne: C. W. Leske, 1979).

The final version of Heine's poem consists of five stanzas.[55] The first stanza presents a picture of the Silesian weavers in their misery. It is written in the first-person plural, suggesting that it is the weavers themselves who are speaking: "In gloomy eyes there wells no tear. / Grinding their teeth, they are sitting here: / Germany, your shroud's on our loom; / And in it we weave the threefold doom. / We weave; we weave." (Im düstern Auge keine Thräne, / Sie sitzen am Webstuhl und fletschen die Zähne: / Deutschland, wir weben Dein Leichentuch, / Wir weben hinein den dreifachen Fluch – / Wir weben, wir weben!) The image is both sad and threatening. While the weavers are portrayed as being in distress, nonetheless they are weaving a funeral shroud for Germany, thus preparing for its death. This suggests that the weavers' uprising will lead the way to a broader revolution that will bring down Prussia and the repressive German states.

The middle three stanzas, the body of the work, each contain a curse on the different forces of oppression: God, the king of Prussia, and the fatherland. These were the three things that Prussians were required to swear allegiance to in the official oath of loyalty. In the second stanza, Heine seems to join in the criticism of religion found in Bruno Bauer and Marx, who claim that religion constitutes a form of oppression since it is used as a tool by the reactionary political forces: "Doomed be the God who was deaf to our prayer / In winter's cold and hunger's despair. / All in vain we hoped and bided; / He only mocked us, hoaxed, derided – / We weave; we weave." (Ein Fluch dem Gotte, zu dem wir gebeten / In Winterskälte und Hungersnöthen; / Wir haben vergebens gehofft und geharrt, / Er hat uns geäfft und gefoppt und genarrt – / Wir weben, wir weben!) The idea that God mocked the weavers implies that religious belief itself is a form of illusory hope that can seduce the oppressed. Religion plays on people's misery and desperation, but in the end there is no reason to believe that it will ever make good on its promises. It simply misleads people and then leaves them to their misery. This negative conception of the oppressive nature of religion is entirely in line with the view of Bauer and Marx.

The second stanza issues a curse on Friedrich Wilhelm IV, who, instead of protecting the poor and oppressed, sided with the merchants in their oppression of the weavers. "Doomed be the king, the rich man's king. / Who would not be moved by our suffering, / Who tore the last coin out of our hands, / And let us be shot by his bloodthirsty bands – / We weave; we weave." (Ein Fluch dem König, dem König der Reichen, / Den unser Elend nicht konnte erweichen, / Der den letzten Groschen von uns erpreßt, / Und uns wie Hunde erschießen läßt – / Wir weben, wir weben!) As noted previously, it was King Friedrich Wilhelm IV who had hired Schelling to fight against left Hegelianism. The king ascended to the throne in 1840, and his policies were

---

[55]  In what follows I quote from this revised version of the poem. Heine, "Die schlesischen Weber" in *Album. Originalpoesien*, pp. 145–146; "The Silesian Weavers," in *The Poetry of Heinrich Heine*, p. 244.

considerably more conservative that those of his predecessor, his father Friedrich Wilhelm III, who was responsible for the creation of the University of Berlin. There was a great sense of anger and betrayal at the fact that the king would use military force to put down the uprising.

Finally, in the third stanza, the "fatherland" is singled out for a special curse: "Doomed be the fatherland, false name, / Where nothing thrives but disgrace and shame, / Where flowers are crushed before they unfold. / Where the worm is quickened by rot and mold – / We weave; we weave." (Ein Fluch dem falschen Vaterlande, / Wo nur gedeihen Schmach und Schande, / Wo jede Blume früh geknickt, / Wo Fäulniß und Moder den Wurm erquickt – / Wir weben, wir weben!) Heine had a complex self-identity as a German Jew. His sense of alienation from the German politics of the Restoration made him much more amenable to having sympathy with France. He had a genuinely cosmopolitan point of view and was critical of petty nationalism and provincialism. In this context his criticism of a German or Prussian fatherland as an antiquated idea makes sense. It is a false fatherland just as religion is a false belief system that only misleads people and plays on their fears and insecurities.

The final stanza emphasizes the never-ending work of the weavers and ominously repeats the refrain, suggesting the fall of God, the king, and the fatherland, the three objects of critique: "The loom is creaking, the shuttle flies; / Nor night nor day do we close our eyes. / Old Germany, your shroud's on our loom. / And in it we weave the threefold doom; / We weave; we weave." (Das Schiffchen fliegt, der Webstuhl kracht, / Wir weben emsig Tag und Nacht / Altdeutschland, wir weben Dein Leichentuch, / Wir weben hinein den dreifachen Fluch, / Wir weben, wir weben!) The message is clear: The days of the Restoration are numbered, and a new time is coming. The fact that the weavers themselves are the speakers suggests a sense of class consciousness or empowerment; through their collective work they can together bring about the fall of Prussia. On this point Heine seems to predict a revolution in Prussia and the German states that is completely in line with what he said in his text from a decade earlier, *On the History of Religion and Philosophy in Germany*.

This poem cemented Heine's reputation as a political poet. Like Heiberg, Heine sees that poetry and art have a valuable role to play in the solution to the crisis of the age. Heine's poem was tremendously popular and helped to bring attention to the plight of the weavers. Historians take the episode of the Silesian weavers to be an important preliminary step on the way to the Revolution of 1848. Thus it can be said that Heine in some way contributed to raising awareness about the issues of oppression that led to this. Likewise, alongside Marx, he helped to develop a sense of class consciousness among the workers, who began to see more clearly their common interests and collective power. The poem was immediately banned in Prussia. The work of Heine, Marx, Engels, and others in the journal *Vorwärts!* caused such consternation that in January 1845 – that is, only a matter of months after the publication of the poem – the French government, under pressure from Prussia, closed down the journal. But Heine's poem continued to be circulated in the form of pamphlets.

## 3.7   Heine's Legacy

Heine's call to freedom was a profound message that had an enduring effect on both thinkers and general readers. Many years later, in 1873, the Russian anarchist Bakunin, in his work *Statism and Anarchy*, refers to the impact of Heine's poem and his prediction of a coming revolution: "an industrial crisis, which condemned tens of thousands of weavers to starvation, aroused an even stronger interest in social issues throughout Germany. The chameleon poet Heine on this occasion wrote a magnificent poem, 'The Weavers,' which predicted an imminent and merciless social revolution."[56] By referring to Heine as a "chameleon," Bakunin perhaps has in mind the change in Heine's religious thinking, which, as has been noted, turned more conservative as he grew older. In any case, Heine is given credit for helping to spread the word about the plight of the Silesian weavers.

In the same book Bakunin praises Heine's *On the History of Religion and Philosophy in Germany* as an insightful if not prescient work. Bakunin tries to give an estimate of the importance of German philosophy. In this context he reflects on Heine's claim that German philosophy, under the aegis of Hegel, will lead to a political revolution in the German states that will rival the French Revolution. Referring to the final pages of Heine's book,[57] Bakunin writes,

> In the 1830s and 1840s it was assumed that when the time for revolutionary action came again, the doctors of philosophy of the school of Hegel would leave the boldest figures of the 1790s far behind them and would amaze the world with their rigorously logical and relentless revolutionism. The poet Heine wrote many eloquent words on this subject. "All your revolutions are as nothing," he said to the French, "compared to our future German revolution. We, who had the audacity to destroy the entire divine world in a systematic, scientific fashion, will not hesitate before any idols on earth and will not rest until, on the ruins of privilege and power, we have won total equality and total liberty for the entire world." In much the same terms Heine proclaimed to the French the future marvels of the German revolution. And many people believed him. Alas, the experience of 1848 and 1849 was enough to shatter that belief.[58]

---

[56] Mikhail Bakunin, *Statism and Anarchy*, trans. by Marshall S. Shatz (Cambridge: Cambridge University Press, 2005), p. 144.

[57] Bakunin paraphrases Heine from the passage quoted above, "De L'Allemagne depuis Luther," *Revue des deux Mondes* (1834), "Troisième Partie," Tome 4, 677; *On the History of Religion and Philosophy in Germany*, p. 116: "A play will be enacted in Germany which will make the French Revolution look like a harmless idyll."

[58] Bakunin, *Statism and Anarchy*, p. 132.

Bakunin points out the enthusiastic tone of Heine's work, claiming that he was naive in trusting in the power of German philosophy to effect social change. The promise of an earthshaking revolution was sadly disappointed. Bakunin refers to Heine's portrayal of Kant's philosophy as destroying religious belief by claiming that knowledge of God was not possible. Bakunin also presumably saw the connection on this point between Heine's account in *On the History of Religion and Philosophy in Germany* and Marx's later praise of German philosophy of religion, which, through the efforts of Feuerbach and others, destroyed the belief in God.[59]

Friedrich Engels, in his work *Ludwig Feuerbach and the Outcome of Classical German Philosophy*, also alludes to Heine's book. Like Marx before him, Engels makes use of Heine's idea that German philosophy will pave the way for a political revolution. But now, writing in retrospect in 1886, Engels believes that this is in fact exactly what happened. At the time it seemed very unlikely that apparently conservative university professors influenced by Hegel would have anything to do with revolutionary politics; however, Engels claims, Hegel's philosophy played a role in preparing for the coming revolution as Heine predicted. Engels writes, "But what neither the government nor the liberals were able to see was seen at least by one man as early as 1833, and this man was indeed none other than Heinrich Heine."[60] Engels thus has a more positive assessment of Heine's prediction than does Bakunin. The point is that there is a revolutionary element in Hegel's philosophy, which Heine correctly perceived,[61] despite the ostensible conservatism of the right Hegelian professors.

There is some pathos in the fact that Heine became seriously ill in May of 1848 and would spend the rest of his life in bed. Although he spent so many years raising awareness of the injustices of the Restoration, when the revolution finally came, he found himself in a state of partial paralysis. He witnessed with disappointment the collapse of the revolution and the rise of Napoleon III. Heine spent his life in a state of constant alienation from the social-political order. This was only partially mitigated by his Parisian exile. He saw an important role for philosophy in understanding this alienation and mobilizing it in the service of social change. Heine was thus inspired by specific ideas in Hegel's philosophy, which he tried to apply by means of his poetic gift.

---

[59] See Chapter 6, Sections 6.1–6.2.

[60] Friedrich Engels, "Ludwig Feuerbach und der Ausgang der klassischen deutschen Philosophie," *Die neue Zeit: Revue des geistigen und öffentlichen Lebens*, vol. 4 (1886) (Parts I–II), no. 4, pp. 145–157 (Parts III–IV), no. 5, pp. 193–209, p. 145. (English translation: *Ludwig Feuerbach and the Outcome of Classical German Philosophy*, ed. by C. P. Dutt [New York: International Publishers, 1941], p. 9.

[61] See Chapter 10, Sections 10.2–10.3.

# 4

# Feuerbach's Doctrine of the Humanity
# of the Divine in *The Essence of Christianity*

One of the most important figures in the first generation of Hegel students was Ludwig Feuerbach (1804–1872).[1] Born in Landshut, in Bavaria, on July 28, 1804, Feuerbach came from a family of scholars. His father was a well-known jurist and legal philosopher, Paul Johann Anselm von Feuerbach (1775–1833). The young Feuerbach received a thorough Lutheran education during his time in school, which he spent in Ansbach. He initially planned to become a pastor and from 1823 to 1824 attended the University of Heidelberg, where he studied theology. It was here that he came into contact with the theologian Karl Daub (1765–1836), from whom he first learned about Hegel's philosophy.

The encounter with Daub inspired Feuerbach to go to Berlin in 1824 in order to attend Hegel's lectures. He remained in the Prussian capital for two years, during which time he immersed himself in the work of Hegel. He became completely enraptured by it, and this resulted in an inward struggle with his plans to become a pastor. In a letter to his father, dated May 24, 1824, he explains, brimming with enthusiasm:

> It is only four weeks since I started on my courses, but they have already been infinitely useful. What was still obscure and incomprehensible while I was studying under Daub, I have now understood clearly and grasped in its necessity through the few lectures of Hegel which I have attended so far; what only smoldered in me like tinder, I see now burst into bright flames.[2]

---

[1] See Eugene Kamenka, *The Philosophy of Ludwig Feuerbach* (London: Routledge & Kegan Paul, 1970); Marx W. Wartofsky, *Feuerbach* (Cambridge: Cambridge University Press, 1982); Van A. Harvey, *Feuerbach and the Interpretation of Religion* (Cambridge: Cambridge University Press, 1997); William J. Brazill, "Feuerbach, Vischer, and the Divinity of Humanity," in his *The Young Hegelians* (New Haven and London: Yale University Press, 1970), pp. 135–174; Josef Winiger, *Ludwig Feuerbach, Denker der Menschlichkeit* (Darmstadt: Lambert Schneider Verlag, 2011); Adolf Kohut, *Ludwig Feuerbach. Sein Leben und seine Werke* (Leipzig: F. Eckardt, 1909).

[2] "Ludwig an den Vater. Berlin, den 24. Mai 1824," in *Ludwig Feuerbach in seinem Briefwechsel und Nachlass sowie in seiner philosophischen Charakterentwicklung*, vols. 1–2, ed. by Karl Grün (Leipzig and Heidelberg: C. F. Winter'sche Verlagshandlung, 1874), vol. 1, p. 181. (English translation in *The Fiery Brook: Selected Writings of Ludwig Feuerbach*, trans. by Zawar Hanfi [Garden City, NY: Anchor Books, 1972], p. 268.)

In September of the same year he writes to his old teacher Daub to say that Hegel's lectures have opened up a new world for him and have marked the turning point in his life.[3] He continues, "the thunder and lightning of [Hegel's] dialectic is the greatest good fortune that could have happened to me."[4] In defiance of the wishes of his father, Feuerbach abandoned the idea of getting a degree in theology and began to devote himself entirely to philosophy.

In 1826 he found himself in financial trouble and was obliged to leave Berlin. He returned to Bavaria and enrolled at the University of Erlangen, where, in 1828, he completed a dissertation entitled *The Unity, Universality and Infinity of Reason.*[5] The main thesis of the book is that reason is the one universal or absolute. The work thus tries to outline a thoroughly secular view, according to which God and immortality are reduced to universal human reason. He sent a copy of the work to Hegel, whom he acknowledges as a great source of inspiration. In his accompanying letter, Feuerbach strikes the tone of a humble student showing great deference to his teacher. However, he ventures a criticism of Christianity, which he says, in contradiction to Hegel's view, cannot "be conceived as the perfect and absolute religion."[6] Anticipating the central idea of *The Essence of Christianity*, he says, "the striving of the individual must now be so directed that through religion Spirit as Spirit may hold forth in appearance as nothing other than itself."[7] The implication seems to be that in the divine, humans should recognize themselves and not some foreign other. It can only be imagined that Hegel was concerned about this interpretation of his philosophy, and he apparently never answered the letter.

After completing his degree, Feuerbach remained in Erlangen as a lecturer. He published his first major book in 1830, *Thoughts on Death and Immortality.*[8] In this work he expanded on the secular view that he presented in his dissertation. While Hegel himself was wary about making any clear and unambiguous statements about the issue of immortality, and this lack of clarity

[3] Günter Nicolin (ed.), *Hegel in Berichten seiner Zeitgenossen* (Hamburg: Felix Meiner, 1970), no. 413, p. 269.
[4] Nicolin (ed.), *Hegel in Berichten seiner Zeitgenossen*, no. 413, p. 269.
[5] Ludovico Andrea Feuerbach, *De ratione, una, universali et infinita. Dissertatio inauguralis philosophica* (Erlangen, 1828).
[6] Letter 592, "Feuerbach an Hegel," in G. W. F. Hegel, *Briefe von und an Hegel*, vols. 1–4, ed. by Johannes Hoffmeister (vols. 4.1 and 4.2 ed. by Friedhelm Nicolin), 3rd ed. (Hamburg: Felix Meiner, 1961–1981), vol. 3, p. 247. (*Hegel: The Letters*, trans. by Clark Butler and Christiane Seiler [Bloomington: Indiana University Press, 1984], p. 549.)
[7] Letter 592, "Feuerbach an Hegel," p. 248; *Hegel: The Letters*, p. 550.
[8] [Ludwig Feuerbach], *Gedanken über Tod und Unsterblichkeit aus den Papieren eines Denkers, nebst einem Anhang theologisch-satyrischer Xenien, herausgegeben von einem seiner Freunde* (Nüremburg: Johann Adam Stein, 1830). (English translation: *Thoughts on Death and Immortality. From the Papers of a Thinker, along with an Appendix of Theological-Satirical Epigrams, Edited by One of His Friends*, trans. by James A. Massey [Berkeley: University of California Press, 1980].)

was later the source of controversy among his students and critics, Feuerbach explicitly criticizes the idea. More precisely, he rejects the notion of the survival of the individual after death, claiming that immortality exists only in the form of universal spirit or consciousness, which absorbs the individual. With death the individual transcends their finite, limited sphere and becomes a part of the universal whole. Like Hegel, Feuerbach understood the collective human mind as spirit or human culture in general. Since this is universal, we become immortal by contributing to human culture and intellectual development. This book appeared anonymously since Feuerbach knew that his criticism of the doctrine of immortality would be controversial. The work was immediately banned by the authorities, and copies of it were confiscated from the bookstores by the police. When it became known that he was the author, his position quickly became tenuous. He discontinued his lectures at the University in Erlangen in the fall of 1832. Although he returned to give another lecture course in the winter semester of 1835–1836, this signaled the end of his academic career. After this time he never held another university position and worked for the rest of his life in relative academic isolation.

Throughout the 1830s Feuerbach published a series of works on the history of philosophy presumably based in part on his lectures at Erlangen: *History of Modern Philosophy from Bacon to Spinoza* (1833), *History of Modern Philosophy: Presentation, Development, and Critique of the Leibnizian Philosophy* (1837), and *Pierre Bayle: A Contribution to the History of Philosophy and Humanity* (1838).[9] In 1837 Feuerbach married Bertha Löw (1803–1883), and the marriage provided him with much-needed financial stability. For years he was able to live off the revenues provided by his wife's porcelain factory in Bruckberg.

Ever since his stay in Berlin, Feuerbach had been interested in and positively disposed toward Hegel's philosophy, but over the course of time he began to develop his own thought, and this put him on a collision course with Hegelian idealism. In 1839 this new direction was expressed in a long article "Towards a Critique of Hegel's Philosophy."[10] This work criticized overenthusiastic assessments of Hegel's philosophy and its pretensions to have reached an

---

[9] Ludwig Feuerbach, *Geschichte der neuern Philosophie von Bacon von Verulam bis Benedict Spinoza* (Ansbach: Carl Brügel, 1833); *Geschichte der neuern Philosophie. Darstellung, Entwicklung und Kritik der Leibnitz'schen Philosophie* (Ansbach: Carl Brügel, 1837); *Pierre Bayle, nach seinen für die Geschichte der Philosophie und Menschheit interessantesten Momenten* (Ansbach: Carl Brügel, 1838).

[10] Ludwig Feuerbach, "Zur Kritik der Hegelschen Philosophie," *Hallische Jahrbücher für deutsche Wissenschaft und Kunst*, ed. by Arnold Ruge and Theodor Echtermeyer (1839), no. 208, pp. 1157–1160; no. 209, pp. 1165–1168; no. 210, pp. 1673–1677; no. 211, pp. 1681–1684; no. 212, pp. 1689–1693; no. 213, pp. 1697–1702, no. 214, pp. 1705–1709; no. 215, pp. 1713–1718; no. 216, pp. 1721–1725. (English translation: "Towards a Critique of Hegel's Philosophy," in Lawrence S. Stepelevich [ed.], *The Young Hegelians: An Anthology* [Cambridge: Cambridge University Press, 1983], pp. 95–128.)

absolute, timeless truth. It also focused in some detail on the claim of Hegel's system to begin without presuppositions. Two years later, in 1841, Feuerbach published his magnum opus, *The Essence of Christianity*, which was the most read book in philosophy and theology of its day.[11] This was a work that had a profound influence on Marx and Engels and others in their generation. It also enjoyed some celebrity among freethinkers in the Anglophone world thanks to the English translation by the novelist Mary Ann Evans. With the publication of *The Essence of Christianity*, Feuerbach's name was often associated with that of Strauss as a leader of the left Hegelian school. Provoked by the great outcry of criticism in response to *The Essence of Christianity*, Feuerbach made a revised and expanded second edition of the work with a new preface that appeared in 1843.[12]

He continued a very productive period, publishing "Provisional Theses for the Reformation of Philosophy,"[13] *Principles of the Philosophy of the Future*,[14] and *The Essence of Religion* in just three years.[15] The extent of Feuerbach's celebrity can be seen in the fact that the publication of a complete works edition of his writings began as early as 1846.[16] In the fall of 1848, a group of students from Heidelberg invited him to come out of his isolation and offer some lectures. When the university refused to allow him the use of a lecture hall, the lectures were given at the City Hall of Heidelberg from December 1848 to March of the following year. These lectures were subsequently published in 1851 as a part of the collected works edition of his writings.[17]

Unlike many of Hegel's other students, Feuerbach played no role in the revolutions of 1848. He reluctantly accepted to serve as a member of the

---

[11] Ludwig Feuerbach, *Das Wesen des Christenthums* (Leipzig: Otto Wigand, 1841).

[12] Ludwig Feuerbach, *Das Wesen des Christenthums*, 2nd ed. (Leipzig: Otto Wigand, 1843). (English translation: *The Essence of Christianity*, trans. by Marian Evans [New York: Calvin Blanchard, 1855].)

[13] Ludwig Feuerbach, "Vorläufige Thesen zur Reformation der Philosophie," in Arnold Ruge (ed.), *Anekdota zur neuesten deutschen Philosophie und Publicistik* (Zürich and Winterthur: Verlag des Literarischen Comptoirs, 1843), vol. 2, pp. 62–86. (English translation: "Provisional Theses for the Reformation of Philosophy," in Stepelevich [ed.], *The Young Hegelians*, pp. 156–171.)

[14] Ludwig Feuerbach, *Grundsätze der Philosophie der Zukunft* (Zürich and Winterthur: Verlag des literarischen Comptoirs, 1843). (English translation: *Principles of Philosophy of the Future*, trans. by Manfred H. Vogel [Indianapolis: Hackett Publishing Company, 1986].)

[15] Ludwig Feuerbach, "Das Wesen der Religion," in *Die Epigonen*, vol. 1 (Leipzig: Otto Wigand, 1846), pp. 117–178; Ludwig Feuerbach, *Das Wesen der Religion*, 2nd ed. (Leipzig: Otto Wigand, 1849). (English translation: *The Essence of Religion*, trans. by Alexander Loos [Amherst, NY: Prometheus Books, 2004].)

[16] Ludwig Feuerbach, *Ludwig Feuerbach's sämmtliche Werke*, vols. 1–10 (Leipzig: Otto Wigand, 1846–1866).

[17] Ludwig Feuerbach, *Vorlesung über das Wesen der Religion*, vol. 8 of *Ludwig Feuerbach's sämmtliche Werke* (Leipzig: Otto Wigand, 1851).

National Assembly in Frankfurt, but he seems to have been wholly unsuited for political life and did not participate in any meaningful way in the political discussions that went on there. After the dissolution of the Assembly, he returned to his isolation in Bruckberg, wholly disillusioned with the political direction of Europe.

In 1857 he published a work entitled *Theogony According to the Sources of Classical, Hebrew and Christian Antiquity*.[18] Although he took this to be an important work, it was largely ignored. In 1860 Feuerbach lost his main source of income when his wife's factory went bankrupt. He lived the last period of his life on a very tenuous financial basis. His publications also slowed down considerably during this time. In 1866 he published his last major work, *Divinity, Freedom and Immortality*, which appeared as the final volume of his collected works edition.[19] Toward the end of his life, he became somewhat more politically engaged, reading Marx's philosophy and joining the German Social Democratic Party. He spent the last years of his life in the small town of Rechenberg, near Nüremburg, where he died on September 13, 1872.

## 4.1    Theology as Anthropology

Feuerbach's *The Essence of Christianity* tries to argue that it is a mistake to think of God as an objective, transcendent entity that is fundamentally different from human beings, as is traditionally done in theology. Instead, God is simply the essence of what is human, projected onto an external entity. When we look closely, we realize that God has nothing but human qualities. Given this, Feuerbach argues that it is necessary to reframe theology from a field that is used to thinking of the divine as something separate and radically different to a field that understands the divine as human. For this reason he refers to his undertaking not as theology or philosophy of religion but as *anthropology*, that is, a study of the human.

The work begins with an extended introduction, and then the body of the text is divided into two large parts. The first half of the book, entitled "The True or Anthropological Essence of Religion," represents the positive side of the analysis. Here Feuerbach goes through different traditional conceptions of the divine in the Christian tradition and tries to demonstrate that all of these can be traced back to a human element. The second half of the work, entitled "The False or Theological Essence of Religion," represents the critical or polemical part of the work. Here Feuerbach endeavors to expose the contradictions

---

[18]  Ludwig Feuerbach, *Theogonie nach den Quellen des classischen, hebräischen und christlichen Alterthums*, vol. 9 of *Ludwig Feuerbach's sämmtliche Werke* (Leipzig: Otto Wigand, 1857).

[19]  Ludwig Feuerbach, *Gottheit, Freiheit und Unsterblichkeit*, vol. 10 of *Ludwig Feuerbach's sämmtliche Werke* (Leipzig: Otto Wigand, 1866).

involved in the traditional Christian dogmas, beliefs, and practices so long as one maintains a conception of the divine as radically separate or different from the human. The work concludes with a long appendix, where he takes up a number of different related issues with short analyses.

The tone of the text has often given critics the impression that Feuerbach's ultimate goal is to undermine Christianity and religion as a whole. But in the preface to the second edition of the work, he is keen to refute reproaches of this kind.[20] Feuerbach points out that the first half of the book is dedicated explicitly to demonstrating the true nature of Christianity. His goal, like that of Hegel, is to put Christianity on a solid footing. For this reason, in the second half of the work, he is keen to criticize what he takes to be mistaken and misleading pictures of Christianity that are presented in the mainstream theology of his day. According to Feuerbach, these views present illusions and thus make Christianity appear contradictory and implausible. By contrast, his own position can be seen as rescuing it. But here the question in the eyes of his critics is whether the remedy is worse than the disease since in order to save Christianity, Feuerbach must interpret it so radically that it seems to have lost almost all of its most defining dogmas.

Although historically placed under the rubric of left Hegelianism, Feuerbach himself understands his work to be a radical denial of Hegel. In the preface to the second edition, he explicitly rejects what he takes to be the abstraction of Hegel's idealism. He writes, "I unconditionally repudiate absolute, immaterial, self-sufficing speculation."[21] By contrast, he portrays his own philosophy as one of materialism, claiming that he is dealing with material things in the real world and not just ideas. He argues that ideas must be based on empirical observation and should not produce their own content from themselves alone. Feuerbach declares his allegiance as follows: "in the sphere of strictly theoretical philosophy, I attach myself, in direct opposition to the Hegelian philosophy, only to realism, to materialism."[22] In view of this explicit rejection of Hegelian idealism, it might seem surprising that historians of ideas have placed Feuerbach in one of the Hegelian schools.

Although historical categorizations of this kind invariably have an element of arbitrariness about them, there is still something that can be said about understanding Feuerbach as a Hegelian. There can be no doubt that his dissertation and treatise on immortality were stamped by a Hegelian influence.

---

[20] Ludwig Feuerbach, *Das Wesen des Christenthums*, pp. xivf (2nd ed., 1843); *The Essence of Christianity*, p. 9. Note that the English translation omits the first part of Feuerbach's preface to the second edition, in which he responds to a critical review of his work.

[21] Feuerbach, *Das Wesen des Christenthums*, p. ix (2nd ed., 1843); *The Essence of Christianity*, p. 4. (All subsequent references are to this second edition of *Das Wesen des Christenthums*.)

[22] Feuerbach, *Das Wesen des Christenthums*, p. ix; *The Essence of Christianity*, p. 4. See also *Das Wesen des Christenthums*, p. xi; *The Essence of Christianity*, p. 6.

The main thesis of *The Essence of Christianity*, that the conception of God is in the end just a reflection of the human, can also be understood as an extension of Hegel's own view in the *Lectures on the Philosophy of Religion*. As we have seen, Hegel's work culminates in the idea that with Christianity, humanity realizes for the first time that the highest, the absolute, God is in fact a human being. But in order to determine Feuerbach's ultimate relation to Hegel, we need to look more closely at the position that he develops.

## 4.2    The Question of the Nature of Human Beings

Feuerbach begins *The Essence of Christianity* by raising the question of "The Essential Nature of Man."[23] This question can be reformulated by asking: what is the difference between humans and animals? Hegel regularly noted that only humans, and not animals, have religion; all of the elements of spirit are unique to *human* culture. So what is it about human beings that makes it possible for them to have religion, whereas animals do not? According to Feuerbach, the answer to this lies in the nature of self-consciousness. Animals are immediately aware of themselves as individuals, but they cannot abstract from this to think of themselves more generally as a species.[24] Human beings, by contrast, have this ability. This means that they can think of human nature or essence in the abstract. It is this ability to abstract, claims Feuerbach, that makes all science and religion possible. To think in terms of scientific laws requires that we abstract from individual cases in order to see the underlying general pattern.

Animals are in a sense one-dimensional since they just have an immediate awareness of themselves as individuals. But humans, by contrast, are complex since they have a double nature.[25] Here Feuerbach echoes Hegel's analysis of the beginning of Genesis, according to which humans were initially at one with themselves and with nature like the animals. Then came the Fall, and human nature became divided and alienated. This means that there is always a distance between our immediate self-relation or our inward self and our abstract relation to ourselves as a species or our outward selves.

The human ability to think and to abstract means that we are able to see ourselves from the perspective of the other, even when the other is not there at the moment. For animals, the relation to the other is always immediate; the other animal must be there physically for them to have this relation. But this is not the case for humans. Since we can think of human nature as an abstract concept, we can think of another human being even when we are alone. We can feel shame at the mere thought of someone observing us doing something

---

[23] Feuerbach, *Das Wesen des Christenthums*, pp. 1–17; *The Essence of Christianity*, pp. 19–31.

[24] Feuerbach, *Das Wesen des Christenthums*, pp. 1f.; *The Essence of Christianity*, pp. 19f.

[25] Feuerbach, *Das Wesen des Christenthums*, p. 2; *The Essence of Christianity*, p. 20.

embarrassing even if there is no one there. Thus humans have the ability to put themselves in the role of another person at any time. We often talk to ourselves, thus assuming the role of another person. It is not uncommon for children to pretend to have an imaginary friend whom they invest with a developed personality. Grieving people sometimes imagine the presence of their deceased loved ones. These phenomena are all the consequences of the nature of human self-consciousness.

Feuerbach argues that this ability is the origin of religious thinking since it means that we can see ourselves from the perspective of another self-consciousness – God – even where none exists. In religion we think of God, an absolute, infinite being. According to Feuerbach, this is simply the aware-ness of ourselves in that part of our nature that is infinite, that is, our consciousness.[26] He goes on to define this more specifically by claiming that human nature consists of three main faculties: reason, will, and affectation.[27] With the faculty of reason we are able to think; with the faculty of will we are able to make choices and act freely; and with the faculty of affectation we are able to feel and love. Feuerbach points out that all three of these can be seen as ends in themselves, and as such they are all infinite. For example, when we want to know something, we use our faculty of reason and thought. We can in principle continue to use this faculty infinitely on any number of different topics. Similarly, we are constantly willing different things and thus exercising our freedom. This can also continue indefinitely. So also there are an infinite number of objects of our feeling and love. Thus, Feuerbach concludes, these faculties represent the infinity in human nature. We can understand this infinity in terms of the concrete cases of the specific objects of our thought, will, and affectation, or we can understand it generally. When we think of infinity in the abstract as a part of our human nature or species, then we think of the divine. The ability to think in terms of abstract concepts is what constitutes infinity since concepts can be interpreted and applied in an infinite number of concrete cases. To think in terms of concepts, such as truth, beauty, and justice, is thus to engage in infinity. Feuerbach then concludes, "The *absolute* to man is his own nature."[28]

One of the points of Hegel's theory of recognition is that we are who we are in relation to others, or, put differently, our nature as individuals is determined by what relation we stand in vis-à-vis other people. So in this sense when I see another person in a specific role, I am also implicitly seeing myself in a corresponding role: When I see a teacher, in that teacher I see myself as a student; when I see a doctor, in that doctor I see myself as a patient, etc. Feuerbach builds on this and claims that all our perceptions of the world are in

---

[26] Feuerbach, *Das Wesen des Christenthums*, pp. 2f.; *The Essence of Christianity*, pp. 20f.

[27] Feuerbach, *Das Wesen des Christenthums*, pp. 3f.; *The Essence of Christianity*, p. 21.

[28] Feuerbach, *Das Wesen des Christenthums*, p. 7; *The Essence of Christianity*, p. 24.

fact inverse reflections of our own human nature. So, for Feuerbach, "In the object the human being becomes conscious *of himself*: the consciousness of the object is the *self-consciousness* of the human being."[29] He uses as an analogy the different relations of the planets to the sun.[30] Since each of the planets in the solar system has a different distance to the sun, they each in effect have a different sun in the sense that the light and heat of the sun are not absolute but relative with respect to distance. So in this way each planet has its own particular nature, which is reflected in its relation to the sun. If the sun were closer or further away, the nature of the planet in question would be different. So, just as with self-conscious subjects, a thing is what it is only as a function of its relation to other things.

Feuerbach argues that every creature is determined by its own natural capacities, and these constitute what it takes to be the highest and the grandest. This is understandable since if one does not have any knowledge or experience of something higher, then it is impossible to conceive of anything higher. There are, therefore, fixed natural limitations on what can be conceived at any given level of existence. Feuerbach writes, "A being's understanding is its sphere of vision. As far as you see, so far extends your nature; and conversely."[31] The idea of limitations is only perceived from a higher perspective. So we might think that the idea of the highest and the grandest in the eyes of a dog or a caterpillar is very limited, but this is only possible since we have a higher perspective. But for the dog and the caterpillar, their conceptions of the highest and the grandest are absolute. So too we take our own conceptions to be absolute, but Feuerbach's decisive critical point is that these are entirely determined by our human nature. What we call "God" as the highest and the grandest is simply a reflection of our own place in the broad scheme of things. Our conception of God is determined by our own highest capacities. One might argue that despite Feuerbach's explicit rejection of Hegel and his affirmation of realism and materialism, this position is in fact idealist. It is the ideas of the human mind that constitute the divine.

Feuerbach takes up the view of Schleiermacher that feeling is the organ by which we become aware of and know God.[32] In the Enlightenment, critical reason had eroded the traditional doctrines of Christianity, which seemed implausible in the face of modern scientific criticism. In response to this, Schleiermacher argued that this criticism was based on a misunderstanding; namely, religion is not about reason and discursive proof, as science is. Rather, religion is about feeling, specifically what Schleiermacher referred to as the

---

[29] Feuerbach, *Das Wesen des Christenthums*, p. 6; *The Essence of Christianity*, p. 23. (Translation modified.)

[30] Feuerbach, *Das Wesen des Christenthums*, p. 6; *The Essence of Christianity*, p. 23.

[31] Feuerbach, *Das Wesen des Christenthums*, p. 12; *The Essence of Christianity*, p. 27. (Translation modified.)

[32] Feuerbach, *Das Wesen des Christenthums*, p. 14; *The Essence of Christianity*, p. 29.

feeling of absolute dependence. In this way Schleiermacher hoped to rescue religion from science. Feuerbach takes up this view and points out that by saying that our relation to God is one of feeling, we in effect reduce God to feeling. In other words, we are saying that there is nothing higher and grander than feeling (a widespread view in the Romantic movement). Feeling is the faculty of the divine. Feuerbach's objection is that, for Schleiermacher and his followers, there is a transcendent being that corresponds to this feeling, but in fact this conclusion is not warranted by the claim. Instead, all that is said is that *feeling* is the highest, the grandest, and the absolute, and this is *per definitione* what we call the divine. But it does not follow that there is anything objective that answers to this. So Feuerbach argues that the conclusion of this view is a form of atheism, but its advocates are too frightened by this result to admit it.[33]

Finally, he observes that this analysis holds true not just of the faculty of feeling but of any other faculty as well. The point is simply that for whatever faculty one decides is that by which we know the divine, this faculty is a natural result of human nature, and our conception of the divine is naturally shaped by it. The conclusion is that these faculties do not allow us to gain access to some different, transcendent, *other* being but rather are simply a reflection of who we are as human beings. So what we are accustomed to calling "God" is simply a reflection of our highest capacities.

## 4.3   The Theory of Objectification and Alienation

Feuerbach continues with the presentation of his thesis and method in a section entitled "The Essence of Religion Considered Generally."[34] He begins by noting that we observe objects outside us in nature by means of perception. But in contrast to this, God is not an object of sense perception. God is a thought and thus not something external but rather something internal to the thinking subject. Given that God is a thought of the human mind, this thought is limited and determined by the usual limitations and determinations of that mind. This means that the thought of God is identical to the thought of the person themselves and not something different or foreign. The idea of God is therefore just an extension of the thoughts of the individual conceiving of him. So God is not something external, in the world, but rather a reflection of the inward life of the person thinking of him.

But this is not something that the individual is aware of or understands. On the contrary, the individual believes that they have before them something given in the external world. We recall how Hegel's theory of self-consciousness

---

[33] Feuerbach, *Das Wesen des Christenthums*, pp. 15f.; *The Essence of Christianity*, p. 30.

[34] Feuerbach, *Das Wesen des Christenthums*, pp. 17–47; *The Essence of Christianity*, pp. 32–55.

stated that the individual sees themselves in another person, and this plays a fundamental role in who we are. Feuerbach continues this line of thinking and claims, "Man first of all sees his nature as if *out of* himself, before he finds it in himself. His own nature is in the first instance contemplated by him as that of another being."[35] Children first become aware that there is something external to themselves, and then only later do they develop a sense of their own being or self. Feuerbach believes that this fundamental feature of child-hood development is also characteristic of religion. In our contemplation of God, we see ourselves objectified in him but are unaware of it: "Man has given objectivity to himself, but has not recognized the object as his own nature."[36] We take God to be something different and other, but in fact he is a reflection of our self-consciousness. This corresponds to Hegel's view that only in the long course of the history of religions do human beings come to recognize that God is spirit.

Feuerbach states his thesis as follows: "The divine being is nothing else than the human being, or, rather the human nature purified, freed from the limits of the individual man, made – objective – i.e., contemplated and revered as another, a distinct being."[37] This is what is often referred to as Feuerbach's theory of projection in the sense that the human mind projects itself onto something in the external world and then imagines that this is a real thing.[38] The word that Feuerbach uses is *vergegenständlichen*, which means not "to project" but literally "to objectify" or to "reify," that is, "to make something into an object or a thing." According to his view, God is not a real being, something external in the world, but rather a collection of human thoughts that have been turned into the idea of something external.

After the Enlightenment's criticisms of religion, it was difficult for scholars to defend the belief in God in traditional ways. Instead, many educated people retreated to the position of Deism, the idea that God created the universe, but otherwise nothing can be known about him. The idea is that humans are finite and limited and cannot gain knowledge of the infinite, transcendent God. Hegel had criticized this view, and his philosophy of religion aims to show that the claimed ignorance of God is both contradictory and harmful to religion. Feuerbach joins Hegel and takes up for critical examination this view, which was popular in his day as it is in our own. He points out that the advocates of this position feign a kind of piety since by saying that we cannot know anything about God, they seem to display a degree of humility in the face of the divine. But Feuerbach argues that by denying that one can ascribe any attribute to God, one in effect denies the very existence of God since any given thing is

---

[35] Feuerbach, *Das Wesen des Christenthums*, p. 19; *The Essence of Christianity*, p. 33.
[36] Feuerbach, *Das Wesen des Christenthums*, p. 19; *The Essence of Christianity*, p. 33.
[37] Feuerbach, *Das Wesen des Christenthums*, p. 20; *The Essence of Christianity*, p. 34.
[38] See also *Das Wesen des Christenthums*, p. 44; *The Essence of Christianity*, pp. 52f.

simply the set of its attributes. A thing with no attributes does not exist. So this view, according to Feuerbach, reduces to "a subtle, disguised atheism."[39] Again, he believes his position can help to save religion from errors of this kind. By saying that God is simply a set of human attributes, this is not a denial of God or a statement of atheism. Feuerbach believes his view sees God for what he truly is, so religion can have a firm basis.

One might argue that Feuerbach's thesis here still sounds rather abstract. There are many different religions with many different conceptions of the divine. Would we not expect more uniformity in these conceptions if God were always just a reflection of human nature? Feuerbach answers this objection by arguing that human self-consciousness is always closely and necessarily connected with a specific historical context. How humans think of themselves is thus not something eternal and fixed. The ancient Greeks thought of themselves in ways very different from our self-conception. Given Feuerbach's thesis that this self-conception is the same as the conception of the divine, it follows that the different views of the gods in history are a function of the historical development of the peoples who worship them. So the ancient Greeks had an immediate and natural relation to the Greek gods since they were an expression of who the people were.[40] So also with other cultures and their religions. Here Feuerbach follows Hegel, who explicitly organized the world religions in a historical manner, with each specific religion being the reflection of one specific people.

Feuerbach argues that what a given people takes to be the highest and the best qualities or predicates is then automatically ascribed to the divine since it lies in the nature of the gods to have the highest and the best properties. He gives the following examples: "Physical strength is an attribute of the Homeric gods: Zeus is the strongest of the gods. Why? Because physical strength, in and by itself, was regarded as something glorious, divine. To the ancient Germans the highest virtues were those of the warrior; therefore, their supreme god was the god of war, Odin."[41] These gods have the qualities they do because these were regarded as the highest qualities in a martial culture. The gods are simply personifications of valued qualities or attributes. It is, according to Feuerbach, an illusion of theology to focus first and foremost on these personifications, that is, on God. The truth of the matter is that it is the predicates themselves that make the divine what it is. God is only God if he has specific qualities.[42]

According to Feuerbach, the highest properties or attributes were revered by a given people and were then combined into specific entities, who became the gods. When these properties became personified, the origin of religion was

[39] Feuerbach, *Das Wesen des Christenthums*, p. 22; *The Essence of Christianity*, p. 36.
[40] Feuerbach, *Das Wesen des Christenthums*, p. 29; *The Essence of Christianity*, p. 41.
[41] Feuerbach, *Das Wesen des Christenthums*, p. 31; *The Essence of Christianity*, p. 42.
[42] Feuerbach, *Das Wesen des Christenthums*, p. 31; *The Essence of Christianity*, p. 43.

forgotten and the focus was placed on the personified deities.[43] There are many different kinds of properties, and for this reason, there are many different conceptions of the gods.

Feuerbach was inspired by Hegel with regard to the idea of alienation that lies at the very heart of the theory of projection or objectification itself.[44] When one projects one's human nature onto something else, this is a form of alienation, that is, a removal of something and a placing of it in the external sphere. In this sense, projection is a separation or a distinction, a splitting up of something that was originally one. Feuerbach characterizes this relation as one of "division" and "disunion."[45] Specifically, this is a form of self-alienation since it involves projecting human qualities onto the divine and presenting them as something foreign or different. Humans are thus not separated from something else or other but rather from themselves or their own nature.

Feuerbach argues that it is a natural aspect of the logic of objectification that when humans conceive of God, they try to understand him as being greater than humans. So they ascribe to him the positive qualities, while they ascribe to themselves the negative ones: "[while] what is positive in the conception of the divine being can only be human, the conception of man, as an object of consciousness can only be negative. To enrich God, man must become poor; that God may be all, man must be nothing."[46] Humans thus deprive themselves of the things that they attribute to God. For example, as we have seen, there is a religious sentiment that says that knowledge is only for God and that we as human beings cannot know anything ultimately. For us to know, God must reveal something to us, but on our own we are incapable of attaining the truth. Similarly, humans are conceived as evil and sinful, where only God is truly good.[47] In this way human beings and God are conceived as being the polar opposites of one another, with God having all of the positive qualities and humans all the negative ones.[48]

According to this view, humans are alienated from their true selves. By placing their positive attributes in another, they leave themselves with only the negative characteristics. Feuerbach refers to this as a form of human "self-humiliation."[49] Humans are thought to have their true being and salvation not in themselves but in God.[50] When one sees oneself from the perspective of God, one does not identify with the picture that is presented. On the contrary, it is a very negative view of what a human being is. But the absurdity is, of

---

[43] Feuerbach, *Das Wesen des Christenthums*, p. 32; *The Essence of Christianity*, pp. 43f.
[44] See Marx W. Wartofsky, *Feuerbach*, pp. 206–215.
[45] Feuerbach, *Das Wesen des Christenthums*, p. 48; *The Essence of Christianity*, p. 56.
[46] Feuerbach, *Das Wesen des Christenthums*, p. 38; *The Essence of Christianity*, p. 48.
[47] Feuerbach, *Das Wesen des Christenthums*, p. 40; *The Essence of Christianity*, p. 50.
[48] Feuerbach, *Das Wesen des Christenthums*, p. 48; *The Essence of Christianity*, p. 56.
[49] Feuerbach, *Das Wesen des Christenthums*, p. 46; *The Essence of Christianity*, p. 55.
[50] Feuerbach, *Das Wesen des Christenthums*, pp. 44f.; *The Essence of Christianity*, p. 53.

course, that it is human beings themselves who have placed the positive attributes in God and the negative ones in themselves.

Feuerbach portrays his own view as serving a liberating function. As long as we continue to conceive of God as something other and transcendent, we will forever be alienated from God and from ourselves. By contrast, when we realize that the divine is just human nature objectified, then we can begin to recognize ourselves in God. Moreover, when we understand this, we can come to recover the positive characteristics of humanity that we had previously abandoned.

It might be claimed that Hegel's theory of alienation is one that starts with the divine, the creator, and then moves to the human. In other words, God, the universal, externalizes or alienates himself by becoming particular in the act of creation. Then he returns to himself again, completing the third element of the Holy Spirit. However, for Feuerbach, the movement is in the other direction – from the human to the divine. Humans start with ideas, which they project onto the divine and then take back for themselves. For Hegel, there is a dialectical relation between universal and particular, divine and human, whereas for Feuerbach the entire movement is human.

## 4.4   The Role of Human Understanding

In the chapter "God as a Being of the Understanding,"[51] Feuerbach makes the case for the claim that God is simply the highest form of human reason or intelligence, conceived as an external being. He states his thesis thus: "The pure, perfect divine nature is the self-consciousness of the understanding, the consciousness which the understanding has of its own perfection."[52] Although the German idealists – for example, Kant and Hegel – distinguish between the faculties of the human mind, such as reason and understanding, Feuerbach seems not to make any distinction but rather to be using these terms in a less technical way more in tune with common usage.

To make his case Feuerbach begins by sketching the virtues of the faculty of reason. This is usually considered to be the highest human faculty because it persuades us to follow abstract laws and principles and to do what is right, even when our personal drives and interests urge us to act in a different way. It is with reason that we can abstract from our emotions and find the right course of action. Feuerbach gives a characterization of the person of reason who, coolly and neutrally, so to speak, puts themselves aside and judges the matter on its own merits. Such a person is not the slave of their desires and emotions but rather can overrule them with reason. The faculty of reason is universal; it is

---

[51] Feuerbach, *Das Wesen des Christenthums*, pp. 48–64; *The Essence of Christianity*, pp. 56–69.
[52] Feuerbach, *Das Wesen des Christenthums*, p. 49; *The Essence of Christianity*, p. 57.

thus what connects us with humanity as a whole, that is, what constitutes humans as a species being.[53] Reason is what allows us to think in terms of abstract principles in contrast to our emotions, which are particular. They are specific to us and do not necessarily build any bridges between us and other people.

Feuerbach then claims that God is simply this faculty of understanding "regarded as objective."[54] In other words, God can be understood as the highest human faculty separated from any specific human being and thus from all human limitations. Since God does not have a physical body, he is free from the passions that dominate so much of human life and that cloud our reason. God is thus simply human thought. Here we have an echo of Aristotle's view of God as thought thinking itself (νόησις νοήσεως), which is described in Book XII of the *Metaphysics*.[55]

In this context Feuerbach takes a polemical jab at Hegel's concept of spirit. He writes, "the idea of spirit is simply the idea of thought, of intelligence, of understanding, every other spirit being a specter of the imagination."[56] The implication is that Hegel has abstracted from the simple faculty of thought and created a metaphysical entity called spirit, which has no reality in the actual world. When Hegel talks of the spirit of a people, world spirit, or Absolute Spirit, these are, for Feuerbach, just meaningless abstractions.

Hegel claimed that the rational is the actual and the actual is the rational,[57] and by this he meant that there is a *logos* or rationality in the world that can be recognized and understood by the human mind. There, of course, exist things that are irrational or contradictory, but these are not the object of human thinking; on the contrary, they seem to defy human thought and comprehension. In Hegel's language, "actuality" is that dimension of the world that is governed by reason, and in this sense the actual is the rational. Feuerbach takes this up and, in agreement with Hegel, writes, "The understanding is to itself the criterion of all reality. That which is opposed to the understanding, that which is self-contradictory, is nothing."[58] Feuerbach then extends this thought to the concept of God. There is a rationality in the world because God is rational. We can discern regularities in nature because God is thought to have created it. It

---

[53] Feuerbach, *Das Wesen des Christenthums*, p. 50; *The Essence of Christianity*, p. 58.
[54] Feuerbach, *Das Wesen des Christenthums*, p. 51; *The Essence of Christianity*, p. 58. See also *Das Wesen des Christenthums*, pp. 52f.; *The Essence of Christianity*, p. 60.
[55] Aristotle, *Metaphysics*, Book XII, chapters 7 and 9.
[56] Feuerbach, *Das Wesen des Christenthums*, p. 51; *The Essence of Christianity*, p. 59.
[57] G. W. F. Hegel, *Naturrecht und Staatswissenschaft im Grundrisse. Grundlinien der Philosophie des Rechts* (Berlin: Nicolaische Buchhandlung, 1821), p. xix. (English translation: *Elements of the Philosophy of Right*, trans. by H. B. Nisbet, ed. by Allen Wood [Cambridge and New York: Cambridge University Press, 1991], p. 20.)
[58] Feuerbach, *Das Wesen des Christenthums*, p. 55; *The Essence of Christianity*, p. 61.

would be absurd to think of God as an irrational being.[59] Thus reason or understanding is one of the criteria for what it is to be God. Feuerbach's ultimate conclusion is that what the individual understands as the rational and the essential is then externalized and reified as a personal being, God.

Feuerbach explains that human thought is the key to freedom and independence.[60] It is only because we think that we are able to make decisions and act on them freely. Through self-conscious thought, we can make ourselves free from nature, repressing our natural desires and drives. If we were mentally incapacitated and could no longer think, then we would be dependent on others. We would not be able to act independently or on our own. To think is what makes us subjects in contrast to objects that exist without thought. Only the thinking being can subject other things to its will. Then at the end of this discussion about the human faculty of thought or reason, Feuerbach introduces God and declares: "To think is to be God. The act of thought, as such, is the freedom of the immortal gods from all external limitations and necessities of life."[61] The point is, once again, that although thinking is a human faculty, it is also a divine faculty, and it is impossible to think of God without it, especially when we consider God as free and powerful over nature.

At the end of the chapter, Feuerbach again connects reason and self-consciousness: "In reason first lies the self-consciousness of existence, self-conscious existence . . . . Reason is existence objective to itself as its own end; the ultimate tendency of things. That which is an object to itself is the highest, the final being . . . ."[62] Self-conscious reason is higher than blind nature. Subjectivity is higher than objectivity. From here it is but a short step to declare that self-consciousness or reason is also what is divine.

### 4.5   God as a Moral Being

At the beginning of the chapter "God as a Moral Being, or Law,"[63] Feuerbach makes the observation that if we conceived of God as a wholly abstract, transcendent being, this would be generally irrelevant for us. For God to be meaningful for human beings, he must have certain human characteristics and concerns. So the important predicates of God are not the abstract ones but rather the human ones, or, as Feuerbach says, "The vital elements of religion are those only which make man an object to man. To deny man is to deny

---

[59] Feuerbach, *Das Wesen des Christenthums*, p. 56; *The Essence of Christianity*, p. 62.
[60] Feuerbach, *Das Wesen des Christenthums*, pp. 57–59; *The Essence of Christianity*, pp. 63–65.
[61] Feuerbach, *Das Wesen des Christenthums*, p. 59; *The Essence of Christianity*, p. 65.
[62] Feuerbach, *Das Wesen des Christenthums*, p. 64; *The Essence of Christianity*, p. 69.
[63] Feuerbach, *Das Wesen des Christenthums*, pp. 64–72; *The Essence of Christianity*, pp. 70–76.

religion."[64] Here one might just as well replace the word "religion" with the word "God." If God did not share certain key features with human beings, how could he be interested in the human world and human salvation? If God were radically separate and other, then how could he be relevant for us? Again, the key is that when we contemplate God, we in fact are only contemplating ourselves as human beings since God is characterized by human features.

Hegel defined freedom and personhood as going out of oneself and finding oneself in another in the way that we do in a relation of love or friendship.[65] This was a key feature of Hegel's interpretation of the role of Christ since he represents not an abstract or transcendent God but a God whom believers can relate to individually. Feuerbach draws on this and notes that to find consolation or peace in God implies that God is not something radically different, since in this case, such consolation or peace would be impossible. Along the lines of Hegel's analysis, he explains:

> Thus, if man feels peace in God, he feels it only because in God he first attains his true nature, because here, for the first time, he is with himself, because everything in which he hitherto sought peace, and which he hitherto mistook for his nature, was alien to him. Hence, if man is to find contentment in God, he must find himself in God.[66]

This would also seem to be a consequence of Hegel's theory of recognition. Since recognition can only be meaningful if it is given freely by an equal and the individual finds their true sense of personhood in God as another entity, this implies that God must be like the individual, that is, he must be human.

The key issue in this short chapter is the Christian understanding of God as morally perfect. According to Feuerbach, this amounts to "the moral nature of man posited as the absolute being."[67] So the understanding of God as a moral agent is simply the transference of the human understanding of morality to something external. But the understanding of God as a moral being is far beyond the human capacity to realize. This conception makes us acutely aware of our own moral shortcomings. When we compare ourselves to the morally perfect being, we always come up short. This underscores the radical disunion

---

[64] Feuerbach, *Das Wesen des Christenthums*, p. 65; *The Essence of Christianity*, p. 70.

[65] G. W. F. Hegel, *Vorlesungen über die Philosophie der Religion*, I–II, ed. by Philipp Marheineke, vols. 11–12 (2nd ed., 1840), in *Georg Wilhelm Friedrich Hegel's Werke. Vollständige Ausgabe*, vols. 1–18, ed. by Ludwig Boumann, Friedrich Förster, Eduard Gans, Karl Hegel, Leopold von Henning, Heinrich Gustav Hotho, Philipp Marheineke, Karl Ludwig Michelet, Karl Rosenkranz, and Johannes Schulze (Berlin: Duncker und Humblot, 1832–1845), vol. 12, pp. 238–240. (*Lectures on the Philosophy of Religion*, vols. 1–3, trans. by E. B. Speirs and J. Burdon Sanderson [London: Routledge and Kegan Paul; New York: Humanities Press, 1962, 1968, 1972], vol. 3, pp. 23–25.) I refer to this older edition because this was Feuerbach's source.

[66] Feuerbach, *Das Wesen des Christenthums*, p. 66; *The Essence of Christianity*, p. 71.

[67] Feuerbach, *Das Wesen des Christenthums*, p. 68; *The Essence of Christianity*, p. 73.

and separation from the divine. When I consider God to be morally perfect, I am obliged to regard myself as a "moral nothingness."[68] In this analysis we can see clear echoes of Hegel's account of the unhappy consciousness, which also ascribes the positive moral qualities to God and the negative ones to itself.

According to the Christian doctrine, it is love that resolves this split and disunion. Out of love, God forgives human sinfulness. So, like moral perfection, love is a divine quality.[69] Here again we have a human property, love, that is ascribed to the divine being. Feuerbach writes, "Love makes man God, and God man."[70] God is like a human being in that he can love and show compassion. While divine moral perfection and the moral law are a reflection of human reason and understanding, divine love, by contrast, is a reflection of human emotion. Humans can show mercy and grant forgiveness, and this quality is then regarded as something divine. Love thus represents another important point of unity between the human and the divine. Feuerbach develops his idea of love further toward the end of the book.[71]

## 4.6   Feuerbach's Critical View of the Revelation

We have seen that the doctrine of the Revelation was the key feature of Christianity for Hegel, and for this reason he referred to it as "the revealed religion." Feuerbach critically discusses this Christian doctrine in his chapter "The Contradiction in the Revelation of God."[72] He begins by noting the traditional understanding of the revelation as the proof or justification of God's existence. The Revelation demonstrates that God is not just a figment of the imagination but instead exists in the real world.

Feuerbach then goes about undermining this traditional view. He repeats his general thesis that religion or God is simply "our own conceptions and emotions," which "appear to us as separate existences, beings out of ourselves."[73] Given that these conceptions are just objectifications of the human mind, it is absurd to regard them as confirmation of some external truth. With this argument, one could equally claim that the stories about the gods in the other world religions are all true. The Greeks also believed with equal conviction that their gods existed and manifested themselves in the world. The revelation can thus hardly be taken as the unique doctrine of Christianity that demonstrates its truth.

---

[68] Feuerbach, *Das Wesen des Christenthums*, p. 69; *The Essence of Christianity*, p. 73.
[69] Feuerbach, *Das Wesen des Christenthums*, p. 70; *The Essence of Christianity*, p. 74.
[70] Feuerbach, *Das Wesen des Christenthums*, p. 71; *The Essence of Christianity*, p. 75.
[71] See Section 4.9.
[72] Feuerbach, *Das Wesen des Christenthums*, pp. 303–316; *The Essence of Christianity*, pp. 263–272.
[73] Feuerbach, *Das Wesen des Christenthums*, p. 304; *The Essence of Christianity*, p. 264.

In line with his previous analyses, Feuerbach attempts to demonstrate that the Christian notion of the Revelation is something entirely human. His argument is that the Revelation is not some arbitrary, spontaneous act of God. Instead, it is specifically aimed at human beings with a specific human purpose. God revealed himself to his human followers in order to make himself known and in order to suffer for human sinfulness. So the form and nature of the Revelation had to take place in such a way that it could be understood by the human cognitive capacity since humans were the desired audience. God addresses himself to human beings. He uses human speech and appeals to common human understandings of things.[74] Feuerbach concludes by saying that "the contents of the divine revelation are of human origin, for they have proceeded not from God as God, but from God as determined by human reason, human wants."[75]

But Feuerbach points out what he takes to be the absurdity or illusion involved in the traditional theological understanding of this doctrine.[76] According to this view, humans are sinful and fallible. They can know nothing of God on their own. For this reason they need God's assistance; God must make himself known to us. But this fails to recognize the fact that all of the features of the Revelation are in fact human. The traditional understanding also fosters religious alienation since it separates human knowing from revealed knowledge. What humans can know is only finite and flawed, always open to correction and revision; by contrast, what God reveals to humans is absolutely true.

Given that the contents of the Revelation are entirely human, the Revelation itself can be conceived as a kind of objectification or projection of the human mind. So Feuerbach claims, "in revelation man goes out of himself, in order, by a circuitous path, to return to himself."[77] Humans first posit the idea of a revelation and, so to speak, go out of themselves. But the point of the Revelation is to convey knowledge to human beings, and so in this, that same knowledge returns to them. As he says in a different passage, in the Revelation, human beings place God between their self-knowledge and themselves.[78] Humans see their own nature outside themselves in God instead of immediately recognizing it as their own. So, oddly, what is revealed in the Revelation is not the nature of God but the nature of human beings.

Feuerbach tries to give his theory a degree of plausibility by explaining this in terms of what we today would call the psychology of religion. Philosophers, theologians, and academics are used to thinking in terms of abstract concepts.

---

[74] Feuerbach, *Das Wesen des Christenthums*, p. 308; *The Essence of Christianity*, p. 266.
[75] Feuerbach, *Das Wesen des Christenthums*, pp. 308f.; *The Essence of Christianity*, p. 267.
[76] Feuerbach, *Das Wesen des Christenthums*, pp. 307f.; *The Essence of Christianity*, p. 266.
[77] Feuerbach, *Das Wesen des Christenthums*, p. 309; *The Essence of Christianity*, p. 267.
[78] Feuerbach, *Das Wesen des Christenthums*, p. 307; *The Essence of Christianity*, p. 265.

But most people are more at home with the world of particular entities given in perception. They have no problem saying that something particular is true, beautiful, or just, but they are not used to contemplating what truth, beauty, and justice are as such. (Thus it is natural to conceive of God as a physical, personal being. At the beginning of Genesis, God is portrayed very much in anthropomorphic terms as walking in the garden with Adam and Eve.) Since most people are focused on the individual and the particular, which they are immediately aware of, they risk running into a kind of relativism; they need something that is universal to give them a higher, more solid truth beyond their own particular ideas. They thus cannot accept that they can determine truth on their own but instead must receive it from a higher being. It is God who provides the universal that trumps the particulars of the individual believer. But this conception is simply the result of the simple believer positing the universal as an external being.[79] From this, one can see that relativism and absolutism grounded in God are in fact closely related to one another. It is fear of relativism that drives one to posit an absolute that is given by God.

Here Feuerbach returns to Hegel's point about the nature of divine command.[80] In Judaism God gives commands along with threats. He does not appeal to human reason to realize the truth and value of his command, but the commands are issued absolutely. For Hegel, this undermines human freedom since it fails to recognize human rationality. Feuerbach makes much the same point. Since the moral rules are thought to come from an external source, God, they are conceived to be separate and distinct from human nature and reasoning. We must obey them not because we know them to be correct and just in themselves but because God commanded them. This deprives moral action of its content since this is a matter of indifference. What is important is that God commanded it.[81] For Feuerbach, it makes much more sense to recognize these moral laws as coming from human beings themselves. To regard these as separate from ourselves undermines our freedom and morality. As Feuerbach says, this "injures [our] moral sense."[82]

Feuerbach concludes this chapter with a discussion of the Bible as the written revelation of God. He states bluntly that such a conception amounts to "superstition and sophistry."[83] His claim is that for something to be truly divine it must be a unified work, free of contradiction. This means that the truth of the Bible is an all or nothing proposition. Either the entire work is a divine revelation or it is not. But insofar as the work obliges us to go through

[79] Feuerbach, *Das Wesen des Christenthums*, p. 310; *The Essence of Christianity*, p. 268.
[80] G. W. F. Hegel, *Vorlesungen über die Philosophie der Religion*, II, 2nd ed., pp. 87–88; *Lectures on the Philosophy of Religion*, vol. 2, pp. 215–216. See Chapter 2, Section 2.3.
[81] Feuerbach, *Das Wesen des Christenthums*, pp. 311f.; *The Essence of Christianity*, p. 269.
[82] Feuerbach, *Das Wesen des Christenthums*, p. 312; *The Essence of Christianity*, p. 269.
[83] Feuerbach, *Das Wesen des Christenthums*, p. 312; *The Essence of Christianity*, p. 269.

and separate the divinely revealed elements from the human corruptions, this cannot be regarded as a divine revelation.[84] He flatly claims, "The Bible contradicts morality, contradicts reason, contradicts itself innumerable times,"[85] and this cannot be squared with the idea that it is the revealed word of God. It lies in God's concept to be moral and true, and he would not suffer such contradictions. The blind belief in every word of the Bible in effect requires us to put our reason and critical thinking aside and simply accept things as divinely revealed, regardless of how absurd or contradictory they might seem. This is a position that Kierkegaard develops, claiming that the Christian Revelation is indeed a paradox, an absurdity, a contradiction, but nonetheless true. This is an idea that Feuerbach would reject. Why should we be obliged to put aside our reason in just this instance alone when it serves us so well in every other aspect of life? Indeed, it is reason itself that is the divine faculty that separates us from the animals, and so it would seem absurd that it should play no role in such an important matter. In this way Feuerbach shows that the traditional understanding of the Revelation as something divine and separate from human beings leads to contradictions and absurdities.

## 4.7   Feuerbach's Critical View of the Nature of God

Feuerbach dedicates a chapter to exploring what he takes to be the contradiction in the Christian conception of God.[86] He identifies the terms of this contradiction by noting that God is conceived, on the one hand, as a transcendent supernatural entity beyond the world and, on the other hand, as a concrete human being who is loving and merciful. In theological terms, this refers to the first and the second parts of the Trinity, God the Father and God the Son. These are two quite different kinds of entities that, for Feuerbach, cannot be united logically.

It makes sense to understand God the Son, according to Feuerbach's theory, since here God is conceived as a human being. The heart of Feuerbach's thesis is that human qualities are transferred to an external being, and the result is an anthropomorphic entity. This way of thinking reaches its culmination in Christianity, which regards a specific human as the incarnation of God. Feuerbach thinks that if we could simply understand this correctly, then there would be no problem. But the contradiction arises in the conception of God as a transcendent, supernatural, nonhuman being, who exists on his own, apart from human beings. It is a mistake, he thinks, to see this conception of God as anything other than a projection of the human mind. When the

---

[84] Feuerbach, *Das Wesen des Christenthums*, p. 313; *The Essence of Christianity*, p. 270.
[85] Feuerbach, *Das Wesen des Christenthums*, p. 315; *The Essence of Christianity*, p. 271.
[86] Feuerbach, *Das Wesen des Christenthums*, pp. 316–336; *The Essence of Christianity*, pp. 273–287.

theologians fail to recognize this and attempt to explain the nature of God, then, according to Feuerbach, this leads to "an inexhaustible mine of false-hoods, illusions, contradictions, and sophisms."[87]

He takes as an example of this sophistry the idea that the nature of God is incomprehensible for human beings. This idea, which Hegel also polemicized against, parades as a kind of religious humility or piety or even a critical philosophical disposition. But Feuerbach thinks that this is false humility since the unknowability of God amounts to an abstraction from what is known. Specifically, he claims that the point of departure is human experience. Humans live in concrete places and have knowledge of specific things. Then with the imagination we can think of a being, in principle like us, but who is not limited by the normal human constraints. Instead of being a finite creature, God is infinite. So one simply takes the human characteristics and thinks of them as infinite. Instead of living in a concrete place, God is omnipresent. Instead of having knowledge only of some things, God has knowledge of everything; that is, he is omniscient. Instead of existing in a concrete time, God is eternal. So, for Feuerbach, there is no difference between humans and God with regard to the essence. The distinction is merely one of degree: "The infinity of God in religion is quantitative infinity; God is and has all that man has, but in an infinitely greater measure."[88]

Given this, it is incorrect to say that God cannot be known. Indeed, we can know God since he is simply a projection of our own experience, which the imagination raises to the power of infinity. But this is only a quantitative difference. With regard to the quality, there is no difference. God knows everything, while I know only a finite number of things, but the knowing itself is qualitatively the same.[89] The imagination simply removes the limits from human experience and then produces the idea of an unlimited being. But since the point of departure is human experience, it is clear that God is hardly something radically different and incomprehensible.

Since this conception of God in Christianity exists only in the human imagination, this means that all human fulfillment in God is deferred to some later time, when it will be achieved in heaven.[90] Although one experiences poverty and misery in this life, in heaven one will have riches and happiness. Feuerbach believes that this undermines the devel-opment of human culture, which aims at fulfilling human needs and realizing human ambitions in this world. But if there is always a promise that these will be fulfilled and realized in heaven, then one is deprived of the motivation for taking action to achieve them here and now in the

[87] Feuerbach, *Das Wesen des Christenthums*, p. 318; *The Essence of Christianity*, p. 274.
[88] Feuerbach, *Das Wesen des Christenthums*, p. 319; *The Essence of Christianity*, p. 275.
[89] Feuerbach, *Das Wesen des Christenthums*, p. 320; *The Essence of Christianity*, p. 276.
[90] Feuerbach, *Das Wesen des Christenthums*, p. 322; *The Essence of Christianity*, pp. 277ff.

mundane sphere. This can also be understood as a form of religious alienation since, due to an act of the imagination, humans are forever separated from the fulfillment of their needs, which is always deferred to an indeterminate future.

## 4.8    Feuerbach's Criticism of Hegel

Feuerbach dedicates a short chapter, entitled "The Contradiction in the Speculative Doctrine of God," to a criticism of Hegel's conception of the divine.[91] One would think that on the face of it Feuerbach would be sympathetic to Hegel's general theory since it is clearly the forerunner of his own idea of projection. He takes as his point of departure Hegel's difficult claim,

> man knows God only in so far as God himself knows Himself in man. This knowledge is God's self-consciousness, but it is at the same time a knowledge of God on the part of man, and this knowledge of God by man is a knowledge of man by God. The spirit of man, whereby he knows God, is simply the spirit of God Himself.[92]

Feuerbach regards Hegel's view as representing an improvement over traditional theological thinking that insists on a radical separation between God and human beings. But he argues that Hegel does not go far enough: "the religious consciousness separates these two properly inseparable sides, since by means of the idea of personality it makes God and man independent existences. Now the Hegelian speculation identifies the two sides, but so as to leave the old contradiction still at the foundation."[93] Feuerbach notes that for objects in the external world, such as rocks or trees, it is a matter of indifference if we think of them or not. A given tree exists if I think of it or if I don't. But the situation with God is different since God is not an external object but a projection of human thought. So it is necessary that we think of God in the sense that his existence, if one wishes to call it that, is dependent on him being thought by the human mind.[94] For Feuerbach, the perspective of God thinking himself, independent of the human mind, is incoherent. God can only be thought by human beings. Here Feuerbach is following Hegel's analysis of the nature of human self-consciousness: We are self-conscious only when we are in interaction with other self-conscious agents.

The problem arises when one conceives of God as a separate self-conscious agent or, as Feuerbach says, another person. We see other people all the time,

---

[91] Feuerbach, *Das Wesen des Christenthums*, pp. 336–344; *The Essence of Christianity*, pp. 288–294.

[92] Hegel, *Vorlesungen über die Philosophie der Religion*, II (2nd ed.), p. 496; *Lectures on the Philosophy of Religion*, vol. 3, pp. 303f.

[93] Feuerbach, *Das Wesen des Christenthums*, pp. 342f.; *The Essence of Christianity*, pp. 292f.

[94] Feuerbach, *Das Wesen des Christenthums*, p. 337; *The Essence of Christianity*, p. 288.

and they seem to be immediately independent of us. But according to Hegel's theory of self-consciousness, what we are as individuals is fundamentally determined by the recognition that we receive from other people. We cannot be who we are without this intersubjective recognition. The situation is oddly similar with respect to the conception of God, even though we do not see God in the empirical world in the way we encounter other human beings. God is thought by humans but does not have any independent existence beyond our thoughts. God is thus only who he is vis-à-vis human beings. This implies that God is not a separate being but rather is fundamentally dependent on the recognition or the thought of human beings. Feuerbach writes, "Man is nothing without God; but also, God is nothing without man; for only in man is God an object as God; only in man is he God."[95]

Feuerbach reproaches Hegel for not stating explicitly that the essence of God is in fact the human. He thus reformulates the passage from Hegel that he referred to at the outset: "Man's knowledge of God is God's knowledge of himself? What a divorcing and contradiction! The true statement is this: man's knowledge of God is man's knowledge of himself, of his own nature."[96] In Feuerbach's view, Hegel's theory, in the end, maintains the dualism. However, Feuerbach's position is very much in line with what Hegel actually says. In the Lectures on the Philosophy of Religion, Hegel traces the history of the world's religions from the religions of nature to the religions of spirit. In this account, he demonstrates how the conception of the divine begins as an object of nature and in the course of time is transformed more and more into something anthropomorphic. For this reason Christianity is the culmination of this process since it alone recognizes God as human. In this sense one might claim that Feuerbach is overstating his criticism.

Feuerbach also sees Hegel as contributing to the problem of alienation, although Hegel's dialectical approach seems to be an effective means of overcoming it. Feuerbach concludes by stating his thesis, "if in the consciousness which man has of God first arises the self-consciousness of God, then the human consciousness is, per se, the divine consciousness."[97] Then he asks rhetorically, as if addressing Hegel directly, "Why then do you alienate man's consciousness from him, and make it the self-consciousness of a being distinct from man ...?"[98] Feuerbach thus believes that Hegel still posits a distinction and separation between God and human beings.[99] This can only be overcome by embracing the idea of theology as a kind of anthropology. Feuerbach's solution to the alienation is to

---

[95] Feuerbach, Das Wesen des Christenthums, p. 339; The Essence of Christianity, p. 290.
[96] Feuerbach, Das Wesen des Christenthums, p. 343; The Essence of Christianity, p. 293.
[97] Feuerbach, Das Wesen des Christenthums, p. 343; The Essence of Christianity, p. 293.
[98] Feuerbach, Das Wesen des Christenthums, p. 343; The Essence of Christianity, p. 293.
[99] Feuerbach, Das Wesen des Christenthums, p. 344; The Essence of Christianity, p. 294.

recognize that God is nothing more than the human, and in this way humans can identify with the divine. But again this seems to be very much what Hegel says, especially in connection with his analysis of the mission of Christ. It can thus be regarded as a matter of debate to what degree Feuerbach actually departs from Hegel.

## 4.9   Feuerbach's Theory of Love

After having eliminated the metaphysical idea of God as something different and other from the human being, Feuerbach tries to replace this with a theory of love, which he believes will solve the problem of alienation. In his analysis, he contrasts the concepts of faith and love, which he takes in a sense to be opposites.[100] His claim is that faith is what causes alienation by separating people from one another, whereas love is what brings them together. He argues, "Faith produces in man an inward disunion, a disunion with himself, and by consequence an outward disunion also; but love heals the wounds which are made by faith in the heart of man."[101] Referring to the title of his work, Feuerbach claims that the true essence of religion, then, is not the abstract idea of God, which is simply a projection of the human mind, but rather love.[102]

Critics will argue that Feuerbach's theory, if true, would destroy religion entirely since it eliminates the idea of God. To this Feuerbach makes the provocative claim that the divine is in a sense love, or love has something divine in it. He writes, "Love has God in itself: faith has God out of itself; it estranges God from man, it makes him an external object."[103] With the projection of God, the human being places their essence in some foreign entity beyond itself. This is alienation. By contrast, with love, one finds oneself again in the other. Love allows us to fully flourish and develop our true self. Thus love is one aspect of Christianity that Feuerbach finds worthy of keeping, although he, of course, gives it his own interpretation.

Faith separates people from one another since it encourages people to distinguish themselves from others who have different beliefs. It thus undermines morality. Religious believers think that they have been given the gift of grace and that they have a special relation with God. This separates them from believers of other religions and those without belief. Feuerbach explains, "The believer finds himself distinguished above other men, exalted above the natural man; he knows himself to be a person of distinction, in the possession of peculiar privileges; believers are aristocrats, unbelievers plebeians."[104] Thus,

---

[100] Feuerbach, *Das Wesen des Christenthums*, p. 382; *The Essence of Christianity*, p. 325.
[101] Feuerbach, *Das Wesen des Christenthums*, p. 367; *The Essence of Christianity*, pp. 313f.
[102] Feuerbach, *Das Wesen des Christenthums*, p. 367; *The Essence of Christianity*, p. 313.
[103] Feuerbach, *Das Wesen des Christenthums*, p. 368; *The Essence of Christianity*, p. 314.
[104] Feuerbach, *Das Wesen des Christenthums*, p. 371; *The Essence of Christianity*, p. 316.

despite all of the Christian rhetoric above love, Christianity in fact undermines love and puts up a wall between people.

Here Feuerbach can be seen as following in the steps of the key figures of the Enlightenment such as Voltaire, who claimed that what set human beings against one another was religious dogma or doctrine.[105] The specific points of dogma were the causes of religious wars and persecutions. Feuerbach agrees that faith is the cause of untold woes in history. The different religions each claim to have the exclusive truth.[106] This means that those who do not share one's faith are regarded as in error or deluded. The dogmas separate one individual from the next, and the Church condemns nonbelievers to damnation. Religious faith is by its very nature intolerant.[107] He claims, "Faith necessarily passes into hatred, [and] hatred into persecution."[108] By contrast, love brings people together since it is indifferent to points of dogma.

Feuerbach indirectly alludes to Hegel's master-slave dialectic in order to explain the psychological nature of faith. He writes:

> As the servant feels himself honored in the dignity of his master, nay, fancies himself greater than a free, independent man of lower rank than his master, so it is with the believer. He denies all merit in himself, merely that he may leave all merit to his Lord, because his own desire of honor is satisfied in the honor of his Lord.[109]

It will be recalled that, for Hegel, the slave received recognition indirectly from the master by fulfilling the master's needs. Despite the slave's lowly status, they take pride in doing their job well since this is what pleases the master. Feuerbach now transfers this psychology from the human realm between two human beings of unequal status to the relation between the human being and God. He claims, then, that religious faith is like this. It contains a deep arrogance that masquerades behind a cloak of humility. While the slave and the religious believer feign a disposition of self-denigration, in fact they are arrogant since they take themselves to be better than other people due to the special relation that they have to their respective masters. Feuerbach explains, "Faith is arrogant, but it is distinguished from natural arrogance in this, that it clothes its feeling of superiority, its pride, in the idea of another person, for

[105] This is the thesis of Voltaire's *Dieu et les hommes, oeuvre théologique, mais raisonnable* (Berlin: Christian de Vos, 1769). (English translation: Voltaire, *God and Human Beings*, trans. by Michael Shreve [Amherst, NY: Prometheus Books, 2010].) Note that Feuerbach also anticipates Nietzsche's criticism of the apostle Paul. *Das Wesen des Christenthums*, p. 373; *The Essence of Christianity*, p. 318.
[106] Feuerbach, *Das Wesen des Christenthums*, p. 368; *The Essence of Christianity*, p. 314. See also *Das Wesen des Christenthums*, p. 373; *The Essence of Christianity*, p. 318.
[107] Feuerbach, *Das Wesen des Christenthums*, p. 379; *The Essence of Christianity*, p. 323.
[108] Feuerbach, *Das Wesen des Christenthums*, p. 386; *The Essence of Christianity*, p. 328.
[109] Feuerbach, *Das Wesen des Christenthums*, p. 371; *The Essence of Christianity*, pp. 316f.

whom the believer is an object of peculiar favor."[110] The key here, however, is that this other person is merely a projection of the individual themselves: "The humility of the believer is an inverted arrogance."[111] The individual still feels superior to others while pretending to be humble. Although a person can accomplish nothing on their own without their master, they are better than everyone else because they have a special relation to the master.

This leads to hypocrisy and bigotry with the idea that "[t]o believe is synonymous with goodness; not to believe, with wickedness."[112] Christians only extend love and fellowship to fellow Christians, but not to those of other faiths or without belief. Feuerbach claims that this represents "a malignant principle" at the very heart of the concept of faith.[113] This is not just an accident that might be different under different circumstances, but rather it is, he believes, an essential aspect of faith as such. He argues, therefore, that "[f]aith abolishes the natural ties of humanity," which we must strive to restore by means of love.[114]

Feuerbach notes that in its separation and exclusiveness, Christianity also excuses itself from the customary sense of morality with an appeal to a higher calling. He explains, "Faith left to itself necessarily exalts itself above the laws of natural morality. The doctrine of faith is the doctrine of duty towards God – the highest duty of faith."[115] Thus terrible crimes and immoral acts can be committed in the name of God. Anything can be justified when one is acting in the service of something higher. Note that this analysis seems to anticipate in a critical manner Kierkegaard's theory of the religious sphere being higher than the ethical sphere. In *Fear and Trembling* he uses the famous example of God's command to Abraham to sacrifice his only son Isaac. This is, of course, in defiance of customary morality, but, Kierkegaard claims, it is a matter of faith that comes from a higher source. Feuerbach would reject this idea. In his eyes this is yet another example of religious alienation: "so far as God is regarded as separate from man, as an individual being, so far are duties to God separated from duties to man."[116] The believer is thus distanced from customary morality and feels that they have the right to break its rules at any time if faith demands it. For Feuerbach, this is alienation since it removes the ethical life of the individual from the human sphere and places it somewhere else with God. In faith we live in contradiction to our own basic moral intuitions.[117]

Feuerbach's claim is that love is what unites human beings in a fellowship of humanity. Christianity distorts this by placing God between us as human beings.

---

[110] Feuerbach, *Das Wesen des Christenthums*, pp. 371f.; *The Essence of Christianity*, p. 317.
[111] Feuerbach, *Das Wesen des Christenthums*, p. 372; *The Essence of Christianity*, p. 317.
[112] Feuerbach, *Das Wesen des Christenthums*, p. 375; *The Essence of Christianity*, p. 319.
[113] Feuerbach, *Das Wesen des Christenthums*, p. 375; *The Essence of Christianity*, p. 320.
[114] Feuerbach, *Das Wesen des Christenthums*, p. 377; *The Essence of Christianity*, p. 321.
[115] Feuerbach, *Das Wesen des Christenthums*, pp. 386f.; *The Essence of Christianity*, p. 328.
[116] Feuerbach, *Das Wesen des Christenthums*, p. 387; *The Essence of Christianity*, pp. 328f.
[117] Feuerbach, *Das Wesen des Christenthums*, p. 389; *The Essence of Christianity*, p. 330.

This destroys the natural immediacy of love and makes my love of my fellow human being dependent on something else.[118] Feuerbach explains the nature of true love as follows: "He therefore who loves man for the sake of man, who rises to the love of the species, to universal love, adequate to the nature of the species, he is a Christian, is Christ himself."[119] Feuerbach controversially claims that love itself is what is primary and not Christ the person himself. Once we have established this true love, then Christ himself falls away, although his essence as love remains.

Feuerbach's recommendation is, then, that we take back all of the energy and focus that has been put into the ephemeral beyond and recover it by putting it where it belongs – in our real lives here and now. We can thus take back what was lost when we placed human essence in God. Our human lives would thus be enriched by this return to ourselves of what was previously placed outside ourselves.

### 4.10   Feuerbach's Conclusion

At the end of the work, Feuerbach calls it a "necessary turning-point of history" that people generally recognize and acknowledge his thesis that "the consciousness of God is nothing else than the consciousness of the species."[120] One might fear that Feuerbach's view, which seems very close to atheism, might well have a pernicious effect. This might bring people to despair or have a negative consequence for ethics. But Feuerbach argues that, on the contrary, this realization will have a liberating effect. This will help people to overcome the delusion of God as an independent, radically different being, along with all the confusions that follow from this. Only with this realization is it possible for people to begin to regard themselves as absolute and not place their highest recognition in some elusive entity beyond themselves.

This has some important consequences. Traditionally, people have been taught to love God as an external, transcendent other. Now, Feuerbach claims, people can begin to love each other, that is, to realize the command to love other human beings.[121] We no longer need to dissipate our love on some illusion, but now it can be given to concrete human beings who are regarded as absolute in themselves. Our mundane world takes on an importance of its own when the true value of the human is realized. We no longer need priests or churches to make certain things sacred. For example, marriage as a relation of love "is sacred in itself" and does not require anything from the outside to gain its authority.[122] We can only fully appreciate the value of this when we realize it with our own

---

[118] Feuerbach, *Das Wesen des Christenthums*, p. 399; *The Essence of Christianity*, p. 338.
[119] Feuerbach, *Das Wesen des Christenthums*, p. 400; *The Essence of Christianity*, p. 339.
[120] Feuerbach, *Das Wesen des Christenthums*, p. 401; *The Essence of Christianity*, p. 340.
[121] Feuerbach, *Das Wesen des Christenthums*, p. 402; *The Essence of Christianity*, p. 341.
[122] Feuerbach, *Das Wesen des Christenthums*, p. 403; *The Essence of Christianity*, p. 341. See also *Das Wesen des Christenthums*, p. 406; *The Essence of Christianity*, p. 344.

understanding and reason. So also we can now realize that moral laws are true in themselves and not because God commands them. We can only become fully free and mature beings when we stop being the slaves of divine command and realize that moral laws issue from our own rationality.

The traditional view of God deceives human beings and robs them of their vigor and energy. All the thoughts, energy, and works that "ought to be devoted to life, to man" are instead bestowed on a fictional deity.[123] We relinquish all that is human to God. Our real relations to other people are sacrificed to our imagined relation to a projected divinity. When one considers all of the cruelties, atrocities, and human suffering that have been caused by people in the name of God,[124] then one begins to appreciate the deep truth of Feuerbach's view. When people claim to be acting on the will of God, they are effectively removing their action from all critical scrutiny or rational discussion. Their action, regardless of how cruel, immoral, or outrageous it may be, is immune from criticism since it is claimed to be the will of God.[125] When one genuinely wants to do what is right and just, then one does not require any additional motivation from God to do so since the truth and rationality of the matter should be motivation enough for the moral person. Feuerbach claims that it is only a form of self-delusion to seek justification for one's actions in God.[126]

Feuerbach's plea is that we restore our energy and efforts to ourselves by, for the first time, dedicating them to ourselves. He dramatically writes, "the work of self-conscious reason in relation to religion is simply to destroy an illusion – an illusion, however, which is by no means indifferent, but which, on the contrary, is profoundly injurious in its effects on mankind; which deprives man as well of the power of real life as of the genuine sense of truth and virtue."[127] Here one can see that Feuerbach believes that his work is no merely theoretical affair but rather has concrete implications for the liberation of humanity from a pernicious illusion that has stunted human development. This is an important matter when we compare it with Hegel's statement about the goal of philosophy at the end of his *Lectures on the Philosophy of Religion*. As we saw, Hegel claimed that philosophy needs to leave it to society or history to work out the problems of alienation in his present day. But Feuerbach, by contrast, seems to ascribe an important liberating role to philosophy. He believes that through reason we can eliminate the illusions of religion and free society from the nefarious shackles that have plagued it for so long. This mood of liberation and revolution was no doubt what inspired the next generation of thinkers such as Marx and Engels, who saw in Feuerbach a great hero of human emancipation.

---

[123]  Feuerbach, *Das Wesen des Christenthums*, p. 404; *The Essence of Christianity*, p. 342.
[124]  Feuerbach, *Das Wesen des Christenthums*, p. 407; *The Essence of Christianity*, pp. 344f.
[125]  Feuerbach, *Das Wesen des Christenthums*, p. 407; *The Essence of Christianity*, p. 345.
[126]  Feuerbach, *Das Wesen des Christenthums*, p. 407; *The Essence of Christianity*, p. 345.
[127]  Feuerbach, *Das Wesen des Christenthums*, p. 408; *The Essence of Christianity*, p. 345.

# 5

# Bruno Bauer's Criticism of Christianity

One of Hegel's most gifted students was Bruno Bauer (1809–1882), who is known, among other things, for being the object of criticism of Karl Marx and Friedrich Engels in "On the Jewish Question," *The Holy Family*, and *The German Ideology*. Due to this famous connection, his work is often thought to be primarily political. While it is true that politics plays an important role, Bauer's thought is far richer than this since he was also keenly interested in questions of religion, especially the question of the origin of Christianity, and even wrote several works on biblical source criticism.[1] He was a prolific author who published a steady stream of works throughout his life.

Historians of ideas have found it difficult to categorize Bauer's work, and he has confusingly been labeled both a right and a left Hegelian. The reason for this is the development of his thinking over the course of many years from a more conservative view to a radical one. Scholars have found it difficult to understand how a young student aspiring to the priesthood could soon afterwards be regarded as a messiah of atheism.[2] But there can be no disagreement about the fact that he played an important role in the development of German philosophy after Hegel. He had personal contact with almost all of the leading philosophical figures of his age. His most radical book, *Christianity Exposed*, takes some of the key ideas from Hegel's account of the master-slave dialectic and the unhappy consciousness in order to develop a theory of religious alienation. The work has been said to anticipate some aspects of Nietzsche's thought.[3]

---

[1] See the chapter on Bauer by Albert Schweitzer, *The Quest of the Historical Jesus: A Critical Study from Reimarus to Wrede*, with an introduction by James M. Robinson (New York: MacMillan, 1961), pp. 137–160.

[2] See Stan M. Landry, "From Orthodoxy to Atheism: The Apostasy of Bruno Bauer: 1835–1843," *Journal of Religion and Society*, 13 (2011), 1–20.

[3] See Ernst Benz, "Nietzsche und Bruno Bauer," in his *Nietzsches Ideen zur Geschichte des Christentums und der Kirche* (Leiden: E. J. Brill, 1956), pp. 104–121. See also Ernst Barnikol (ed.), "Einleitung. Bruno Bauer als Kritiker des Urchristentums," in *Das entdeckte Christentum im Vormärz. Bruno Bauers Kampf gegen Religion und Christentum und Erstausgabe seiner Kampfschrift* (Jena: Eugen Diederichs, 1927), p. 78.

Bauer was born in 1809 in Eisenberg in the Duchy of Saxony-Altenburg.[4] He moved with his family to Berlin in 1815, where he attended school. He enrolled in the University of Berlin in 1828 in order to prepare himself for a career as a Protestant pastor. There he attended Hegel's lectures and those of the theologians Philipp Marheineke, August Neander, and Schleiermacher. Hegel was impressed by the young student, and in 1829 he helped Bauer to win an essay prize offered by the Philosophical Faculty for a work on Kant.[5] Bauer's meticulous notes on Hegel's lectures were adopted by the editors of the complete edition of Hegel's writings published after his death. Indeed, Bauer himself helped Marheineke with the editorial work of the second edition of the *Lectures on the Philosophy of Religion*.[6] At an early age, Bauer completed his dissertation and received his degree in 1834. Immediately thereafter he was given a teaching post as privatdocent in theology at the University of Berlin, where he taught until 1839. The young Marx attended Bauer's lectures there.

David Friedrich Strauss published *The Life of Jesus Critically Examined* in 1835–1836, in which he tried to show that the New Testament narratives were largely myths. This was a scandalous claim, and many outside observers believed that this was a natural conclusion of Hegel's philosophy. Bauer made his polemical debut by writing a critical review of this work in the *Jahrbücher für wissenschaftliche Kritik*.[7] Here he plays the role of a conservative follower of Hegel, arguing that, according to Hegel, Jesus was a necessary

---

[4] For works on Bauer's life and works, see Douglas Moggach, *The Philosophy and Politics of Bruno Bauer* (Cambridge: Cambridge University Press, 2003); Karl Löwith, *From Hegel to Nietzsche: The Revolution in Nineteenth-Century Thought*, trans. by David E. Green (London: Constable and Co., 1965), pp. 105–110, pp. 299–301, pp. 343–350; William J. Brazill, *The Young Hegelians* (New Haven: Yale University Press, 1970), pp. 177–207; Martin Kegel, *Bruno Bauer und seine Theorien über die Entstehung des Christentums* (Leipzig: Quelle & Meyer, 1908); Zvi Rosen, *Bruno Bauer and Karl Marx: The Influence of Bruno Bauer on Marx's Thought* (The Hague: Martinus Nijhoff, 1977); David McLellan, *The Young Hegelians and Karl Marx* (New York: F. A. Praeger, 1969), pp. 48–84; Massimiliano Tomba, *Krise und Kritik bei Bruno Bauer. Kategorien des Politischen im nachhegelschen Denken* (Frankfurt am Main: Peter Lang, 2005); Antonio Gargano, *Bruno Bauer* (Naples: Città del Sole, 2003); Massimiliano Tomba, "Exclusiveness and Political Universalism in Bruno Bauer," in Douglas Moggach (ed.), *The New Hegelians: Politics and Philosophy in the Hegelian School* (Cambridge: Cambridge University Press, 2006), pp. 91–113; Klaus-M. Kodalle and Tilman Reitz (eds.), *Bruno Bauer (1809–1882): Ein "Partisan des Weltgeistes"?* (Würzburg: Königshausen & Neumann, 2010).

[5] This essay appears in English as an appendix, "On the Principles of the Beautiful," in Moggach, *The Philosophy and Politics of Bruno Bauer*, pp. 188–212.

[6] G. W. F. Hegel, *Vorlesungen über die Philosophie der Religion*, I–II, ed. by Philipp Marheineke, vols. 11–12 (2nd ed., 1840), in *Hegel's Werke*. See Bruno Bauer, *Briefwechsel zwischen Bruno und Edgar Bauer während der Jahre 1838–1842 aus Bonn und Berlin* (Charlottenburg: Verlag von Egbert Bauer, 1944), pp. 48–51.

[7] Bruno Bauer, "Rezension: *Das Leben Jesu, kritisch bearbeitet* von David Friedrich Strauss," *Jahrbücher für wissenschaftliche Kritik*, (December 1835), no. 109, pp. 879–880; no. 111, p. 891; no. 113, pp. 905–912; (May 1836), no. 86, pp. 681–688; no. 88, pp. 697–704.

development in the movement of spirit, the particular arising from the universal, the Son from the Father. This was not captured by Strauss' theory of mythology. Strauss' analysis concerned only the question of historical contingencies about whether something happened or not. But it never entered into the Hegelian issue of conceptual necessity.

In 1838 Strauss published a response to Bauer in a booklet entitled *In Defense of My Life of Jesus against the Hegelians*.[8] Here Strauss distances himself from the Hegelians and famously creates a scheme for understanding the different directions of the Hegelian school. In his classification of right, left, and center, Strauss places Bauer in the camp of the right Hegelians. This classification was often repeated by later historians of ideas and eventually led to confusion since the tag continued to be used even though Bauer's position had changed completely.

Perhaps inspired by the critical exchange with Strauss, Bauer's early work is concerned primarily with biblical criticism. He published an impressive series of writings in quick succession. His first major work appeared in 1838, a two-volume book, *Criticism of the History of the Revelation: The Religion of the Old Testament Presented in the Historical Development of Its Principles*.[9] Here he portrays the fundamental principle of Judaism as the absolute split between the transcendent God and the world of creation. This division was overcome with the coming of Jesus, who unites the two spheres.

Bauer was among the intellectuals who constituted the so-called "Doctors' Club," which met regularly at cafes to discuss Hegel's philosophy. Bauer's relation to Marx took place during this period in 1839.[10] In the same year Bauer unadvisedly dedicated an entire book to criticizing a senior scholar at the university of Berlin, the conservative theologian Ernst Wilhelm Theodor

---

[8]  David Friedrich Strauss, *Streitschriften zur Vertheidigung meiner Schrift über das Leben Jesu und zur Charakteristik der gegenwärtigen Theologie* (Tübingen: Osiander, 1837). (English translation: *In Defense of My Life of Jesus against the Hegelians*, trans. by Marilyn Chapin Massey [Hamden, CN: Archon Books, 1983].)

[9]  Bruno Bauer, *Kritik der Geschichte der Offenbarung. Die Religion des alten Testaments in der geschichtlichen Entwickelung ihrer Principien dargestellt*, vols. 1–2 (Berlin: Ferdinand Dümmler, 1838).

[10]  For Bauer's relation to Marx, see Zvi Rosen, *Bruno Bauer and Karl Marx*; David McLellan, *The Young Hegelians and Karl Marx*; Ruedi Waser, *Autonomie des Selbstbewußtseins. Eine Untersuchung zum Verhältnis von Bruno Bauer und Karl Marx (1835–1843)* (Tübingen: Francke Verlag, 1994); Sidney Hook, *From Hegel to Marx: Studies in the Intellectual Development of Karl Marx* (New York: Humanities Press, 1958), pp. 98–125; Kathleen L. Clarkson and David J. Hawkin, "Marx on Religion: The Influence of Bruno Bauer and Ludwig Feuerbach on His Thought and Its Implications for the Christian-Marxist Dialogue," *Scottish Journal of Theology*, 31 (1978), 533–555; Jürgen Gebhardt, "Karl Marx und Bruno Bauer," in Alois Dempf, Hannah Arendt, and Friedrich Engel-Janosi (eds.), *Politische Ordnung und menschliche Existenz. Festgabe für Eric Voegelin zum 60. Geburtstag* (Munich: C. H. Beck, 1962), pp. 202–243.

Hengstenberg (1802–1869).[11] This was the beginning of his difficulties in academic politics. The Prussian Minister of Education, Karl Altenstein, was positively disposed toward Bauer's work and, in an effort to help him, arranged a position for Bauer as privatdocent in theology at the University of Bonn in the same year. Altenstein presumably hoped to remove Bauer from the polemics of Berlin and to use him to promote Hegel's philosophy in Bonn.[12] However, the more conservative Faculty of Theology at the university there was suspicious of Bauer from the start. His teaching was provocative and perceived by many to be an advocation of atheism. Believing, however, that he had the support of Altenstein, Bauer felt no inhibitions about provoking his new colleagues. For his next work he turned to the New Testament with *The Critique of the Evangelical History of John*.[13] Here he contrasts the Gospel of John with the Synoptics. While the latter represent a historical account of Jesus, John is, he argues, a philosophical writer who ascribes to Jesus certain then-current philosophical views in the Greco-Roman world. This portrayal of Jesus is thus more fiction than fact. Therefore, he claims, the Gospel of John should not be regarded as a historical record of Jesus but should rather be treated as a kind of artistic creation.

He then expanded his interpretation to include the Synoptic authors in the three-volume *Critique of the Evangelical History of the Synoptic Gospels* from 1841–1842.[14] This was his most famous work, and in it he returns to his earlier criticism of Strauss' *The Life of Jesus*. While Strauss claimed that the myths found in the New Testament are natural, unconscious outgrowths of the culture in which they written, Bauer argues that these are intentional fictions created for specific purposes. In these works he thus attempts to undermine the foundation of the idea of the historical Jesus. The Synoptic writers were, like John, more creative artists than scholarly historians.

Bauer was keen to make use of the method of biblical criticism, which he adopted as his own principle, and here we can discern a Hegelian element in his work. He believes that by means of a critical study of the biblical text, it is possible to determine the deeper conceptual truth of religion by separating it from the fictions of the gospel writers.[15] Bauer develops this into a more general idea of a critical method that can be applied to anything at

---

[11] Bruno Bauer, *Herr Dr. Hengstenberg. Kritische Briefe über den Gegensatz des Gesetzes und des Evangelium* (Berlin: Ferdinand Dümmler, 1839).

[12] See Max Lenz, *Geschichte der Königlichen Friedrich-Wilhelms-Universität zu Berlin*, vols. 1–2.2 (Halle: Verlag der Buchhandlung des Waisenhauses, 1910–1918), vol. 2.2, pp. 25–39.

[13] Bruno Bauer, *Kritik der evangelischen Geschichte des Johannes* (Bremen: Carl Schünemann, 1840).

[14] Bruno Bauer, *Kritik der evangelischen Geschichte der Synoptiker*, vols. 1–3 (Leipzig: Otto Wigand, 1841–1842).

[15] See Brazill, *The Young Hegelians*, pp. 198–200.

all.[16] This should be the principle of philosophy since it allows the faculty of reason to develop and flourish while at the same time identifying and undermining repressive ideas, traditions, and institutions. Bauer's whole-hearted embracing of the idea of criticism or the critical method was the subject of Marx's critique, and in *The Holy Family*, Bauer is referred to satirically as Absolute Criticism. Bauer's continued loyalty to Hegel at this time can be seen from the anonymous publication in 1841 of *The Trumpet of the Last Judgement against Hegel the Atheist and Antichrist: An Ultimatum.*[17] Here he defends Hegel against the criticisms that had been raised by the conservative forces of Prussia by pretending ironically to be a reactionary critic of Hegel.

During this time Bauer had been under the watchful eye of the new Prussian Minster of Education, Johann Albrecht Friedrich von Eichhorn (1779–1856), who had assumed his post on the death of Altenstein in 1840. Bauer's contro-versial *Critique of the Evangelical History of the Synoptic Gospels* compelled him to take action. Eichhorn asked the Faculties of Theology at the Prussian universities their opinion on the matter. What exactly was Bauer's view with respect to Christianity and should he be allowed to continue to teach at a Faculty of Theology? Although there were differing opinions on the matter from the different universities, the Faculty of Theology in Bonn, where Bauer had his appointment, was the most critical, concluding that he should be barred as an instructor.[18] Based on the reports, the Prussian Ministry revoked Bauer's license to teach in Prussia, in effect firing him from his position in March of 1842.

This action in a sense radicalized Bauer, who prior to this time had believed himself to be promoting a true picture of Christianity. Now that he had been dismissed from his position and forbidden from finding another one, he no longer had any incentive to hold himself back. He must have felt that he had nothing left to lose. He thus became more and more strident in his religious views. Bauer's reputation as a left Hegelian comes from this period when his works were openly critical of Christianity. In the end he openly declared himself an atheist.

Angered by the abrupt end to his university career, Bauer published a detailed account of the affair in 1842, entitled *The Good Cause of Freedom*

---

[16] See, for example, his "Was ist jetzt der Gegenstand der Kritik?" *Allgemeine Literatur-Zeitung. Monatsschrift,* ed. by Bruno Bauer, 8 (June 1844), pp. 18–26.

[17] Bruno Bauer, *Die Posaune des jüngsten Gerichts über Hegel den Atheisten und Antichristen. Ein Ultimatum* (Leipzig: Otto Wigand, 1841). (English translation: *The Trumpet of the Last Judgement against Hegel the Atheist and Antichrist: An Ultimatum,* trans. by Laurence Stepelevich [Lewiston, NY: Edwin Mellon Press, 1989].)

[18] See *Gutachten der Evangelisch-theologischen Facultäten der Königlich Preußischen Universitäten über den Licentiaten Bruno Bauer in Beziehung auf dessen Kritik der evangelischen Geschichte der Synoptiker* (Berlin: Ferdinand Dümmler, 1842).

*and My Own Case.*[19] This was the first of a number of works in which Bauer argues for the principle of academic freedom of expression. Also in 1842, Bauer anonymously published *Hegel's Doctrine of Religion and Art,*[20] which was another ironic defense of Hegel against his critics. He believes that Hegel's philosophy leads to atheism, precisely the view that the Prussian authorities feared and for which reason they tried to repress the Hegelians. Bauer's movement from an orthodox right Hegelianism to open atheism culminated in 1843 with the publication of *Christianity Exposed: A Recollection of the Eighteenth Century and a Contribution to the Crisis of the Nineteenth Century.*[21]

Bauer led the existence of an independent scholar after the end of his teaching career. He left Bonn and lived on a farm in Rixdorf, a small village outside Berlin. The return to Berlin had the advantage that he was able to be exposed to the more stimulating intellectual environment of the capital in contrast to the provincial academic life of Bonn. Together with his brothers Egbert Bauer (1809–1882) and Edgar Bauer (1820–1886), he was a part of the literary circle "Die Freien" ("The Free"), which included Marx, Engels, Stirner, and Ruge. He also frequented the literary salon of Bettina von Arnim (1785–1859). During this time, he published several articles in different newspapers, including Arnold Ruge's *Rheinische Zeitung.* Together with his brother Egbert, Bauer edited a literary monthly entitled *Allgemeine Literatur-Zeitung* from 1843 to 1844. The articles in this journal constitute the subject of the satire of Marx and Engels in *The Holy Family.* Bauer was understandably disappointed that his dismissal did not turn into a rallying point for the left Hegelians in a way that would unify them and mobilize them for action. On the contrary, they spent much of their time criticizing one another.

As the years passed, Bauer's influence began to recede, although he regularly produced a number of weighty tomes. He wrote several works on the changing politics of the times.[22] Despite being such a firebrand in matters of religion and

---

[19] Bruno Bauer, *Die gute Sache der Freiheit und meine eigene Angelegenheit* (Zürich and Winterthur: Verlag des literarischen Comptoirs, 1842).

[20] Bruno Bauer, *Hegels Lehre von der Religion und Kunst von dem Standpuncte des Glaubens aus beurtheilt* (Leipzig: Otto Wigand, 1842).

[21] Bruno Bauer, *Das entdeckte Christenthum. Eine Erinnerung an das 18. Jahrhundert und ein Beitrag zur Krisis des 19.* (Zürich and Winterthur: Verlag des literarischen Comptoirs, 1843). (English translation: *An English Edition of Bruno Bauer's 1843 Christianity Exposed: A Recollection of the Eighteenth Century and a Contribution to the Crisis of the Nineteenth Century,* ed. by Paul Trejo, trans. by Esther Ziegler and Jutta Hamm [Lewiston, NY: Edwin Mellon Press, 2002] [*Studies in German Thought and History,* vol. 23].)

[22] See his *Geschichte der Politik, Kultur und Aufklärung des 18ten Jahrhunderts,* vols. 1–2 (Charlottenburg: Verlag von Egbert Bauer, 1843–1845); together with Edgar Bauer and Ernst Jungnitz, *Geschichte der französischen Revolution,* vols. 1–3 (Leipzig: Voigt und Fernau's Separat-Conto, 1847); *Die bürgerliche Revolution in Deutschland seit dem*

for all of his high-sounding rhetoric about the development of human freedom, Bauer was something of a reactionary in political matters. He was against
the Jewish emancipation,[23] and he has traditionally been read as critical of the
Revolution of 1848, although recent research has called this view into question
and shown the issue to be more complicated.[24]

In the 1850s Bauer then returned to his New Testament studies with
*A Critique of the Gospels and a History of Their Origin*.[25] Here he claims that
Jesus never existed but was a fiction of later writers from the second century. In
1852 he published his *Critique of the Pauline Epistles*,[26] in which he claimed
that these letters were not written by Paul but by someone else almost two
centuries later. In 1874 his *Philo, Strauss, Renan and Original Christianity*
appeared,[27] in which he argues that Philo's philosophy was the true source of
inspiration of the gospel writers, who made use of it and created the figure of
Jesus as a fictional character to present their views. *Christ and the Caesars* from
1877 recapitulates many of his earlier views, including now Seneca and the
Stoics as sources of the gospel writers.[28] In this work Bauer again attempts to
demonstrate the influence of Greece and Rome on the development of
Christianity. He denies anew the very historicity of Jesus, claiming that he
was a fiction made up by later writers interested in Greek and Roman philosophy. Much of the same material was recast yet again three years later in *The
Original Gospel and the Opponents of the Book: Christ and the Caesars*.[29] These

*Anfang der deutsch-katholischen Bewegung bis zur Gegenwart* (Berlin: Gustav Hempel,
1849); *Der Untergang des Frankfurter Parlaments. Geschichte der deutschen constituirenden Nationalversammlung* (Berlin: Friedrich Gerhard, 1849); *Rußland und das
Germanenthum*, vols. 1–2 (Charlottenburg: Verlag von Egbert Bauer, 1853); *Rußland
und England* (Charlottenburg: Verlag von Egbert Bauer, 1854); *Disraelis romantischer
und Bismarcks socialistischer Imperialismus* (Chemnitz: Schmeitzner, 1882).

[23] See David Leopold, "The Hegelian Antisemitism of Bruno Bauer," *History of European
Ideas*, 25 (1999), 179–206; Yoav Peled, "From Theology to Sociology: Bruno Bauer and
Karl Marx on the Question of Jewish Emancipation," *History of Political Thought*, 13(3)
(1992), 463–485.

[24] See Brazill, *The Young Hegelians*, p. 203. Douglas Moggach, "Republican Rigorism and
Emancipation in Bruno Bauer," in Moggach (ed.), *The New Hegelians*, pp. 114–135;
Douglas Moggach, "Post-Kantian Perfectionism," in Douglas Moggach (ed.), *Politics,
Religion, and Art: Hegelian Debates* (Evanston: Northwestern University Press, 2011), pp.
179–200.

[25] Bruno Bauer, *Kritik der Evangelien und Geschichte ihres Ursprungs*, vols. 1–4 (Berlin:
Gustav Hempel, 1850–1852).

[26] Bruno Bauer, *Kritik der paulinischen Briefe* (Berlin: Gustav Hempel, 1852).

[27] Bruno Bauer, *Philo, Strauß, Renan und das Urchristentum* (Berlin: Gustav Hempel, 1874).

[28] Bruno Bauer, *Christus und die Cäsaren. Der Ursprung des Christentums aus dem
römischen Griechentum* (Berlin: Eugen Grosser, 1877). (English translation: *Christ and
the Caesars: The Origin of Christianity from Romanized Greek Culture*, trans. by Frank
E. Schacht [Charleston, SC: Charleston House Publishing, 1998].)

[29] Bruno Bauer, *Das Urevangelium und die Gegner die Schrift: "Christus und die Caesaren"*
(Berlin: Eugen Grosser, 1880).

works all have the same general tendency of trying to demonstrate that the origin of Christianity comes from a later period and that the authors were inspired by Greco-Roman philosophers. Despite the increasing radicalism in Bauer's works, his corpus shows a tremendous amount of continuity with regard to his works on religion. After so many productive years, Bauer died at Rixdorf in 1882. He was eulogized by Engels, who sees his most important contribution being his research on the historical origins of Christianity.[30]

## 5.1   The Context of Bauer's *Christianity Exposed*

As noted, in 1843 Bauer published *Christianity Exposed: A Recollection of the Eighteenth Century and a Contribution to the Crisis of the Nineteenth Century*.[31] This work was immediately banned by the Prussian government, which confiscated the book from the bookstores and tried to destroy the entire print run. In his *Outline of the History of Philosophy*, Erdmann, another Hegel student, claims that only a single copy survived.[32] Bauer's publisher, Julius Fröbel (1805–1893), was immediately arrested. Some copies, however, were circulated clandestinely, and the text was known at the time, as is evidenced by the fact that it was cited by Marx in *The Holy Family*. Today this work is rare. Most scholars use the modern edition printed by Ernst Barnikol in 1927.[33]

The work itself purports to be an account of some of the key texts on religious critique from the Enlightenment. Bauer's text is full of long quotations from writers of the eighteenth century. He refers most frequently to the work of Johann Christian Edelmann (1698–1767), *Confession of Faith*.[34] Also important is the book by Paul-Henri Thiry, Baron d'Holbach (1723–1789) (under the pseudonym Boulanger), *Christianisme Dévoilé*, from which Bauer presumably drew the title for his own work.[35] Holbach's *Système de la nature* is

---

[30] Frederick Engels, "Bruno Bauer und das Urchristentum," *Der Sozialdemokrat*, 19–20 (May 4 and 11, 1882) (no page numbers). (English translation: "Bruno Bauer and Early Christianity," in *Marx/Engels Collected Works*, vols. 1–50 [Moscow: Progress Publishers, 1975–2004], vol. 24, pp. 427–435. *Marx-Engels-Gesamtausgabe*, vols. 1– [Berlin: Dietz], 1975ff, vol. 19, pp. 297–305.)

[31] Bauer, *Das entdeckte Christenthum*; *An English Edition of Bruno Bauer's 1843 Christianity Exposed*.

[32] Johann Eduard Erdmann, *Grundrisse der Geschichte der Philosophie*, vols. 1–2 (Berlin: Wilhelm Hertz, 1866), vol. 2, *Philosophie der Neuzeit*, § 338, p. 668. (English translation: *A History of Philosophy*, vols. 1–3, trans. by Williston S. Hough [London: George Allen & Unwin; New York: Macmillan, 1889], vol. 3, *German Philosophy Since Hegel*, § 338, p. 78.)

[33] Barnikol (ed.), *Das entdeckte Christentum im Vormärz*.

[34] *Johann Christian Edelmanns Abgenöthigtes jedoch andern nicht wieder auf genöthigtes Glaubens-Bekenntnis* (Neuwied: no publisher given, 1746).

[35] [Paul-Henri Thiry, Baron d'Holbach] under the pseudonym Boulanger, *Le Christianisme dévoilé, ou Examen des principes et des effets de la religion chrétienne* (Nancy, Switzerland: de L'Imprim. Philosophique, 1761). (English translation: *Christianity Unveiled, Being an*

also an important work that Bauer often cites to illustrate the view of materialism.[36] Also frequently referenced is a work entitled *Examen de la religion dont on cherche l'Eclairissement de Bonne Foi*,[37] the authorship of which is uncertain. It has been attributed to, among others, Charles de Marguetel de Saint-Denis, seigneur de Saint-Évremond (1613–1703), and Voltaire. Bauer also references Balthasar Bekker's (1634–1698) *Enchanted World*.[38] The point of this return to the Enlightenment is the idea that the eighteenth century shares with Bauer's own age a sense of religious alienation. This had been repressed in the Restoration but was now emerging in ever stronger forms during Bauer's time.

*Christianity Exposed* can be seen as a part of Bauer's protest against his firing and as the culmination of his radicalization. The situation seems to have embittered him and encouraged him to write things that he knew would be particularly provocative and incendiary to the powers that be. The work is an uninhibited attack not just on Christianity and religious sectarianism but also on the repressive forces of the Prussian government, which, Bauer argues, undermine human freedom and development. Bauer criticizes Christianity as being antithetical to everything that is natural. It is an illusion that humans impose on themselves, thus creating the conditions for a miserable, mundane existence. There is a clear anti-clerical strain in the work, and this can be explained by the fact that Bauer felt that he had been betrayed by his colleagues, the narrow-minded and provincial theologians at the University of Bonn. This seems to be implied by his reference to his work from the previous year, *The Good Cause of Freedom and My Own Case*.[39] At the end of the work, he also critically raises the question of intellectual freedom among theologians, whom he regards as hypocrites.[40] He entitles this section "The Last Supports of Religion," by which he seems to mean the secular powers such as the government, the university officials, and even the police department, which all work together to stamp out any views that might be critical of religion.

*Examination of the Principles and Effects of the Christian Religion*, trans. by W. M. Johnson [New York: (no publisher given), 1835].)

[36] [Paul-Henri Thiry, Baron d'Holbach] under the pseudonym Jean-Baptiste de Mirabaud, *Système de la Nature ou Des Loix du Monde Physique et du Monde Moral*, vols. 1–2 (London [Amsterdam]: [no publisher given], 1770).

[37] *Examen de la religion dont on cherche l'Eclairissement de Bonne Foi* (no date, place of publication or publisher is listed). See C. J. Betts, "The *Examen de la Religion* and Other Clandestine Works," chapter 11 in *Early Deism in France: From the So-Called "déistes" of Lyon (1564) to Voltaire's "Lettres philosophiques" (1734)* (The Hague: Martinus Nijhoff, 1984), pp. 157–171.

[38] Balthasar Bekker, *De betoverde Weereld* (Amsterdam: Daniel Van Den Dalen, 1691). (In German: *Die bezauberte Welt* [Amsterdam: Daniel von Dahlen, 1693].)

[39] Bauer, *Das entdeckte Christenthum*, p. 103; *Christianity Exposed*, p. 98. Bauer, *Die gute Sache der Freiheit und meine eigene Angelegenheit*.

[40] Bauer, *Das entdeckte Christenthum*, p. 117; *Christianity Exposed*, p. 114.

The work can also be seen as a movement away from a scholarly form of writing to a kind of political activism – a call for action. It does not contain well-worked-out analyses but consists largely of very broad claims and assertions. Bauer relies heavily on quotations to give the work its provocative edge. He seems to hope that this book will mobilize readers to reject Christianity and the oppressive political status quo of the Prussian state. After his dismissal, Bauer's struggle was no longer about making an abstract academic point but rather about toppling hypocrisy, corruption, and oppression. Whatever stood in the way of the development of human freedom must be destroyed. People would only be free when Christianity was eliminated and replaced with a humanism.

## 5.2   The Atheistic Enlightenment

In the Introduction, signed February 3, 1843, Bauer explains that the work is about the atheistic Enlightenment of the eighteenth century, which, he claims, has recently seen a revival. He distinguishes the atheistic strand of the Enlightenment from the less radical deistic one. The atheistic Enlightenment he traces to the revival of Spinozism, which disabused the deistic view of its religious vestiges. This radical trend was then thwarted for a time by the Restoration.

Bauer further contrasts the English and the French Enlightenment, associating the former with deism and the latter with atheism. (This is not so straightforward since he mentions Voltaire as a leader of the deist movement as well as Robespierre's attempt to create a cult of the Supreme Being.) He argues that English deism in the end still wanted to preserve religion, albeit in a more limited form. By contrast, the more radical atheism of the French was determined to eliminate religion altogether. He writes, "The French atheistic Enlightenment proved that religion in general is the self-obscuring of the human mind. It taught the human mind to know itself, its truths and its former falsehoods."[41] The idea is that the human mind was previously unclear to itself and required a form of awakening. It did not truly know itself and was unaware of the errors that it lived in. It was alienated from itself until the new atheistic movement showed it the way. Then the oppressed were able to overcome the tyranny of religion that had been imposed again by the Restoration: "The downtrodden mind arose with strengthened elasticity to complete what French atheism was not able to accomplish. It fought the final fight with the anti-spiritual, the anti-human, the mindlessness and the whole past of man's inhumanity to man."[42]

---

[41] Bauer, *Das entdeckte Christenthum*, pp. vi–vii (note that all references are to the first edition pagination); *Christianity Exposed*, p. 2.

[42] Bauer, *Das entdeckte Christenthum*, p. vii; *Christianity Exposed*, p. 2.

Bauer sees his own work to be making common cause with the goals of the French atheistic movement. He says that he wants to let "the atheism of the eighteenth century and modern criticism fight as allies the very Christian Restoration."[43] By "modern criticism," he means his own work or the critical movement of which he is a part. Bauer's idea is that the proper philosophical view should not just be critical of specific things but rather should issue a universal criticism, sparing nothing, regardless of how sacred it might be. Likewise, criticism should not be limited to a specific field such as religion or history; instead, it must be applied generally. Erdmann describes Bauer's position as follows: "the doctrine proclaimed that there is no truth in anything but man and that therefore even the word 'atheism,' because it contains a relation to the object denied, is not the correct designation for the views of the free man. For this reason the free man must not assume that anything has absolute value."[44] For Bauer, this view completes the destruction caused by the Enlightenment's critical reevaluation of all traditional beliefs and forms of society. With this methodological disposition, Bauer can be said to anticipate the thought of the Russian nihilists in the 1860s, who were also keen to reject all previously accepted truths.

With the term "criticism," Bauer also seems to be drawing on the work of Strauss and others in the field of biblical criticism. The Bible scholars critically examine the scriptures to learn about their sources and the date and context of their composition. Bauer believes that this spirit can be applied to other aspects of religion and indeed society in general. Nothing should be taken for granted, and everything should be exposed to the critical test of reason. Bauer raises the question of why the Enlightenment did not ultimately complete its task. Why did it give way to the Restoration? This is ostensibly the purpose of the work.

It should be noted that throughout the work Bauer uses Hegel's language from *The Phenomenology of Spirit*, speaking of "religious consciousness." He thus seeks to sketch a certain religious mindset or worldview and the consequences that follow from it. In this context he builds on Hegel's account of the unhappy consciousness as a form of religious alienation. The focus on consciousness also implies the unity of subject and object. Every object is an object of consciousness, including the divine.[45] This linguistic point is relevant for Marx's criticism of Bauer. Marx takes this to be an indication of the fact that Bauer is still under the spell of Hegel's idealism and thus continues to operate with abstractions.

In the very title of the work, Bauer also echoes Hegel's belief that the present is an age of crisis, and this is what it has in common with the religious tumult of

---

[43] Bauer, *Das entdeckte Christenthum*, p. vii; *Christianity Exposed*, p. 3.

[44] Erdmann, *Grundrisse der Geschichte der Philosophie*, vol. 2, *Philosophie der Neuzeit*, § 341, p. 681; *A History of Philosophy*, vol. 3, *German Philosophy since Hegel*, § 341, p. 92.

[45] See Brazill, *The Young Hegelians*, p. 190.

the Enlightenment in the eighteenth century. Later in the text Bauer refers to "the current spiritual revolution" and "the current crisis."[46] By this he seems to mean the doubt cast upon traditional religious belief by the criticisms of thinkers such as Strauss and Feuerbach. History has reached a point where people can begin for the first time to realize the negative effects that religion has had on humanity. Hegel claimed that the Enlightenment was the period in which spirit became aware of itself. Strauss, Feuerbach, and Bauer seize on this idea for their own critical agenda. For the first time people have begun to realize that they have been oppressed by religion, which has prevented them from exercising their freedom and rationality and thus from fully developing themselves as human beings. Therefore the new criticism can make common cause with the atheism of the Enlightenment in order to combat the repressive forces of the Restoration.

### 5.3  The Necessary Alienation of the Religious Consciousness

Bauer begins his analysis by pointing out what he takes to be an innate intolerance found in religious belief. He claims that while there are cycles of war and peace in the political sphere, in the religious sphere there is perpetual conflict that can never be reconciled due to the differences of religious dogma. Each religious sect takes its own beliefs to be the sole true ones and thus excludes everyone else, declaring them to be in error. The result of this is the alienation of one human from another: "This alienation [*Entfremdung*] must continue until the other party is as foreign to each as one animal species is to another."[47]

Bauer believes that this disposition leads to a demonizing of others who belong to a sect different from oneself. Each party condemns the other in order to preserve the idea that it alone is in sole possession of the truth. Bauer's claim is that this is not an accident that depends on the individual believer, but instead it is "a necessary consequence of religious consciousness."[48] In other words, all religious belief sooner or later ends in intolerance. Every religion wants to prop itself up as the true one, and this ipso facto means regarding the others as false. Every religion is a particular that claims to be a universal.

The obvious contradiction in this view is that when a religious sect condemns the others as wallowing in error, it must realize at the same time that its rival sect holds exactly the same view of it. Any given sect is thus condemned by all others. Here we can discern a vestige of Hegel's theory of recognition.[49]

---

[46]  Bauer, *Das entdeckte Christenthum*, p. 105; *Christianity Exposed*, p. 101. See also *Das entdeckte Christenthum*, p. 119; *Christianity Exposed*, p. 117.
[47]  Bauer, *Das entdeckte Christenthum*, p. 1; *Christianity Exposed*, p. 5.
[48]  Bauer, *Das entdeckte Christenthum*, p. 2; *Christianity Exposed*, p. 6.
[49]  This has been noted by Moggach, *The Philosophy and Politics of Bruno Bauer*, pp. 139f.

In order to be recognized meaningfully, we must recognize the other. But when we reject the other, then they will also reject us. So the sectarian disposition of any given religious group inevitably serves to undermine itself. By rejecting the views of others, this disposition condemns itself to being rejected by them. Unlike Hegel's master-slave relation, which develops dialectically, there is no development in the rejection of one religious sect from another. For this reason religious sects are always in conflict, and none of them will ever be recognized as universal. Deep down, religious believers are acutely aware of the relative nature of their belief, and this is an irritation that they cannot get rid of. They know that it is a delusion to believe that theirs is the sole truth, and this is unsettling. This awareness leads to a form of the unhappy consciousness: "So, by being a particularity each one is in its own pain, plague and misery. This is an eternal misery because each one damns the other forever and can only secure one's self-assurance by enjoying the other's eternal damnation."[50] It suffers the pain of being aware of the relativity of its belief and not enjoying the universal recognition of its truth. The pain is the nagging uncertainty that one's own beliefs might be wrong, as the other sects think they are.

This then leads to the impulse to repress and persecute others whose beliefs are not in harmony with one's own. Through the persecution of the other, as in Hegel's master-slave dialectic, one attempts in vain to overcome the sense of separation and alienation from the other. Bauer writes, "Species of animal tear each other to pieces and devour each other to neutralize the feeling of alienation [Fremdheit]."[51] But once the victory has been won and the other is eliminated, the sense of alienation returns since there are always others to take the place of the person who has just been defeated. The religious believer thus lives in a constant state of alienation from other people.

Thus, despite all claims to the contrary, at the heart of religion lies a deep-seated hatred for the other. Once again, Bauer makes a provocative claim that hatred is not something accidental or dependent on the specific individual; instead, it is a necessary element of all religion given the fact that each religion makes an exclusive absolute claim to truth. This hatred also fuels the sense of alienation and despair that the religious believer feels.

Religious hatred and persecution are necessary for the individual religious believer. Just as the master needed the slave whom he must defeat, so also any given religious sect needs other sects to capitulate and recognize its own truth: "Each particularity has to hate the other but cannot survive precisely without the other. From this evolves the miserable feeling of insecurity that dominates religious consciousness – a feeling of insecurity and alienation that it has in common only with animals."[52] The individual sect needs an opposing one by

---

[50] Bauer, *Das entdeckte Christenthum*, p. 3; *Christianity Exposed*, pp. 6f.
[51] Bauer, *Das entdeckte Christenthum*, p. 4; *Christianity Exposed*, p. 7.
[52] Bauer, *Das entdeckte Christenthum*, p. 5; *Christianity Exposed*, p. 8.

means of which it can define itself. The one necessarily produces its opposition. But when the opposing sect is defeated, then a new enemy must be created in order to take its place. A given sect or belief system is thus constantly determined by this dialectic of identity and difference. It needs another in order to determine itself: "Religious fighting is a gruesome game, with many victims of hate, but in its feverish exaggeration and weakness, it takes care that it always has enough victims. If there were no more to be used up, it would collapse. If the other was no longer alive, the sect itself would be lost along with the other."[53] It is thus, like the master and the slave, unknowingly dependent on the other.

## 5.4   The Sacrifice of the Believer's Reason

Bauer notes that religious sects must also persecute any form of critical or independent thinking. Members of religious groups must be unthinking and docile, simply going along readily with whatever is dictated to them. Religion thus demands that individuals sacrifice their faculty of reason, which amounts to their very humanity: "Whoever wants to be human, to think, to be free, commits the worst betrayal of his sect."[54] Reason dictates that one examines things from different perspectives and that one tries to look at evidence and build consensus for solutions. This kind of thing represents a threat to a sect, which claims for itself the sole possession of the truth. Religious sects must thus reject any rational or scientific approach to things. Therefore, when it finds this kind of spirit among its followers, the sect brands it betrayal or conspiracy. Anyone perceived not to go along with the key dogmas blindly is regarded as sinful.

This discussion provides Bauer with the occasion to castigate the practice of censorship. This was presumably a highly sensitive issue for him at the time, given that he had himself been barred from teaching at the university by the Prussian authorities. He describes censorship as a kind of crime against humanity. He argues that thinking and using our reason are the very things that make us human. In thinking, we use universals by means of which we are connected with others. Understanding these universals – for example, laws or concepts – is possible for all human beings. He recalls the formulations of Feuerbach and Marx about humans as "species beings": "In thinking, in writing, in the fiery drive of criticism I no longer live for the sect and its limited preconditions, but for the species and its freedom. Thinking is the true species-process [*Gattungsprozeß*] which creates an intellectual human, yes, even humanity itself."[55] It will be recalled from Chapter 4 that this was precisely

---

[53]   Bauer, *Das entdeckte Christenthum*, p. 7; *Christianity Exposed*, p. 10.
[54]   Bauer, *Das entdeckte Christenthum*, p. 8; *Christianity Exposed*, p. 11.
[55]   Bauer, *Das entdeckte Christenthum*, p. 9; *Christianity Exposed*, p. 12.

Feuerbach's definition of self-consciousness: the ability to think oneself not as individual but as species, or to think the universal.[56] For Bauer, by preventing people from expressing their thoughts, censorship undermines this fundamental aspect of what it is to be human. Those who practice censorship fear the full development of human freedom and thus actively work to prevent it.

Bauer seems to echo Hegel's account of the historical context in which Christianity arose in the Roman world. He claims, "Christianity appeared when the world was distressed and the supports which had maintained it so far were broken."[57] This was the world of the unhappy consciousness. Therefore, he claims that the origin of religion is anxiety. When people are anxious and fearful, it is natural that they seek in God some fixed point of truth and certainty. Bauer claims that religion "is the highest suffering that man was able to inflict on himself."[58] Religion undermines the full development of human reason and freedom. It thus prevents humans from fulfilling their natural human potential. Instead, with the imagined transcendent God, it places them in a world of misery and sin, as described in the figure of the unhappy consciousness. The idea of God represents a limitation or oppression of human thinking.

Since the oppression of the sect is interpreted as the will of God, it is understood that it is God's wish that people do not use their reason and do not exercise their faculty of critical thought. God does not want people to think or act freely since that would undermine the sect. Given this, it appears that God's intention is that human beings remain ignorant and unhappy, destined never to rise out of their lowly condition. Here we find an echo of Hegel's criticism of the story of the Fall in Genesis, which in effect says that God created humans to be like the animals and wanted to prevent them from eating from the tree that granted them knowledge. Bauer extends this criticism to Christianity itself. With the imagined idea of God, humans thus enslave themselves and condemn themselves to misery. The belief in God represents "a thousandfold bondage and falsehood that penetrates all human relations."[59] According to Bauer's view, with the fictional idea of God, the religious believer conceals the truth from themselves that they are the origin of their own oppression. Bauer radically departs from Hegel's view that Christianity is the religion of freedom, which emancipates humans from the constraints of nature. Instead of being a force of human liberation, Christianity, according to Bauer, is a pernicious agent of oppression.

---

[56] Ludwig Feuerbach, *Das Wesen des Christenthums*, 2nd ed. (Leipzig: Otto Wigand, 1843), pp. 1f. (English translation: *The Essence of Christianity*, trans. by Marian Evans [New York: Calvin Blanchard, 1855], pp. 19f.)

[57] Bauer, *Das entdeckte Christenthum*, p. 10; *Christianity Exposed*, p. 12.

[58] Bauer, *Das entdeckte Christenthum*, p. 10; *Christianity Exposed*, p. 13.

[59] Bauer, *Das entdeckte Christenthum*, p. 12; *Christianity Exposed*, p. 14.

In this context Bauer criticizes the Christian dogma of the Revelation, which was so important to Hegel. According to Bauer, the message of the idea of Revelation is that the human mind itself cannot determine the truth. Instead, it must wait and passively receive the truth from some outside source. This disposition discourages all scientific or scholarly investigation. This prevents people from developing their critical reasoning in order to understand the world around them. The revelation simply presents a truth that they are obliged to believe without further ado.[60] This involves believers passively accepting absurdities and outright contradictions. Once again he portrays religion as having a repressive element that prevents humans from developing their faculties and fully realizing their potential.

Bauer sketches his own version of the unhappy consciousness. Religion keeps people miserable in the present world, preventing them from developing their human reason and freedom. By contrast, it promises a great reward in another world. This leads to a form of self-alienation since we cannot be who we truly are: free, rational beings. He claims, "we are completely torn apart within ourselves."[61] Instead, we remain in a state of misery, with the lure of something much better to come. But this means that people spend their entire lives in this alienated state. We live haunted by the idea that we are inveterate sinners and thus deprive ourselves of natural pleasures. Christianity teaches the virtues of chastity and celibacy, and people are told that the enjoyment of our physical side is sinful.[62] As a result humans are alienated from their own bodies and natural drives. True happiness and fulfillment must wait until after we are dead. Once again, for Bauer, the absurdity of all of this is that it is self-created. Humans have themselves dreamed up the religious belief systems and as a result have oppressed themselves and made their own lives miserable. The religious believer is obliged to regard the world as nothing.[63] It contains no lasting truth or meaning, which is reserved for the divine and the transcendent realm. Religious belief thus implies an alienation from this world. The believer "must alienate [entfremden] his heart from the world, from human relations and from history."[64] Christianity is a negation and denial of the world.[65]

Bauer observes the contradiction between fear and love. A tyrant rules by fear and intimidation. People go along with them and flatter them, putting on a show of love and affection, but deep down they resent them since the tyrant keeps them in fear. This resentment prevents any feeling of genuine affection from ever arising. It is thus absurd, he claims, when religion teaches that we should simultaneously love and fear God. The two mutually exclude one

---

[60] Bauer, *Das entdeckte Christenthum*, p. 14; *Christianity Exposed*, p. 16.
[61] Bauer, *Das entdeckte Christenthum*, pp. 17f.; *Christianity Exposed*, p. 18.
[62] Bauer, *Das entdeckte Christenthum*, pp. 68–72; *Christianity Exposed*, pp. 63–66.
[63] Bauer, *Das entdeckte Christenthum*, p. 59; *Christianity Exposed*, p. 55.
[64] Bauer, *Das entdeckte Christenthum*, p. 60; *Christianity Exposed*, p. 56.
[65] Bauer, *Das entdeckte Christenthum*, p. 83; *Christianity Exposed*, p. 79.

another. Here again Bauer refers to a motif from Hegel's master-slave dialectic. It is impossible for the slave to love the master. Instead, the slave secretly disdains the master while serving them. The slave comes to hate themselves for lacking integrity and making themselves subservient to the master and not revolting. The slave can never respect themselves so long as they are a slave. In this condition there is no reconciliation either with the master or with oneself.

Bauer applies Hegel's dialectics to the concept of God, arguing that the very idea of an all-good God necessarily implies its opposite principle: evil, incarnated in the form of the devil. A part of the definition of God is as a principle that combats evil. But if evil did not exist, then God would lose his raison d'être. God needs some negative principle in opposition to himself in order to exist.[66] God represents being and the devil nothingness, which mutually imply one another. The devil plays an important role in the psychology of religion since he inspires fear, which, according to Bauer, is the basis for religious belief. With the support of the thinkers of the Enlightenment, Bauer claims that the idea of evil or the devil is necessary for religion. This is a surprising outcome for Christianity, which claims to be a religion of love.

## 5.5   Christianity's Undermining of Freedom, Equality, and Love

Bauer notes that Christianity has been praised for being based on three things: freedom, equality, and love. However, he claims that upon closer analysis, this turns out to be an illusion, and these things turn into their opposites.[67] With respect to freedom, Bauer objects that the freedom offered by religion separates individuals from the world and their interests. True freedom means the ability to develop one's faculties, but religion prevents this and discourages any form of critical thinking or scientific or scholarly pursuit.[68] Thus Christian freedom is an unthinking bondage.

With respect to equality, it is claimed that Christianity makes all people equal before God and thus historically played a role in the elimination of slavery and the development of democracy. However, despite this, Christianity in fact divides people into two groups, the believers and the nonbelievers, with the former being the privileged class. It thus undermines genuine equality. On the contrary, it established a kind of caste hierarchy with the believers on the top. Finally, while Christianity seems at face value to teach a belief system based on love, it is in fact a religion of hate. Christianity discourages people from thinking the universal since this involves reflection. This is the form of scientific thinking, which places particular cases under the universal. While it is true that Christianity says that we should love God, a particular, this is very

---

[66] Bauer, *Das entdeckte Christenthum*, pp. 26f.; *Christianity Exposed*, p. 25.

[67] Bauer, *Das entdeckte Christenthum*, p. 33; *Christianity Exposed*, p. 31.

[68] Bauer, *Das entdeckte Christenthum*, pp. 61–65; *Christianity Exposed*, pp. 57–60.

different from a love of the human. The love of God is in fact a hatred for humanity and the human sphere. As we have seen, Christianity encourages hatred for those who hold different beliefs or who wish to examine the Christian belief system with critical reason. Thus the high-sounding claims about love quickly turn into the very opposite. The development of Christianity has thus warped Christ's original message of love. Instead of uniting people through a common sense of humanity, it constantly divides and separates them. One can see here a criticism of Feuerbach's appeal to love as the true essence of Christianity that is worth preserving. Bauer argues that this view is mistaken since the idea of Christian love is sheer hypocrisy.

Bauer further objects to the use of the word "religion" to mean simply a deep devotion or dedication to a specific profession in the sense that one would say of someone that their job is their religion. This usage implies particularity; that is, it is a specific job that is said to be per analogy a kind of religion. But this is misconceived. Religion is supposed to be about the highest things, something that fulfills us as human beings. But our work at meaningless jobs can never do this. He raises the critical question: "Can the work . . . fulfill the complete soul of humanity? Can we find our religion by doing nothing more than controlling a certain machine that produces a certain screw our whole life long?"[69] These kinds of specific tasks can never speak to our universal humanity. Thus the analogy of work with religion is misplaced. Here we can catch a brief glimpse of Bauer's politics. His idea here seems to anticipate Marx's notion of alienated labor.[70] All productive and meaningful human activities are regarded as vain signs of self-love by the Christian belief system, which sees truth and meaning only in the beyond. It thus deprives people of finding satisfaction and self-affirmation in their work and accomplishments.[71] The idea of God, according to Bauer, in the end amounts to "the perfect rejection of humanity, the sacrifice of humanity, the negation of humanity."[72]

Likewise, it is a mistake to refer to the enthusiasm for art, science, and the state in terms of religion. While these represent the highest of human interests, they are in fact antithetical to religion. It is true that people can find their fulfillment in such things, but religion undermines this since it prevents self-actualization. In these spheres of human interest, we act and work based on the universal – our humanity. But this is precisely what religion prevents by not allowing us to develop our true human faculties. Christianity is thus self-alienation since it separates us from our humanity. In Bauer's words, "Thus

---

[69] Bauer, *Das entdeckte Christenthum*, p. 36; *Christianity Exposed*, p. 34. (Translation modified.)

[70] See Zvi Rosen, "The Influence of Bruno Bauer on Marx's Concept of Alienation," *Social Theory and Practice*, 1 (1970), 50–68.

[71] Bauer, *Das entdeckte Christenthum*, pp. 72–80; *Christianity Exposed*, pp. 67–71.

[72] Bauer, *Das entdeckte Christenthum*, pp. 75f.; *Christianity Exposed*, p. 70.

religion is a misfortune and a self-division [*Selbstentzweiung*] of humanity."[73]
It is therefore ill-advised to transfer the name of religion to other spheres.

The key to overcoming alienation is not religion since that is the very cause
of it. Religion will never be able to bring people together since its very nature
separates them. Therefore we should aim not merely to reform religion, which
has become corrupt over time, but to eliminate it altogether since the problem
of alienation lies at its very root. Feuerbach believes that if we can just eliminate
the idea of a transcendent God, it would still be possible to rescue the key
aspect of Christianity, which is Christian love. Bauer rejects this claim.
Christian love is in fact hate. It prevents people from connecting with other
people. It instead divides people into believers and nonbelievers and hostile
sects. There is thus no point in trying to retain some aspect of Christianity. The
solution to modern alienation can only be achieved with its elimination.

## 5.6   Religion and Historical Development

In examining the contradictions of the religious consciousness, Bauer reveals
his debt to Hegel's understanding of the nature of historical change. He notes
that the contradictions are not accidental. Instead, they are a natural part of
human development, which is characterized by the continuous overcoming of
contradictions. Following Hegel, he claims, "it lies in the nature and destin-
ation of humans that in their historical development they must come to odds
with themselves and drive this contradiction to extremes before they are able to
achieve self-harmony."[74] Here we can see Hegel's dialectical methodology,
according to which there is an original unity, then a separation or alienation,
and finally a reconciliation in a higher unity. Bauer explains that this means
that humans are not born with a fixed human nature right from the start.
Instead, this is something that develops over time: "The human being as
a human is not a product of nature but the work of his own freedom."[75]
Through their education and upbringing, humans must learn to control their
natural desires and to develop their higher faculties. Humans are thus the
result of a process that is both personal and historical.

In religion people posit a divinity – something nonhuman. This is
a necessary step in human development. People must first see the human
in something external, foreign to themselves, and only later realize that this is
a reflection of their own nature. Thus to become fully human, this external
other must be overcome. This is a process of human liberation and self-
actualization. On this point Bauer seems clearly to follow Feuerbach's
account.

---

[73]   Bauer, *Das entdeckte Christenthum*, p. 38; *Christianity Exposed*, p. 35.
[74]   Bauer, *Das entdeckte Christenthum*, p. 78; *Christianity Exposed*, p. 73.
[75]   Bauer, *Das entdeckte Christenthum*, pp. 78f.; *Christianity Exposed*, pp. 73f.

The basic law of human history is the old Greek motto that humans must come to know themselves. Again following Hegel, Bauer claims that the course of history is the story of this process. Humans become aware of themselves in the sense that they realize that they, and not some external deity, are the locus of truth. But as Hegel indicated, the path is not an easy or straightforward one. There are many difficulties that are experienced along the way. The oppression caused by religion is one of these that must be overcome before humans can reach their full potential.

Bauer criticizes the abovementioned theologian August Neander for his failure to understand key elements of Hegel's thought. Neander had attacked the Hegelians for reifying the Idea or the Concept, which, it is claimed, amounts to a form of self-deification. Bauer grants in the first instance that there was a tendency in Hegel to give too much importance to abstract ideas. However, this has been corrected by the subsequent work of people like Feuerbach. This new work has returned from abstract ideas to the human sphere:

> Modern criticism has finally brought the human to himself. It made him get to know himself, it freed humans from their illusions and got to know self-consciousness as the sole and creative power of the universe – as the universe itself. Should modern criticism reminisce to idolize humanity, that is, to alienate himself and teach people to pray to their chimerical, inflated, distorted image? It has rather proved that especially in religion the human idolizes himself and that means he has lost himself and prays to his own loss.[76]

Far from deifying itself by means of abstract ideas, philosophy has undermined the self-deification involved in projecting the human image onto the divine. Modern philosophy has shown that this is the source of alienation and tries to correct it. Bauer quotes from the account of the origin of religious belief in Holbach's *System of Nature*.[77] The view sketched in the quotations is strikingly reminiscent of that of Feuerbach. Bauer's gloss on this is as follows: "Then God is only the human being alienated from humanity [*der den Menschen entfremdete Mensch*] and as such cannot let go of humanity."[78] The idea of God is simply that of a "fantastic, chimerical human."[79] It is thus the theologians and not the Hegelians who are guilty of self-deification since it is the former who have created the fictional idea of God from their own human image.

Bauer continues his discussion of Holbach's *System of Nature* and praises the materialist view that the work puts forth. He provocatively hails atheism as

[76] Bauer, *Das entdeckte Christenthum*, pp. 105f.; *Christianity Exposed*, p. 102.
[77] Bauer, *Das entdeckte Christenthum*, pp. 106f.; *Christianity Exposed*, pp. 102f.; [Baron d'Holbach], *Système de la Nature ou Des Loix du Monde Physique et du Monde Moral*.
[78] Bauer, *Das entdeckte Christenthum*, p. 107; *Christianity Exposed*, p. 103.
[79] Bauer, *Das entdeckte Christenthum*, p. 107; *Christianity Exposed*, p. 103.

"the first liberation of humanity, of eternal meaning."[80] The idea is that religion has oppressed the human being since time immemorial. Now, with the rejection of the idea of God, it is possible to realize our true human potential and escape from the tyranny of the Church and its belief system. However, while Bauer recognizes the historical importance of the rise of scientific materialism and its criticism of religion, he believes it has a shortcoming. Materialism reduces human beings to objects of nature with no free will. It fails to account for human culture, history, and social and political life. It does not fully understand the nature of human self-consciousness as developed in Hegel's philosophy. This seems to be a part of Bauer's answer to the question that he raised at the outset about why the Enlightenment did not manage to sustain and complete its critical mission. Bauer's criticism of materialism and adherence to idealism is a key point in Marx's criticism of him. Marx claims that despite Bauer's radicality, he still clings to the abstractions of idealism and has yet to see the truth of a fully materialist view.

Bauer ends the work with a triumphant tone. His point seems to be that Hegelian philosophy will complete the work of the Enlightenment and will ultimately free humanity from the oppression of religion. Following Hegel's account of the development of freedom in history, he writes, "self-consciousness has arrived at the certainty of its freedom" and "[i]t will overcome the world with freedom."[81] The historical process thus allows humans to realize their humanity fully after millennia of oppression. The work of the Enlightenment is thus being completed in his own day, as people throw off the last vestiges of religion. This is the nature of the current crisis of the age. Then, departing from Hegel, Bauer claims, "After the crisis, history will no longer be religious, no longer Christian."[82] The self-realization of human beings and the overcoming of religious alienation mean leaving behind Christianity. Bauer takes this to be the work of his age.

## 5.7 The Radicalism of Bauer's Criticism

Feuerbach's criticism of Christianity and his analysis of the origin of religion with the idea of projection seemed radical to the readers of the time. Bauer agrees with it to a large extent. According to his view, Feuerbach's understanding of the nature of God as a form of self-alienation is entirely accurate. Bauer writes, "Can there be anything more contradictory than that a free being closes himself off from his own being and turns his own existence over

---

[80] Bauer, *Das entdeckte Christenthum*, p. 111; *Christianity Exposed*, p. 108.
[81] Bauer, *Das entdeckte Christenthum*, p. 119; *Christianity Exposed*, p. 117.
[82] Bauer, *Das entdeckte Christenthum*, p. 119; *Christianity Exposed*, p. 117.

to a foreign subject whose depraved slave he becomes and from whose grace he lives?"[83]

However, Bauer's alternative theory goes even further. While Feuerbach attempts to see the human element in religion and thereby to reconcile the human sphere with the divine, Bauer's conclusion is just the opposite. While, to be sure, the idea of God and religion is an entirely human invention, it is a form of oppression that must be rejected since no reconciliation is possible. Bauer's view is that in Christianity, we as humans completely lose ourselves. It alienates us from our very essence as human beings: our freedom, rationality, etc. It is thus necessary to reject religion entirely if we are to develop as humans. Complete liberation can only occur with the complete destruction of religion and the oppression that it creates.

While Feuerbach tries to preserve what he takes to be the key element in Christianity, Bauer can find no redeeming feature in it whatsoever. Feuerbach wants to eliminate the transcendent element of Christianity but maintain the idea of Christian love, which he takes to be beneficial. Bauer, on the contrary, thinks that this too is an illusion and that Christian love is sheer hypocrisy. It does not help us to overcome alienation but just the opposite since it turns to hatred of others. Religion dehumanizes us; that is, it robs us of our very humanity.

While Feuerbach thus wants to maintain Christianity in a modified form, Bauer openly declares his own atheism. The only solution to the oppression caused by Christianity is to eliminate it altogether. While Strauss and Feuerbach reject Hegel's idealism, Bauer maintains it. He claims that "criticism" is the tool that is needed to disabuse people of the errors of religion. It will strip religion of its historical contingencies and allow us to see the conceptual truth beneath.[84] The proper development of reason, our critical faculty, is the key to overcoming human alienation. This continued interest in what Hegel calls the Idea and the Concept is one of the main things that Marx objects to in his criticism of Bauer.

Strauss, Feuerbach, and Bauer all became famous very young and early in their careers. After the controversies surrounding their works, they were excluded from academic life. Then over time they all gradually faded away as they got older. This is not coincidental. It tells us something about the times in which they lived. In their youth, there was something exciting and innovative about the criticism of religion that they were proposing. But then, as they grew older, this became more and more commonplace and lost something of its novelty. By the time they were old men, it was no longer scandalous to criticize religion.

Bauer's theory also anticipates Marx's views on the nature of alienation in religion. Bauer clearly sees how political power makes use of religion to

---

[83] Bauer, *Das entdeckte Christenthum*, p. 78; *Christianity Exposed*, p. 73.
[84] See Brazill, *The Young Hegelians*, p. 199.

advance its own agenda. The state employs religion as a tool of manipulation and oppression of the people it governs. The difference between their positions is one of focus. For Bauer, religion is the key issue that determines things in the social order. By contrast, for Marx, it was the other way around. It was the fundamental economic and political realities that determined everything, including religion. Thus while Marx agreed with Bauer's atheism, he disagreed with his use of it as an explanatory tool in the understanding of history and the social order.

Bauer's work represents a good case in point of how closely connected religion was to philosophy during this period. Indeed, in his case they were indistinguishable. The questions of the conceptual meaning of the divine, the nature of mythology, and the role of history in religion all have philosophical implications. Bauer is equally important for the history of philosophy and for the history of biblical criticism.

# PART III

## The Second Generation

# 6

# Marx's View of Religious and Political Liberation

Another towering figure in the history of nineteenth-century philosophy was Karl Marx (1818–1883).[1] Beginning in 1836, Marx attended the University of Berlin, where, following in the footsteps of his father, he studied law. When he arrived in the Prussian capital, Hegel had been dead for five years, but there were still active discussions about his philosophy among his students. As noted in Chapter 5, Marx attended the lectures of, among others, the young Bruno Bauer, with whom he struck up a friendship. He also took courses from Eduard Gans, whose main interest was Hegel's political philosophy. In a letter to his father from November of 1837, Marx reports on his first year of studies in Berlin. He begins by talking dramatically about arriving at a turning point in his life. He then goes on to tell how he became caught up in the mood of excitement about Hegel's philosophy: "I got to know Hegel from beginning toend, together with most of his disciples."[2] He recounts having long discussions with fellow students, and during this time he became a part of the aforementioned "Doctors' Club," where Hegel's philosophy was the subject of endless debate. Marx was reported to be a very intense and passionate

---

[1] For Marx's life and times, see Isaiah Berlin, *Karl Marx: His Life and Environment* (New York: Oxford University Press, 1959); Franz Mehring, *Karl Marx: The Story of His Life*, trans. by Edward Fitzgerald (Ann Arbor: University of Michigan Press, 1962); Otto Rühle, *Karl Marx: His Life and Work* (London: George Allen & Unwin Ltd., 1929); Leopold Schwarzschild, *The Red Prussian* (New York: Charles Scribners, 1947); Boris Nicolaevsky and Otto Mänchen-Helfen, *Karl Marx: Man and Fighter* (London: Methuen, 1936); Maximilien Rubel and Margaret Manale, *Marx without Myth: A Chronological Study of His Life and Work* (New York: Harper & Row, 1975). For useful introductions to the thought of Marx, see Louis Dupré, *The Philosophical Foundations of Marxism* (New York: Harcourt Brace Jovanovich, 1966); Erich Fromm, *Marx's Concept of Man* (New York: Frederick Ungar Publishing, 1961); Shlomo Avineri, *The Social and Political Thought of Karl Marx* (Cambridge: Cambridge University Press, 1968); Louis Althusser, *For Marx*, trans. by Ben Brewster (New York: Vintage, 1970); Michael Quante and David P. Schweikard (eds.), *Marx Handbuch: Leben, Werke, Wirkung* (Stuttgart: J. B. Metzler, 2016).

[2] "Brief an den Vater in Trier," Berlin, den 10ten November [1837], in *Marx-Engels-Werke*, vols. 1–46, ed. by the Institut für Marxismus-Leninismus (Berlin: Dietz, 1956–2018), vol. 40, p. 10. (English translation: "Letter from Marx to His Father in Trier," in *Marx/Engels Collected Works*, vols. 1–50 [Moscow: Progress Publishers, 1975–2004], vol. 1, p. 19.)

person, often working through the night.[3] When his father died in 1838, Marx gave up the idea of becoming a lawyer and dedicated himself entirely to philosophy.

In 1841 Marx completed his dissertation on Greek philosophy (*The Difference between the Democritean and Epicurean Philosophies of Nature*), for which he received his PhD as an external student from the University of Jena. He initially hoped to obtain a position at the University of Bonn, but his radical reputation and his association with left Hegelians such as Bruno Bauer prevented him from obtaining academic employment. Instead, in 1842 he moved to Cologne and became an editor for the newspaper the *Rheinische Zeitung*. When the newspaper was subjected to severe censorship laws and the authorities threatened to shut it down, Marx resigned his position and moved to Paris in November 1843.

With his collaborator Arnold Ruge, he began publication of the *Deutsch-Französische Jahrbücher* in 1843. It was during this time that Marx began his collaboration with Friedrich Engels, who was living in England at the time. Their first joint work was a criticism of Bruno Bauer under the title *The Holy Family*, which appeared in 1845. In Paris, Marx came into contact with Joseph-Pierre Proudhon, Mikhail Bakunin, and Heinrich Heine. Since the *Jahrbücher* were highly critical of Prussia, the Prussian authorities asked France to expel Marx, a request with which the French happily complied, forcing Marx to leave the country in January of 1845.

Marx then moved with his family to Brussels, where he worked with Engels on *The German Ideology*, a text that was only published posthumously. In July 1845 Marx accompanied Engels to England, where he spent six months. In 1846 they founded the Communist Correspondence Committee, which was in contact with communists throughout Europe. Later, after the Communist League was formed, their group became the Brussels chapter of that organization. In 1847 Marx, again together with Engels, wrote *The Communist Manifesto* for the fledgling Communist League. He traveled to London in November of 1847 for the Second Congress of the organization. The Revolution of 1848 broke out, and for his active encouragement of the uprising, he was arrested in Brussels and expelled from Belgium.

After a short stay in Paris, Marx returned to Cologne, where he briefly edited the *Neue Rheinische Zeitung*. After a series of radical articles, many of the shareholders of the newspaper withdrew their support and left it in a financial crisis. In September of 1848 the journal was shut down, and many of its editors, including Engels, left Cologne in order to avoid being arrested. The journal resumed publication but was soon in trouble again. In May of 1849 Marx was expelled from Prussia and forced into exile.

---

[3]  At the end of his aforementioned letter to his father, Marx apologizes for his handwriting, saying that it is four o'clock in the morning and he cannot see any more since the candle has burnt itself out.

In August of 1849 he moved to London, where he spent the rest of his life. During this time his financial situation would have been dire if it had not been for the generous assistance of Engels, who had money from his family's textile mills. Marx worked long hours in the reading room of the British Museum and had very little contact with the English. In 1859 he published *A Contribution to the Critique of Political Economy*. In 1864 he played a key role in founding the International Working Men's Association, which held a series of periodical congresses. For years he labored quietly on his magnum opus, *Capital*, a massive work that he never finished. The first volume appeared in 1867, and the second and third volumes were published posthumously by Engels. During the last decades of his life, Marx's work began to be increasingly influential as translations of *Capital* became available in French and Russian. This corresponded to the rise of the workers' movement, which embraced his ideas. Marx died in London in 1883, never knowing the enormous impact his thought would have.

Marx's oeuvre is a complex matter.[4] Although he was a tireless writer, he had difficulty finishing projects that he started. As a result, some of what are regarded today as his most famous works, such as *The German Ideology*, are in fact unfinished texts that were not known during his lifetime and were only published after his death. The massive edition of the collected writings of Marx and Engels, the *Marx-Engels-Gesamtausgabe*, was launched in 1975 and is still ongoing.[5]

### 6.1   Marx's Religious Inspiration and the Task of Philosophy

Marx published his "Introduction to the Contribution to the Critique of Hegel's *Philosophy of Right*" in the *Deutsch-Französische Jahrbücher* in 1844 when he was living in Paris.[6] This explains why the article is full of comparisons of French and German history and politics. He had apparently conceived this to be a part of a monograph-length manuscript on Hegel's political philosophy based on Hegel's *Elements of the Philosophy of Right or Natural Law and Political Science*

---

[4] For the complex history of publication of the works of Marx and Engels, see Karl Marx, *The Marx-Engels Reader*, ed. by Robert C. Tucker (New York and London: W. W. Norton & Company, 1978), pp. xxxix–xlii.

[5] Karl Marx, *Marx-Engels-Gesamtausgabe*, vols. 1– (Berlin: Dietz, 1975ff) (commonly abbreviated as *MEGA*). See also the invaluable English translation: *Marx/Engels Collected Works*, vols. 1–50 (Moscow: Progress Publishers, 1975–2004) (commonly abbreviated *MECW*). See also *Marx-Engels-Werke*, vols. 1–46.

[6] Karl Marx, "Zur Kritik der Hegel'schen Rechts-Philosophie. Einleitung," *Deutsch-Französische Jahrbücher*, 1–2 (1844), 71–85. (English translation: "Contribution to the Critique of Hegel's *Philosophy of Right*: Introduction," in *The Marx-Engels Reader*, ed. by Robert C. Tucker [New York and London: W. W. Norton & Company, 1978], pp. 53–65.)

*in Outline.*[7] While he never managed to complete or publish the full text, parts of his manuscript do survive, which include his commentary on sections 261–313 of Hegel's book.[8] His "Introduction to the Contribution to the Critique of Hegel's *Philosophy of Right*" is an important statement of his relation to both Hegel and Feuerbach.[9] While he clearly appreciates Hegel, Marx in this text perhaps owes an even deeper debt to Feuerbach.[10] Indeed, Marx sent a copy of the published piece to Feuerbach and in the accompanying letter openly acknowledges Feuerbach as a source of inspiration. He tells Feuerbach that his readings provide "a philosophical basis for socialism."[11]

Marx begins with the claim that "the criticism of religion has been largely completed,"[12] and by this he refers to the work of Feuerbach, but presumably also to that of David Friedrich Strauss and Bruno Bauer. The issues concerning the philosophy of religion had been the main points of contention concerning the proper interpretation of Hegel's philosophy in the 1830s and early 1840s. These discussions, as we have seen, ended in a radical criticism of traditional understandings of Christianity. Marx welcomes and salutes the achievements made in this area.

He can be seen to take up where Feuerbach left off. He echoes Feuerbach's thesis about the divine being a reflection of human qualities, writing, "Man, who has found in the fantastic reality of heaven, where he sought a supernatural being, only his own reflection, will no longer be tempted to find only the

[7] G. W. F. Hegel, *Naturrecht und Staatswissenschaft im Grundrisse. Grundlinien der Philosophie des Rechts* (Berlin: Nicolaische Buchhandlung, 1821). (English translation: *Elements of the Philosophy of Right*, trans. by H. B. Nisbet, ed. by Allen Wood [Cambridge and New York: Cambridge University Press, 1991].)

[8] Marx, "Zur Kritik der Hegelschen Rechtsphilosophie," in *Marx-Engels-Werke*, vol. 1, pp. 201–333. (English translation: *Critique of Hegel's "Philosophy of Right,"* trans. by Annette Jolin and Joseph O'Malley [Cambridge: Cambridge University Press, 1970].)

[9] For Marx's complex relation to Hegel and Hegelianism, see Norman Levine, *Divergent Paths: The Hegelian Foundations of Marx's Method* (Lanham and Oxford: Lexington Books, 2006); David McLellan, *The Young Hegelians and Karl Marx* (New York: F. A. Praeger, 1969); Lucio Colletti, *Marxism and Hegel*, trans. by Lawrence Garner (London: New Left Books, 1973); Tom Rockmore, *Marx after Marxism: The Philosophy of Karl Marx* (Oxford: Blackwell, 2002).

[10] For Marx's relation to Feuerbach, see Klaus Bockmühl, *Leiblichkeit und Gesellschaft. Studien zur Religionskritik und Anthropologie im Frühwerk von Ludwig Feuerbach und Karl Marx* (Göttingen: Vandenhoeck & Ruprecht, 1961); Robert C. Tucker, *Philosophy and Myth in Karl Marx* (Cambridge: Cambridge University Press, 1972), pp. 95–105; Werner Schuffenhauer, *Feuerbach und der junge Marx. Zur Entstehungsgeschichte der marxistischen Weltanschauung*, 2nd revised ed. (Berlin: VEB Deutscher Verlag der Wissenschaften, 1972).

[11] "Marx an Ludwig Feuerbach in Bruckberg, Paris, d. 11 August 1844," in *Marx-Engels-Werke*, vol. 27, p. 425. (English translation: "To Ludwig Feuerbach in Bruckberg, Paris, August 11, 1844," in *Marx/Engels Collected Works*, vol. 3, p. 354.)

[12] Marx, "Zur Kritik der Hegel'schen Rechts-Philosophie. Einleitung," p. 71; "Contribution to the Critique of Hegel's *Philosophy of Right*: Introduction," p. 53.

semblance of himself – a non-human being – where he seeks and must seek his true reality."[13] In other words, once people have realized the truth of Feuerbach's claim, they will no longer have recourse to imaginary deities, and their focus will no longer be on heaven but on the world of actuality here and now.

Like Feuerbach and Bauer, Marx sees religion as an oppressive force that needs to be overcome. People have recourse to superstition when they are oppressed, and religion gives them solace by redirecting their attention to the illusory world of God in heaven. In a famous passage, he writes, "*Religious* suffering is at the same time an *expression* of real suffering and a *protest* against real suffering. Religion is the sigh of the oppressed creature, the sentiment of a heartless world, and the soul of soulless conditions. It is the *opium* of the people."[14] Religion contributes to human oppression insofar as it presents illusions and fantasies that provide people with a misguided sense of hope. Like Feuerbach, Marx thinks that the goal should rather be to direct that energy to the real world and attempt to address the root causes of human suffering and oppression there. It is only when the illusions are eliminated that one can go to work on the real problems: "The abolition of religion as the *illusory* happiness of men is a demand for their *real* happiness."[15]

While we are used to associating Marx more or less exclusively with social-political philosophy and economics, this text shows that he, surprisingly, draws a large part of the inspiration for his thinking from the contemporary discussions about the philosophy of religion that stem from Hegel. Indeed, he takes the idea of emancipation in the sphere of religion as his model for a general emancipation of humanity in the social and political spheres. In the first line of this article, he claims "the criticism of religion is the premise of all criticism,"[16] which means that people such as Feuerbach and Strauss are not only criticizing traditional forms of religion but are also paving the way for a broader criticism of society. Not an isolated element of human thought, religion is intimately connected to the rest of society.

For Feuerbach, the goal was to demonstrate that all the things that we know as God are in fact human qualities, and the task was to recognize this and embrace the human as something absolute. Marx echoes this when he declares, "It is the *task of history*, therefore, once the *other-world of truth* has vanished, to establish the *truth of this world*."[17] Likewise, Feuerbach wanted to help people

---

[13] Marx, "Zur Kritik der Hegel'schen Rechts-Philosophie. Einleitung," p. 71; "Contribution to the Critique of Hegel's *Philosophy of Right*: Introduction," p. 53.

[14] Marx, "Zur Kritik der Hegel'schen Rechts-Philosophie. Einleitung," pp. 71f.; "Contribution to the Critique of Hegel's *Philosophy of Right*: Introduction," p. 54.

[15] Marx, "Zur Kritik der Hegel'schen Rechts-Philosophie. Einleitung," p. 72; "Contribution to the Critique of Hegel's *Philosophy of Right*: Introduction," p. 54.

[16] Marx, "Zur Kritik der Hegel'schen Rechts-Philosophie. Einleitung," p. 71; "Contribution to the Critique of Hegel's *Philosophy of Right*: Introduction," p. 53.

[17] Marx, "Zur Kritik der Hegel'schen Rechts-Philosophie. Einleitung," p. 72; "Contribution to the Critique of Hegel's *Philosophy of Right*: Introduction," p. 54.

to overcome religious alienation, which was the result of conceiving of God as a foreign, external entity, radically different from human beings. Marx then urges that we apply this line of thought to overcome the alienation that exists in society in general: "The immediate *task of philosophy*, which is in the service of history, is to unmask human self-alienation in its *secular form* now that it has been unmasked in its sacred form."[18] Like Heine, Marx has a clear sense that philosophy has a specific role to play in the contemporary crisis of the age, and in a certain sense their visions of that role are quite similar. As we will see, Marx also makes an appeal to philosophy to provide the theoretical underpinning of the revolutionary movement that will be actualized by the proletariat.

Marx clearly sees himself as following in the footsteps of Feuerbach and extending the latter's analysis from the sphere of religion to that of society in general. He writes, "the criticism of heaven is transformed into the criticism of earth, the *criticism of religion* into the *criticism of law*, and the *criticism of theology* into the *criticism of politics*."[19] This is, of course, an allusion to Bruno Bauer's program of universal "criticism" that was discussed in Chapter 5. Marx takes his work on Hegel's political philosophy to be an important step in this project. In these few pages one can begin to get a sense of the enormity of Feuerbach's influence on Marx's project in general.

In his Introduction to the "Contribution to the Critique of Hegel's *Philosophy of Right*," Marx issues a merciless criticism of politics in Prussia and the German states. He claims that the historical development there lags far behind that of France. In contrast to that country, Germany never had a revolution. Thus he associates the current governments in Germany with the *ancien régime* in pre-revolutionary France.[20] He regards the current state of political affairs in Germany and Prussia as reactionary and comical.[21]

But while he has nothing but negative things to say about politics in Germany, Marx is in many ways positively disposed toward German philosophy, which he takes to be theoretically well ahead of the actual historical development. German philosophy can be regarded as having kept up with the times, in contrast with German politics.[22] While in practical terms the Germans were stuck with a reactionary political situation, in their work on political philosophy they were able to advance beyond this and point in the

---

[18] Marx, "Zur Kritik der Hegel'schen Rechts-Philosophie. Einleitung," p. 72; "Contribution to the Critique of Hegel's *Philosophy of Right*: Introduction," p. 54.

[19] Marx, "Zur Kritik der Hegel'schen Rechts-Philosophie. Einleitung," p. 72; "Contribution to the Critique of Hegel's *Philosophy of Right*: Introduction," p. 54.

[20] Marx, "Zur Kritik der Hegel'schen Rechts-Philosophie. Einleitung," p. 74; "Contribution to the Critique of Hegel's *Philosophy of Right*: Introduction," p. 56.

[21] Marx, "Zur Kritik der Hegel'schen Rechts-Philosophie. Einleitung," p. 75; "Contribution to the Critique of Hegel's *Philosophy of Right*: Introduction," p. 57.

[22] Marx, "Zur Kritik der Hegel'schen Rechts-Philosophie. Einleitung," pp. 76f.; "Contribution to the Critique of Hegel's *Philosophy of Right*: Introduction," p. 58.

MARX'S VIEW OF RELIGIOUS AND POLITICAL LIBERATION     149

direction of a more progressive view. Marx hails Hegel as the leading figure in this regard: "This criticism of the German philosophy of right and of the state ... was given its most logical, profound and complete expression by Hegel."[23]

But unfortunately this development is one that has only remained theoretical. He explains, "In politics, the Germans have *thought* what other nations have *done*. Germany has been their *theoretical consciousness*."[24] What German philosophy has lacked, according to Marx, is a practical side, and he sees it as his task to provide this: "the criticism of the speculative philosophy of right does not remain within its sphere, but leads on to tasks which can only be solved by *means of practical activity*."[25] Marx claims that his philosophy will not be satisfied with just developing a theoretical structure but instead will be concerned with actualizing this in the real world by means of the action of real human beings. Here one can hear an echo of Feuerbach's criticism of Hegel's philosophy as overly abstract. Moreover, from this perspective Hegel's philosophy appears complacent or disinterested in the events in the real world. Once again we can recall here Hegel's comments at the end of his *Lectures on the Philosophy of Religion* about the reconciliation of philosophical thought despite the enduring alienation in the real world. An obvious source of inspiration for the motif of a German philosophical revolution or revolution of thought in comparison to the real French Revolution was Heine's *On the History of Religion and Philosophy in Germany*. As we have seen,[26] in this work Heine develops in some detail exactly this comparison and in the final pages predicts a coming revolution in the German states.

Marx thus makes even more explicit Feuerbach's view that philosophy should have some practical result and specifically that it should aim at the liberation of humanity. Alluding indirectly to Feuerbach, Marx explains, "The criticism of religion ends with the doctrine that man is the supreme being for man. It ends, therefore, with the categorical imperative to overthrow all those conditions in which man is an abased, enslaved, abandoned, contemptible being."[27] While philosophy cannot in itself cause a revolution, Marx believes it can play an important role in one by making the masses aware of the injustices that they suffer from. Moreover, the revolution in Germany can already be

---

[23] Marx, "Zur Kritik der Hegel'schen Rechts-Philosophie. Einleitung," p. 78; "Contribution to the Critique of Hegel's *Philosophy of Right*: Introduction," p. 59.

[24] Marx, "Zur Kritik der Hegel'schen Rechts-Philosophie. Einleitung," p. 78; "Contribution to the Critique of Hegel's *Philosophy of Right*: Introduction," p. 59.

[25] Marx, "Zur Kritik der Hegel'schen Rechts-Philosophie. Einleitung," p. 78; "Contribution to the Critique of Hegel's *Philosophy of Right*: Introduction," p. 60.

[26] See Chapter 3, Sections 3.1–3.3.

[27] Marx, "Zur Kritik der Hegel'schen Rechts-Philosophie. Einleitung," p. 79; "Contribution to the Critique of Hegel's *Philosophy of Right*: Introduction," p. 60.

thought to have begun with the criticism of religion that aims to undermine repressive religious illusions.[28]

In order for the theoretical side of German philosophy to become real in the context of revolutionary action, the theory needs practical action carried out by the oppressed class of people, the workers, or, as Marx says, the proletariat. Philosophy can make them aware of the sources of their oppression and stimulate them to action. The proletariat as a class can then work as a representative of society in general for positive social change.[29] Marx claims that the proletariat class during his time is being formed in Germany in step with the process of industrialization. But as this process moves forward, the proletariat will increase in power and constitute a viable revolutionary force. Thus Marx concludes that philosophy and the proletariat will work together as reciprocal elements in the revolutionary movement: "just as philosophy finds its material *weapons* in the proletariat, so the proletariat finds its *intellectual* weapons in philosophy."[30] Marx repeats his claim that the key is to bring into action and practice the insight that Feuerbach provided in the sphere of religion, specifically, "The emancipation of Germany is only possible in practice if one adopts the point of view of that theory according to which man is the highest being for man."[31] So, for Marx, it is not just a matter of improving working conditions or the physical welfare of the proletariat class, but it is also a matter of disabusing them of the illusions of religion, which is a condition for their liberation in the social-economic sphere.

## 6.2    Alienated Labor

Marx wrote the so-called "Economic and Philosophic Manuscripts" between April and August 1844, also while he was living in Paris.[32] It was apparently a draft for a book. He never published this work in his lifetime, but it remained among his papers and was published posthumously. The manuscripts clearly represent work in progress. Although many of the analyses remain to be developed, nonetheless the text contains a number of ideas of great interest,

[28] Marx, "Zur Kritik der Hegel'schen Rechts-Philosophie. Einleitung," p. 79; "Contribution to the Critique of Hegel's *Philosophy of Right*: Introduction," p. 60.

[29] Marx, "Zur Kritik der Hegel'schen Rechts-Philosophie. Einleitung," p. 81; "Contribution to the Critique of Hegel's *Philosophy of Right*: Introduction," p. 62.

[30] Marx, "Zur Kritik der Hegel'schen Rechts-Philosophie. Einleitung," p. 85; "Contribution to the Critique of Hegel's *Philosophy of Right*: Introduction," p. 65.

[31] Marx, "Zur Kritik der Hegel'schen Rechts-Philosophie. Einleitung," p. 85; "Contribution to the Critique of Hegel's *Philosophy of Right*: Introduction," p. 65.

[32] Karl Marx, "Ökonomisch-philosophische Manuskripte aus dem Jahre 1844," in *Marx-Engels-Werke*, vol. 40, pp. 465–588. (Partial English translation: "Economic and Philosophic Manuscripts of 1844," in *The Marx-Engels Reader*, pp. 66–125.) See the useful edition by Michael Quante, *Karl Marx. Ökonomisch-Philosophische Manuskripte. Kommentar von Michael Quante* (Frankfurt am Main: Suhrkamp, 2009).

including the theory of alienated labor.[33] Here we can see Marx applying ideas from Hegel and Feuerbach to the sphere of social-political philosophy.

He begins by explaining that this work is conceived as a continuation or supplement to his previous article, "Contribution to the Critique of Hegel's *Philosophy of Right.*" It is intended to contain a critical discussion of a number of topics such as law, ethics, and politics.[34] Marx lists the sources that he drew upon in the work, and here he mentions explicitly Feuerbach and Hegel.[35] He further indicates that his study will end with a critical account of Hegel's philosophy that differs from those currently in vogue among the so-called critical theologians, by which he means Bruno Bauer and his followers.

Under the heading "Alienated Labor" or "Estranged Labor," Marx examines four different forms of alienation. The first of these is the alienation of the product. According to Marx, the labor of the worker becomes objectified in their product, and this involves alienation.[36] The worker invests their skill, time, and energy in creating the product. But the product belongs to the owner of the factory and not the worker. Thus the product confronts the worker "as *something alien*" (*ein fremdes Wesen*)[37] or "an *alien* object" (*einem fremden Gegenstand*).[38] The worker is unable to identify with the product of their labor and take pride in it. It is not like a work of art or something that the worker would create of their own free volition; instead, it is something that they are obliged to produce in order to earn a living. The object takes on a specific meaning and value on its own, which is beyond the control of the worker. Since the worker does not own their product, they are not free to do with it what they wish. The value of the worker and their labor are reduced to the market value of the product. Marx explains that the more of themselves that the worker puts into their product, the more impoverished they become. This is illustrated by an analogy drawn directly from Feuerbach's theory of religious alienation: "It is the same in religion. The more man puts into God, the less he retains in himself. The worker puts his life into the object; but now his

---

[33]  For Marx's theory of alienation, see Bertell Ollman, *Alienation: Marx's Conception of Man in Capitalist Society* (New York: Cambridge University Press, 1971); Istvan Meszaros, *Marx's Theory of Alienation* (New York: Harper & Row, 1972); Allen W. Wood, "Part One, Alienation," in his *Karl Marx* (London: Routledge & Kegan Paul, 1981), pp. 1–59; Herbert Marcuse, "Marx: Alienated Labor," in his *Reason and Revolution: Hegel and the Rise of Social Theory* (Boston: Beacon, 1960), pp. 273–287.

[34]  Marx, "Ökonomisch-philosophische Manuskripte aus dem Jahre 1844," p. 467; "Economic and Philosophic Manuscripts of 1844," p. 67.

[35]  Marx, "Ökonomisch-philosophische Manuskripte aus dem Jahre 1844," p. 468; "Economic and Philosophic Manuscripts of 1844," p. 68.

[36]  Marx, "Ökonomisch-philosophische Manuskripte aus dem Jahre 1844," pp. 511f.; "Economic and Philosophic Manuscripts of 1844," pp. 71f.

[37]  Marx, "Ökonomisch-philosophische Manuskripte aus dem Jahre 1844," p. 511; "Economic and Philosophic Manuscripts of 1844," p. 71.

[38]  Marx, "Ökonomisch-philosophische Manuskripte aus dem Jahre 1844," p. 512; "Economic and Philosophic Manuscripts of 1844," p. 72.

life no longer belongs to him but to the object."[39] Marx uses the same language as Feuerbach with the term "objectification."

Since the product of the worker's labor becomes something external and independent, with a value of its own, the worker becomes dependent upon it. It is only through their labor and thus through their product that they can earn a living. They are obliged to continue to work in order to sustain themselves. The worker is thus made into a "slave of his object" and subjected to the "bondage" of the marketplace.[40] But this reduces the worker simply to a creature with only certain basic physical needs. In Hegel's language, the full conception and appreciation of "personhood" is lacking. The individual is regarded simply as an object of nature and is deprived of the higher aspects of spirit.[41]

Marx then introduces the second form of alienation, that is, alienation from the act of production.[42] The worker is alienated not only from the product of their labor but also from the process of producing it. We like to think that we can use the time allotted to us in life as we wish. However, we are compelled out of economic necessity to surrender a large part of our time and energy to someone else who hires us to do a job. When we are working for the other person, our time is no longer our own, and we cannot do what we would like. Instead, for that time the owner tells us what we should do since they own our time and energy. The worker understandably finds no sense of pleasure or satisfaction in the work that they are assigned to do. The work itself is demeaning and does not speak to their true self or their inner being. The work does not provide the worker with the possibility of developing their own skills and faculties in a meaningful and constructive manner. The worker disdains the work itself and performs it only out of economic distress. In short, the work also has an alien character that the worker does not identify with. Again Marx draws an analogy to Feuerbach's theory of religion: "Just as in religion the spontaneous activity of the human imagination, of the human brain and heart, operates independently of the individual – that is, operates on him as an alien, divine or diabolical activity – in the same way the worker's activity is not his spontaneous activity. It belongs to another; it is the loss of his self."[43] According to Feuerbach, it is the human mind that projects a conception of God as an external entity that then determines and controls human activity, as it were, from the

---

[39] Marx, "Ökonomisch-philosophische Manuskripte aus dem Jahre 1844," p. 512; "Economic and Philosophic Manuscripts of 1844," p. 72.

[40] Marx, "Ökonomisch-philosophische Manuskripte aus dem Jahre 1844," p. 513; "Economic and Philosophic Manuscripts of 1844," p. 73.

[41] Marx, "Ökonomisch-philosophische Manuskripte aus dem Jahre 1844," p. 513; "Economic and Philosophic Manuscripts of 1844," p. 73.

[42] Marx, "Ökonomisch-philosophische Manuskripte aus dem Jahre 1844," p. 514; "Economic and Philosophic Manuscripts of 1844," pp. 73f.

[43] Marx, "Ökonomisch-philosophische Manuskripte aus dem Jahre 1844," p. 514; "Economic and Philosophic Manuscripts of 1844," p. 74.

outside. For Marx, the same dynamic takes place in the activity of labor. Workers perform the labor, which originally is their own, but, due to the social institutions and market forces, it confronts them as something alien and belongs to someone else. Just like Feuerbach's conception of God, this alienated activity of labor negatively determines many aspects of human life.

The third form of alienation is, according to Marx, self-alienation.[44] Here the worker feels alienated from their own essence. In this context Marx draws on Feuerbach's term, referring to humans as "a species being."[45] Human essence involves the desire to use objects of nature and to transform them into something else. There is a fundamental human impulse that is evident even in the youngest children to create and to make things. This is human nature. We desire to create regardless of whether this will make us any money or provide us with any other material benefit. However, in labor relations, this basic human nature – or, as Marx says, the "universality of man" – becomes distorted.[46] The laborer is now obliged to work and to create out of economic necessity. They do not do so freely as an expression of their species being or human nature, but instead they have to do it. In this way, when people work, they feel alienated from themselves in the sense that they feel alienated from their true human nature. They would prefer to work freely and spontaneously in a context of their own choosing, rather than under compulsion and duress. Work, which should be interesting and gratifying, is reduced simply to fulfilling a basic need to eat and survive physically.

Here Marx can be seen to be drawing on Hegel's understanding of what it is to be a human being. Marx writes, "The whole character of a species – its species character – is contained in the character of its life-activity; and free, conscious activity is man's species character."[47] To be fully human means not merely to exist physically but rather to be a free human being able to use one's rationality and judgment to determine one's actions. Being human thus means more than merely physical survival as with the animals. While animals in a sense work to fulfill their basic natural needs, humans produce for its own sake even when the production is irrelevant for the fulfillment of the natural needs or goes far beyond what is required to meet them. With humans there is much more to life than mere physical existence: "Man makes his life-activity itself the object of his will and of his consciousness."[48] Humans have the ability

---

[44] Marx, "Ökonomisch-philosophische Manuskripte aus dem Jahre 1844," p. 515; "Economic and Philosophic Manuscripts of 1844," p. 75.

[45] Marx, "Ökonomisch-philosophische Manuskripte aus dem Jahre 1844," p. 515; "Economic and Philosophic Manuscripts of 1844," p. 75.

[46] Marx, "Ökonomisch-philosophische Manuskripte aus dem Jahre 1844," p. 515; "Economic and Philosophic Manuscripts of 1844," p. 75.

[47] Marx, "Ökonomisch-philosophische Manuskripte aus dem Jahre 1844," p. 516; "Economic and Philosophic Manuscripts of 1844," p. 76.

[48] Marx, "Ökonomisch-philosophische Manuskripte aus dem Jahre 1844," p. 516; "Economic and Philosophic Manuscripts of 1844," p. 76.

to freely think and create without any further motivation than this. They can also decide how to earn their living, but, for Marx, when we are forced into demeaning jobs just to survive, we are alienated from our human nature and our life-activity. This deprives us of our freedom and the use of our rationality. This discussion recalls Hegel's analysis of the Fall, where he made a similar point that the curse of Adam having to earn his living through hard work is precisely what separates humans from animals and thus should not be conceived as a curse.[49] To work in a free and fulfilling way of one's own choosing is to be human. Thus to subject the worker to the conditions of labor in capitalism is to deprive them of their humanity and to reduce them to the level of an animal.

The fourth and final form of alienation is that between one human being and another.[50] Since the worker is alienated from the products of their own labor, so also they are alienated from the products of other people. These products also confront the worker as something alien in the world. The worker does not, so to speak, find themselves in another person. They cannot see in other people the fulfillment of their common species being. Moreover, once again, the product of the worker belongs not to them but to the factory owner who employs them. The worker is thus alienated from the owner. Here Marx draws on Hegel's theory of recognition: "man's relation to himself only becomes objective and real for him through his relation to the other man."[51] But the negative recognition that the worker receives from the owner resembles that which the slave receives from the master. This leads Marx to an analysis of the alienated relation between the capitalist and the laborer, and in this we find the beginnings of Marx's theory of the conflict of the classes.

### 6.3　Marx's Criticism of Hegel's Philosophy

In the section of the "Economic and Philosophical Manuscripts" entitled "Critique of the Hegelian Dialectic and Philosophy as a Whole," Marx gives a detailed critical analysis primarily of The Phenomenology of Spirit.[52] At the outset Marx claims that many sympathetic readers of Hegel, such as David Friedrich Strauss and Bruno Bauer, have remained uncritical with regard to

---

[49] Genesis 3:17–18. See G. W. F. Hegel, Vorlesungen über die Philosophie der Religion, Parts I–III, ed. by Walter Jaeschke (Hamburg: Felix Meiner, 1983–1985, 1993–1995), Part II, Die Bestimmte Religion, vol. 4a, p. 340n. (English translation: Lectures on the Philosophy of Religion, vols. 1–3, ed. by Peter C. Hodgson, trans. by Robert F. Brown, P. C. Hodgson, and J. M. Stewart with the assistance of H. S. Harris [Berkeley: University of California Press, 1984–1987], vol. 2, Determinate Religion, p. 440n.)

[50] Marx, "Ökonomisch-philosophische Manuskripte aus dem Jahre 1844," pp. 517f.; "Economic and Philosophic Manuscripts of 1844," p. 77.

[51] Marx, "Ökonomisch-philosophische Manuskripte aus dem Jahre 1844," p. 519; "Economic and Philosophic Manuscripts of 1844," p. 78.

[52] Marx, "Ökonomisch-philosophische Manuskripte aus dem Jahre 1844," pp. 568–588; "Economic and Philosophic Manuscripts of 1844," pp. 106–125.

Hegel's conception of the dialectic, and for this reason he intends to focus on it as one of the main points in his discussion. Marx hails Feuerbach alone as the one who has been critical of this aspect of Hegel's philosophy and who has genuinely moved past the Hegelian paradigm.[53]

Marx lists three points where Feuerbach rightly criticizes Hegel. First, Feuerbach has shown that "philosophy is nothing else but religion rendered into thoughts and thinking expounded, and that it has therefore likewise to be condemned as another form and manner of existence of the estrangement of the essence of man."[54] In the *Principles of the Philosophy of the Future*, Feuerbach criticizes Hegel for reifying the concept of spirit.[55] Because of this, Hegel's philosophy is also the result of a form of intellectual projection, just like religious thinking. It has created a fiction from the human imagination and then regards it as something real.

Second, Marx is especially appreciative of Feuerbach's attempt to get away from the abstraction of idealism and to make philosophy something concrete, thus establishing "true materialism" and "real science."[56] Feuerbach also issues this criticism in the *Principles of the Philosophy of the Future*.[57] Marx's language very much resembles that of the preface to the second edition of *The Essence of Christianity*, where Feuerbach was in a polemic against all forms of what he regarded as speculative abstraction. Along the same lines, Marx believes that Feuerbach has opened the way to a genuine social philosophy with his attempt to eliminate the relation of humanity to God and replace it with one of person to person.

Third, he praises Feuerbach's criticism of Hegel's principle of the negation of the negation.[58] This seems to be the point that Marx refers to when he talks about Hegel's dialectic. Hegel's famous method operates with a three-step procedure: something is posited, then it is negated, and then the negation itself is negated, thereby producing something positive – a higher unity. For example, in the first triad of Hegel's logic, the concept of being is posited, then it is negated by its opposite, the concept of nothingness. Then this negation is itself

---

[53]  Marx, "Ökonomisch-philosophische Manuskripte aus dem Jahre 1844," p. 569; "Economic and Philosophic Manuscripts of 1844," p. 107.

[54]  Marx, "Ökonomisch-philosophische Manuskripte aus dem Jahre 1844," p. 569; "Economic and Philosophic Manuscripts of 1844," pp. 107f.

[55]  Ludwig Feuerbach, *Grundsätze der Philosophie der Zukunft* (Zürich and Winterthur: Verlag des literarischen Comptoirs, 1843), pp. 39f., § 23. (English translation: *Principles of Philosophy of the Future*, trans. by Manfred H. Vogel [Indianapolis: Hackett Publishing Company, 1986], p. 36, § 23.)

[56]  Marx, "Ökonomisch-philosophische Manuskripte aus dem Jahre 1844," p. 570; "Economic and Philosophic Manuscripts of 1844," p. 108.

[57]  Feuerbach, *Grundsätze der Philosophie der Zukunft*, p. 55, § 30; *Principles of the Philosophy of the Future*, pp. 48f., § 30.

[58]  Feuerbach, *Grundsätze der Philosophie der Zukunft*, pp. 49–55, §§ 29–30; *Principles of the Philosophy of the Future*, pp. 44–49, §§ 29–30.

negated with the third step when the concept of becoming unites the concepts of being and nothingness. This issue seems to be the main one that Marx wishes to explore here. His critical point is that alienation is conceived as the second step – that is, negation – but then the third step, the negation of the negation, does not meaningfully do away with alienation since this third step is simply an abstract thought.[59] The first step in Hegel is universality or ideas, and then the second step is concrete particulars, which are juxtaposed with this. For Marx's materialism, the empirically perceived particulars are what is truly real, so this second step should be the real focus. But instead, in Hegel, it is sublated and there is a move to the third step, where the particular is united with the universal. This is a mistake, according to Marx, since with this third step Hegel abandons concrete actuality and returns to the abstractions of thought.

Using *The Phenomenology of Spirit* as his point of departure, Marx initially raises two objections to Hegel's philosophy. First, when Hegel talks about people being alienated from different things, institutions, and practices in the *Phenomenology*, these things are merely "thought-entities" (*Gedankenwesen*).[60] But this means that the entire process of alienation is not one that takes place in the real world but rather only in the realm of abstract thought. This ignores the relations that humans have to the real world. Second, given this, the reconciliation that Hegel proposes is empty since it is not a real reconciliation of a real person with a concrete practice or institution; instead, it is a reconciliation of one abstract thought with another – in other words, an empty and illusory form of reconciliation.[61] The so-called "natural consciousness" that works through the different stages of the *Phenomenology* is not a real person but a thought construction. Marx cannot accept any talk of reconciliation and resolution as long as there is still alienation and injustice in the real world. Hegel's reconciliation in thought rings hollow so long as there are still institutions and practices that alienate human beings. Marx can thus never accept Hegel's statement at the end of his *Lectures on the Philosophy of Religion* about a reconciliation with the world *in the minds of* the philosophers in contrast to a reconciliation in reality.

Marx then turns his attention to a critical analysis of the short final chapter of the *Phenomenology* entitled "Absolute Knowing."[62] This is where all of the different elements of Hegel's previous analyses of ethics, history, and religion come together in a conceptual unity and the truth of the whole is finally grasped. Here Marx in a sense seems to praise Hegel for recognizing the

---

[59] Marx, "Ökonomisch-philosophische Manuskripte aus dem Jahre 1844," pp. 584f.; "Economic and Philosophic Manuscripts of 1844," p. 122.

[60] Marx, "Ökonomisch-philosophische Manuskripte aus dem Jahre 1844," p. 572; "Economic and Philosophic Manuscripts of 1844," p. 110.

[61] Marx, "Ökonomisch-philosophische Manuskripte aus dem Jahre 1844," p. 573; "Economic and Philosophic Manuscripts of 1844," p. 111.

[62] Marx, "Ökonomisch-philosophische Manuskripte aus dem Jahre 1844," pp. 574–585; "Economic and Philosophic Manuscripts of 1844," pp. 112–122.

importance of both labor in the development of human beings and the complex structure of objectification and alienation in this context. Here he apparently has in mind not just the dialectic of the lord and the bondsman but also the analysis that Hegel gives of history as the development of human nature or "species being."[63] But, Marx complains, this is not a question of real labor relations since "the only labor which Hegel knows and recognizes is abstractly mental labor."[64] Again Hegel is concerned solely with the abstractions of thought and not real action in the real world.

Marx refers to the way in which there are in the *Phenomenology* a progressive series of models of otherness or objectivity. At each stage the analysis begins with a form of realism, whereby the subject is confronted by some other external entity – a thing, another subject, an institution, etc. The subject is thus said to be alienated from the other in the different spheres. Then in the course of the analysis it turns out that the other is in fact fundamentally related to the subject. This is what Marx refers to as "the movement of *surmounting the object of consciousness*."[65] In each case the subject is said to appropriate the object and make it a part of itself. But for Marx this is something that takes place only in the sphere of thought. It is with *knowledge* or philosophical insight that one realizes that what seemed to be an external other is in fact related to oneself.[66] Thus the final chapter in Hegel's work is called "Absolute *Knowing*." But this creates a false, ideal reality of thought alongside the real one. For Marx, alienation concerns real people and real relations, and it is in the real world that it should be overcome and not just in the mind of the philosopher. It is not just a matter of knowing.

Here one can see the analogy with Feuerbach's theory of religious alienation. For Feuerbach, initially one thinks of God as an external, foreign other. Then one realizes that God is just a projection of human characteristics. When one reaches this realization, then the goal is to take back or reappropriate the focus and energy that one took from oneself and placed in God as other. So also for Hegel in the *Phenomenology*, the goal is to take back the world of the other for the human mind. But in this context it is not easy to see why Marx believes that Feuerbach is more concrete than Hegel since for Feuerbach as well what is at issue is a thought, a realization that God is a projection. In other words, one reappropriates the thought of an external God or the human qualities that one has ascribed to God. But there is nothing here that can be regarded as

---

[63] Marx, "Ökonomisch-philosophische Manuskripte aus dem Jahre 1844," p. 574; "Economic and Philosophic Manuscripts of 1844," p. 112.

[64] Marx, "Ökonomisch-philosophische Manuskripte aus dem Jahre 1844," p. 574; "Economic and Philosophic Manuscripts of 1844," p. 112.

[65] Marx, "Ökonomisch-philosophische Manuskripte aus dem Jahre 1844," p. 575; "Economic and Philosophic Manuscripts of 1844," p. 113.

[66] Marx, "Ökonomisch-philosophische Manuskripte aus dem Jahre 1844," p. 580; "Economic and Philosophic Manuscripts of 1844," p. 117.

a concrete object in the real world. It seems that in both cases it is a matter of ideas and thoughts. To overcome alienation means not just taking back *an idea*, as with Hegel and Feuerbach, but rather taking back, for instance, the products of one's labor or the concrete means of production, which belong to another person. Only by recovering these *physical things* can real progress be made.

Marx further objects that Hegel's idealism forgets the natural side of human beings by reducing them to self-consciousness. He writes flatly, "Man is directly a *natural being*."[67] Humans have natural drives such as hunger that are only satisfied by real things in the real world. Just as humans are physical entities, so also they have a relation to other physical entities: "To say that man is a *corporeal*, living, real, sensuous, objective being full of natural vigor is to say that he has *real, sensuous objects* as the objects of his being or of his life, or that he can only *express* his life in real, sensuous objects."[68] Marx believes that Hegel's idealism ignores this physical side. Moreover, by seeing everything as a unity of thought, it denies the existence of any external, physical other. Hegel's idea of self-consciousness is not a physical being and has no physical being outside it. For Marx, this means that this is an illusory subject and not a real existing one in the world.[69]

Marx raises an objection to Hegel's notion of reconciliation, which he regards as one of "the illusions of speculation."[70] For Hegel, reconciliation means finding oneself in another or being at home with another. According to Hegel's view, there is, as noted, a three-step dialectical process of position, negation, and negation of negation, with the third step being the reconciliation. For Marx, in terms of religion, this can be understood as first an understanding of oneself (position), then a traditional understanding of God as other (negation and alienation), and then a reconciliation of the two (negation of the negation). But this means betraying the negative element:

> the self-conscious man ... again confirms [the spiritual world] in its alienated shape and passes it off as his true mode of being – re-establishes it, and pretends to be *at home in his other-being as such*. Thus, for instance, after annulling and superseding religion, after recognizing religion to be a product of self-alienation, he yet finds confirmation of himself in *religion as religion*.[71]

---

[67] Marx, "Ökonomisch-philosophische Manuskripte aus dem Jahre 1844," p. 578; "Economic and Philosophic Manuscripts of 1844," p. 115.

[68] Marx, "Ökonomisch-philosophische Manuskripte aus dem Jahre 1844," p. 578; "Economic and Philosophic Manuscripts of 1844," p. 115.

[69] Marx, "Ökonomisch-philosophische Manuskripte aus dem Jahre 1844," pp. 578f.; "Economic and Philosophic Manuscripts of 1844," p. 116.

[70] Marx, "Ökonomisch-philosophische Manuskripte aus dem Jahre 1844," p. 580; "Economic and Philosophic Manuscripts of 1844," p. 118.

[71] Marx, "Ökonomisch-philosophische Manuskripte aus dem Jahre 1844," p. 581; "Economic and Philosophic Manuscripts of 1844," p. 118.

Marx thus objects to Hegel's ultimate defense of Christianity as something true. If it is the source of alienation, how can one find oneself at home in it and be reconciled with it? How can we reconcile ourselves with something that is irrational? So the negation of the negation is not a negation of alienation but rather an affirmation of it. After the criticism of religion has been made and the alienation that religion causes has been exposed, does it really make sense to return to religion again by negating this negation? The criticism shows that religion should simply be rejected, but, according to Hegel, there is a higher truth that, once seen, restores it.

While Marx has some appreciation for Hegel's theory of history, he ultimately objects that it falls victim to abstraction as well. Hegel rightly sees history as the development of human beings through the process of labor and alienation.[72] However, Hegel becomes overly metaphysical when he calls the development of history a "divine process" and when he associates the spirit of humanity, called Absolute Spirit, with God.[73] Here, according to Marx, Hegel reifies an abstraction and leaves real human beings out of the account: "This result ... is therefore *God – Absolute Spirit – the self-knowing and self-manifesting Idea*. Real man and real nature become mere predicates – symbols of this esoteric, unreal man and of this unreal nature."[74]

Marx has a number of objections to Hegel, but they all seem to come in the end to the same thing: Hegel is too abstract, too much of an idealist, and this deprives his analyses of their truth and value. What is needed is a discussion of real people in the real world and not self-conscious subjects. Marx sees Feuerbach as taking the important first step in overcoming Hegel's abstraction and exploring real relations in the real world. Marx's goal is to continue this project of Feuerbach in the sphere of social-political philosophy.

### 6.4   Alienation and the Proletariat in *The Holy Family*

Marx and Engels jointly wrote *The Holy Family* in the fall of 1844 in Paris.[75] The book is a critical response to the work of Bruno Bauer and his circle, as is indicated by the full title: *The Holy Family or Critique of Critical Criticism*

---

[72] Marx, "Ökonomisch-philosophische Manuskripte aus dem Jahre 1844," p. 584; "Economic and Philosophic Manuscripts of 1844," p. 121.

[73] Marx, "Ökonomisch-philosophische Manuskripte aus dem Jahre 1844," p. 584; "Economic and Philosophic Manuscripts of 1844," p. 121.

[74] Marx, "Ökonomisch-philosophische Manuskripte aus dem Jahre 1844," p. 584; "Economic and Philosophic Manuscripts of 1844," p. 121.

[75] Friedrich Engels and Karl Marx, *Die heilige Familie, oder Kritik der kritischen Kritik. Gegen Bruno Bauer & Consorten* (Frankfurt am Main: Literarische Anstalt, 1845). (English translation: *The Holy Family or Critique of Critical Critique*, trans. by Richard Dixon [Moscow: Foreign Languages Publishing House, 1956]. Also *The Holy Family*, trans. by Richard Dixon and Clemens Dutt, in vol. 4 of *Marx/Engels Collected Works*, vols. 1–50 [Moscow: Progress Publishers, 1975–2004], pp. 5–211.)

*against Bruno Bauer and Company.* The satirical use of the term "the holy family" refers to Bruno Bauer and his brothers. In this work Marx and Engels respond to a number of articles printed by Bauer and others in the *Allgemeine Literatur-Zeitung* in 1843–1844.[76] They are particularly attentive to the notion of "criticism" or "critical criticism" that Bauer develops in these articles.[77] *The Holy Family* is highly ironic and satirical, and its many references and allusions to the articles of Bauer and others often make it difficult to follow if one is unfamiliar with the works being referred to. In this text Marx's debt to both Hegel and Feuerbach is again apparent. Perhaps most importantly, he develops further the theory of alienation.

In the foreword to the work, Marx and Engels immediately state their main thesis, namely that Bauer's work, while pretending to be something new and radical, in fact is still deeply entrenched in Hegel's abstractions. Specifically, it is a form of "*speculative idealism,* which substitutes '*self-consciousness*' or the '*spirit*' for the *real individual man.*"[78] Marx and Engels believed that they had discovered the true principle of historical movement: material relations. Thus, for them, any talk of self-consciousness or spirit was just a meaningless abstraction that explained nothing. They take this tendency of trading in abstractions to be typical of German philosophy, a point developed further in *The German Ideology.* The goal of *The Holy Family* is thus to expose and illuminate "the illusions of speculative philosophy."[79]

In this text the proletariat is opposed not to the bourgeoisie but to wealth in general.[80] One might expect that only the proletariat would be depicted as the object of alienation, but interestingly the oppressors – that is, the owners of the means of production – are also portrayed as victims of alienation:

> The propertied class and the class of the proletariat present the same human self-estrangement. But the former class feels at ease and strengthened in this self-estrangement as *its own power* and has in it the *semblance*

---

[76] *Allgemeine Literatur-Zeitung. Monatsschrift,* ed. by Bruno Bauer, 1 (1843), 2–12 (1844). The journal is reprinted (with no author listed) as *Streit der Kritik mit den modernen Gegensätzen* (Charlottenburg: Verlag von E. Bauer, 1847).

[77] Especially Bruno Bauer, "Was ist jetzt der Gegenstand der Kritik?," *Allgemeine Literatur-Zeitung. Monatsschrift,* ed. by Bruno Bauer, 8 (June) (1844), 18–26. See also Szeliga (a pseudonym for Franz Zychlin von Zychlinski), "Die Kritik," *Allgemeine Literatur-Zeitung. Monatsschrift,* ed. by Bruno Bauer, 11–12 (October) (1844), 25–46.

[78] Engels and Marx, *Die heilige Familie,* p. iii; *The Holy Family,* in vol. 4 of *Marx/Engels Collected Works,* p. 5. (All quotations are from the English translation found in the *Collected Works* edition. I have occasionally eliminated the excessive use of italics when it distracts from the reading.)

[79] Engels and Marx, *Die heilige Familie,* p. iv; *The Holy Family,* in vol. 4 of *Marx/Engels Collected Works,* p. 5.

[80] Engels and Marx, *Die heilige Familie,* p. 43; *The Holy Family,* in vol. 4 of *Marx/Engels Collected Works,* pp. 35f.

of a human existence. The latter feels annihilated in estrangement; it sees in it its own powerlessness and the reality of an inhuman existence.[81]

While the owners enjoy the recognition of the proletariat since it seems to confirm them in their power, as Hegel has shown in the analysis of the lord and the bondsman, this recognition is not meaningful because it is not given freely. The owners are themselves alienated, although they do not realize it or see their situation as something negative.

Marx and Engels characterize the proletariat as living in a condition of dehumanization.[82] They refer to Hegel's depiction of self-alienated spirit from the *Phenomenology*: The proletariat "is, to use an expression of Hegel, in its abasement the *indignation* at that abasement, an indignation to which it is necessarily driven by the contradiction between its human *nature* and its condition of life, which is the outright, resolute and comprehensive negation of that nature."[83] We saw earlier that Marx outlined a number of forms of alienation in the condition of the proletariat, one of which is the alienation from oneself and one's universal human nature as an intelligent, creative being. The key here is that the awareness of this contradiction leads to indignation and alienation. This awareness is then what develops into a sense of class consciousness for the proletariat that can play a critical role in social change. When the proletariat class becomes aware of the injustice of their condition, then they can collectively rise up against the owners of the means of production and cause a revolution that changes the entire system.

Here again we can see a parallel with Feuerbach's theory of religious alienation and his proposed solution to it. For Feuerbach, the key to overcoming alienation was to realize that one had simply externalized and reified human attributes in God. When one realizes this, then one will be able to take back all of the things that rightly belong to one as a human being. The realization of this view of Feuerbach is what is essential. This corresponds to Marx's idea of class consciousness. It is only when the proletariat class realizes its own self-alienation and the root causes of it that it is able to take concrete steps to overcome it. For Marx, this is an important point where his view goes beyond that of Feuerbach. As he says in the fourth thesis on Feuerbach, just realizing the contradiction is not enough; instead, concrete revolutionary action must follow.

It can also be argued that another forerunner of the idea of class conscious is Hegel's theory of spirit becoming aware of itself in history. Hegel's idea is that

---

[81] Engels and Marx, *Die heilige Familie*, p. 43; *The Holy Family*, in vol. 4 of *Marx/Engels Collected Works*, p. 36.
[82] Engels and Marx, *Die heilige Familie*, p. 44; *The Holy Family*, in vol. 4 of *Marx/Engels Collected Works*, p. 36.
[83] Engels and Marx, *Die heilige Familie*, p. 43; *The Holy Family*, in vol. 4 of *Marx/Engels Collected Works*, p. 36.

human beings have subjective freedom, but they have not been able to understand this fully or realize it in the real world until fairly recently. When humans
become aware of their subjective freedom, they for the first time become aware
of their true humanity. This is a collective form of self-awareness that has only
taken place in the modern world. The idea of class consciousness is also a form
of coming to awareness of oneself in a broader context. It also involves a new
consciousness of one's true self and how one has been prevented from realizing
this in the past. For both Hegel and Marx, this new awareness is the trigger for
social change and historical development.

## 6.5    The Criticism of Bauer in *The Holy Family*

One of the most illuminating parts of *The Holy Family* is the section "The
Speculative Cycle of Absolute Criticism and the Philosophy of Self-
Consciousness." Here Marx and Engels discuss explicitly Bauer's works
*Critique of the Evangelical History of the Synoptic Gospels* and *Christianity
Exposed*.[84] This focus shows a somewhat surprising interest in religion and
theology in the thought of Marx. In the criticism of Strauss in the *Critique of
the Evangelical History of the Synoptic Gospels*, Bauer describes the current
philosophical movement (including his own work) as undermining Spinoza's
principle of substance. In other words, Spinoza, with his famous thesis from
the *Ethics* that the world consists of nature, which is synonymous with God,
focuses on the physical world around us. For Bauer, this is the principle that
Strauss is operating with since he believes that the gospels are a natural growth
of the spirit of a people. This follows Hegel's language of customs and traditions constituting the ethical substance of communities. Unfortunately,
according to Bauer, this fails to take into account the subjective side of things,
that is, the human subject, which consciously creates the myths of the gospel
stories. Thus we read in *The Holy Family*, "by overcoming *Spinozism, Criticism*
ended up in *Hegelian idealism*" and "from 'substance' it arrived at another
*metaphysical monster*, the '*subject*.'"[85] Here Marx and Engels do not refer to
Bauer directly by name but instead satirically personify his principle of

---

[84] Bruno Bauer, *Kritik der evangelischen Geschichte der Synoptiker*, vols. 1–3 (Leipzig: Otto
Wigand, 1841–1842); Bruno Bauer, *Das entdeckte Christenthum. Eine Erinnerung an das
18. Jahrhundert und ein Beitrag zur Krisis des 19.* (Zürich and Winterthur: Verlag des
literarischen Comptoirs, 1843). (English translation: *An English Edition of Bruno Bauer's
1843 Christianity Exposed: A Recollection of the Eighteenth Century and a Contribution to
the Crisis of the Nineteenth Century*, ed. by Paul Trejo, trans. by Esther Ziegler and Jutta
Hammn [Lewiston, NY: Edwin Mellon Press, 2002] [*Studies in German Thought and
History*, vol. 23].)

[85] Engels and Marx, *Die heilige Familie*, p. 216; *The Holy Family*, in vol. 4 of *Marx/Engels
Collected Works*, p. 137.

criticism. In his letter to Feuerbach, Marx dwells on this criticism of Bauer as follows:

> "Criticism" is transformed into a transcendental being. These Berliners do not regard themselves as *men* who *criticize*, but as *critics* who, *incidentally*, have the misfortune of being men. They therefore acknowledge only one *real* need, the need of *theoretical* criticism . . . . This criticism therefore lapses into a sad and supercilious intellectualism. Consciousness or self-consciousness is regarded as the only human quality.[86]

In his article "Contribution to the Critique of Hegel's *Philosophy of Right*," Marx argued that the philosophers would join forces with the proletariat to bring about the revolution, with the former being the theoretical or intellectual side and the latter the actual or material side.[87] He thus acknowledges the importance of the theoretical side. However, the revolution needs to be realized in the real world. Bauer, by contrast, has become fixated on the theoretical side alone, which renders his thought impotent. Marx portrays Bauer's project of "criticism" as wholly negative. Bauer "only exposes contradictions and, satisfied with this occupation, he departs with a contemptuous 'Hm.' He declares that criticism does not give anything, it is far too spiritual for that."[88] Bauer has nothing positive to offer in order to replace that which he has torn down. He represents only the negative side of Hegel's dialectical method without the so-called negation of the negation, which ends in a positive third step.

Marx and Engels object that Bauer falls victim to the same problem as Hegel by taking certain abstract categories from metaphysics – for example, substance – and then reifying them by regarding them as real existing things in the world. It is a fundamental principle of Hegel's idealism that whatever is regarded as some external entity or substance can in fact always be shown to be necessarily connected to the subject, and what we know as objectivity in the world is a product of the human cognitive apparatus. It is claimed that Bauer follows this Hegelian principle: "Bauer's *self-consciousness*, too, is *substance raised* to self-consciousness or *self-consciousness* as *substance*; self-consciousness is transformed from an *attribute of man* into a *self-existing subject*."[89] Bauer thus by sleight of hand changes the thought of self-consciousness into a living and

---

[86] "Marx an Ludwig Feuerbach in Bruckberg, Paris, d. 11 August 1844," in *Marx-Engels-Werke*, vol. 27, p. 427; "To Ludwig Feuerbach in Bruckberg, Paris, August 11, 1844," in *Marx/Engels Collected Works*, vol. 3, p. 356.

[87] Marx, "Zur Kritik der Hegel'schen Rechts-Philosophie. Einleitung," p. 391; "Contribution to the Critique of Hegel's *Philosophy of Right*: Introduction," p. 65.

[88] "Marx an Ludwig Feuerbach in Bruckberg, Paris, d. 11 August 1844," in *Marx-Engels-Werke*, vol. 27, p. 427; "To Ludwig Feuerbach in Bruckberg, Paris, August 11, 1844," in *Marx/Engels Collected Works*, vol. 3, p. 356.

[89] Engels and Marx, *Die heilige Familie*, p. 218; *The Holy Family*, in vol. 4 of *Marx/Engels Collected Works*, p. 138.

breathing human being. For however important self-consciousness might be, it is only a part of what makes us human. Of paramount importance is, of course, the physical body, which is not mentioned in this account. Thus Bauer's understanding of the human being is simply a *"metaphysical-theological* carica-ture of man in his *severance* from nature. The *being* of this self-consciousness is not *man*, but *the idea* of which self-consciousness is the *real existence."*[90]

If Strauss can be accused of focusing on the objective and thus being a follower of Spinoza's philosophy of substance, then Bauer is guilty of the opposite sin, namely focusing on the subjective at the expense of the objective. Marx and Engels thus characterize Bauer as following Fichte's subjective idealism. They point out that the actual Hegelian dialectical principle is one that intends to unite these two views:

> In Hegel there are three elements, Spinoza's substance, Fichte's self-consciousness and Hegel's necessarily antagonistic unity of the two, the Absolute Spirit. The first element is metaphysically disguised nature separated from man; the second is metaphysically disguised spirit separated from nature; the third is the metaphysically disguised unity of both, real man and the real human species.[91]

Here the Hegelian idea of separation or alienation of spirit from nature clearly emerges. Likewise, we have here a clear statement of the origin of the idea of humans as species beings, that is, beings who have the ability to abstract and see themselves as a universal or a species. Hegel's idea of Absolute Spirit is precisely this abstraction.

Marx and Engels thus demonstrate that Strauss and Bauer mistakenly cling to one side of the equation – Strauss to the objective side and Bauer to the subjective side. Hegel unites these two. By contrast, Feuerbach is hailed as the thinker who overcame this dualism and the abstraction of Hegel "by resolving the metaphysical Absolute Spirit into 'real man on the basis of nature.'"[92] It is, however, not clear how Marx and Engels take Feuerbach's position, with its focus on the nature, to be different from Strauss' Spinozism.

They then turn to Bauer's criticism of the materialism of the French Enlightenment thinkers that appears at the end of *Christianity Exposed*. They quote two passages from Bauer's text. The first is as follows:

> If the truth of materialism, the philosophy of self-consciousness is found out, and self-consciousness is recognized as the universe, as the solution to the riddle of Spinoza's substance and as the true *causa sui*, then the great

---

[90] Engels and Marx, *Die heilige Familie*, p. 218; *The Holy Family*, in vol. 4 of *Marx/Engels Collected Works*, p. 138.
[91] Engels and Marx, *Die heilige Familie*, p. 220; *The Holy Family*, in vol. 4 of *Marx/Engels Collected Works*, p. 139.
[92] Engels and Marx, *Die heilige Familie*, p. 220; *The Holy Family*, in vol. 4 of *Marx/Engels Collected Works*, p. 139.

work of materialism, the disintegration of the religious theological business, is brought to an end. Why does spirit exist? For what reason is there self-consciousness? Because self-consciousness does away with the distinction between what is brought forth and itself, and because self-consciousness can exist only in bringing forth and in movement (in fact it is this movement), we declare: in fact, this self-consciousness that made a distinction with the world and with what it itself brings forth, has its own purpose and first possesses itself!"[93]

In their gloss on this, Marx and Engels claim that Bauer's statement amounts to saying that there is nothing that exists outside of self-consciousness. This is the Hegelian principle of immanence, whereby everything is an object of consciousness and there is no truly transcendent other. For Marx and Engels, this is an absurd idealism that lives in abstractions and fails to do justice to the real material world around us.

The second quotation from *Christianity Exposed* concerns Bauer's treatment of French materialism, which he believes did not grasp the nature of spirit or self-consciousness. The passage quoted runs as follows:

> [The French materialists] understood the movement of self-consciousness, however, both as the movement of common being and of matter, but could not yet see that the movement of the universe, first as the movement of self-consciousness, has really become itself and has come together as a unity with itself.[94]

The objection is that the materialists failed to appreciate the way in which the categories of the human mind shape our conception of objectivity. In short, they did not appreciate that what is real is not the physical things, which are rather illusions or mere appearances. Instead, what is most real is the movement of thought that determines objectivity. Marx and Engels find it absurd to reduce the material world to the product of the human mind and to call it mere appearance. They refer to this as Hegel's theory of creation, according to which the world is created by the externalization or alienation of spirit. As evidence of this, two passages from the "Absolute Knowing" chapter of the *Phenomenology* are quoted.[95] They believe that Bauer has fully embraced Hegel's theory of self-

---

[93] Engels and Marx, *Die heilige Familie*, p. 221; *The Holy Family*, in vol. 4 of *Marx/Engels Collected Works*, p. 140. (Instead of using the translation of Bauer's text in the translation of *The Holy Family*, I use that which appears in *An English Edition of Bruno Bauer's 1843 Christianity Exposed: A Recollection of the Eighteenth Century and a Contribution to the Crisis of the Nineteenth Century*, pp. 109f. *Das entdeckte Christenthum. Eine Erinnerung an das 18. Jahrhundert und ein Beitrag zur Krisis des 19.*, p. 113.)

[94] Engels and Marx, *Die heilige Familie*, p. 222; *The Holy Family*, in vol. 4 of *Marx/Engels Collected Works*, p. 140. (*Christianity Exposed*, p. 111. *Das entdeckte Christenthum. Eine Erinnerung an das 18. Jahrhundert und ein Beitrag zur Krisis des 19.*, pp. 114f.)

[95] Engels and Marx, *Die heilige Familie*, pp. 223f.; *The Holy Family*, in vol. 4 of *Marx/Engels Collected Works*, p. 141. Marx and Engels quote from the second printing of the

consciousness and spirit and thereby rendered any meaningful account of the actual world impossible.

Marx and Engels return to this criticism again in the section "The Revealed Mystery of the 'Standpoint.'" Here they refer to Bauer's understanding of science as a movement through and sublation of individual standpoints by means of criticism. Marx and Engels point out that here again he appropriates the methodology of *The Phenomenology of Spirit*.[96] In that work Hegel traces the different forms of spirit, showing at each stage their inadequacy, which then compels the dialectical movement forward to the next stage. At each step along the way, some element of external reality is shown to be necessarily connected with spirit. In this way the reality of the material world gradually dissolves. Thus by the end of the work everything external has been eliminated, and what is left is Absolute Spirit. Marx and Engels point out that Bauer has simply replaced the Hegelian term "Absolute Spirit" with his own term "criticism," but the point is the same. Here we see once again the idealist dogma of the unity of being and thought.[97]

This criticism of Bauer is illuminating for the position that Marx and Engels themselves wish to develop. In contrast to idealism, they want to focus on the concrete material conditions in the world that determine people's lives. In the end, much of the idealist analysis ends up explaining only thoughts that it itself has created instead of going to work to understand the real world and real human relations. Idealism ends in empty abstractions, whereas materialism leads to true insight and prepares the road for real action and practice in contrast to dwelling forever in the realm of sterile theory.

## 6.6 Marx's Theses on Feuerbach

Another interesting but fragmentary text by Marx is the "Theses on Feuerbach,"[98] which was written in 1845 and published posthumously by Engels. The work consists of a series of eleven short passages or theses, most

---

*Phenomenology* in the collected works edition: *Phänomenologie des Geistes*, ed. by Johannes Schulze, vol. 2 (2nd printing 1841), in *Georg Wilhelm Friedrich Hegel's Werke. Vollständige Ausgabe*, vols. 1–18, ed. by Ludwig Boumann, Friedrich Förster, Eduard Gans, Karl Hegel, Leopold von Henning, Heinrich Gustav Hotho, Philipp Marheineke, Karl Ludwig Michelet, Karl Rosenkranz, and Johannes Schulze (Berlin: Duncker und Humblot, 1832–1845), pp. 574f., pp. 582f. (*Hegel's Phenomenology of Spirit*, trans. by A. V. Miller [Oxford: Clarendon Press, 1977], p. 479, p. 486.)

[96] Engels and Marx, *Die heilige Familie*, p. 305; *The Holy Family*, in vol. 4 of *Marx/Engels Collected Works*, p. 192.

[97] Engels and Marx, *Die heilige Familie*, p. 307; *The Holy Family*, in vol. 4 of *Marx/Engels Collected Works*, p. 193.

[98] Karl Marx, "Thesen über Feuerbach," in *Marx-Engels-Werke*, vol. 3, pp. 5–7. (English translation: "Theses on Feuerbach," in *The Marx-Engels Reader*, pp. 143–145.)

of which name Feuerbach directly in a critical manner. This text seems to be the outline for the Introduction to *The German Ideology*. In any case it is insightful for appreciating how Marx sees himself as moving beyond Feuerbach's theory of religious alienation. While in the other texts that we examined, Marx tended to put Feuerbach up on a pedestal, here in the "Theses on Feuerbach" there is a critical tone. Instead of Feuerbach being portrayed as the great pioneer of social criticism who pointed the way forward, now he is criticized for falling short and not going far enough.

Marx does not make a big issue of whether his work is philosophical as such, and he does not seem particularly invested in being regarded as a philosopher. However, he does clearly see his work as a part of the development of the tradition that runs from Hegel to Feuerbach. In the "Theses on Feuerbach" one can see the outlines of his view of the meaning of, if not philosophy as such, then knowledge. In the first thesis, Marx objects that Feuerbach rests complacently with an understanding of things in terms of contemplation and not real life action.[99] He refers explicitly to Feuerbach's *The Essence of Christianity*, which, he claims, presents "the theoretical attitude as the only genuinely human attitude,"[100] while rejecting practice. Here he seems to have in mind Feuerbach's idea of the theoretical understanding of God as a projection of human attributes.

Marx continues this train of thought in the second thesis, which raises the issue to a more general level about the nature of knowledge as such. He states, "The question whether objective truth can be attributed to human thinking is not a question of theory but is a *practical* question. Man must prove the truth, that is, the reality and power, the this-sidedness of his thinking in practice."[101] The implication is clearly that Feuerbach has not appreciated this point and remains at the level of contemplation without any practical relevance. This view seems to state that all knowledge must have some practical import if it is to be meaningful at all. This makes sense in the context of social-economic theory that is of primary concern to Marx. In this sphere, for something to be true, it must be proven successful in practice. So the measure of truth is how well the idea can be used to resolve concrete human problems in specific contexts. This view seems to work less well in other contexts such as quantum physics or cosmology, where the actual practical implications are more uncertain and indeterminate. Yet we still want to claim that the ideas of these fields have some kind of truth value. Marx's view can be seen as directly opposed to that of Hegel, who, as we saw, argued that the goal of philosophy was simply to understand the world. While Hegel was skeptical about the ability of philosophical ideas or insights to change things directly in the world, Marx is much

---

[99] Marx, "Thesen über Feuerbach," p. 5; "Theses on Feuerbach," p. 143.
[100] Marx, "Thesen über Feuerbach," p. 5; "Theses on Feuerbach," p. 143.
[101] Marx, "Thesen über Feuerbach," p. 5; "Theses on Feuerbach," p. 144.

more optimistic with his theory of class consciousness, which can be the vehicle for concrete social change and revolution. Here again we have two fundamentally different intuitions about the nature and use of knowledge.

Marx continues along the same lines in the fourth thesis, where he claims, "Feuerbach starts out from the fact of religious self-alienation, of the duplication of the world into a religious imaginary world and a real one. His work consists in resolving the religious world into its secular basis. He overlooks the fact that after completing this work, the chief thing still remains to be done."[102] Feuerbach reduced the religious world to the secular one by showing that God is just a projected image of the human. Once one realizes that religion is simply an illusion, one must look into the cause of the illusion: the corrupt and oppressive society that creates the illusion. The criticism of religion should precipitate one to a criticism of the social order. This should lead to concrete practice in the world in order to overturn the oppressive elements in society, which have led to religious alienation in the first place. For Marx, it is an absurdity to think that once one comes to the realization that God is just a projection of the human mind, then all the problems are thereby resolved. This is a complacent and contemplative attitude. The reconciliation that Feuerbach proposes is only the reconciliation of an idea. With this, nothing is changed about the concrete conditions of human beings. No real reconciliation has taken place.

Marx also criticizes Feuerbach for taking human beings as individuals and not seeing them in a broader social context. The point might be made by saying that Feuerbach is interested in a kind of religious psychology, whereas Marx is interested in a kind of sociology or social theory that sees individuals in interaction with one another. In Thesis VI, Marx argues that Feuerbach has an atomic conception of the individual and abstracts the individual from history and society. But religion is in fact a social product (Thesis VII) and not the result of the work of people as individuals. Marx writes, "human essence is no abstraction inherent in each single individual. In its reality it is the ensemble of the social relations."[103] To grasp this fully, one has to see humans as members of society in concrete social relations. This criticism is particularly striking because this was something that was cited as one of Feuerbach's positive achievements in the "Economic and Philosophic Manuscripts of 1844."[104]

In the ninth thesis Marx finds Feuerbach's theory too abstract and critically labels it a "contemplative materialism,"[105] with the word "contemplative" intended

---

[102] Marx, "Thesen über Feuerbach," p. 6; "Theses on Feuerbach," p. 144.

[103] Marx, "Thesen über Feuerbach," p. 6; "Theses on Feuerbach," p. 145.

[104] Marx, "Ökonomisch-philosophische Manuskripte aus dem Jahre 1844," p. 570; "Economic and Philosophic Manuscripts of 1844," p. 108: "Feuerbach also makes the social relationship 'of man to man' the basic principle of the theory."

[105] Marx, "Thesen über Feuerbach," p. 7; "Theses on Feuerbach," p. 145. See also the criticism of Feuerbach's materialism as "contemplation" in the first thesis ("Thesen über Feuerbach," p. 5; "Theses on Feuerbach," p. 143).

to be a critical echo of Hegel's idealism. This criticism contrasts sharply with Marx's claim in the "Economic and Philosophic Manuscripts of 1844" that Feuerbach has established *true materialism* and *real science.*[106] Here again his disposition toward Feuerbach seems, in a short period of time, to have turned critical.

Marx's final thesis is the most famous one, and we have alluded to it before: "The philosophers have only *interpreted* the world in various ways; the point, however, is to *change* it."[107] Here he speaks explicitly of "philosophers," and, given the immediate context, he clearly has in mind both Feuerbach and Hegel (although the claim, strictly speaking, could certainly refer to many others). His point is one about the nature of philosophy. Since this sentence is repeated so often, it is easy to lose a feel for its polemical force. When one looks at the history of philosophy, it is clear that the discipline has always been about learning and discovering new things. Etymologically, the word "philosophy" just means the love of wisdom, and in this definition there is no reference to any practical element. In a sense Marx can be seen as calling into question the entire tradition of philosophy. His practice-oriented view represents an entirely new conception. Of course, there have been many philosophers who were interested in social-political philosophy before Marx, but their goal was primarily to understand social-political phenomena or to develop theories of the state or justice. There were also philosophers who were interested in fomenting revolution in one form or another; here one can think of the French *philosophes* during the Enlightenment who supported both the French and the American revolutions, or John Stuart Mill's revolutionary appeal for the rights of women, or Sartre's political engagement on behalf of communism. In these cases one can see philosophers using their knowledge and argumentative skills in order to attempt to bring about social change. But Marx seems to formulate this even more radically by apparently claiming it is the primary vocation and goal of philosophy to make social changes. In any case, his eleventh thesis on Feuerbach encapsulates this issue in a nutshell by raising the fundamental question of what is the proper vocation of the philosopher or what is the value of knowledge of any kind.[108]

## 6.7   The Polemic with the Young Hegelians in *The German Ideology*

*The German Ideology* is a text that was penned jointly by Marx and Engels in 1845–1846 and published posthumously for the first time in the twentieth

---

[106] Marx, "Ökonomisch-philosophische Manuskripte aus dem Jahre 1844," p. 570; "Economic and Philosophic Manuscripts of 1844," p. 108.

[107] Marx, "Thesen über Feuerbach," p. 7; "Theses on Feuerbach," p. 145.

[108] For a recent discussion of this topic, see Jon Stewart, "El oficio de la filosofía. La dialéctica de la teoría y la práctica," in Hans Hiram Pacheco García and Victor Hugo Robledo Martínez (eds.), *Las preguntas de la Esfinge 5. Psicoanálisis y figuras de la interpretación* (Zacatecas: Taberna Libraria Editores, 2020), pp. 169–192.

century.[109] The work is known primarily as their most detailed statement of the
nature of historical development. It contains a broad range of different topics,
which are not always organized in any obvious way. It is important to keep in
mind that this text is more of an example of work in progress or a pastiche than
a polished, definitive statement of the views of Marx and Engels. The word
"ideology" in the title refers to a number of thinkers in the wake of Hegel's
philosophy, such as David Friedrich Strauss, Bruno Bauer, and Max Stirner. The
work begins by noting that, according to these figures, there has been a great
intellectual revolution in recent years, that is, from 1842 to 1845. This revolution
has consisted of overthrowing Hegel's philosophy and moving beyond it. Marx
and Engels believe that these claims are ideological and amount to "philosophic
charlatanry."[110] They argue that these thinkers are all still deeply dependent on
Hegel, despite all claims to the contrary. Instead of issuing a real criticism of
Hegel's philosophy, these figures simply take a part of his system and blow it up
as the most important part at the expense of the rest.[111] This one part is then
paraded in front of competing theories as something new. In this way individual
thinkers come and go, factions develop, and the mistaken appearance of philosophical progress is given as each subsequent thinker battles for Hegel's heritage.
   Marx and Engels rightly note the centrality of religion in these debates. The
consequences of Hegel's philosophy for religious belief constituted the main issue
in the formation of the Hegel schools during this time. It is claimed that these
"Young Hegelians consider conceptions, thoughts, ideas, in fact all the products of
consciousness . . . as the real chains of men."[112] The idea here is that traditional
ways of thinking have stood in the way of human progress, and so in order to
move forward, one must expose these as fallacious and disabuse people of the
errors that they contain. Here we might think of Feuerbach's attempt to demonstrate that the traditional conception of God is just a projection of the human
mind. It will be recalled that Feuerbach believes that when this becomes generally
known, people will abandon their traditional ways of thinking about both God
and themselves, and a radical change will take place in society. Marx and Engels
object that the results of these theories have been quite limited since they have
missed the real point. People have not been enslaved by false ideas but rather by

---

[109] Karl Marx and Friedrich Engels, *Die deutsche Ideologie. Kritik der neuesten deutschen
Philosophie in ihren Repräsentaten Feuerbach, B. Bauer und Stirner, und des deutschen
Sozialismus in seinen verschiedenen Propheten*, in *Marx-Engels-Werke*, vol. 3, pp. 9–530.
(English translation: *The German Ideology* [London: Lawrence & Wishart, 1965;
Moscow: Progress Publishers, 1964]. Partial translation: *The German Ideology*, Part I,
in *The Marx-Engels Reader*, pp. 146–200.)
[110] Marx and Engels, *Die deutsche Ideologie*, p. 18; *The German Ideology*, Part I, p. 147. (Here
and in what follows, all references to the English translation refer to the text in *The Marx-
Engels Reader*.)
[111] Marx and Engels, *Die deutsche Ideologie*, pp. 18f.; *The German Ideology*, Part I, p. 148.
[112] Marx and Engels, *Die deutsche Ideologie*, pp. 19f.; *The German Ideology*, Part I, p. 149.

concrete conditions in the world. The Young Hegelians, they claim, have operated at a highly abstract level of philosophy and have never really applied themselves to actual reality. It is a mistake to think that people will be liberated by mere thoughts or insights alone. Instead, true human liberation can only take place by means of a change in the concrete modes of the organization of production and the work conditions of real people in the world.

In Hegel's *Lectures on the Philosophy of History*, he argues that history represents the gradual coming to awareness of the idea of freedom. As cultures and societies develop, humans overcome different kinds of oppressive influences that fail to recognize the importance and value of the individual. Initially humans thought of themselves simply as products of nature, and so they tried to conceive of their specific form of social organization, for example, the Indian caste system, as something that was given by nature. Thus individuals were subordinated to the customs, traditions, and laws of society that were all conceived as natural. In this conception there is little room left for subjective development in any way that contradicts the roles ascribed to the individual by society. If individuals are dissatisfied or unhappy with the role that they find themselves in, then this has no significance whatsoever. Their personal desires and interests are not recognized as important. According to Hegel, in the course of history this conception is gradually overturned as people come to realize that humans are higher than nature. Only in time are individuals given a value on their own terms. As noted at the end of Section 6.4, this development is what Hegel refers to as the coming to awareness of the idea of freedom in history. Marx and Engels object to this precisely because it is *an idea*. They argue that ideas or thoughts are vacuous and cannot be the motor of history.

The thesis in *The German Ideology* is that it is not ideas or abstractions that move history but actual conditions in the real world.[113] The authors explain in some detail how from the beginning of history humans have had to develop ways to produce what they need to survive. Initially this involved simple activities such as hunting or fishing, but in time these became more complex as populations grew and technologies developed. In this context humans are obliged to cooperate with one another for mutual benefit. They thus create different forms of production that organize people and their individual tasks in different ways. As society grows, these roles in the economic sphere are mirrored in all aspects of culture, that is, politics, law, ethics, religion, etc. (Here one can see an echo of Hegel's idea of spirit, which constitutes the organic whole of a people, including all of its different practices and forms of culture.) Thus the different forms of interaction among people are fundamentally dictated by the modes of production that are developed. For Marx and Engels, these are the concrete conditions of real life that determine how people

---

[113] See Marx and Engels, *Die deutsche Ideologie*, p. 36, p. 39; *The German Ideology*, Part I, p. 163, p. 166.

act in the world. This sphere of work relations is, they believe, far more fundamental than any abstract thought. The Young Hegelians have it the wrong way around since they believe that the abstract ideas that people have are the key, and if these are changed, then social change will result. By contrast, Marx and Engels claim that it is the actual conditions of labor that determine how people think in the first place, and thus change must begin here with the real cause of the problem and not just with one of its effects. Ideas do not arise spontaneously; instead, they are created by human beings in concrete situations determined by their role in the relations of production and labor.

In this context one finds a criticism of Hegel's view of consciousness. As we have seen, Hegel develops his theory of consciousness and self-consciousness in terms of an abstract scenario of the lord and the bondsman in *The Phenomenology of Spirit*. This was a kind of thought experiment and made no pretense of being any kind of analysis of actual historical events. By contrast, here in *The German Ideology*, Marx and Engels claim, "Consciousness can never be anything else than conscious existence, and the existence of men is their actual life-process."[114] To be a self-conscious human being is to be immediately involved in concrete relations with other human beings, and the primary modality for this is in the context of relations of production. Consciousness is not something that exists ahead of time and then is applied to one's circumstances in life; rather, it arises from the conditions of life in one's concrete interactions with the world and other people: "Consciousness is, therefore, from the very beginning a social product."[115] The goal that Marx and Engels set for themselves in the work is to examine these concrete relations as they appear in the context of historical development. They thus criticize what they take to be the mistaken methodology of both Hegel and the Young Hegelians when they write, "In direct contrast to German philosophy which descends from heaven to earth, here we ascend from earth to heaven."[116] The point is clearly that one should not start from abstract ideas (heaven) but instead with empirically observable facts about human life (earth). If one starts with abstract ideas, which are not in harmony with the empirical world, then one risks a theory that explains nothing. By contrast, if one starts with the observable facts and develops a theory from this, then it is certain that what one is describing at the theoretical level is in fact a reality and not a fiction of one's own mind.

### 6.8   Alienation in *The German Ideology*

Marx and Engels continue their analysis with a reference to early religion, which Hegel calls natural religion.[117] According to their view, early humans

---

[114] Marx and Engels, *Die deutsche Ideologie*, p. 26; *The German Ideology*, Part I, p. 154.
[115] Marx and Engels, *Die deutsche Ideologie*, p. 31; *The German Ideology*, Part I, p. 158.
[116] Marx and Engels, *Die deutsche Ideologie*, p. 26; *The German Ideology*, Part I, p. 154.
[117] Marx and Engels, *Die deutsche Ideologie*, p. 31; *The German Ideology*, Part I, p. 158.

are born into a hostile world and are confronted with the forces of nature, which are often violent and detrimental to human goals. These forces are unpredictable and the object of fear. In the course of time they become personified as deities. This is the immediate relation that humans have with nature, which leaves them with a deep sense of helplessness and vulnerability. Nature appears to people as "a completely alien, all-powerful and unassailable force."[118] Only in the course of time do humans begin to develop ways to avoid the negative effects of nature and to make themselves in part independent of them. In this manner they come to get a sense of their own freedom, and the feeling of alienation from nature is gradually overcome. This account has been largely derived from Hegel's *Lectures on the Philosophy of Religion* with the movement from natural religion to the religions of spirit. In natural religion the gods and goddesses are conceived as objects of nature, that is, the sun, the moon, a river, a tree, or an animal. This recognizes the powerful force of the natural world and conceives of the human world as subordinate to it. By contrast, the religions of spirit conceive of the gods and goddesses in human form, that is, as anthropomorphic entities. This conception sees the human world as dominant over the forces of nature.

Marx and Engels take this discussion, which in Hegel is primarily about religion, and transfer it to the social sphere. They claim that this is the beginning of social life and the development of self-consciousness as humans begin to interact with others in increasingly large groups for the purpose of satisfying their needs. As societies become more complex, so also do the forms of social organization and the division of labor. This is, it is claimed, the beginning of inequality and oppression. This is made worse by the inequalities in the distribution of products and property rights, with some having a greater share than others.

With the gradual growth of society, new ways of thinking develop. These include ethics, religion, philosophy, and so forth.[119] These form an integral and constitutive part of the common consciousness of a people and are developed collectively. Marx and Engels are generally critical of these ways of thinking since they regard them as a reflection of the oppressive social forces from which they arose. The ethics, religion, and philosophy of a society legitimatize the status quo and the established forms of production in a given society. They provide people with a way of understanding their lot in life. But these areas of thought hide from people the basic conditions that determine their oppression.

As a result of this, individuals perceive a sense of alienation with regard to their participation in the work activity of their society. Their own work is not perceived as something that they freely choose or have control over. On the

---

[118] Marx and Engels, *Die deutsche Ideologie*, p. 31; *The German Ideology*, Part I, p. 158.
[119] Marx and Engels, *Die deutsche Ideologie*, p. 31; *The German Ideology*, Part I, p. 159.

contrary, "man's own deed becomes an alien power opposed to him, which enslaves him instead of being controlled by him. For as soon as the distribution of labor comes into being, each man has a particular, exclusive sphere of activity, which is forced upon him and from which he cannot escape."[120] Individuals are obliged to do the work that is dictated by their society and its leaders. They do not have the opportunity to choose their profession for themselves. Their personal interests are subordinated to the demands of the modalities of production of society.

Here Marx and Engels can be seen as expanding Hegel's theory of subjective freedom, according to which the right of the individual must be recognized and taken into account. According to Hegel, this was not the case in ancient societies, where the personal wishes of individuals were not regarded as legitimate. Instead, the professions that they had or the people they married were in effect assigned to them by their family, their tribe, or their society. The personal desires and interests of the individuals in the matter were not recognized as important. For Hegel, the recognition of the value of the individual is something that only emerges in the modern world. Similarly, for Marx and Engels, it is only in a communist society that the individual is able to choose freely what profession they wish to pursue. According to their view, the economy will be regulated by the state, and individuals will be free to follow their own hearts with regard to the form of work that they find most interesting and personally fulfilling. They will not be obliged to take a job just in order to earn a minimal living. In such a situation the individual will be able to overcome the sense of alienation that is felt in a society that has a strict division of labor that is in effect forced on people.

According to Marx and Engels, people feel a deep-seated intuition of alienation with regard to the sphere of labor and production because it is perceived as something apart from their own wishes and will. Just as early humans perceived the forces of nature as something simply given and alien, so also later humans perceive the sphere of labor as something foreign, from which they feel estranged. The interest of society with regard to the production of goods is "imposed on them as an interest 'alien' to them, and 'independent' of them."[121] Like a force of nature, "the social power, i.e., the multiplied productive force ... appears to these individuals ... not as their own united power, but as an alien force existing outside them, of the origin and goal of which they are ignorant, which they thus cannot control."[122] The labor market has a power of its own, dictating who works when and where. Like a jealous god, it seems arbitrary and unjust in its actions, sometimes demanding intensive labor and an enlarged workforce and sometimes laying off hundreds of

---

[120] Marx and Engels, *Die deutsche Ideologie*, p. 33; *The German Ideology*, Part I, p. 160.
[121] Marx and Engels, *Die deutsche Ideologie*, p. 34; *The German Ideology*, Part I, p. 161.
[122] Marx and Engels, *Die deutsche Ideologie*, p. 34; *The German Ideology*, Part I, p. 161.

workers. The particular interests of the individuals are entirely disregarded. The workers are simply obliged to adapt themselves as well as they can to the fiat of the market and hope for the best.

Marx and Engels believe that it is only with a communist economy that individuals will overcome their sense of alienation. Since they will be able to choose their own work freely, they will no longer have the sense that they are being obliged to do something that they are disinclined to do merely for the sake of making a living. Moreover, they will feel a sense of enfranchisement or empowerment since the sphere of work and production will no longer strike them as a mysterious alien force to be feared, but rather it will be regarded as a rational construction under human regulation that can be controlled and steered for the benefit of all. In this way humans overcome, so to speak, the angry gods that were thought to govern the universe. Now it is humans who are in control based on their rationality and technical ability. This is what Hegel refers to as spirit overcoming nature. For Marx and Engels, history is the story of the gradual emancipation of people from the tyranny of the market forces as an alien power.[123]

## 6.9   The Theory of Ideology

While Marx and Engels are consistently critical of abstract ideas in contrast to the actual modes of production in society, they do claim that there is a connection between them. Specially, the organization of production in a society creates different social classes. The ruling class then develops a series of ideas and views that legitimate its position and defend the existing state of affairs as rational and beneficial for all. Thus in *The German Ideology* it is claimed, "The ideas of the ruling class are in every epoch the ruling ideas."[124] In short, the ruling class develops an ideology to justify its own position. When seen from a historical perspective, the leading ideas of any given age are simply a reflection of the worldview and set of priorities of the ruling class: "during the time that the aristocracy was dominant, the concepts honor, loyalty, etc. were dominant, during the dominance of the bourgeoisie the concepts freedom, equality, etc. [were dominant]."[125]

But this is ideological since it does not accurately reflect the true situation of society. The picture that it presents is slanted in favor of the leaders of the society. Such views are thus oppressive since they help to keep the disenfranchised classes in line by deceiving them about what is in their best interests. The goal of the ruling ideology is to convince the workers that the system is working for them, whereas in fact they are victimized by it. The ruling class universalizes its interests as a specific class and presents them as the interests of society as

---

[123] Marx and Engels, *Die deutsche Ideologie*, p. 36; *The German Ideology*, Part I, p. 163.

[124] Marx and Engels, *Die deutsche Ideologie*, p. 46; *The German Ideology*, Part I, p. 172.

[125] Marx and Engels, *Die deutsche Ideologie*, p. 47; *The German Ideology*, Part I, p. 173.

a whole: "it has to give its ideas the form of universality, and represent them as the only rational, universally valid ones."[126] If anyone challenges these views, then *they* are charged with representing *special interests*, which are not valid for the whole of society. The irony is that the ruling class has managed to portray its special interests as also being in the interest of everyone else, but their promotion of their special interests is never called into question.

Marx and Engels claim that in advanced societies, intellectuals make their living as ideologues directly or indirectly in the service of the state. The intellectuals develop views and theories that support the privileged class to which they belong. It is claimed that Hegel is one such intellectual and that his theory of historical development is simply an ideological justification of the status quo. At the end of his *Lectures on the Philosophy of History*, Hegel describes his theory as a "theodicy," that is, a justification of God's plan in history.[127] Despite wars, persecutions, and great human suffering, there is a reason in history that can be uncovered and understood by the philosopher. Once one understands this, then one will be reconciled with history. The goal of Hegel's theory is thus to overcome a sense of alienation with the world by bringing about a reconciliation.

According to Marx and Engels, this theory serves the purpose of the ruling class since it attempts to demonstrate that things are as they should be – that the existing social order is the result of a divine plan. Moreover, it even tries to account for the perception of injustice and inequality, which it then dissolves with an argument about how this fails to see the big picture. In order to make this view sound plausible, Hegel is obliged to use very abstract language, referring to "spirit," "freedom," "the concept," etc. Hegel attempts to make things appear concrete by using terms such as "self-consciousness" as if this were a specific person, but this is simply an illusion. This abstract language can give the impression of giving the arguments a degree of plausibility, but when one looks more closely, one sees that these are pure fictions that have nothing to do with real life and human interaction in the world.

According to Marx and Engels, Hegel's theory begins and ends with ideas. It must abstract from the concrete empirical facts of existence right from the start. Then, in working with pure ideas, Hegel finds certain connections that can be developed into a theory about the alleged movement of spirit. This is the basis of the narrative about the development of human freedom in history. But the objection is that this theory has no relation to reality. It simply uses abstract ideas to justify a certain state of things under the banner of human freedom

---

[126] Marx and Engels, *Die deutsche Ideologie*, p. 47; *The German Ideology*, Part I, p. 174.

[127] G. W. F. Hegel, *Vorlesungen über die Philosophie der Geschichte*, ed. by Eduard Gans, vol. 9 (1837) (2nd ed. by Karl Hegel, 1840), in *Georg Wilhelm Friedrich Hegel's Werke. Vollständige Ausgabe*, p. 446. (English translation: *The Philosophy of History*, trans. by J. Sibree [New York: Willey Book Co., 1944], p. 457.) See Marx and Engels, *Die deutsche Ideologie*, pp. 48f.; *The German Ideology*, Part I, p. 175.

and self-determination. In fact, the truth of the matter is that the workers in modern society are not free but rather subject to the arbitrary conditions of the market. For Marx and Engels, such theories should be exposed as ideological and as representing the interests of only a specific group of people. The goal should be to discern the truth about society and history on its own terms, independent of the interests of the ruling class.

## 6.10    Marx's Debt to Hegel

Here one can see that Marx's theory of self-consciousness, alienation, and even historical development owes a great debt to Hegel, specifically to Hegel's theory of self-consciousness in the lord-bondsman dialectic and Hegel's theory of the movement of history and religion. While Marx is well known for his criticism of Hegel for abstraction, which he refers to as "idealistic humbug,"[128] nonetheless this should not be allowed to overshadow the deeper resonance of Hegel's philosophy that one can find in Marx's theories. Marx draws from Hegel a developmental and teleological sense of history that ultimately leads to the fulfillment of human freedom. For Hegel, this means achieving the correct balance of the subjective freedom of the individual and the identification with the rational laws and customs of the state and society as a whole. For Marx, this means the attainment of a communist society that eliminates all forms of inequality by doing away with the division of labor and private property.

Marx and Hegel agree that the individual can only be truly free in the context of a larger group, that is, the society or the state. The individual becomes who they are by identifying with the larger social whole and seeing its truth and rationality. However, there is an interesting divergence in their concrete assessment of this. According to Hegel, the different stages of history represent different stages of the awareness of human freedom.[129] At the beginning of history in China, there is only an awareness that one person is free, namely the Emperor of China. In the Greco-Roman world, democracy is invented, and there is an awareness that some people are free, whereas others remain slaves. Finally, in the Germanic world, with the rise of Christianity, there is an awareness that everyone is free and that each human being has an absolute irreducible value. For Marx, this conception is ideological since it is clear that in contemporary society not everyone is free. On the contrary, the proletariat class is enslaved by the current mode of production and is at the mercy of market forces. They do not have the possibility of freely determining their own work conditions. In *The German Ideology*, Marx and Engels, in agreement with Hegel, readily grant that "only in the community ... is

---

[128] Marx and Engels, *Die deutsche Ideologie*, p. 38; *The German Ideology*, Part I, p. 164.
[129] Hegel, *Vorlesungen über die Philosophie der Geschichte*, vol. 9, p. 20; *The Philosophy of History*, p. 18.

personal freedom possible."[130] But they then hasten to add a qualification to this: "In the previous substitutes for the community, in the state, etc., personal freedom has existed only for the individuals who developed within the relationships of the ruling class, and only insofar as they were individuals of this class."[131] So Hegel's conception that everyone is free in modern society is an illusion. As long as society consists of different classes in conflict with one another, the individuals in the oppressed classes can never be free. According to this view, Hegel does not realize that modern society represents merely an "illusory community" (*scheinbare Gemeinschaft*) and not a real one.[132] Where there are different classes, there can never be a fully free development of one's abilities in the different human relations and forms of interaction. One class will always oppress another.

Marx has no patience for the Hegelian view that history is the development of the idea of human freedom since he believes that ideas are not what is primary but rather what is secondary. It is, he claims, instead concrete work relations and the organization of labor in civil society that is the true driving force of history. It is only from these concrete relations that any philosophical ideas about freedom or anything else can arise. But Hegel would be quick to point out that ideas and concrete relations cannot be as readily separated as Marx believes. In every mode of production there is an idea about how things should be organized and done. Even in something as concrete as money, there is always a necessary element of thought since money itself as a physical object is worthless paper or metal. It only attains a value when the thought is added to it that it represents a specific value, which is itself an idea, for example, twenty dollars or euros. This is a value that can be used to buy concrete goods, but it is also a value in itself, an idea in one's mind. So, for Hegel, ideas and concrete objects or actions in the real world cannot be separated. The goal of philosophy is precisely to understand the relationship between the two. In history this means not simply dwelling on an abstract idea but rather seeing it concretely instantiated in specific historical movements and developments. This is granted when Marx and Engels describe their own methodology in *The German Ideology* as one that wishes to "overcome the dead facts as it is with the empiricists" and the "imagined activity of imagined subjects as with the idealists."[133] Their point here is exactly that of Hegel: Pure facts on their own without any thought to make sense of them are meaningless; likewise, pure thoughts on their own in the absence of any relation to the real world are also meaningless. The goal should be to combine the two. In this sense Marx, despite his overt polemic against Hegel, can be seen as, in fact, following a Hegelian methodology in his view of history and society.

---

[130] Marx and Engels, *Die deutsche Ideologie*, p. 74; *The German Ideology*, Part I, p. 197.
[131] Marx and Engels, *Die deutsche Ideologie*, p. 74; *The German Ideology*, Part I, p. 197.
[132] Marx and Engels, *Die deutsche Ideologie*, p. 74; *The German Ideology*, Part I, p. 197.
[133] Marx and Engels, *Die deutsche Ideologie*, p. 27; *The German Ideology*, Part I, p. 155.

# 7

# Kierkegaard's Analysis of the Forms of Despair and Alienation

Søren Kierkegaard (1813–1855) was a Danish religious writer who had a profound influence on philosophy and a number of other fields such as theology, religious studies, psychology, and literature. Born in Copenhagen in the Kingdom of Denmark,[1] Kierkegaard had a melancholy youth and witnessed the early deaths of all of his siblings with the exception of his elder brother. His father, a profoundly religious man, belonged to the nouveau riche of Copenhagen, and Kierkegaard never had to worry about earning a living for himself. His thought is in many ways closely connected to the city of Copenhagen, where he lived his entire life. In his works he frequently refers to well-known places in the city and sketches certain characters that are intended to reflect the general ways of thinking of the Copenhagen bourgeoisie. His polemics often have a very local character and are directed against leading Danish cultural or religious figures of the day.

Kierkegaard's elder brother, Peter Christian Kierkegaard, attended Hegel's lectures in Berlin in 1828 and 1829.[2] During the 1830s Hegel's philosophy became an increasingly popular trend in Denmark due to the work of Johan Ludvig Heiberg and the young theologian Hans Lassen Martensen. Although Kierkegaard initially cultivated a personal relation to Heiberg, he was critical of the many easily excitable followers of Hegel, whom he saw among his fellow students. But he nonetheless maintained a great respect for certain aspects of Hegel's philosophy. In his dissertation, *The Concept of Irony*, from 1841, he used Hegel's works extensively in his research, and they play a central role in the formation of his own thinking in the text.[3]

---

[1] For Kierkegaard's life and works, see Alastair Hannay, *Kierkegaard: A Biography* (Cambridge: Cambridge University Press, 2001); Walter Lowrie, *Kierkegaard* (London: Oxford University Press, 1938); Walter Lowrie, *A Short Life of Kierkegaard* (Princeton: Princeton University Press, 1942); Ronald Grimsley, *Søren Kierkegaard: A Biographical Introduction* (London: Studio Vista, 1973) (*Leaders of Modern Thought*); Jon Stewart, *Søren Kierkegaard: Subjectivity, Irony and the Crisis of Modernity* (Oxford: Oxford University Press, 2015).

[2] See Jon Stewart, *A History of Hegelianism in Golden Age Denmark*, Tome I, *The Heiberg Period: 1824–1836* (Copenhagen: C. A. Reitzel, 2007) (*Danish Golden Age Studies*, vol. 3), pp. 327–331.

[3] See Jon Stewart, *Kierkegaard's Relations to Hegel Reconsidered* (New York: Cambridge University Press, 2003), pp. 132–181; Jon Stewart, *A History of Hegelianism in Golden Age Denmark*, Tome II, *The Martensen Period: 1837–1842* (Copenhagen: C. A. Reitzel, 2007)

After the completion of his dissertation, Kierkegaard left Copenhagen and travelled to Berlin in order to attend the lectures of, among others, Schelling at the university there. Kierkegaard's journey was in part triggered by his notorious break-up with his fiancée Regine Olsen, an event that had become the talk of the town. Although Kierkegaard quickly tired of Schelling's lectures, he ended up spending almost five months in Berlin.[4] This stay in the Prussian capital gave him first-hand insight into the world of Germanophone philosophy a decade after Hegel's death. As we have seen, this period was dominated by discussions concerning, above all, Hegel's philosophy of religion, and Kierkegaard was familiar with the works of people like Feuerbach, Strauss, and Bruno Bauer. He sat in the same classroom as Engels and Bakunin and attended the courses of the Hegelian logician Karl Werder and the Hegelian theologian Philipp Marheineke.[5]

During this time Kierkegaard began work on what can be regarded as his breakthrough book, the two-volume *Either/Or*, which he published in 1843 after he returned to Copenhagen. This work inaugurated an amazingly productive period, in which he rapidly produced a series of books on philosophical and religious topics. In quick succession he published *Repetition* (1843), *Fear and Trembling* (1843), *Philosophical Fragments* (1844), *The Concept of Anxiety* (1844), *Prefaces* (1844), and *Stages on Life's Way* (1845). Like *Either/Or*, these works were published under different pseudonyms that Kierkegaard created. Parallel to these famous works, he penned a number of collections of edifying discourses in his own name. His strategy was to appeal to different kinds of readers with different interests and levels of education. While the pseudonymous works are more complex and philosophical, the edifying works tend to be more straightforward and less technical, in many ways resembling sermons.

One reason for this productivity might be found in Kierkegaard's conviction that he would die before he reached the age of thirty-four. The sad story of the death of his siblings at early ages had led him to believe that his family

(*Danish Golden Age Studies*, vol. 3), pp. 564–634; Jon Stewart, "Hegel's Historical Methodology in *The Concept of Irony*," *Kierkegaard Studies Yearbook* (2011), 81–100; Jon Stewart, "Hegel: Kierkegaard's Reading and Use of Hegel's Primary Texts," in Jon Stewart (ed.), *Kierkegaard and His German Contemporaries*, Tome I, *Philosophy* (Aldershot and Burlington: Ashgate, 2007) (*Kierkegaard Research: Sources, Reception and Resources*, vol. 6), pp. 97–165.

[4] See Stewart, *A History of Hegelianism in Golden Age Denmark*, Tome II, *The Martensen Period: 1837–1842*, pp. 641–678.

[5] See Jon Stewart, "Werder: The Influence of Werder's Lectures and *Logik* on Kierkegaard's Thought," in Stewart (ed.), *Kierkegaard and his German Contemporaries*, Tome I, *Philosophy*, pp. 335–371; Heiko Schulz, "Marheineke: The Volatilization of Christian Doctrine," in Jon Stewart (ed.), *Kierkegaard and His German Contemporaries*, Tome II, *Theology* (Aldershot and Burlington: Ashgate, 2007) (*Kierkegaard Research: Sources, Reception and Resources*, vol. 6), pp. 117–142.

was under some kind of curse, perhaps due to some misdeed of his father, and that he too would share their fate. So he hastened to write as many works as he could while he could still do so. As his thirty-fourth birthday approached, he rushed to complete the *Concluding Unscientific Postscript* (1846), another pseudonymous work, which he planned to be his final work. In a short appendix at the end of the book, called "A First and Last Explanation," Kierkegaard, believing that he would soon die, reveals to his readers that he is the author behind all of the pseudonymous works. This was in some ways a bold move since up until that point he had been meticulous about concealing his identity, although it was probably known by most of his readers.

To his great surprise, however, his thirty-fourth birthday came and went, and he remained in good health. He thus resumed writing and continued to develop his thought. Scholars usually divide Kierkegaard's authorship into two periods – an early period including the *Concluding Unscientific Postscript* and all the works that preceded it, and a late period that includes everything that he wrote after the *Postscript* up until his death in 1855. This later period includes famous books such as *The Sickness unto Death* (1849) and *Practice in Christianity* (1850) and a number of other religious works. It is usually said that the first half of his authorship is not explicitly religious in aim but has more of a negative or exploratory focus. By contrast, Kierkegaard is thought to have become more explicit about his Christian agenda after 1847.

In the last few years of his life, Kierkegaard was engaged in a bitter public polemic against the Danish State Church. He published a series of articles in the newspaper *The Fatherland* and in his own publication, *The Moment*, in which he gave a vitriolic rebuke of the Church for deviating from what he called true New Testament Christianity. He believed that the leaders of the Church had become corrupt and complacent, preaching a distorted and watered-down version of the Christian message. Kierkegaard tried to counter this by presenting a harsh and highly demanding vision of Christianity that involved things such as suffering and martyrdom. He died on November 11, 1855 in the midst of the controversy, and in his final days he refused to receive a pastor of the Danish Church.

Kierkegaard remained a controversial figure after his death. He was known as an important writer and thinker in the Scandinavian countries in the second half of the nineteenth century, but his real international breakthrough came at the beginning of the twentieth century when German translations of his works became more widespread. He has been seen as a major source of inspiration for movements such as dialectical theology, existentialism, and deconstruction. The complexity and ambiguity of his works continue to provide fertile ground for academic disagreement and interpretation.

## 7.1  The Unhappiest One and Hegel's Unhappy Consciousness

Kierkegaard's *Either/Or* is divided into two parts and ostensibly published by the pseudonymous editor Victor Eremita. The first part contains a series of aphorisms and essays on different topics written by an unnamed aesthetic writer, referred to simply as A. The second part is presented as the work of a civil servant, Judge William, who writes long essays to his friend, the aesthete, in which he argues for the virtues of bourgeois life. In Part I of the work there is a short chapter entitled "The Unhappiest One."[6] The chapter takes as its point of departure a purported grave in England that instead of giving the name of the deceased on the tombstone gives simply the inscription "The Unhappiest One." This is then the occasion for a meditation on different forms of unhappiness. The aesthete is concerned to find out what can be considered the greatest unhappiness, or, put differently, what this person experienced in life to make his unhappiness greater than that of other people. He imagines a kind of competition among unhappy people in order to decide who can justly be said to deserve the title of the unhappiest one.[7] The contestants are divided into different categories and classes in order to determine more clearly their degree of unhappiness.

In this context the aesthete brings up Hegel's idea of the unhappy consciousness for comparison.[8] As we have seen in our analysis of *The Phenomenology of Spirit*, the unhappy consciousness represents a form of religious alienation.

---

[6] Søren Kierkegaard, *Enten-Eller, Første Deel*, in *Søren Kierkegaards Skrifter*, vols. 1–28, K1–K28, ed. by Niels Jørgen Cappelørn, Joakim Garff, Jette Knudsen, Johnny Kondrup, and Alastair McKinnon (Copenhagen: Gad Publishers, 1997–2012) (hereafter *SKS*), vol. 2, pp. 211–223. (English translation: *Either/Or*, Part I, trans. by Howard V. Hong and Edna H. Hong [Princeton: Princeton University Press, 1987], pp. 217–230.) See Dorothea Glöckner, "'The Unhappiest One' – Merely an Inscription? On the Relationship between Immediacy and Language in the Work of Kierkegaard," in Paul Cruysberghs, Johan Taels, and Karl Verstrynge (eds.), *Immediacy and Reflection in Kierkegaard's Thought* (Leuven: Leuven University Press, 2003) (*Louvain Philosophical Studies*, vol. 17), pp. 41–53; John E. Hare, "The Unhappiest One and the Structure of Kierkegaard's *Either/Or*," in Robert L. Perkins (ed.), *Either/Or*, Part I (Macon, GA: Mercer University Press, 1995) (*International Kierkegaard Commentary*, vol. 3), pp. 91–108; Karsten Harries, *Between Nihilism and Faith: A Commentary on "Either/Or"* (Berlin and New York: De Gruyter, 2010) (*Kierkegaard Studies Monograph Series*, vol. 21), pp. 71–75.

[7] Kierkegaard, *SKS*, vol. 2, p. 215; *Either/Or*, Part I, p. 221.

[8] Kierkegaard, *SKS*, vol. 2, pp. 215f.; *Either/Or*, Part I, p. 222. See W. Richard Comstock, "Hegel, Kierkegaard, Marx on 'The Unhappy Consciousness,'" *Internationales Jahrbuch für Wissens- und Religionssoziologie*, 11 (1978), 91–119; Matthew Edgar, "Deer Park or the Monastery? Kierkegaard and Hegel on Unhappy Consciousness, Renunciation, and Worldliness," *Philosophy Today*, 46 (2002), 284–299; Liesbet Samyn, "How to Cure Despair: On Irony and the Unhappy Consciousness," *Kierkegaard Studies Yearbook* (2009), 317–351; Liesbet Samyn, "Yearning for the Grave: The Unhappy Consciousness in Hegel's *Phenomenology of Spirit* and in Kierkegaard's *Either/Or*," in Andreas Arndt (ed.), *Geist? Zweiter Teil* (Berlin: Akademie Verlag, 2011), pp. 255–261.

The reason for its unhappiness is that the unhappy consciousness is forever separated from God. The individual remains in a finite, sinful world, while God is in a transcendent beyond. The unhappy consciousness finds its truth and meaning in God yet is radically separated from him. This can be a relationship to *the past* since the unhappy consciousness looks back with longing to the time of Jesus and regrets that now that time has gone. It desperately attempts to recapture this past by collecting splinters of the cross or the funeral shroud of Jesus, but for all of this, the unhappy consciousness remains alienated and unfulfilled. But this can also be a relationship to *the future*. The unhappy consciousness is in a sense trapped in the sinful mundane world until it dies and is united with God in heaven. So here the focus is on a future life, which is regarded as the real life, where the separation from the divine will be overcome.

Hegel's account of the unhappy consciousness provides the key categories for unhappiness that Kierkegaard draws on. Based on Hegel's discussion, Kierkegaard's aesthete then takes up an analysis of these forms of alienation with respect to the past and the future. The aesthete explains, "The unhappy one is the person who in one way or another has his ideal, the substance of his life, the plentitude of his consciousness, his essential nature, outside himself."[9] This can serve as a definition of alienation, which, as we have seen, is characterized as some kind of separation. So *self*-alienation is a separation from oneself. The aesthete continues by explaining this in more detail: "The unhappy one is the person who is always absent from himself, never present to himself. But in being absent, one obviously can be in either past or future time."[10] So one can imagine one's essence or the focus of one's life to be something that was in the past and is now gone, and for this reason one is separated from it. Or it can be something in an indeterminate future that one seemingly will never reach, and for this reason one is separated from it. One is condemned to live in the present, so all longing for the past or hope for the future represents some kind of separation or alienation. One can only be happy if one is present to oneself, that is, if one's sense of self is in the present that one lives in. Unhappiness arises from the split between the temporal spheres: One must live in the present, but one's focus is constantly on the past or the future.

The aesthete then goes on to explore both of these temporal modalities in turn. He examines first the individual who lives in the hope of a future. Here he recalls Hegel's discussion of the unhappy Christian consciousness looking forward to a life in heaven with God: "A person who hopes for eternal life is certainly in a sense an unhappy individuality, insofar as he renounces the present."[11] To retreat from this life in the hope of an afterlife is a betrayal of religion. It is important that one not try to escape the here and now. To live in

---

[9] Kierkegaard, *SKS*, vol. 2, p. 216; *Either/Or*, Part I, p. 222.
[10] Kierkegaard, *SKS*, vol. 2, p. 216; *Either/Or*, Part I, p. 222.
[11] Kierkegaard, *SKS*, vol. 2, p. 217; *Either/Or*, Part I, p. 223.

the hope of a future life is thus a form of unhappiness, although it does not qualify as the highest form.

Yet the aesthete qualifies this claim, saying that not everyone who lives with hope is unhappy.[12] It is indeed possible to be hopeful of an eternal life in such a way that this does not undermine one's existence in the present. So one can say that there is a dialectical relation at work here. It is natural and normal that one has hopes and dreams and to this extent thinks of the future. But the key is not to become obsessed with this to the point that this focus on the future comes to obscure the present. One can thus still be present to oneself when one thinks of a future, but one should avoid taking this too far.

The aesthete states that the same dynamic is at work with regard to someone who is focused on the past. We all have treasured recollections and life-defining memories of the past, and it is normal that we think of them from time to time. The problem arises when we turn these into fixations and they come to occupy our minds more than the present. For example, an old person might think of their life as a young person and regard this as their true self, whereas their current self, as old and diminished, is somehow less real or important. So once again it is a matter of having the right degree of focus on the present along with a relation to the past.

The aesthete says that with the past and the future, the different forms of unhappiness seem to be exhausted, and for "this firm limitation, we thank Hegel."[13] Here he refers to the two temporal dimensions of the unhappy consciousness, just discussed. But then he in a sense applies Hegel's own methodology to go Hegel one better. He combines the first and the second term, which Hegel had mentioned in his analysis of the unhappy conscious-ness, into a synthesis or higher unity.

Kierkegaard's author explains that there can be a combination of the two forms of unhappiness, that is, as relating to both the future and the past. At first this seems impossible since one is oriented either toward the past or toward the future, and the two are mutually exclusive. How can one be oriented toward both at the same time? The aesthete explains that the individual's "hope is continually being disappointed, but he discovers that this disappointment occurs not because his objective is pushed further ahead but because he is past his goal, because it has already been experienced or should have been experienced and thus passed over into recollection."[14] The aesthete explains that real unhappiness occurs when one focuses on a past or a future that is not possible. He gives the example of someone who had no real childhood, but

---

[12] Kierkegaard, *SKS*, vol. 2, p. 217; *Either/Or*, Part I, p. 223: "strictly speaking, he is nevertheless not unhappy, because he is present to himself in this hope and does not come into conflict with the particular elements of finiteness."
[13] Kierkegaard, *SKS*, vol. 2, p. 216; *Either/Or*, Part I, p. 222.
[14] Kierkegaard, *SKS*, vol. 2, p. 218; *Either/Or*, Part I, p. 225.

then in later life, through his work as a teacher, comes to experience the true meaning of childhood in his young students.[15] Upon comparing this new experience with his own life experience, the individual feels an infinite sense of loss. There is something in the past that he has missed out on forever. Or likewise if someone knew no joy in life and only discovered this in old age before dying, then this recollection of his own life without joy would be a bitter one. These are the real cases of profound unhappiness, according to the aesthete.

Examples like this represent the dialectical third term that unites the first and the second, that is, the past and the future. An individual regrets that he has had no joyful childhood, and this is a focus on the past. But it is also in a sense a hope for the future in that one hopes for a better childhood. But this is not something that lends itself to being a hope for the future in the way that one can hope for a million dollars or a new friend – hopes that can in principle always be realized no matter how old one is or where one finds oneself in life. But this is not the case with a lost childhood since once one is old, it is impossible that one will ever have the chance to go back and relive one's childhood. One's childhood is irretrievably gone, and no one has a second chance to live it again. So one relates both to a future that can never be and a past that never was. One is unable to be present to oneself in the here and now because of a fixation on a regret about both the past and the future.

A pendant to this position can be found in an impossible wish for the future; for example, someone might wish that their dead parents could be present to celebrate their upcoming wedding, which is obviously impossible. Here the orientation is toward the future, but again the wish is different from wishing something that could really be realized. Like the recollection of the childhood that never was, this hope is for a future that can never be. Also like the other example, there is regret about something in the past – that is, the death of one's parents – that one wishes had been different.

The aesthete goes on to list a number of examples of well-known unhappy figures from the Bible and Greek mythology. Specifically, he refers to Niobe, Antigone, and Job, who all seem to be victims of the unhappiness of recollection since they all recall a happy time in the past that has been taken from them. By contrast, he mentions the father of the prodigal son from Luke 15:11–32, who is an example of the unhappiness of hope since he is constantly hoping for some time in the future when his son will return to him.

He mentions an anonymous young woman whose lover has been faithless,[16] which is presumably an allusion to his former fiancée Regine Olsen. When Kierkegaard was alone in Berlin writing *Either/Or* immediately after his break-up, he must have thought a lot about what happened. He seems to use his

[15] Kierkegaard, *SKS*, vol. 2, p. 218; *Either/Or*, Part I, p. 224.
[16] Kierkegaard, *SKS*, vol. 2, p. 220, p. 222; *Either/Or*, Part I, p. 227, pp. 228f.

writing as a way of communicating with Regine, knowing that she would read
his published books and that she would recognize certain passages that were
addressed to her. The brief sketch of the unnamed young woman seems to be
just one such passage. She falls into the third category of unhappiness. Her
grief is focused on the past. In the sadness of the present, she recollects a time
when she was together with her lover and they had a good relationship. But one
might argue that they are still young, and there might be some chance that he
would return to her and they would be reconciled. But this possibility is ruled
out for unexplained reasons. It is impossible for the lover ever to return or for
Kierkegaard ever to be reunited with Regine. So Regine and presumably
Kierkegaard as well regret a past that they wish could have been different
and hope for a future that can never be. Kierkegaard's author wants to grant
the young woman second place in the competition.

Finally, the author sketches, as the winner of the title of the unhappiest one,
an unnamed figure who seems to be Christ, although he is not mentioned
explicitly. This figure is said to have lived many centuries ago, to have been
"nailed to the cross," and to have seen "heaven open."[17] Further, it is written,
"he denied his Lord and himself,"[18] which refers to Jesus' words on the cross,
"My God, my God, why hast thou forsaken me?"[19] Reference is also made to
the stone having been rolled away from the entrance to the tomb of Jesus.[20]
The author then writes of his wish to see people seek comfort and solace in this
figure as a Christian would in Jesus: "may those who are pregnant turn to you
in their anxiety; may the mothers trust you; may the dying seek consolation in
you; may the young people attach themselves to you; may the men rely upon
you; may the aged reach for you as for a cane – may the whole world believe
that you are able to make it happy."[21] With this figure the dialectical analysis
comes to a head, and the categories become indistinguishable from one
another. Kierkegaard's author writes, "Farewell, then, unhappiest one! But
what am I saying? I ought to say 'the happiest,' for this is indeed precisely
a gift of fortune that no one can give himself. See, language breaks down, and
thought is confused, for who indeed is the happiest but the unhappiest and
who the unhappiest but the happiest."[22] Just as in Hegel's logic the categories
of being and nothing turn out to be identical mirror images of one another, so
also happiness and unhappiness merge and constitute a higher category. Here
lies the paradoxical Christian message that Jesus suffered a terrible, unjust
death, yet this should be regarded as a joyous event since it was an atonement
for human sin and thus made salvation possible. Kierkegaard himself agrees

---

[17] Kierkegaard, *SKS*, vol. 2, p. 221; *Either/Or*, Part I, p. 228.
[18] Kierkegaard, *SKS*, vol. 2, p. 221; *Either/Or*, Part I, p. 228.
[19] Matthew 27:46.
[20] Matthew 28:2, Mark 16:4, Luke 24:2, John 20:1.
[21] Kierkegaard, *SKS*, vol. 2, p. 223; *Either/Or*, Part I, p. 230.
[22] Kierkegaard, *SKS*, vol. 2, p. 223; *Either/Or*, Part I, p. 230.

that this is contradictory or even absurd when judged by human reason. Seen from this perspective, "faith [is] but foolishness."[23] The text thus ends with a Christian idea that would seem to be far away from the world of the aesthete.

In the analysis of the unhappiest one, Kierkegaard has his aesthete not merely take up Hegel's motif of the unhappy consciousness but also offer an analysis of different forms of alienation. Moreover, he imitates Hegel's systematic and dialectical form of analysis that explores first one possibility, then its opposite, and then a combination of the two. In short, Kierkegaard seems to have been inspired both by the actual content of analysis of the unhappy consciousness and Hegel's methodology. He expands Hegel's analysis of alienation to include the complex forms of self-alienation.

## 7.2   Kierkegaard's Criticism of the Present Age

In 1846, only three years after *Either/Or*, Kierkegaard published a long book review of a novel entitled *Two Ages*, which was the work of Thomasine Gyllembourg, who belonged to one of Denmark's most celebrated cultural families and was the mother of Johan Ludvig Heiberg. The novel explores the changes in Danish life that took place during two periods: that of the French Revolution (The Age of Revolution) and that of the Restoration (The Present Age). In his critical assessment of the work, which is often referred to as *A Literary Review of Two Ages* or simply *A Literary Review*, Kierkegaard examines not just the novel but also certain social-political tendencies in his own age. For this reason, this work is often hailed as his statement of political philosophy, although this somewhat overstates the case since it is by no means a theoretical work about the state as such.

In his chapter dedicated to "The Present Age," he issues a criticism of different modern trends.[24] Kierkegaard begins with a general characterization: The age of revolution was characterized by its passion, whereas the present age

---

[23] Kierkegaard, *SKS*, vol. 2, p. 223; *Either/Or*, Part I, p. 230.
[24] Kierkegaard, *SKS*, vol. 8, pp. 66–106. (English translation: *Two Ages: The Age of Revolution and the Present Age, A Literary Review*, trans. by Howard V. Hong and Edna H. Hong [Princeton: Princeton University Press, 1978], pp. 68–112.) See Daniel W. Conway, "Modest Expectations: Kierkegaard's Reflections on the Present Age," *Kierkegaard Studies Yearbook* (1999), 21–49; Daniel W. Conway and K. E. Gover (eds.), *Social and Political Philosophy: Kierkegaard and the "Present Age"* (London and New York: Routledge, 2002) (*Søren Kierkegaard: Critical Assessments of Leading Philosophers*, vol. 4); George Pattison, "The Present Age: The Age of the City," *Kierkegaard Studies Yearbook* (1999), 1–20; Milan Petkanič, "Passion and Age: Kierkegaard's Diagnosis of the Present Age," *Human Affairs: A Postdisciplinary Journal for Humanities and Social Sciences*, 14(2) (2004), 165–182; Husain Sarkar, *The Toils of Understanding: An Essay on "The Present Age"* (Macon, GA: Mercer University Press, 2000); John R. Wilson, "'Signs of the Times' and 'The Present Age': Essays of Crisis," *Western Humanities Review*, 26 (1972), 369–374.

is characterized by its cool calculation, reflection, and lack of passion. This
might at first glance sound like criticism of the age of revolution and praise of
the present age, but in fact just the opposite is the case. Kierkegaard objects to
what he regards as the overemphasis on reflection, which he believes leads
away from important aspects of a person. He argues that by reflecting and
calculating the whole time, people fail to act, and for this reason he describes
the present age as one characterized by inertia, indolence, and laziness.[25]
Although people make a big show of being busy with important matters, all
of their time and effort is spent reflecting and calculating, and not taking real
action. In the present age this is regarded as sensible and prudent, but this is
based on a misunderstanding since the lack of passion undermines making
decisions and acting freely in the world.

While in the age of revolution people took to the streets to demand their
rights, in the present age people have quiet meetings and discuss minor
measures of reform dispassionately. Passionate revolutionary people try to
tear down things in order to start again, but people in the age of reflection stage
their revolution by allowing old habits and institutions to remain yet rendering
them meaningless.[26] Revolutions take place because there are clear principles
in conflict with one another. However, reflection undermines these sharp
distinctions and oppositions; they become wishy-washy, or, in Kierkegaard's
language, they equivocate.[27] He claims that it is a characteristic of the modern
age that it has annulled the law of contradiction;[28] that is, nothing is absolutely
contradictory any more, or, put differently, the contradiction between any two
positions can always be overcome. In a passionate age, one finds passionate
individuals who are ready to fight for one cause or another. By contrast, in
a reflective age, people have no character since they undermine opposition and
contradiction. Clear lines and sharp distinctions are lost in the present age, and
everything remains blurred and ambiguous. People are no longer capable of
bold and daring action that requires choice and resolution. In such an age,
there are no heroes. In the age of reflection, young people no longer struggle
for love or fame but instead for money.[29]

In the age of reflection, individuality is undermined. In the age of revolution,
people passionately participate in events that are important to them. By
contrast, people who live in reflection are not participants but rather specta-
tors. They tend not to relate themselves to the events around them but instead
distance themselves from them.[30] Since they have no personal relation to the
issue, they lack inwardness and thus have no character. They see the issue, so to

[25] Kierkegaard, *SKS*, vol. 8, p. 67; *Two Ages*, p. 69.
[26] Kierkegaard, *SKS*, vol. 8, pp. 74f.; *Two Ages*, p. 77.
[27] Kierkegaard, *SKS*, vol. 8, p. 75; *Two Ages*, p. 78.
[28] Kierkegaard, *SKS*, vol. 8, p. 92; *Two Ages*, p. 97.
[29] Kierkegaard, *SKS*, vol. 8, p. 72; *Two Ages*, p. 75.
[30] Kierkegaard, *SKS*, vol. 8, p. 76; *Two Ages*, p. 79.

speak, from the outside. Instead of emphasis being put on individual action, the reflective age appoints one committee after another to discuss the issue. In a sense this criticism of reflection anticipates Nietzsche's critique of the reflectivity of the modern age some years later. According to Nietzsche this reflection has separated us from our natural instincts and led us to a distorted morality and system of values.

Whereas great actions are admired in the age of revolution, they are treated as objects of envy in the age of reflection. The person who does something bold and daring is regarded as reckless. Kierkegaard regards envy as one of the defining characteristics of the present age.[31] Envy prevents people from acting decisively and boldly since individuals fear what others might think of such action. They are prudently advised by their friends and relatives not to undertake anything rash. The prudent people drag down anyone who stands out above them. This is what Kierkegaard refers to as the phenomenon of leveling, that is, bringing down the outstanding and the extraordinary to the common mean.[32] Excellence is ridiculed and persecuted by people who are weak, petty, and envious. Leveling is a phenomenon whereby an abstract group or crowd in general undermines and diminishes the achievements of specific individuals. Here again Kierkegaard anticipates an important concept in Nietzsche.

Kierkegaard's notion of leveling is also bound up with Hegel's concept of intersubjective recognition. While the weak and spiteful person undermines the achievement of another person, it might on the face of things seem that it is only the other person who is hurt by this. But in fact this also has a negative effect on the person who is doing the leveling. Kierkegaard says, "although the individual selfishly enjoys the abstraction during the brief moment of pleasure in the leveling, he is also underwriting his own downfall."[33] For one to be who one is as an individual, one must respect and recognize others in their individuality. If one undermines the abilities and achievements of others, then one undermines oneself since this erodes the possibility of one receiving meaningful recognition from the other for one's own abilities and achievements. Leveling is a contest that has no winner.

What Kierkegaard calls "the public" plays a negative role in the process of leveling.[34] The idea of the public is, for Kierkegaard, a grotesque abstraction. What exists is a manifold of particular individuals with particular interests and dispositions. However, the idea of the public levels all of this and objectifies an abstraction. People speak a lot about *the public interest* or make political

---

[31] Kierkegaard, *SKS*, vol. 8, p. 78; *Two Ages*, p. 81.
[32] Kierkegaard, *SKS*, vol. 8, p. 80; *Two Ages*, p. 84.
[33] Kierkegaard, *SKS*, vol. 8, p. 83; *Two Ages*, p. 86. See also ibid.: "for the individual who levels is himself carried along."
[34] Kierkegaard, *SKS*, vol. 8, pp. 86ff.; *Two Ages*, pp. 90ff.

decisions based on *public opinion*, but in the end this idea has no reality, and no responsibility can be ascribed to it as to a real person. When we interact with one another in society, we do so in concrete ways and situations that involve different interests and opinions. The idea of the public makes no sense in this context. It does not reflect any of the complexity of human relations in societies or communities.

The phenomenon of the public is created and preserved by the press.[35] Envious people in a reflective age see in the press an organ by which they can level what is outstanding and distinguished. They gain a perverse pleasure in seeing a talented person being torn down by the attacks of the press. Kierkegaard saw himself as a victim of this kind of persecution in connection with a conflict with the local journal *The Corsair*, which criticized him and printed satirical images of him. Kierkegaard points out that attacks of this kind are created by envious people, who are not held to account and thus do not have to take any responsibility for their actions. While they support the press and read these kinds of criticisms with great pleasure, they are always quick to distance themselves from it, saying that it was just the responsibility of a particularly mean-spirited editor or journalist. Even though they may sub-scribe to the journal and read it religiously, they can always distance them-selves from any given attack and claim that they had nothing to do with it.

### 7.3   The Political and Religious Dangers of the Present Age

There is also an important political dimension to Kierkegaard's analysis since this was the age when there were calls for equality and democracy throughout Europe, which eventually led to the Revolutions of 1848. Kierkegaard was critical of this move since he believed that these principles undermined individuality by eroding important social distinctions. Democracy means leveling. The opinion of everyone, including the greatest expert and the least-informed person, counts for the same since everyone has just one vote. In democracy, members of parliament are elected who are intended to represent the others. Kierkegaard objects to this form of representation because it undermines the value of the individual. The idea of a consensus or public opinion insidiously becomes reified as if it were a kind of collective person or individual.[36] Likewise, democracy can lead to the tyranny of the majority and of public opinion, which undermines the minority and anyone who has a view that differs from this. The individual on their own counts for nothing, and their views and values are only meaningful if they are shared by others in the context of a political party or faction. Moreover, everyone naturally wants to be liked and accepted, and so there is a tendency to go along with the crowd

---

[35]  Kierkegaard, *SKS*, vol. 8, pp. 89ff.; *Two Ages*, pp. 93ff.
[36]  Kierkegaard, *SKS*, vol. 8, p. 81; *Two Ages*, p. 85.

without even considering the issue seriously for oneself. Peer pressure can make people do things in groups that they would never dream of doing on their own as individuals. For these reasons Kierkegaard was wary of the new political trends that were breaking out in his own day.

The tendencies of the modern age are particularly troublesome for Kierkegaard with regard to religion. According to his view, in Christianity each individual is special and unique before God. For Christianity, each of us is a single individual, and this is a positive concept. Each person must make the decision of faith on their own and take responsibility for it. The modern age, however, undermines this sense of individuality and responsibility. Christian belief involves passion and inwardness, which are repressed in the age of reflection. The modern age tells us that we as individuals do not count for much if we are not a part of a larger group. But one cannot have Christian faith based on the arguments and reasoning of a larger group; instead, one must believe on one's own. People in the modern age, Kierkegaard argues, continue to regard themselves as Christian and to use Christian terminology, but they no longer know what they mean. He thus sees the social crisis of his day as related to the religious confusion that he finds in his contemporaries. Kierkegaard thus follows his contemporary Heiberg in his assessment of the crisis of the present age.[37] He refers to his time as the "age of disintegration."[38]

The symptoms of the modern age that Kierkegaard outlines can be understood as forms of alienation. When one stops regarding oneself as a participant, actively engaged in events, and starts regarding oneself as a spectator to them, then one is alienated from oneself as an individual. One's own desires and interests are undermined. Likewise, when one associates oneself with the crowd and eschews one's individuality, one is alienated from one's true self. The things that make us different as individuals no longer have any value, and we become characterless. This also means that we become alienated from others since it is not clear who they are or what they stand for either. Kierkegaard seems to have identified the source of alienation that many people feel today with large democracies, where one cannot go along with the majority view and sees that one's own opinion or vote has no value whatsoever in the big picture. In the modern age the idea of individuality is eliminated and

---

[37] Johan Ludvig Heiberg, *Om Philosophiens Betydning for den nuværende Tid. Et Indbydelses-Skrift til en Række af philosophiske Forelæsninger* (Copenhagen: C. A. Reitzel, 1833). (English translation in *Heiberg's On the Significance of Philosophy for the Present Age and Other Texts*, ed. and trans. by Jon Stewart [Copenhagen: C. A. Reitzel, 2005] [*Texts from Golden Age Denmark*, vol. 1], pp. 85–119.)

[38] Søren Kierkegaard, *Søren Kierkegaards Papirer*, vols. I to XI–3, ed. by Peter Andreas Heiberg, Victor Kuhr, and Einer Torsting (Copenhagen: Gyldendalske Boghandel, Nordisk Forlag, 1909-1948), IX B 63:7; *Papers and Journals: A Selection*, trans. with introductions and notes by Alastair Hannay (London and New York: Penguin, 1996), p. 350.

replaced with abstractions such as the crowd, public opinion, national interest, the majority, etc.

## 7.4   The Motif of the Sickness unto Death and Self-Consciousness

Kierkegaard published *The Sickness unto Death* in 1849 under the name of the pseudonymous author, Anti-Climacus. This work was followed a year later by *Practice in Christianity*, which was ostensibly penned by the same author. The title of *The Sickness unto Death* is inspired by the story of Lazarus in the New Testament (John 11:1–44).[39] Jesus is asked to come and heal the gravely sick Lazarus, but instead he says that the sickness is not mortal or unto death. So he delays two days before going to Lazarus, who dies in the interim. Jesus then miraculously revives him from death. Christ explains that this is "for the glory of God" (John 11:4). Kierkegaard interprets this to mean that the miracle of raising Lazarus from the dead demonstrates God's power and indicates to the believer that death can be overcome by Christian faith.

The point for Anti-Climacus is that this demonstrates that death is not the end for the Christian, but instead there is an eternal life in Christianity. Although we may fall mortally ill and die, this is not real death in the sense of the end of our existence. So the idea of sickness is used as a metaphor for mundane existence. Life itself is a sickness that many believe will only end in death. But for the Christian, this sickness is not unto death but rather the beginning of a new life. The so-called natural human – that is, the person without religion – regards death as the worst thing that can happen. It is to be feared every day of one's life. The Christian, by contrast, is not alarmed by this since they know that death is not the end. The divine requirement is to live right here and now with a consciousness grounded in God. The Lazarus story is about despair in this life. Jesus tells his disciples not to worry because Lazarus does not have the sickness unto death, yet he dies physically. The point is that Lazarus was not dead to the call of spirit; he was living in balance, and this is far more important than mere physical life. The problem for the despairing living person is that right now, in life, they cannot get rid of the sense of self that they ought to become, even though they want to do so. But the self is eternal, and this is why they can never get rid of it. Sickness is a metaphor for despair, which is the key topic of the work. Much of the first part of the book is dedicated to outlining the different forms of despair that humans can fall victim to.

---

[39] Kierkegaard, *SKS*, vol. 11, pp. 123–125. (English translation: *The Sickness unto Death*, trans. by Howard V. Hong and Edna H. Hong [Princeton: Princeton University Press, 1980], pp. 7–9.) See also *SKS*, vol. 11, pp. 133–137; *The Sickness unto Death*, pp. 17–21. See Robert L. Perkins (ed.), *The Sickness unto Death* (Macon, GA: Mercer University Press, 1987) (*International Kierkegaard Commentary*, vol. 19).

Kierkegaard's pseudonymous author examines these in a systematic fashion in a way that is highly reminiscent of Hegel's dialectical methodology.

From this we can see that the work is framed in a Christian context right from the outset. Indeed, this is indicated in the subtitle of the work: *A Christian Psychological Exposition for Upbuilding and Awakening.* The key Christian dogmas such as the divinity of Christ, immortality, God as a creator, and humans as created beings are all presupposed without argument. Some might argue that this undermines the *philosophical* value of the work since philosophy is not allowed to make assumptions of this kind. While this objection has some merit to it, there can be little doubt that within this broader Christian context there are some philosophically valuable analyses. The work is known for its philosophical anthropology, that is, its view of what the nature of human beings is.

At the beginning of *The Sickness unto Death*, Anti-Climacus immediately announces the influence of Hegel by using some of his key terms.[40] Specifically, the term "spirit" is employed to refer to human beings (in contrast to plants, animals, or other things). He goes on to indicate that the individual self is synonymous with spirit. His much-discussed definition of the self is as follows: "The self is a relation that relates to itself or is the relation's relating to itself in the relation; the self is not the relation but is the relation's relating to itself."[41] As we saw in Hegel, human beings are self-conscious and have the ability to reflect. They can see themselves from the outside and evaluate who they are, constantly revising this evaluation in terms of experience. In this sense the individual is both subject and object, that is, the subject making the evaluation and the object being evaluated. The point for Anti-Climacus seems to be in agreement with Hegel: Humans are specifically characterized by just this kind of reflection and self-evaluation. This results in a complex mental life, which, it is thought, only humans have. This is Anti-Climacus' pendant to Hegel's theory of self-consciousness.

Anti-Climacus then introduces a set of opposite terms, which also define the self: "A human being is a synthesis of the infinite and the finite, of the temporal and the eternal, of freedom and necessity, in short, a synthesis."[42] Here again we can see the shadow of Hegel's dialectic. Hegel shows that humans are aware of finite and temporal things via their senses, but they can think the infinite and the eternal with ideas. Human beings are not just one-sided; rather, qualities that might seem immediately to be contradictory are contained in the same consciousness. Kierkegaard refers to this with reference to Hegel's analysis in his unfinished work, *Johannes Climacus, or De omnibus dubitandum est.*[43]

---

[40] Kierkegaard, *SKS*, vol. 11, p. 129; *The Sickness unto Death*, p. 13.
[41] Kierkegaard, *SKS*, vol. 11, p. 129; *The Sickness unto Death*, p. 13.
[42] Kierkegaard, *SKS*, vol. 11, p. 129; *The Sickness unto Death*, p. 13.
[43] Kierkegaard, *SKS*, vol. 15, p. 58; *Johannes Climacus, or De omnibus dubitandum est*, trans. by Howard V. Hong and Edna H. Hong (Princeton: Princeton University Press, 1985), p. 171: "Here is the contradiction, for that which is, is also in another mode. That the

Anti-Climacus uses these dual terms to organize his analysis of the concept of despair. Since human beings are complex entities, they can be regarded from different points and in different aspects. For example, we can see humans as physical beings continuous with nature or as self-conscious entities raised higher than mere nature. Similarly, humans can also think of themselves in different aspects, isolating the one side from the other, and then reversing this. Thus, for Kierkegaard, as for Hegel, self-consciousness is not something static but rather represents a constant dynamic movement: "every moment that a self exists, it is in a process of becoming."[44]

A religious or Christian element can also be found in the analysis in that human beings are conceived from the outset as created beings, that is, created by God. Anti-Climacus writes, "The human self is such a derived, established relation, a relation that relates itself to itself and in relating itself to itself relates itself to another."[45] The idea seems to be that because we are created beings, we also have a necessary relation to our creator since our very essence is determined by the fact that we are created. It is impossible to separate ourselves from this relation to the creator because it is a part of who we are. This also echoes Hegel's theory of self-consciousness, by which individuals are who they are in the dialectic of recognition with other self-conscious agents. This also applies to the relation to God, who is spirit. Who we are as human beings is determined by what our conception of God is, and vice versa.

The idea that human beings are created by God is key to understanding the idea of despair as a conception of alienation. The fact that humans are created as a synthesis makes humans the complex beings that they are and separates them from nature. But this also makes despair possible. So in a sense it lies in human nature or human self-consciousness to despair: Animals do not despair. Despair is simply a feature of the human condition. The forms of despair can be understood as forms of alienation. In a draft, Kierkegaard says of sections A and B of *The Sickness unto Death*, "Both forms are forms of an unhappy consciousness."[46] By referring to Hegel's notion of the unhappy consciousness, he implies that his analysis also involves some form of

---

external is, that I see, but in the same instant I bring it into relation with something that also is, something that is the same and that also will explain that the other is the same. Here is a redoubling; here it is a matter of repetition. Ideality and reality therefore collide – in what medium? In time? That is indeed an impossibility. In eternity? That is indeed an impossibility. In what, then? In consciousness – there is the contradiction."

[44] Kierkegaard, *SKS*, vol. 11, p. 146; *The Sickness unto Death*, p. 30. See G. W. F. Hegel, *System der Wissenschaft. Erster Theil, die Phänomenologie des Geistes* (Bamberg and Würzburg: Joseph Anton Goebhardt, 1807), p. 103; *Hegel's Phenomenology of Spirit*, trans. by A. V. Miller (Oxford: Clarendon Press, 1977), p. 105: "As self-consciousness, it is movement . . .."

[45] Kierkegaard, *SKS*, vol. 11, p. 130; *The Sickness unto Death*, pp. 13f.

[46] *Søren Kierkegaards Papirer*, vol. VIII-2 B 150.8; *The Sickness unto Death*, Supplement, p. 150.

separation that is characteristic of alienation. Despair is characterized by a lack of balance of the synthesis: One aspect is accepted and the other ignored. The individual identifies with one element and is alienated from the other. To overcome alienation, one must accept and embrace the dialectical nature of human existence in its contradictory forms.

## 7.5   The Forms of Despair: Infinity-Finitude and Possibility-Necessity

Since human beings are a synthesis of different contradictory elements, despair occurs when the individual takes one of these elements unilaterally, that is, to the exclusion of the other. In Anti-Climacus' language, the individual relates themselves to themselves in a mistaken, one-sided manner. This means that there are different forms of despair in accordance with which element the individual chooses to emphasize. Anti-Climacus refers to the different elements of the self in Hegelian language as "dialectical opposite[s]."[47] For Hegel, as for Anti-Climacus, the truly dialectical view is the one that sees the legitimacy and validity of both opposites and regards the individual as a synthesis of them.

The first categories that are treated are the finite and the infinite. Human beings are a synthesis of both. We have a physical, limited, finite side that makes us continuous with the rest of nature, but we also have an infinite, spiritual side that we have in common with God. Humans are a special combination of both aspects. However, one can choose to deny this and to focus exclusively on the one side or the other, and when one does this, then one is in despair because this unilateral focus means a denial of what one truly is, that is, a synthesis.

Anti-Climacus begins by exploring the person who takes themselves to be pure infinity and to lack finitude.[48] Each form of despair is defined by a lack or denial of one aspect of the self. The despair of infinity means to conceive of oneself as infinite and unlimited. This form of despair is closely related to the imagination since in the imagination everything is possible and we are not held back by the limitations of our finitude. The individual who lives in the fantasy of the imagination is in despair because they are not who they really are. They are living a dreamed role in a dream world and not their real life in the real world. In Anti-Climacus' language, this means that the individual "lacks a - self."[49] The individual fails to recognize their finite, limited side. In a sense this form of despair can be an exaggerated kind of religiosity, by which one has an imaginary relation to God. Such a relation is a kind of "intoxication" that leads one away from oneself.[50]

---

[47] Kierkegaard, *SKS*, vol. 11, p. 146; *The Sickness unto Death*, p. 30.
[48] Kierkegaard, *SKS*, vol. 11, pp. 146–148; *The Sickness unto Death*, pp. 30–33.
[49] Kierkegaard, *SKS*, vol. 11, p. 148; *The Sickness unto Death*, p. 32.
[50] Kierkegaard, *SKS*, vol. 11, p. 148; *The Sickness unto Death*, p. 32.

There is also the opposite form of despair, according to which the individual focuses exclusively on the finite to the exclusion of the infinite.[51] This is the despair of finitude. In this form of despair, the individual focuses on themselves simply in terms of their limited, finite side. One is reduced to a physical being with no ability to transcend this. This view is typical of the secular way of thinking, which conceives of human beings simply as a part of nature. Humans are limited just like everything else in nature. Such a person becomes lost in the petty affairs of daily life and fails to see anything higher. Anti-Climacus claims that this is a form of conformism, and thus by following this unreflective modern practice, one becomes "a copy, a number, a mass man."[52] In other words, by ignoring the infinite element in the self, one ceases to be who one is as an individual. In short, one is in despair. Such an individual ignores the divine and dedicates themselves solely to mundane things.

It will be noted that for both of these initial forms of despair there is nothing that stands in the way of the individual being a flourishing and successful member of society. In fact, the despair of finitude can actually lead to great material prosperity in the world since one is focused solely on mundane affairs. The fact that the individual is in despair is irrelevant for their success in family or business. Indeed, no one would ever think to regard such people as being in despair.

The next set of dialectical opposites that Anti-Climacus explores is possibility and necessity. As was the case with the previous forms of despair, the issue here is the exclusive focus on the one category to the exclusion of the other. Human beings are a synthesis of both possibility and necessity, yet the person in despair can forget or deny this by dwelling exclusively in the one or the other.

By focusing on possibility, this form of despair denies that there is a necessary element in the self.[53] According to this view, the individual is always open to an infinite number of possibilities. One can do and be absolutely anything that one wants. This is similar to the despair of infinitude since it conceives the individual to be without limitation. The individual who dwells in possibility has difficulty completing projects because for them, everything in the realm of possibility is just as good as if it were actuality. Thus in a sense the possibilities become real in the mind of the person in this form of despair. The book that one will write or the piece of music that one will compose are brilliant, but this always remains in possibility and not in actuality, where such products can actually be criticized. This is a form of despair since it fails to recognize certain necessary elements in what it is to be human. We cannot overcome certain factual aspects of our physical being and our existence in the

---

[51] Kierkegaard, *SKS*, vol. 11, pp. 149–151; *The Sickness unto Death*, pp. 33–35.
[52] Kierkegaard, *SKS*, vol. 11, p. 149; *The Sickness unto Death*, p. 34.
[53] Kierkegaard, *SKS*, vol. 11, pp. 151–153; *The Sickness unto Death*, pp. 35–37.

world. While there is, to be sure, possibility, it is never absolute or unlimited. There are natural limitations of time and energy that prevent one from carrying out every single project. Failing to recognize this element of necessity in life means the individual is in despair.

The dialectical opposite of this form of despair is the despair of necessity, whereby one denies the element of possibility.[54] In other words, one conceives of everything as necessary and does not see any room for real possibility. We exist as physical beings in a physical universe, which is governed by the laws of cause and effect that nothing can escape. Like the despair of finitude, the despair of necessity reflects a secular view. This is the notion of materialism, which claims we are determined by the functions of our brain, and free will is an illusion. When one sees the world in terms of necessity, then one denies the realm of possibility, and this means, according to Anti-Climacus, to deny God since for God everything is possible.[55] In this form of despair, when one reaches a crisis or a disaster occurs, one despairs since this is the result of cause and effect, and there seems to be nothing that can alleviate the situation. In this way one denies the possibility of God. If one believes that there is only necessity, then prayer does not make any sense because prayer presupposes the idea of God and possibility. One personality type that falls victim to the despair of necessity is the "philistine-bourgeois mentality."[56] Like the victim of the despair of finitude, this kind of person is wholly focused on the affairs of daily life, which seem predictable and thus reliable. The bourgeois mentality raises these things to matters of the utmost importance and fails to see that there is something higher. Anti-Climacus refers to this as a focus on "triviality."[57] Only when things go seriously wrong is this kind of person jarred out of their complacency. The bourgeois philistine lives in the mistaken belief that they can control the world and thus have no need for God. By denying possibility, this kind of person is also in the despair of necessity.

All of these forms of despair can be understood as forms of self-alienation. The individual is a synthesis of contradictory elements, which must be held together. The alienation occurs when one of these elements is insisted upon at the expense of the other, and thus the two elements are thrown out of balance. One is not who one is unless the contradictory elements are held together in the correct balance. When they are out of balance or one side is denied, then one is in despair and alienated from oneself. Moreover, since we are created beings and thus always have a relation to God, when we are alienated from ourselves, we are ipso facto alienated from God. For this reason, the opposite of despair is faith.[58]

---

[54] Kierkegaard, SKS, vol. 11, pp. 153–157; The Sickness unto Death, pp. 37–42.
[55] Kierkegaard, SKS, vol. 11, p. 153; The Sickness unto Death, p. 38.
[56] Kierkegaard, SKS, vol. 11, p. 156; The Sickness unto Death, p. 41.
[57] Kierkegaard, SKS, vol. 11, p. 156; The Sickness unto Death, p. 41.
[58] Kierkegaard, SKS, vol. 11, p. 164; The Sickness unto Death, p. 49.

## 7.6  The Forms of Despair as Defined by Consciousness

We have explored so far only the first forms of despair that are defined simply by the categories of infinity and finitude and possibility and necessity. Now Anti-Climacus introduces another set of forms that is determined by whether or not the individual is conscious of being in despair. He claims that there is an ascending scale, whereby "the greater the degree of consciousness, the more intensive the despair."[59] He thus begins to explore the low end of the scale, where there is no consciousness of despair, and proceeds to the high end of the scale, where there is full consciousness of it. With each new stage of despair, one comes closer to full awareness and salvation.

The first of this set of forms of despair that Anti-Climacus explores is what he refers to as "the despair that is ignorant of being despair, or the despairing ignorance of having a self and an external self."[60] This form of despair corresponds to the secular person who is not much interested in God. Anti-Climacus also states that this is the form of "paganism and the natural man,"[61] that is, the person who has no religion or knowledge of Christianity. He claims that this is the most widespread form of despair. Such a person is focused exclusively on the mundane sphere and the realm of the senses. They do not believe in anything higher than this. Such a person is in despair because they have this unilateral focus and do not see themselves as a synthesis that includes a spiritual element as well as a physical one. According to Anti-Climacus, such a person chooses to focus on the lowest elements of the human being instead of the highest; that is, humans are simply their physical natures. This is what they have in common with animals but not God. They fail to recognize the element of spirit that they have within themselves. In short, they fail to recognize that they have an eternal self; they fail to recognize that they are created beings and have a relation to God, and this is a form of despair.

Here we can see the special way in which the word "despair" is being used. Usually when we talk about despair, we understand it as a kind of mood or mental state that one experiences when one feels a sense of hopelessness or deep depression. In such cases the person who feels this knows it quite well, and it would be absurd to talk about despair that the person is unaware of. But for Anti-Climacus' understanding, it is quite possible for someone to be in despair but not be aware of it or not be conscious of it. Such a person could lead a normal life and from the outside seem apparently happy and flourishing. Despair lies beneath the surface. Again we are reminded of his special defin-ition of despair as a lack of balance in the dialectical relation between two contradictory elements. This lack of balance can certainly be present without someone being aware of it, as in the case that Anti-Climacus sketches.

[59] Kierkegaard, *SKS*, vol. 11, p. 157; *The Sickness unto Death*, p. 42.
[60] Kierkegaard, *SKS*, vol. 11, pp. 157–162; *The Sickness unto Death*, pp. 42–47.
[61] Kierkegaard, *SKS*, vol. 11, p. 160; *The Sickness unto Death*, p. 45.

One would think, given that the individual who does not know God or the spiritual is in despair, that the one who does know these things would, according to Anti-Climacus, not be in despair. But this is not the case since the next form of despair is the despair of being conscious of having an eternal self. For Anti-Climacus, one can know that one has an eternal self yet still have a mistaken relation to this or, put differently, can misunderstand the nature of this. He then proceeds to sketch two forms of this: not to will to be oneself and to will to be oneself, both of which are forms of despair.[62]

The form of despair of not willing to be oneself Anti-Climacus refers to as "feminine despair."[63] He divides this into two further forms: despair over the earthly and despair of the eternal.[64] With regard to the despair over the earthly, the individual lives in the mundane world of the senses and is focused on the goods of the world. When some disaster strikes and the individual happens to lose some of these goods, they fall into despair. Unlike the previous form of despair that we just discussed, this individual knows that they are in despair: They despair because they have lost some of their property or possessions. But, according to Anti-Climacus, this is a mistaken conception of despair since true despair is about losing God or what is eternal and not about losing something finite and temporal.[65] The individual might be said to have lost some of their property, but this is not real despair. This can in no way be compared with the infinite loss of God. This form of despair evinces an exaggerated emphasis on the goods of this world and a blindness to the infinite importance of God and spirit. Anti-Climacus even indicates that such a person can be a professing Christian yet still not have any idea of what this means.[66] This is a form of Christian hypocrisy and confusion that he takes to be typical of his own day. Focused on the mundane world, this form of despair does not will to be itself, that is, a created being before God. This can take the form of wishing to be someone else, for example, envying someone who enjoys the goods of bourgeois life unimpeded.

In explicating this form of despair, Anti-Climacus presents an analysis that recalls the forms of alienation that we saw in the discussion of "the unhappiest one" in *Either/Or*, Part I. Anti-Climacus argues that, while it is often thought that despair is a kind of childhood phase that one can grow out of, this is in fact an error. Both young people and old people can be in despair. While the despair of young people is oriented toward the future, the despair of old people is oriented toward the past. For young people this involves the illusion of hope

---

[62] Kierkegaard, *SKS*, vol. 11, pp. 165–181, pp. 181–187; *The Sickness unto Death*, pp. 49–67, pp. 67–74. See Stewart, *Kierkegaard's Relations to Hegel Reconsidered*, pp. 572–595.

[63] Kierkegaard, *SKS*, vol. 11, p. 165; *The Sickness unto Death*, p. 49.

[64] Kierkegaard, *SKS*, vol. 11, pp. 165–175, pp. 175–181; *The Sickness unto Death*, pp. 50–60, pp. 60–67.

[65] Kierkegaard, *SKS*, vol. 11, p. 167; *The Sickness unto Death*, p. 51.

[66] Kierkegaard, *SKS*, vol. 11, p. 168; *The Sickness unto Death*, p. 52.

and for old people the illusion of recollection.[67] These were the very categories of the analysis of the unhappiest one. In neither case is the individual living in the present so long as they nourish an illusion in hope of recollection. Both cases are forms of despair and alienation. If the true self is the created being that one is before God, then this is completely obscured by a focus on the mundane goods of either the past or the future. One fails to be who one is: a synthesis of the different, conflicting elements.

The second form of the despair of not willing to be oneself is the despair of the eternal or despair over oneself. According to Anti-Climacus, this form of despair is in fact already implicit in the despair over the earthly in the sense that despairing of the goods of mundane life is a despairing over oneself. In contrast to the previous stage, here the individual recognizes that it is their own weakness that makes them despair the goods of the world. The individual despairs of having an eternal self that can overcome this weakness.[68] In other words, at the previous stage when the individual lost one of the goods of the world, they despaired and ascribed this to a shortcoming or bad luck in the world. Now at this stage there is a dialectical shift, and when this happens, the individual realizes that in fact the shortcoming lies with themselves and not the world since they are the one who is attached to such external things in an inappropriate manner. The individual despairs of their own weakness and of not being able to will themselves. This is clearly an individual in conflict with themselves. Anti-Climacus uses the somewhat odd term "inclosing reserve" to characterize this individual. This means simply that the person suffering from this form of despair withdraws or closes themselves off from the world in a certain sense. They keep their inward reflections about their own weakness to themselves. They somewhat arrogantly regard other people as unreflective and thus take it as a waste of time to discuss such matters with them. This person seeks solitude and avoids groups of people. This fixation on one's own weakness can end in suicide.

The final form of despair is defiance or the despair of willing to be oneself.[69] At this stage the individual is focused on themselves as before, but now they are able to will themselves. They regard themselves as infinite and eternal, but, most importantly, they do not acknowledge the necessary relation to God. So they will themselves in the absence of this relation, thus in a sense attempting to create themselves. This is what Anti-Climacus refers to as defiance.

Two aspects of this form of despair are distinguished: despair as acting self and despair as being acted upon,[70] that is, active and passive. When the

[67] Kierkegaard, *SKS*, vol. 11, p. 173; *The Sickness unto Death*, p. 58.
[68] Kierkegaard, *SKS*, vol. 11, p. 176; *The Sickness unto Death*, p. 62.
[69] Kierkegaard, *SKS*, vol. 11, pp. 181–187; *The Sickness unto Death*, pp. 67–74.
[70] Kierkegaard, *SKS*, vol. 11, pp. 182–183, pp. 183–185; *The Sickness unto Death*, pp. 68–70, pp. 70–71.

individual who is victim of this form of despair *acts in the world*, they do not acknowledge God or any higher power. They believe that they themselves are the highest. But without any deeper grounding, the acts of the individual appear arbitrary and meaningless. The individual tries to ascribe importance to them, but they are unable to do so since they are unwilling to appeal to God or any higher authority than themselves. In all of their actions there is nothing that holds firm, and thus they live in a world of "imaginary constructions"[71] and build "castles in the air."[72] When the individual in this form of despair *is acted upon* by some outside force, they do not wish to recognize it. The world often presents us with obstacles and impediments that make it difficult for us to reach our goals. The individual in defiance in a sense acknowledges this, but they defiantly pretend that this is not a problem for them. They do not wish to appeal to help from God or anyone else to overcome such obstacles and must instead minimize them based on their own strength and will. To accept help from someone else is regarded as a form of humiliation and a recognition that one is limited. They accept a godless world with all of its defects and defiantly will themselves in this context. They thus accept their own suffering in order to maintain the ability to will themselves and create themselves.

This is defiance, and it ends, in its extreme form, in the demonic. For such a person, the problems of the individual's life become a fixation that the individual refuses to give up. They regard themselves as a victim that the world had wronged, and they wish to maintain the source of their problem to demonstrate this. Such an individual disdains the world and regards themselves as vastly superior to other people. They thus end up in a monumental and irresolvable struggle with the world. Defiance is the highest form of despair and thus the end of the ascending list that Anti-Climacus has traced.

These forms of despair as defined by consciousness can also be seen as forms of alienation, either from oneself or from the world or both. In each case, the individual has an incorrect relation to the world and to themselves, and this results in distortions in one's self-relation and in one's relation to others. This invariably involves a mistaken relation to God, and for this reason, in the second part of the work, despair is understood as sin.

## 7.7    Kierkegaard, Hegel, and Alienation

Traditionally, works on the history of nineteenth-century philosophy tend to juxtapose Kierkegaard and Hegel and to cast Kierkegaard in the role of a great anti-Hegelian.[73] However, as we have seen, in *The Sickness unto Death* there is

---

[71] Kierkegaard, *SKS*, vol. 11, p. 182; *The Sickness unto Death*, p. 68.
[72] Kierkegaard, *SKS*, vol. 11, p. 183; *The Sickness unto Death*, p. 69.
[73] See, for example, Niels Thulstrup, *Kierkegaard's Relation to Hegel*, trans. by George L. Stengren (Princeton: Princeton University Press, 1980).

much evidence that in fact Kierkegaard was in some ways inspired by Hegel. Kierkegaard has his pseudonymous author make use of a philosophical language that often recalls that of Hegel, with one of the key terms being spirit. Moreover, the dialectical methodology that Anti-Climacus follows in Part I of the work very much resembles that of Hegel, whereby one category is explored on its own until its contradictions are revealed, and then its opposite is explored in the same way. Thus pairs of categories such as finitude/infinitude and possibility/necessity are explored in a way that shows their dialectical relations to each other. These analyses can be seen as a form of Hegelian phenomenology, according to which one follows the experience of consciousness of an individual who is defined by one category or the other.[74]

One can also find in *The Sickness unto Death* an allusion to the dialectic of recognition and the lordship and bondage analysis in *The Phenomenology of Spirit*. For Hegel, recognition must be freely given among equals in order for it to be meaningful. For this reason the compelled recognition of the master does not count for anything. Likewise, being recognized by someone inferior cannot be valid. Kierkegaard's Anti-Climacus takes up this point in his discussion of what it means to say that one exists *before God*. He writes:

> A cattleman who . . . is a self directly before his cattle is a very low self, and, similarly, a master who is a self directly before his slaves is actually no self – for in both cases a criterion is lacking. The child who previously has had only his parents as a criterion becomes a self as an adult by getting the state as a criterion, but what an infinite accent falls on the self by having God as the criterion![75]

It is impossible to receive meaningful recognition from cattle or from a slave. The conception of selfhood produced by this form of recognition would be subhuman. But the recognition of God is something completely different. Here Anti-Climacus agrees with Hegel's praise of Christianity for its conception of God as a loving being who recognizes human beings as infinitely valuable and free. It will be recalled that in Hegel this is contrasted to the Jewish conception of God as a tyrant, who threatens and punishes the believers if they fail to follow the law instead of appealing to their free, rational consent.

---

[74] For attempts to connect Kierkegaard with the tradition of phenomenology, see Jeffrey Hanson (ed.), *Kierkegaard as Phenomenologist: An Experiment* (Evanston: Northwestern University Press, 2010); Stephen N. Dunning, "Love Is Not Enough: A Kierkegaardian Phenomenology of Religious Experience," *Faith and Philosophy*, 12 (1995), 22–39; Claudia Welz, "Kierkegaard and Phenomenology," in John Lippitt and George Pattison (eds.), *The Oxford Handbook of Kierkegaard* (Oxford: Oxford University Press, 2012), pp. 432–455; Vincent A. McCarthy, *The Phenomenology of Moods in Kierkegaard* (The Hague and Boston: Martinus Nijhoff, 1978); Jon Stewart, "Kierkegaard's Phenomenology of Despair in *The Sickness unto Death*," *Kierkegaard Studies Yearbook* (1997), 117–143.

[75] Kierkegaard, *SKS*, vol. 11, p. 193; *The Sickness unto Death*, p. 79.

For Anti-Climacus the conception of the self is also intimately and necessarily bound up with the conception of God. In order to have a self, one must acknowledge that one is a being created by God. The fact that "the other" is God is important since this raises the value of the individual above what it is in the forms of despair that deny God and thus force the individual to try to stand on their own. Anti-Climacus writes, "Despair is intensified in relation to the consciousness of the self, but the self is intensified in relation to the criterion for the self, infinitely when God is the criterion. In fact, the greater the conception of God, the more self there is; the more self, the greater the conception of God."[76] There is thus a dialectical relation between the self and God.

With these examples we can see that far from being an ardent critic of Hegel, Kierkegaard is in fact profoundly receptive to certain aspects of his thought, which he appropriates for his own purposes. This shows that there is not a radical break in the history of philosophy in the nineteenth century as is sometimes thought.[77] Instead, the century can be largely understood as a variety of attempts to come to terms with some of the key analyses of Hegel concerning issues such as alienation, recognition, religion, and the individual.

According to Anti-Climacus, the solution to this is to embrace Christian faith and enter into a proper relation to God. Only in this way can alienation be overcome. Only by recognizing that we are beings created by God can we hope to get past the problems of despair that are so common in the world. This is an important point of contrast with writers such as Feuerbach, Marx, and Nietzsche, for whom religion and Christianity specifically are not the solution to alienation but rather its root cause.

Another point of contrast can be seen in Kierkegaard's use of the metaphor of despair as a form of sickness. The idea is that we are all sick, and for this reason the different forms of despair represent different forms of this sickness. Christianity can heal us from this sickness by helping us attain the right balance of the different elements that make us who we are. The goal is not transferred to some other sphere since to want to escape to a life after death is once again the mark of an unhappy or despairing consciousness. God's demand is that we live before him, grounded in faith in the present. The demand is that we become who we are in this time, in this place, right now. Nietzsche uses the metaphor of sickness as well but in a quite different way. For him, Christianity is not the cure for the sickness but rather its main cause.

---

[76] Kierkegaard, *SKS*, vol. 11, p. 194; *The Sickness unto Death*, p. 80.

[77] See Jon Stewart, *Idealism and Existentialism: Hegel and Nineteenth- and Twentieth-Century European Philosophy* (New York and London: Continuum International Publishing, 2010).

Christianity is a cancerous growth that has infected European culture by alienating us from our natural instincts.

While much of the nineteenth century is characterized by a biting criticism of Christianity, Kierkegaard attempts to defend it, although admittedly not in any way that we are used to seeing it defended. To defend Christianity usually means showing that it is in harmony with *logos* and reason. But Kierkegaard insists that to defend Christianity in this sense is to betray it. This approach always implies that if one cannot make the defense, disbelief is justified. Kierkegaard says Christianity will never be justified because it is absurd, paradoxical, etc. Belief must be the result of a fundamental response to a call from God, which is absurd and indefensible rationally (like Abraham's response). In other words, he agrees with all the critics who say it is absurd. He just thinks it must be accepted nonetheless, but on other grounds than reason. So he is obliged to reconceive Christianity in important ways.

Somewhat oddly, in this regard he makes common cause with Hegel. It will be recalled that Hegel's stated goal in his *Lectures on the Philosophy of Religion* was to defend Christianity from the criticisms of the Enlightenment. He believes that this defense can be made with philosophical tools. Kierkegaard differs from Hegel in his tactics because he does not want to issue a philosophical defense of Christianity as such; indeed, he denies that such a defense is even possible. Instead, he wants to show that there is an inward, subjective sphere of religious life that escapes the criticisms of science and Enlightenment reason. So while their approaches are radically different, as are their conceptions of Christianity, Hegel and Kierkegaard can nonetheless be seen as responding to the same problem. Together they represent the minority voice in the nineteenth century in their attempt to defend Christianity and its traditional doctrines.

# 8

# Dostoevsky's Criticism of Modern Rationalism and Materialism

Fyodor Mikhailovich Dostoevsky (1821–1881) was a Russian writer who penned a number of novels, novellas, and essays with profound philosophical and psychological meaning. An Orthodox Christian, he treated issues concerning the self, human freedom, and the negative depths of the human psyche. Although he is not a philosopher in the traditional sense, his writings had an important influence on later thinkers associated with the existentialist tradition. For example, Nietzsche wrote that Dostoevsky was "the only psychologist from whom I had anything to learn."[1] Dostoevsky anticipates the problems of existentialist ethics with the famous line that he puts in the mouth of one of his most compelling characters, Ivan Karamazov: if God does not exist, then "everything is allowed."[2] For Sartre, this is a formula for human liberation, but for Dostoevsky it is a negative formula of nihilism: The idea of a world without God is a terrifying prospect.

Born in Moscow in 1821, Dostoevsky had a difficult life.[3] His father, Mikhail Dostoevsky, was a doctor and a devout Christian. In 1833 the young Dostoevsky was sent to a French boarding school. His mother died in 1837

---

[1] Friedrich Nietzsche, *Götzen-Dämmerung oder Wie man mit dem Hammer philosophirt*, in *Nietzsche's Werke*, vols. 1–20 (Leipzig: C. G. Naumann, 1889), "Streifzüge eines Unzeitgemässen," § 45, p. 120. (English translation: *Twilight of the Idols or How to Philosophize with a Hammer*, in *Twilight of the Idols/The Anti-Christ*, trans. by R. J. Hollingdale [Harmondsworth: Penguin, 1968], "Expeditions of an Untimely Man," § 45, p. 99.) See also Friedrich Nietzsche, *Der Antichrist. Versuch einer Kritik des Christenthums*, in *Nietzsche's Werke*, vol. 8 (1895), § 31, p. 255. (English translation: *The Anti-Christ* in *Twilight of the Idols or How to Philosophize with a Hammer*, in *Twilight of the Idols/The Anti-Christ*, § 31, p. 143.)

[2] Fyodor Dostoevsky, *The Brothers Karamazov*, vols. 1–2, trans. by David Magarshack (Harmondsworth: Penguin, 1958), vol. 2, p. 691.

[3] The standard scholarly biography of Dostoevsky is Joseph Frank's five-volume study: *Dostoevsky: The Seeds of Revolt, 1821–1849* (Princeton: Princeton University Press, 1976); *Dostoevsky: The Years of Ordeal, 1850–1859* (Princeton: Princeton University Press, 1983); *Dostoevsky: The Stir of Liberation, 1860–1865* (Princeton: Princeton University Press, 1986); *Dostoevsky: The Miraculous Years, 1865–1871* (Princeton: Princeton University Press, 1995); *Dostoevsky: The Mantle of the Prophet, 1871–1881* (Princeton: Princeton University Press, 2002). This work has been condensed into one volume as *Dostoevsky: A Writer in His Time* (Princeton: Princeton University Press, 2009).

of tuberculosis. In the same year Dostoevsky was enrolled in a military engineering school in St. Petersburg. After graduating in 1843, he spent a year in the
Engineering Corps of the Russian army. At this time he began his literary
career by publishing a series of translations of French literature. His first novel,
which enjoyed some success, was *Poor Folk* (1846), which portrays the life of
poverty in a naturalistic and humanistic manner. Around this time he developed an interest in the socialist movement and soon became a follower of
Charles Fourier, Saint-Simon, and their Russian exponent Vissarion Belinsky
(1811–1848). He became a member of the "Petrashevsky Circle," a group
surrounding the radical intellectual and reformer Mikhail Petrashevsky (-
1821–1866). The group read and debated leading political and philosophical
writers of the day. During this time Feuerbach was the most discussed philosopher, while Marx still remained unknown. In 1849 the group was infiltrated
by czarist spies, and its members were arrested and sentenced to death by firing
squad. A mock execution was staged, whereby at the last moment when the
order was to be given to shoot the condemned men, a messenger arrived on the
scene with a message from the Czar to rescind the order and stop the execu-
tions. Dostoevsky was instead sentenced to four years of hard labor in Siberia.
After he was released in 1854, he was obliged to serve a term of five further
years of military service. For many years afterwards, he continued to be
watched by the police. All in all, the episode cost Dostoevsky almost
a decade of his life. After his experience in prison, he abandoned his scientific,
enlightenment, rationalist orientation and became a critic of liberalism and
socialism. He became a religious thinker and psychologist. Like some of his
literary characters, Dostoevsky had epilepsy, which became worse in Siberia.

Upon his release, he returned to St. Petersburg. In 1861 he published *The
House of the Dead*, which is an account of his experience in prison. The
next year he embarked on an extensive trip to Western Europe, which included
stops in Germany, Belgium, France, England, Switzerland, and Italy. A second
trip followed in 1863. He met the Russian socialist author Alexander Herzen
(1812–1870) in London and became critical of capitalism and modern materialism. Together with his brother, he founded a couple of literary magazines,
which failed to enjoy any commercial success. For one of these, entitled *The
Epoch*, he wrote *Notes from Underground*, which appeared in 1864. After
another trip abroad, Dostoevsky returned to Russia and published *Crime
and Punishment* (1866). He left Russia yet again to travel for four full years
in Europe. Although he suffered from great poverty, he wrote prolifically
during this period, publishing *The Idiot* in 1868. These works were also initially
published serially in literary journals. Despite his literary success, Dostoevsky
was dogged by financial problems, which were exacerbated by his gambling
addiction.

After years of travel he returned to Russia in 1871. In the same year he
published *The Possessed* (or *The Devils*). Only in the last decade of his life did

his works begin to enjoy a wider reading public, and his financial situation finally improved. In 1876 he began publication of his own literary magazine, *Writer's Diary*, which increased his fame. His last great novel was *The Brothers Karamazov* (1880), which is considered by many to be his masterpiece. His health became increasingly fragile, and he died in 1881. By this time he was lionized as a national hero. While Dostoevsky was never one of Hegel's students in Berlin, he was influenced by Hegel's thought and fits well with the general trajectory of European thinking in the nineteenth century that we have been tracing.

## 8.1   The Context and Structure of *Notes from Underground*

In Dostoevsky's time there was a group of thinkers in Russia who were fascinated by the progress of the West. The Industrial Revolution and modern science had transformed life in Western Europe, and it seemed that Russia had been left behind. This group was excited about modern trends such as rationalism, utilitarianism, and materialism and attempted to introduce them to their Russian audience. They believed that these movements would transform society and improve the lot of the individual. One of the leading ideologues for this movement was Nikolai Chernyshevsky (1828–1889), who, in 1863, published the highly popular novel *What Is to Be Done?*[4] This work made a case for socialism, which is portrayed as a kind of future utopia. The novel was profoundly influential among a number of well-known later thinkers and activists of the socialist and communist movements.

Dostoevsky wrote *Notes from Underground* as a critical response to this work by Chernyshevsky. During his stay in London in 1862, Dostoevsky saw first-hand the misery and human price of the Industrial Revolution. He became critical of attempts to portray the mentioned modern movements as the path toward utopia. He initially published his reflections on this topic in the essay *Winter Notes on Summer Impressions* (1863).[5] He saw Western European culture as corrupt and driven by greed. He was thus critical of Chernyshevsky's attempts to introduce it in Russia. By contrast, Dostoevsky was an advocate of a Slavic-Russian identity that, he believed, should resist Western influence and instead return to traditional Russian religion and values.

In *Notes from Underground* Dostoevsky challenges Chernyshevsky's underlying philosophical assumptions about the nature of human beings and human society. Thus *Notes from Underground* finds its place in the context of a debate

---

[4] Nikolai Chernyshevsky, *What Is to Be Done?"* trans. by Michal R. Katz (Ithaca and London: Cornell University Press, 1993).
[5] Fyodor Dostoevsky, *Winter Notes on Summer Impressions*, trans. by David Patterson (Evanston: Northwestern University Press, 1988).

about social reform in Russia. The views represented by Chernyshevsky belong to their specific time in Russian intellectual history; however, echoes of many of these ideas can still be found. The schools of rationalism and materialism are still alive and well in modern philosophical thinking, and this is what gives Dostoevsky's reflections a relevance and topicality today. Many of his criticisms of these thinkers can be easily translated into a criticism of modern tendencies of thought. His vision of what a human being is represents an important challenge to our modern thinking.

*Notes from Underground* is divided into two parts. The first part, "The Underground," contains the reflections of the underground man, who speaks in the first person (sections 1–11). His name is never given, but we learn that he is forty years old and was formerly a civil servant. He lives a humble life in St. Petersburg in the 1860s. He was able to retire the previous year and live off an inheritance he received from a distant relative. He is referred to as the underground man because he lives in a basement. This has been interpreted as a symbol of his isolation and alienation. In this part of the work, which is a long monologue, the underground man in effect describes his worldview. He critically examines the modern notions of what a human being is, that is, the ideas promoted by Chernyshevsky and his followers. This first part reads in some passages like a kind of polemical philosophical treatise.

By contrast, the second part of the work, entitled "A Story of the Falling Sleet," reads more like a traditional novel. Here the protagonist recounts different episodes from his life as a young man in the 1840s, that is, twenty years before the time of the narration. He cynically describes his relations with other people, and his accounts evince an utter alienation from all forms of social life. This second part can be divided into three narratives: in the first, the underground man portrays his animosity toward an officer and his attempts to gain the officer's respect (section 1); in the second, he describes his volatile interaction with his former school comrades (sections 2–5); and in the third, he recounts his attempt to reform and at the same time antagonize the young prostitute Liza (sections 6–10).

The underground man is claimed to be the first antihero in world literature, and Dostoevsky himself coins the term.[6] In his introductory note to the work he writes, "The author of these Notes, and the Notes themselves, are both, of course, imaginary. All the same, if we take into consideration the conditions

---

[6] Fyodor Dostoevsky, *Notes from Underground*, in *"Notes from Underground" and "The Double,"* trans. by Jessie Coulson (London: Penguin, 1972), p. 122. (All the following references to *Notes from Underground* will be to this translation.) For analyses of this work, see Bernard J. Paris, *Dostoevsky's Greatest Characters* (New York: Palgrave Macmillan, 2008), pp. 3–47; James P. Scanlan, *Dostoevsky the Thinker* (Ithaca and London: Cornell University Press, 2002); René Girard, *Resurrection from the Underground: Feodor Dostoevsky,* trans. by James G. Williams (East Lansing: Michigan State University Press, 2012).

that have shaped our society, people like the writer not only may, but must exist in that society."[7] Dostoevsky thus seems to imply that the underground man represents a certain modern type of human being. He represents something common in the European culture or spirit: a caricature of the alienated intellectual, the disillusioned idealist of the 1840s who once believed in truth, beauty, and social justice. The implicit point is that the alienating, dehumanizing society of the modern world produces this kind of figure. The underground man is thus a symbol of the modern human condition. He illustrates the different forms of estrangement and alienation of the self in ways reminiscent of Kierkegaard.

## 8.2   The Underground Man's Disease of Reflection

The underground man begins his confessions with the statement, "I am a sick man."[8] Thus, like Kierkegaard, Dostoevsky develops the metaphor of sickness. The modern human being is not just physically ill but somehow mentally or psychologically ill. He is alienated from his true nature, and this causes him to be twisted and distorted. But the nature of his illness remains something of a mystery to him: "I don't understand the least thing about my illness, and I don't know for certain what part of me is affected."[9] So the cultural problems that affect him remain as yet undiagnosed.

The underground man explains that he is unable to do anything meaningful. He explains enigmatically, "a wise man can't seriously make himself anything, only a fool makes himself anything. Yes, a man of the nineteenth century ought, indeed is morally bound, to be essentially without character."[10] The underground man cannot do anything because he is a highly reflective person, and once one begins to reflect critically on the world around one – that is, people, society, customs – things begin to lose their value. One begins to see through the hypocrisies of human life, the absurdities of traditions and conventional wisdom. Everything that one has learned and taken for granted as a child is called into question. Given this, it is impossible to take anything seriously and thus to embark upon any projects or to try to make something out of oneself. Only a fool can do such things since a fool has not seen the world through the eyes of a critical thinker. The fool still believes in the folly of the world and has not understood it for what it really is.

The underground man claims that reflection or a heightened sense of consciousness is the cause of the problem, and he identifies this as the disease that affects him: "I swear to you that to think too much is a disease, a real,

---

[7]   Dostoevsky, *Notes from Underground*, p. 13.
[8]   Dostoevsky, *Notes from Underground*, p. 15.
[9]   Dostoevsky, *Notes from Underground*, p. 15.
[10]   Dostoevsky, *Notes from Underground*, p. 16.

actual disease."[11] He continues, "I'm firmly convinced that not only a great deal, but every kind, of intellectual activity is a disease."[12] Why does he call thinking and reflection a disease? For the philosophers of the tradition of German Idealism, rational thinking was the highest form of human cognition. For Hegel, it was the faculty that separates us from the animals and makes us like God. But for Dostoevsky, reflection and thought can have a *negative* effect.

Once, through reflection, one begins to call into question accepted customs and traditional practices, one can no longer participate in them in the same way as before. As a result, one either refuses to participate in them at all or one does so with a cynicism or irony that most people, who are unreflective, cannot understand. In this sense being reflective is a kind of disease that affects the individual in many different ways and undermines their ability to function in the world. There is no firm intellectual base to stand on. The person of common sense can act, but the intelligent, hyperconscious person must think twice. All reasons to act are undermined by reflection. Reflection dissolves action. This is also a form of self-alienation since one is alienated from one's own feelings. One cannot act emotionally or immediately since everything must pass through the test of reflection and critical reason.

One cannot become anything since hyperconsciousness or "intensified awareness" leads to inertia.[13] Once one has seen the vanity of all human striving, it is difficult to motivate oneself to do anything at all. Reason paralyzes. The underground man has nothing but disdain for "men of action" or "doers," since they ascribe to themselves a sense of importance that is absurd.[14] They do not realize that their projects and goals are ultimately hollow and worthless. This is a condition that is typical of the nineteenth century, where the fast pace of social change and the development of science have eaten away at traditional customs and beliefs. To act in the world implies that one is certain of what one is doing, but reflection leads to doubt. If one is forever in doubt, then this prevents one from acting forcefully and purposely in the world.[15] If one continues to reflect, then one can always raise new questions, and all foundations are undermined. The underground man recounts that this disease of consciousness has caused him to withdraw from social life, and he has remained in his isolated condition for some twenty years.

Once one begins to think critically about the world, one is immediately separated and alienated from other people who do not think critically. One cannot take other people seriously who continue slavishly to follow customs and traditions that one has seen the absurdity and hypocrisy of. The

---

[11] Dostoevsky, *Notes from Underground*, p. 17.
[12] Dostoevsky, *Notes from Underground*, p. 18.
[13] Dostoevsky, *Notes from Underground*, p. 19, p. 26.
[14] Dostoevsky, *Notes from Underground*, p. 20, p. 26.
[15] Dostoevsky, *Notes from Underground*, p. 27.

underground man says that he is "cleverer than anybody else" and this undermines his ability to interact meaningfully with others.[16] His reflection and critical rationality always put him in an elevated position where he can only regard them with condescension.

Moreover, once one has begun to think critically, it is impossible to return to one's former life of innocence. One can no longer simply go along with accepted custom and tradition as one did as a child. The individual's immediate relation to society and other people has been broken forever. The underground man says, "you could never make yourself into a different person";[17] that is, one can never go back and be an unreflective person after having been through the process of critical reflection.

Like Kierkegaard, Dostoevsky also describes this condition as a form of despair or hopelessness.[18] But paradoxically, the underground man derives a perverse sense of pleasure from it. This corresponds to Kierkegaard's notion of being in despair without knowing it. The underground man says that there is a pleasure that comes "from being too clearly aware of your own degradation."[19] Although one feels alienated from other people, there is a sense of liberation in being freed from all of the traditional customs and practices that hold other people forever in a form of self-imposed slavery. The reflective person can then intentionally act in ways that contradict conventional norms and values and thereby shock or offend other people. From this the reflective person gains a kind of guilty pleasure since they are amused at the effect that their behavior has on other people. Moreover, their actions are an expression of their own freedom from accepted custom and public opinion. They do not care what anyone thinks of them. In terms of Hegel's theory of recognition, the underground man attempts to show his indifference to the recognition of the other and thus to "negate" the other by acting in ways that contradict normal social behavior. The underground man repeatedly says that he does not care what his readers will think of his views.[20]

The reflective person can see themselves at a distance and observe their interaction with others in a detached manner, regarding it as a kind of game. By contrast, the person of immediacy or common sense never steps out of their own first-person perspective and takes seriously all of their relations and forms of interaction with others. For this reason they are vulnerable to being baited by the person of reflection.

The move from immediacy to reflection, from common sense to critical reasoning, mirrors the story of the Fall. At first Adam and Eve lived like

---

[16] Dostoevsky, *Notes from Underground*, p. 19.
[17] Dostoevsky, *Notes from Underground*, p. 19.
[18] Dostoevsky, *Notes from Underground*, p. 19.
[19] Dostoevsky, *Notes from Underground*, p. 19.
[20] E.g., Dostoevsky, *Notes from Underground*, p. 22.

children in the Garden of Eden. But then, after the original sin, they were cast out
into the real world, where they were forced to live as adults and to face the hard
realities of life. As we have discussed, this was a story of alienation since human
beings were separated from their original nature. Hegel criticized this picture
since true human nature lies on the other side of the Fall with critical reason and
reflection and not prior to it, when humans were simply continuous with
animals.[21] For Dostoevsky as well, this movement toward reflectivity is
a movement away from what is natural and normal. He says that the "spontaneous man is the real man."[22] Even though the underground man regards such
natural people as stupid, he confesses that he is envious of them. He wishes that
he could revert to the natural condition of human beings, but this is impossible
for him,[23] just as Adam and Eve cannot return to the Garden of Eden. Thus the
condition of reflection and critical thinking is de facto one of alienation. While
other people can act and function normally in society, the reflective person
always stands apart as something different and alien. Normal people can walk
and live in the sun, while the reflective person lives in the underground.

## 8.3   The Laws of Nature and Modern Scientific Rationalism

The underground man constantly refers to the laws of nature, and by this he
addresses the question of our relation to the universe at large. We are born into
an already created world that is not of our own making. This world imposes on
us natural limitations. The underground man notes that we frequently run up
against walls that we cannot surmount. Our bodies limit what we are capable of
doing. This is not something that we decided but something that we were
simply confronted with.

Moreover, nature is entirely indifferent to our wishes and hopes. It does not
care what we think: "Nature doesn't ask you about it; she's not concerned with
your wishes or with whether you like her laws or not."[24] These things simply
belong to the actual relations that exist in the world, which is sometimes
referred to as "facticity." In Dostoevsky's time Darwin's theory of evolution
was still something new that was being digested. Many people found the idea
offensive that human beings are continuous with animals and descended from
more primitive beings. We may find evolutionary theory distasteful, but there
is no point to this. Nature has made it that way: "When it is proved, for
example, that you are descended from an ape, it's no use scowling about it –
accept it as a fact."[25] Dostoevsky refers to the necessity or inevitability of nature

[21] See Chapter 2, Sections 2.1–2.2.
[22] Dostoevsky, *Notes from Underground*, p. 20.
[23] Dostoevsky, *Notes from Underground*, pp. 20f.
[24] Dostoevsky, *Notes from Underground*, p. 23.
[25] Dostoevsky, *Notes from Underground*, p. 23.

in a number of ways. He often speaks of it in terms of mathematics and the simple formula that 2 plus 2 is equal to 4. There is no debating this and no getting around it. It is just what it is.

While the underground man of course understands these laws of nature and accepts them, he refuses to be reconciled with them: "Naturally I shan't break through a wall with my head, if I'm really not strong enough, but I won't be reconciled to it simply because it's a stone wall and I haven't enough strength to break it down."[26] He continues, "The point is to understand everything, to realize everything, every impossibility, every stone wall; not to reconcile yourself to a single one of the impossibilities and stone walls if the thought of reconciliation sickens you."[27] It will be recalled that reconciliation was one of the goals of Hegel's philosophy. For him, understanding and philosophical insight lead to reconciliation. When we understand the dynamics of history, then we are reconciled with it. When we understand the development of the forms of religion, then we are reconciled with God. For the underground man, this is a mistake and even a betrayal of what it is to be human. The individual can issue a protest against the universe even if they know full well that they cannot do anything about it. This is the beginning of the existentialist motif of the individual in revolt. The groaning of a cultured person of the nineteenth century represents a protest against the universe and its laws.[28] While such a person knows that their complaining and protesting will do no good since the universe will not change its laws because of them, they remain in a position of defiance and protest.

Like Kierkegaard, Dostoevsky acknowledges that this revolt against the universe means that one must suffer and must live one's life in suffering. This is the human condition. The world seems not to be made for us and to be immune to our wishes. As a result we suffer and are in despair because we desire it to be different: "you ache with it all, and the more mysterious it is, the more you ache."[29] Humans feel themselves helpless in this situation and despair that although they have control over so many things in life, they are utterly impotent when it comes to the basic laws of nature: life, death, and suffering. There is no escaping these fundamental facts of human existence. An awareness of this is the result of reflection.

Beginning with section 7, the underground man critically examines the views of Chernyshevsky, and the text takes on a decidedly polemical aspect, even though he is never mentioned by name. Chernyshevsky argued that humans are, so to speak, programmed to act for their own advantage. When

---

[26] Dostoevsky, *Notes from Underground*, p. 23.
[27] Dostoevsky, *Notes from Underground*, p. 23.
[28] Dostoevsky, *Notes from Underground*, p. 24.
[29] Dostoevsky, *Notes from Underground*, p. 24.

one sees one's true advantage, one will naturally pursue it. With science and technology it is possible to perceive more and more clearly one's true advantage. No one knowingly acts contrary to their own advantage. This is an echo of the old view of Socrates that no one does evil willingly and knowingly. Evil only takes place due to ignorance, when people act without knowing that their actions are evil since if they knew, they would not act in this way. For Chernyshevsky the focus is on both the moral question of evil and that of what is advantageous, and this is defined as what is useful. We are all by nature utility maximizers. This, of course, refers to the doctrine of utilitarianism that was popular at this time, especially in England.

The underground man radically rejects this view, which he finds naive and utterly out of touch with what human nature really is. He raises a series of critical questions in an attempt to undermine Chernyshevsky's position. In the first of these, he asks, "when in all these thousands of years have men acted solely in their own interests?"[30] The underground man claims that people act all the time in ways that are contrary to their advantage and self-interest, and indeed they know this. Here one might think of people who smoke, knowing all the while that smoking is bad for their health. They have been told this repeatedly, and they know and accept the clear scientific evidence for this, yet they continue to smoke. One might also think of people who put themselves at risk of personal harm for the sake of loved ones or their countries or some specific cause, even if it might lead to their own demise. People often help friends or loved ones in need, even if they know that they personally might suffer some harm from this, but their loyalty or love overrides their self-interest. Examples like this defy explanation from the point of view of enlightened self-interest. It is impossible to understand this kind of behavior in terms of a utility scale. Paradoxically, people often desire and choose what is actually harmful to them. So as a psychological thesis, the view of Chernyshevsky is simply wrong and can be proven as such empirically. There are many things that people place higher than their own personal advantage, strictly speaking.

This leads to the second question: "can you undertake to define exactly where a man's advantage lies?"[31] The view of Chernyshevsky assumes that enlightened human self-interest is something immediately obvious and even foundational. But is it? For example, one common assumption is that it is in our self-interest to acquire as much wealth as possible and that this will lead to our happiness. But in fact all experience shows that people who have accumulated a great amount of wealth are much more prone to certain kinds of problems such as depression, alcoholism, marital infidelity, and other such things than people with a normal income. Of course, this is not to say that the happiest people are those who live in poverty since they too are confronted

---

[30] Dostoevsky, *Notes from Underground*, p. 29.
[31] Dostoevsky, *Notes from Underground*, p. 29.

with their own set of problems that undermines their happiness. So while it is true that a certain amount of wealth is important for one to be happy, there is a tipping point beyond which it tends to have a counterproductive effect. Therefore, desiring more wealth could very well be bad for people in the end. The underground man points out that when one gets right down to it, it is not so easy to define clearly and unambiguously what human self-interest really is since humans are such complex creatures.

The underground man argues that if people in fact acted toward their own advantage and this led them to do what is right and virtuous, then one would expect in the course of history that the clearer and clearer awareness of what is to people's advantage would make them less violent and aggressive. We could expect civilization to be less affected by wars and bloodshed. But, as history has shown, in Dostoevsky's time and our own, this is simply not the case. The knowledge that scientific and industrial development has brought us has not led to any fundamental change in human nature. It has only led to the development of more sophisticated weapons and forms of warfare. Here it is difficult not to think of the Holocaust, which Dostoevsky's remarks seem in a sense to anticipate. The underground man asks, "Have you noticed that the most refined shedders of blood have been almost always the most highly civilized gentlemen ... ?"[32] After the Holocaust this was something that puzzled many thinkers. So once again, Chernyshevsky's assumptions about human nature and civilization seem woefully naive and off-target.

At length the underground man reveals what he thinks Chernyshevsky and his followers have missed in their calculation of human self-interest:

> doesn't there, in fact, exist something that is dearer to almost every man than his own very best interests, or – not to violate logic – some best good ... which is more important and higher than any other good and for the sake of which man is prepared if necessary to go against all the laws, against, that is, reason, honor, peace and quiet, prosperity – in short against all those fine and advantageous things ... ?[33]

As is seen a few pages later, what is referred to here is free will. The underground man continues his assessment of human nature by claiming,

> a man, whoever he is, always and everywhere likes to act as he chooses, and not at all according to the dictates of reason and self-interest .... One's own free will and unfettered volition, one's own caprice, however wild, one's own fancy, inflamed sometimes to the point of madness – that is the one best and greatest good, which is never taken into consideration because it will not fit into any classification.[34]

---

[32] Dostoevsky, *Notes from Underground*, pp. 31f.
[33] Dostoevsky, *Notes from Underground*, pp. 30f.
[34] Dostoevsky, *Notes from Underground*, pp. 33f.

All of the talk of human rational self-interest and advantage makes no sense if freedom does not play a role in the analysis. It is freedom that makes human behavior difficult to predict and understand. It makes it possible for people to value other things higher than what, with all things being equal, should be in their enlightened self-interest. Chernyshevsky has completely failed to appreciate this central element of the human psyche.

## 8.4   The Criticism of Scientific Materialism

While the underground man began with a criticism of Chernyshevsky's assumptions about the psychological nature of human beings, he continues with a criticism of the metaphysical view that lies behind this, that is, the view of human nature as such. Chernyshevsky is operating with a form of scientific materialism. In other words, human beings are simply products of nature, and this has been proven by biology. In nature everything works by means of cause and effect. Animals behave the way they do in the world since they have been programmed to do so by their biology. When we understand this, we can easily predict their behavior in the same way that we know a bull will always charge a red cloth or a lion will always chase its fleeing prey. Although humans are more complex and their behavior is not so easy to predict, nonetheless it is in the end the same forces that are at work. Humans are conditioned by their biology. They act in certain ways because their brain tells them to do so.

We like to think that we can act freely, but this idea is an illusion, which is maintained because we do not understand our brains and our biology well enough. We believe, for example, that we freely choose the people we love, but in fact we are compelled to do so due to certain chemical reactions taking place in our brains. In short, humans have no free will and are determined by nature. The underground man portrays this materialist view of human nature as follows:

> science will teach men . . . that they have not, in fact, and never have had, either will or fancy, and are no more than a sort of piano keyboard or barrel-organ cylinder; and that the laws of nature still exist on the earth, so that whatever man does he does not of his own volition but, as really goes without saying, by the laws of nature.[35]

This might seem to be a radical view, but it is in fact widely held in the modern field of philosophy of mind today. It is argued that the more we learn about the brain, the more persuasive this position will become, and the illusion of freedom will gradually disappear. Understanding human behavior will always be a complex matter because the human brain is a complex organ, but it is

---

[35] Dostoevsky, *Notes from Underground*, p. 32.

a mistake to think that it operates in a way that is fundamentally different from the rest of nature.

Once the mysteries of the human mind have been uncovered by science and reduced to the matter of the brain, the next step will be to apply this same method to society as a whole. When one knows how humans function as individuals, then one simply needs to expand the analysis to sociology to see how they act in groups. According to Chernyshevsky's view, this knowledge will help us to create a utopian society, where people lead happy lives and the needs of everyone are met. The underground man describes this as follows: "Then ... a new political economy will come into existence, all complete, and also calculated with mathematical accuracy, so that all problems will vanish in the twinkling of an eye .... Then the Palace of Crystal will arise."[36] When Dostoevsky was in London in 1862, he visited the Crystal Palace that had been built for the World Fair in 1851. It was for him a great symbol of modern science and industry. For Dostoevsky, it represented the illusion of a perfect human society and social order in the future.

According to the materialist thesis about human nature, it would be possible, using scientific means, to create a utopian society in which all human needs are met. For Chernyshevsky and the socialists, this should be the goal; indeed, it is the only enlightened and rational goal. But the counterargument of the underground man is that humans are more complex than this. Just meeting their physical needs will never be enough to satisfy them. People need more than this. We cannot live in a Crystal Palace because there is nothing to do, no obstacles to overcome, and nothing to live for. There will always be other kinds of needs that are not taken into account. Here the key again is human freedom: "What a man needs is simply and solely *independent* volition, whatever that independence may cost and wherever it may lead."[37] This is something that Chernyshevsky cannot understand. According to his view, it would seem fundamentally irrational to act in a way that contradicts one's self-interest or to desire anything beyond the satisfaction of one's natural needs. The underground man attempts to argue that the true metaphysical nature of human beings is more complex than this simplistic view allows.

It might be claimed that the underground man does not actually refute the argument for scientific materialism in the sense that he does not demonstrate that it is wrong. But rather he argues that humans could never accept such a view, even if it were proven to be correct. This view sees humans as simply objects of nature like rocks and trees. The idea is that if we could understand all of the human natural drives and desires as well as we understand the chemistry of other objects of nature, then we will have understood the human being completely. But for the underground man, this is to reduce human beings to

---

[36] Dostoevsky, *Notes from Underground*, p. 33.
[37] Dostoevsky, *Notes from Underground*, p. 34.

objects.[38] Humans would be just complex natural machines and nothing more. In this sense we could learn from some kind of scientific calculation what our best interests are, and our will would amount to simply carrying out the result of this calculation.

The underground man clarifies his position by pointing out that he is not against reason per se. He agrees that on the whole, reason is a good thing, but he denies that this is the whole story of what it is to be human:

> reason is only reason and satisfies only man's intellectual faculties, while volition is a manifestation of the whole of life . . . . After all, I . . . quite naturally want to live so as to fulfill my whole capacity for living and not so as to satisfy simply and solely my intellectual capacity, which is only one-twentieth of my whole capacity for living.[39]

The spirit of scientific rationalism has led its followers to overestimate the role of reason in human life and to underestimate the many other complex factors that make up human beings.

It is our ability to act in ways that greatly differ from our rational self-interest that makes humans beings what they are. This is what makes us all special as individuals since we have different values and priorities and are not all mechanically governed by rationality. The underground man concedes that it might well be stupidity to act in contradiction to one's self interest, yet "this height of stupidity, this whim, may be for us, gentlemen, the greatest benefit on earth . . . . because it does at any rate preserve what is dear and extremely important to us, that is our personality and our individuality."[40] For the underground man, human nature consists precisely in the assertion of one's will and freedom, in demonstrating that one is not an object of nature but something else.[41]

## 8.5   The Criticism of the Idea of Historical Progress

In his *Lectures on the Philosophy of History*, Hegel defended the thesis that although history appears at first glance to be a confusing chaos of wars, migrations, and kings, with no deeper meaning, in fact upon closer examination, history contains a deep rationality that can be discerned by the human mind. By this he meant specifically that human history tends toward the development of subjective freedom, that is, the idea of the individual. The idea of progress in history was an old one, but in Dostoevsky's time it seemed

---

[38] Dostoevsky, *Notes from Underground*, p. 34.
[39] Dostoevsky, *Notes from Underground*, pp. 35f.
[40] Dostoevsky, *Notes from Underground*, p. 36.
[41] Dostoevsky, *Notes from Underground*, p. 38: "the whole business of humanity consists solely in this – that a man should constantly prove to himself that he is a man and not a sprig in a barrel-organ!"

to have a certain plausibility since during the second half of the nineteenth century, Europe enjoyed a fairly long period of peace and prosperity. The population of the continent grew rapidly, and the development of science and industry was radically transforming urban life. Chernyshevsky shared this view of human progress and development in the course of history. Dostoevsky refers explicitly to the writings of the English historian Henry Thomas Buckle (1821–1862), who, the underground man writes, claimed "civilization renders man milder and so less bloodthirsty and addicted to warfare."[42]

The underground man challenges this belief, which he again takes to be naive. He begins by asking how one can characterize the history of humanity. He entertains a few different interpretations briefly and then concludes, "anything can be said of world history, anything conceivable even by the most disordered imagination. There is only one thing that you can't say – that it had anything to do with reason."[43] He thus denies the idea that there is any *logos* or rational principle in historical development at all. His argument for this denial, he claims, can be found in human nature itself. Even if by some chance history had created certain conditions for human beings to thrive and be happy and fulfilled, strangely enough, humans will always manage to tear this down:

> Shower [man] with all earthly blessings, plunge him so deep into happiness that nothing is visible but the bubbles rising to the surface of his happiness; give him such economic prosperity that he will have nothing left to do but sleep, eat gingerbread, and worry about the continuance of world history – and he . . . even then . . . will commit some abomination.[44]

He continues his tirade, "He will jeopardize his very gingerbread and deliberately will the most pernicious rubbish, the most uneconomic nonsense, simply and solely in order to alloy all this positive rationality with the element of his own pernicious fancy."[45] So even if there were some reason in history, human beings would destroy it. Again it is difficult not to think of the events of the World Wars and the Holocaust in the twentieth century. These events led many thinkers to wholly abandon any notion of human progress in history.

The underground man continues his criticism of the modern view of rational and enlightened self-interest by granting that human beings are so constructed that they naturally set goals for themselves and strive for them and to this extent are constructive creatures.[46] Dostoevsky uses an example from his own experience: engineering. Humans like to construct roads, even though it does not matter where the road leads. But then he raises the critical question:

[42] Dostoevsky, *Notes from Underground*, p. 31.
[43] Dostoevsky, *Notes from Underground*, p. 37.
[44] Dostoevsky, *Notes from Underground*, pp. 37f.
[45] Dostoevsky, *Notes from Underground*, p. 38.
[46] Dostoevsky, *Notes from Underground*, p. 39.

"But how is it that [man] is so passionately disposed to destruction and chaos?"[47] According to his view, no one who knows anything about human psychology, social life, or history can deny that humans possess this destructive impulse. But this seems clearly and straightforwardly to contradict the positive, constructive impulse. How can one account for this?

The underground man postulates that while they love to create and construct, human beings are in fact fearful of attaining their goals. There is something fixed and final about the goal once it has been achieved, and this then leads to a sense of dissatisfaction. At the beginning the goal might have seemed to be a good one, but once it is achieved, it looks different from how one originally conceived it. Often goals are created in response to perceived problems, and so the idea is that once the solution is found and the goal achieved, then the problem will disappear. But experience shows that while this is true in many cases, new problems arise that cause people at least the same amount of vexation as the old ones.

In many ways the nineteenth-century vision of a utopian society has in fact been realized in some of our modern nations. We have beautiful shopping malls where one can buy almost anything; we have a multitude of restaurants where one can indulge the most specialized of tastes. Some countries have good welfare and health care systems. People from Dostoevsky's time would presumably be astonished at such modern societies. But in a sense the social problems that we see today seem to vindicate the truth of some of Dostoevsky's psychological insights. While it is true that many of the social ills of our day come from problems of poverty, many of them do not. One often hears of young people from perfectly well-off middle-class homes turning to drugs, alcohol, or gang violence. These young people live, comparatively speaking, in a utopia. They have all of their physical needs met. Yet they are dissatisfied and feel a kind of emptiness that they seek to fill in other kinds of ways. Parents, teachers, and other members of the older generation have a difficult time grasping this. They cannot seem to understand what drives young people to such things; if they are so well off, then they should not have any problems. The parents and people from the earlier generation worked to create a well-functioning welfare state; this was their goal, which, once achieved, would resolve all of the major problems, or so they believed. But to their surprise, this proves not to be the case. Humans cannot accept a situation in which, with the goals achieved, "there will . . . be nothing left to do."[48] Despite prosperity and a high standard of living, there is thus still a sense of dissatisfaction among many people. There is a negative, destructive impulse in human beings that will show itself even if there is no particular reason for it and even if they are wealthy and have no material needs. The underground man writes that even in

[47] Dostoevsky, *Notes from Underground*, p. 40.
[48] Dostoevsky, *Notes from Underground*, p. 41.

the best of situations, people "will contrive to create destruction and chaos, invent various sufferings."[49]

So for the underground man, "mankind is comically constructed" in the sense that although our nature tells us to go out and set goals and accomplish them, it also tells us to be destructive and tear down whatever we have built up.[50] As long as human beings are in the process of reaching a goal or constructing something, then things are fine. People are busy with the task at hand and are captivated by the illusion that everything will be better when it is completed. But the problems arise once the task is completed and the building is erected. Then dissatisfaction sets in, and the destructive impulse comes out. Humans will never be able to sit quietly and live in a world where all problems are solved and everything is conveniently at hand. They will always perceive new problems that require new solutions. While ants live in anthills and have always done so and will always do so in the future, humans are always changing their form of life.[51] For them there is no rationally determinable, optimal way of living that, once achieved, will resolve all human cares and problems. Humans cannot live in an anthill but must constantly change the key elements of their lives. Dostoevsky states, "consciousness is man's supreme misfortune."[52] It will be recalled from Hegel's analysis of the story of the Fall that the coming to self-consciousness of human beings is what separates us from the animals and makes us like God. Therefore, according to his view, this should be regarded as something positive and not, as in Genesis, as something negative. But for the underground man, consciousness is what leads to suffering. Humans cannot, like ants, be satisfied with the achievement of any goal. They cannot ever remain in a stationary situation but, motivated by suffering caused by new problems, must continue to move on. Here we can see a fundamentally different evaluation of the meaning and significance of human self-consciousness from the positive view given by Hegel.

The modern advocates of utilitarianism and pragmatism believe that the goal should be human welfare and prosperity, but the underground man points out that humans also need just the opposite: "perhaps prosperity isn't the only thing that pleases mankind, perhaps he is just as attracted to suffering. Perhaps suffering is just as good for him as prosperity."[53] The underground man explains, "suffering is doubt, negation,"[54] and by this he seems to mean that regardless of how much prosperity or welfare people have, there will always be room for doubt. There will always be new problems that even the

---

[49] Dostoevsky, *Notes from Underground*, p. 38.
[50] Dostoevsky, *Notes from Underground*, pp. 40f.
[51] Dostoevsky, *Notes from Underground*, p. 40.
[52] Dostoevsky, *Notes from Underground*, p. 41.
[53] Dostoevsky, *Notes from Underground*, p. 41.
[54] Dostoevsky, *Notes from Underground*, p. 41.

greatest amount of prosperity cannot solve, and this will lead to chaos and destruction.

## 8.6    The First Conflict with Others: The Slave

Chapter 2 of *Notes from Underground*, entitled "A Story of the Falling Sleet," makes frequent reference to wet snow. This dominant image is a symbol for everything that is wrong in human society and with humans in interaction with others. This chapter explores the underground man's personal relations to a number of different kinds of people. These different relations can be divided into two fundamental sorts. First, the underground man has a relation of inferiority or subordination to those people who stand above him in the social hierarchy, those who enjoy more respect and status in the world. This is depicted in the first story that is recounted here, where he engages in a one-sided conflict with an unnamed officer (section 1), and in the second story, when he tells the reader about his relations with his old friends from school (sections 2–5). In both cases he is in a position of inferiority and is generally regarded with disdain. Second, the underground man has a relation of superiority to the young prostitute Liza (sections 6–10) and his servant (section 8).

In these stories one can see the shadow of Hegel's analysis of the lord and the bondsman. As has been discussed, one cannot be for oneself without being recognized by the other. My independence and selfhood is a function of what I am for the other. As Hegel showed, we all attempt to gain positive recognition from others that reflects and confirms our own self-image. However, this is undermined in relations where there is a form of hierarchy, with one person being in a position of power and the other in a position of weakness. In such cases, recognition only flows in one direction, from the weak person to the strong person or, in Hegel's terms, from the slave to the master. For Hegel, the dialectic of the lord and the bondsman is dynamic and indeed only the beginning of genuine social relations. In time humans can overcome these kinds of relations and reach a situation where the two parties are regarded as equals and can mutually give and receive recognition. But Dostoevsky seems more cynical about the possibility of ever reaching such a positive view. He explores different kinds of relations that the underground man has – those in which he is in a position of power and those in which he is in a position of weakness – but there is never any hint that it is ever possible to overcome these kinds of social asymmetries. In other words, all human relations reduce to either one side or the other, and no equal relation is possible in which freely given recognition is imparted from both sides. Human beings are fundamentally condemned to be alienated from one another.

The underground man represents a kind of defiant independence: He claims that he does not care about others and that he is independent of them, yet the events constantly prove that he is the most dependent. He urgently seeks the recognition of the officer and his former schoolmates, although he claims to disdain them. Thus there is a dialectic at work in his relation to others. The more he tries to show that he is independent, the more he shows that he is in fact dependent. The underground man hates the way in which he is seen in the eyes of others and is determined to change their views of him so that they come to respect him for one positive trait or another.

The first story concerns a perceived insult by an officer that is blown entirely out of proportion. The story is prefaced by the underground man's description of his workplace, where he is universally despised. He struggles with this in his own self-image and attempts to convince himself that although the others are superior to him, he nonetheless is superior to them in different ways. But he can never quite manage to convince himself of this since he knows down deep that he is "a coward and a slave."[55]

The story of the officer begins with an account of how in a bar the officer gently moves the underground man out of the way in order to move past him. The underground man is infuriated by the fact that the officer does not seem even to acknowledge his existence: "I had been treated like an insect."[56] Being a coward, the underground man of course does not have the courage to say anything but instead smolders with anger and resentment. To the officer he is such an insignificant being that he hardly even exists. His disdain for the officer becomes an obsession lasting more than two years, which shows the urgency of the underground man's need for recognition. He subsequently spends an enormous amount of time and goes to great lengths plotting different ways in which he can take his revenge and force the officer to respect him. These include writing a caricature of the officer and publishing it or challenging the officer to a duel, but of course none of these ever comes to fruition.[57] In his imagination he pictures himself having great triumphs, but he never has the resolve to carry through any of his ideas.

He sees the officer along with other nobles taking their regular walks on Nevsky Prospect, the main avenue in the city of St. Petersburg, and he finds himself constantly yielding and giving way so that the others can pass, while no one ever makes way for him. This confirms that they regard him as unworthy of recognition, while he, the slave, recognizes them. It is a visible demonstration of their power over him. He writes, "It was an agonizing torment, a never-ending unbearable humiliation, caused by the suspicion, constantly growing into clear-cut certainty, that compared to them I was a fly, a nasty obscene fly."[58] The underground man sees the officer and constantly gives way to him and resents himself for doing so. He decides to stand up to the officer and not

[55] Dostoevsky, *Notes from Underground*, p. 48.
[56] Dostoevsky, *Notes from Underground*, p. 52.
[57] Dostoevsky, *Notes from Underground*, p. 54.
[58] Dostoevsky, *Notes from Underground*, p. 55.

yield, waiting until the officer gives way. After a couple of failed attempts where
he always capitulates and yields at the last minute, the underground man
resolves to stick with his plan. In the end, he manages to hold his ground
and in fact collides with the officer, getting a knock on the shoulder.[59] The
underground man regards this as a great triumph. The reader, however, cannot
help but see this as a pathetic and vain attempt of a slave to gain recognition
from the master. The underground man's description of the whole affair is
comic.

The second episode where the underground man is portrayed as being in
a relation to superiors is when he meets some old school acquaintances. It
becomes immediately clear that none of his old schoolmates likes him at all,
and, indeed, they hold him in disdain. He is the least popular and the least
successful professionally. He harbors great resentment and anger toward them
but nonetheless craves their recognition in one form or another. Upon learning that his schoolmates will be meeting together for a dinner the next day, he
invites himself to join them, although he is clearly not welcome. As was the
case with the officer, the underground man's relations to his old acquaintances
resemble that of the slave and the master. He tries to show his imagined
superiority over them and his indifference toward them, although he is clearly
inferior. Predictably, his efforts fail miserably every time. He regards the
dinner as his opportunity to show the others that he is really better than they
are.[60] He is made to endure one insult and humiliation after another, reinfor-
cing his lowly status instead of revising it. His relationships to his former
schoolmates appear completely hopeless.

## 8.7   The Second Conflict with Others: The Master

The final story in the work concerns the underground man's relation to the
young prostitute Liza. She is the main figure here, but it is also in this same part
of the text that we are told about the underground man's servant Apollon.
While the first two stories – about the officer and the underground man's
schoolmates – represented the underground man's relations to superiors, this
last one represents his relation to those who stand lower than him in the social
hierarchy. Now he is the master and the others the slaves. Here as well he is
unsuccessful at achieving any kind of meaningful relation.

In the story of his dinner with his old schoolmates, the underground man
recounts that he was also disdained back in his school days and that everyone
was his superior. However, there was a single person, whom he refers to as
a "friend," over whom he was superior. But the underground man recounts
that he acted like a true master toward a true slave: "I was a tyrant at heart;

---

[59] Dostoevsky, *Notes from Underground*, p. 58.
[60] Dostoevsky, *Notes from Underground*, p. 70.

I wanted unlimited power over his heart and mind."[61] But he notes that he also disdained his friend precisely for his submissiveness; in short, the master cannot have true respect or give true recognition to his slave: "he was a simple-hearted and submissive soul, but when he became wholly devoted to me I immediately took a dislike to him and repulsed him."[62] One cannot respect someone whom one regards and treats as a slave.

The underground man's relation to his servant Apollon also very much resembles the master-slave dialectic. Ostensibly the underground man is the master and Apollon his slave – literally his servant. Apollon does the bidding of the underground man, cleaning his shoes, running his errands, etc. Yet the servant turns out to be the real master. The underground man is in need of recognition, which he never really manages to get from Apollon. He constantly interprets the silence of his servant as a form of disrespect or disdain. But by means of this silence, the servant manages to bring out the underground man's need for recognition and thus dependence. The servant needs to do almost nothing at all to infuriate the underground man, and this clearly shows a masterful way of handling his master, who ostensibly is in the position of power. The underground man says that he hates his servant, yet he never fires him.[63] Despite being in the role of the master, the underground man is thus dependent on him and his recognition. The underground man attempts to do things such as withhold Apollon's wages in order to demonstrate that he is the boss and can do what he pleases, but these efforts have no effect and cause more vexation to the underground man than to his servant.[64] The silent glance of Apollon drives the underground man to despair. The servant does not have to say anything, but his gaze alone is enough to unsettle his master. All of the underground man's attempts to intimidate him are in vain. The slave has become the master.

The main story in this part of the text is, however, the encounter with Liza. The underground man for the first time comes under the gaze of another who seems to take him seriously and not ignore him. He says, "I saw two eyes open, regarding me with curiosity and fixed attention. Their look was coldly indifferent, sullen, like something utterly alien."[65] Unlike his former schoolmates, who simply ignored him and found him obnoxious, Liza seems to be interested in him. But this look of the other makes the underground man feel uncomfortable and gives him an "eerie feeling."[66] He does not feel confirmed by this look of the other, but rather he feels uncertain about what Liza's view of him might be. Instead of using Liza's interest as a basis to build a true friendship or

---

[61] Dostoevsky, *Notes from Underground*, p. 69.
[62] Dostoevsky, *Notes from Underground*, p. 69.
[63] Dostoevsky, *Notes from Underground*, p. 107.
[64] Dostoevsky, *Notes from Underground*, p. 109.
[65] Dostoevsky, *Notes from Underground*, p. 86.
[66] Dostoevsky, *Notes from Underground*, p. 86.

love relation, he begins to torment her in an attempt at control and domination. He succeeds in his sport of manipulating her and makes her feel badly about her life as a prostitute. He portrays her as a slave and reduces her to despair.[67] Yet, as with his sole friend from his schooldays, he disdains her in her role as a slave.[68] As with his servant Apollon, there is an inversion of roles between the underground man and Liza. He becomes her slave. He needs her recognition and cannot bear feeling humiliated in her eyes.[69] She thus holds great power over him, despite his efforts to humiliate and crush her. At the end he himself realizes this: "The idea came also into my overwrought mind that our roles had definitely been reversed, she was the heroine and I was just such another crushed and degraded creature as she had been that night – four days before."[70] His account of his capacity to love reveals his master-slave approach to relationships.

Just as the underground man is alienated from others who were his master, so also he is alienated from others for whom he is the master. All human relations can be divided into these categories, masters and slaves, and in no case is a real relation of love or friendship possible. The underground man exclaims, "Without power and tyranny over somebody I can't live."[71] The theme of romantic love is made the object of satire.[72] The underground man confesses: "I could no longer fall in love, because, I repeat, with me to love meant to tyrannize and hold the upper hand morally."[73] He continues, "I sometimes think now that the whole of love consists in the right, freely given to the lover, to tyrannize over the beloved. Even in my underground dreams I did not picture love otherwise than as a struggle, always beginning with hatred and ending with moral subjugation."[74] According to his view, love itself is a master-slave relation. We are forever alienated from one another.

## 8.8   Two Interpretations

With regard to its final message, *Notes from Underground*, like any great work of literature, leaves the reader with some interpretative ambiguities to untangle. What does Dostoevsky really mean to say with this work? There are two main lines of interpretation here that we can follow: a negative one and a positive one.

---

[67]   He says to her: "But you have to admit that you've been a slave from the start. Yes, a slave!" (Dostoevsky, *Notes from Underground*, p. 90).

[68]   Dostoevsky, *Notes from Underground*, p. 96.

[69]   Dostoevsky, *Notes from Underground*, p. 116.

[70]   Dostoevsky, *Notes from Underground*, p. 118.

[71]   Dostoevsky, *Notes from Underground*, p. 118.

[72]   Dostoevsky, *Notes from Underground*, p. 94.

[73]   Dostoevsky, *Notes from Underground*, p. 119.

[74]   Dostoevsky, *Notes from Underground*, p. 119.

On the negative interpretation, one might argue that the underground man and his cynical worldview is, for Dostoevsky, the lamentable truth about human existence. According to this view, all human relations reduce to master-slave relations. As the underground man says, "Either a hero, or dirt, there was nothing in between."[75] We are all in different kinds of relations in society, but these always have some hierarchical aspect. It is not just the case that the underground man happens to be cynical about this with regard to his own lowly status, but in fact it is something universal. While the unnamed officer does not yield or give way to the insignificant underground man, he does so immediately for nobility or people above him in the social hierarchy.[76] While the underground man's old acquaintances from school give the appearance of friendship, this is an illusion since their small group is also structured by a hierarchy, with Zverkov as its clear leader.[77] Human beings are inevitably locked in power relations, and there is no escaping this. This is the view taken up later by figures such as Sartre and Foucault. In a sense these thinkers take Hegel's analysis of the lord and the bondsman as their point of departure, but then they deny Hegel's subsequent analysis about how this relation is overcome through the further mediation of social relations. According to this view, relations such as love and friendship are in the end an illusion since they presuppose an impossible relation of equality and mutual respect.

This negative or even cynical interpretation seems to be supported at the end of the work, when it is objected to the underground man that he is only describing his own cynical condition but that this is not valid for everyone else. The imagined critic argues, "You are talking only about yourself and your underground miseries, don't dare speak of 'all of us!'"[78] To this the underground man responds, "I have only carried to a logical conclusion in my life what you yourselves didn't dare take more than half-way; and you supposed your cowardice was common sense, and comforted yourselves with the self-deception."[79] This implies that the rest of society suffers from naiveté and self-delusion since it does not want to face the grim reality of social relations that the underground man has discovered. Seen from this perspective, the work is a harsh criticism of mainstream society and ways of thinking.

But there is also a possible positive interpretation. According to this view, the work is a specific case study of a demonic personality and thus is not intended to be valid for everyone. The demonic reflects the fate of the human conscience without God. For Kierkegaard, the alternatives are faith or despair. For Dostoevsky, the options are between the God-man or Christ and the man-

---

[75] Dostoevsky, *Notes from Underground*, p. 59.
[76] Dostoevsky, *Notes from Underground*, p. 55.
[77] Dostoevsky, *Notes from Underground*, p. 63, p. 72.
[78] Dostoevsky, *Notes from Underground*, pp. 122f.
[79] Dostoevsky, *Notes from Underground*, p. 123.

God: that is, the conception of man as deified by modernity – in short, the demonic man. The *Notes* can thus be understood as a philosophy of tragedy. This is the tragedy of modern man, man without God and thus without a moral center. Here we see the inner tragedy of consciousness: the sinfulness of fallen man.

One aspect of this positive interpretation is that a Christian resolution or redemption is possible. While there is no explicit reference to Christian categories in the text, in a letter to his brother, Dostoevsky complains that the censors enigmatically took out the religious message of the work. They removed his claim for "the necessity of faith and Christ,"[80] and for whatever reason Dostoevsky never put this material back in the later editions. Thus, despite everything, there is an intended Christian message, and in this regard the work can be read as an extension of Kierkegaard's analysis in *The Sickness unto Death*.

The theme of alienation is absolutely fundamental to the work, specifically, alienation toward other people. Since human relations always end in either lordship or bondage, genuine human recognition and solidarity is undermined. Hegel's idea of finding oneself in another person and thus having a richer self is dismissed as naive. The theme of self-alienation is also very much present. The underground man knows full well that he is a coward and a morally depraved person, and in his moments of transparency he admits this. But much of the time he engages in fantasies and dreams in which he portrays himself in much more flattering terms. Similarly, he knowingly lies to others in order to cast himself in a more positive light. His identity is in a sense uncertain, and he is himself constantly self-deceived about it.

At the end of this work, this is thematized again with the claim that people in the nineteenth century "have all got out of the habit of living" and are alienated from "real life."[81] Here Dostoevsky seems to echo Kierkegaard's claim that modern human beings are lost in abstractions and have forgotten what it is to exist. People do not want to be vulnerable individuals; instead, they "are always striving to be some unprecedented kind of generalized human being."[82] As Kierkegaard argued in *A Literary Review*, people escape into the crowd or the "they" and thus eschew their individuality. People oddly want to be rational utility maximizers and statistics instead of individuals invested with freedom. Modern humans are thus alienated from themselves and have forgotten what it is to act freely in the real world. Dostoevsky offers a terrifying vision of the modern human experience in the face of the rise of science and technology.

[80] See "Excerpts from Dostoevsky's Letters," in Fyodor Dostoevsky, *"Notes from Underground" and "The Grand Inquisitor"*, trans. by Ralph E. Matlaw (Harmondsworth: Penguin, 1991), "To his brother Michael, March 26, 1864," p. 195.
[81] Dostoevsky, *Notes from Underground*, p. 122.
[82] Dostoevsky, *Notes from Underground*, p. 123.

# 9

# Bakunin's Theory of Anarchy

The Russian revolutionary thinker Mikhail Aleksandrovich Bakunin (1814–1876) is best known today for his theory of anarchism. Due to his wide travels, he had contact with many of the most important intellectuals in Europe. Moreover, because of his activism, he was also important in the political debates of the day. His role in the development of the history of philosophy in the nineteenth century should not be overlooked. He had a lifelong interest in Hegel's philosophy, which he regularly returned to and made use of in the service of his own thinking. Bakunin represents a broad group of Russian intellectuals of his generation who were all influenced by Hegel, including Ivan Turgenev, Alexander Herzen, and Vissarion Belinsky, and, as was seen in Chapter 8, Dostoevsky.[1]

Bakunin began his study of philosophy at the University of Moscow in 1835.[2] There he came under the influence of the circle of students surrounding

---

[1] See Andrzej Walicki, "The Russian Hegelians: From 'Reconciliation with Reality' to 'Philosophy of Action,'" in his *A History of Russian Thought from the Enlightenment to Marxism*, trans. by Hilda Andrews-Rusiecka (Stanford: Stanford University Press, 1979), pp. 115–134; Guy Planty-Bonjour, *Hegel et la pensée philosophique en Russie 1830–1917* (The Hague: Martinus Nijhoff, 1974); Dmitrij Cyzevskyj, "Hegel in Rußland," in Dmitrij Cyzevskyj (ed.), *Hegel bei den Slaven* (Bad Homburg vor der Höhe: Gentner, 1954), pp. 145–396; Boris Jakowenko (ed.), *Geschichte des Hegelianismus in Rußland. Erster Band* (Prague: Josef Bartel, 1934); Boris Jakowenko (ed.), *Zweiter Beitrag zur Geschichte des Hegelianismus in Rußland. Hegel und die Anfänge des Slawophilentums (1839–1849)* (Prague: Josef Bartel, 1935); Alexandre Koyré, "Hegel en Russie," in his *Études sur l'historie de la pensée philosophique en Russie* (Paris: Librairie philosophique J. Vrin, 1950), pp. 103–170; Janko Janeff, "Zur Geschichte des russischen Hegelianismus," *Deutsche Vierteljahrsschrift für Literaturwissenschaft und Geistesgeschichte*, 10 (1932), 45–73.

[2] Edward H. Carr, *Michael Bakunin* (London: Macmillan, 1937); Mark Leier, *Bakunin: The Creative Passion: A Biography* (New York: Thomas Dunne Books, 2006); Madeleine Grawtiz, *Bakounine: biographie* (Paris: Plon, 1990); Paul MacLaughlin, *Mikhail Bakunin: The Philosophical Basis of His Anarchism* (New York: Algora Publishing, 2002); Arthur P. Mendel, *Michael Bakunin: Roots of Apocalypse* (New York: Praeger Publishers, 1981); Aileen Kelly, *Mikhail Bakunin: A Study in the Psychology and Politics of Utopianism* (New York: Clarendon Press, 1982); Brian Morris, *Bakunin: The Philosophy of Freedom* (Montreal: Black Rose Books, 1993); Eugene Pyziur, *The Doctrine of Anarchism of Michael A. Bakunin* (Milwaukee: Marquette University Press, 1955).

the poet and philosopher Nikolai Stankevich (1813–1840), who was the key figure in disseminating Hegel's ideas at the time in Russia.[3] Bakunin had an interest in German philosophy from a fairly early age, and he made his first study of Kant, Fichte, Schelling, and Hegel there. In 1836 he translated Fichte's *Lectures on the Vocation of the Scholar* into Russian. Two years later he published a translation of Hegel's *Gymnasial-Reden*.[4] These were lectures that Hegel gave in his capacity of headmaster at a secondary school in Nuremberg. They had then recently been published for the first time in 1834 in the first volume of Hegel's *Vermischte Schriften*, which constituted a part of the new collected works edition.[5] In his preface to his translation, Bakunin shows excitement about Hegel's philosophy as a critical tool, which he uses to criticize the educational system in Russia. In this text he also broaches the issue of modern alienation.

In 1840 Bakunin traveled to Prussia and attended the University of Berlin. There he came into contact with some of Hegel's leading students. In his work *Statism and Anarchy* from many years later, Bakunin recounts how the University of Berlin, under the guidance of the abovementioned Prussian Minister of Education Karl Freiherr vom Stein zum Altenstein, became the leading institution for progressive ideas during the period of the Restoration. Altenstein tried to bring to the new university the leading scholars in the different fields from all over the Germanophone world. Bakunin speaks from first-hand experience that he gained during his stay in the Prussian capital.[6] Together with Kierkegaard and Friedrich Engels, he attended the lectures of the Hegelian logician Karl Werder.[7] He also heard the famous lectures of

[3] Stankevich himself went to Berlin in 1838 to study with Hegel's students. See Serge N. Evanow, *N. V. Stankevich and His Circle: The Idealistic Movement of the 1830's* (Berkeley: University of California Press, 1953); Edward J. Brown, *Stankevich and His Moscow Circle, 1830–1840* (Stanford: Stanford University Press, 1966); John Randolph, *The House in the Garden: The Bakunin Family and the Romance of Russian Idealism* (Ithaca: Cornell University Press, 2007).

[4] See Martine Del Giudice, "Bakunin's Preface to Hegel's Gymnasial Lectures: The Problem of Alienation and the Reconciliation with Reality," *Canadian-American Slavic Studies*, 16 (2) (1982), 161–189.

[5] G. W. F. Hegel, "Fünf Gymnasial-Reden, gehalten zu Nürnberg," in *Vermischte Schriften*, I–II, ed. by Friedrich Förster and Ludwig Boumann, vols. 16– 17 ( 1834– 1835), in *Georg Wilhelm Friedrich Hegel's Werke. Vollständige Ausgabe*, vols. 1– 18, ed. by Ludwig Boumann, Friedrich Förster, Eduard Gans, Karl Hegel, Leopold von Henning, Heinrich Gustav Hotho, Philipp Marheineke, Karl Ludwig Michelet, Karl Rosenkranz, and Johannes Schulze (Berlin: Duncker und Humblot, 1832–1845), vol. 16, pp. 131–199.

[6] Mikhail Bakunin, *Statism and Anarchy*, trans. by Marshall S. Shatz (Cambridge: Cambridge University Press, 2005), p. 130.

[7] See Lawrence S. Stepelevich, "Hegelian Nihilism: Karl Werder and the Class of 1841," *Philosophical Forum*, 46(3) (2015), 249–273, especially 267–271; Jon Stewart, "Werder: The Influence of Werder's Lectures and *Logik* on Kierkegaard's Thought," in Jon Stewart (ed.), *Kierkegaard and His German Contemporaries*, Tome I, *Philosophy* (Aldershot and

Schelling, but, like many others in attendance, he soon grew tired of them. Also in Berlin, Bakunin met and befriended his fellow Russian, the novelist Turgenev, who was also interested in Hegel. Like others of his generation, Bakunin was caught up in the excitement surrounding the publication of Feuerbach's *The Essence of Christianity* in 1841, and this work was a source of inspiration for him.

Scholars tend to ascribe great importance to Bakunin's time in Berlin. His thought is usually divided into two parts: the early period in which he was still struggling to find his own views, and the later part when he became radicalized and developed his theory of anarchism. It is often claimed that it was his encounter with the intellectual milieu in Berlin surrounding Hegel's philosophy that lit the spark that ended in his new radical political orientation. However, it has also been argued that there is more continuity in Bakunin's thought than might appear to be the case at first glance.[8] This view has some plausibility given the fact that Bakunin was already familiar with Hegel's writings before he came to Berlin. So while the experience of studying in Berlin with some of Hegel's own students must have been profound, this in itself does not necessarily imply a radical shift of thought.

In 1842 Bakunin moved to Dresden and began a collaboration with Arnold Ruge in the publication of the *Deutsche Jahrbücher für Wissenschaft und Kunst.* His early excitement about Hegel's philosophy is evident in one of his articles published pseudonymously in the journal, entitled "The Reaction in Germany: A Fragment from a Frenchman." There he writes,

> Contradiction and its immanent development constitute a keynote of the whole Hegelian system, and since this category is the chief category of the governing spirit of our times, Hegel is unconditionally the greatest philosopher of the present time, the highest summit of our modern, one-sided, theoretical cultural formation. Indeed, just like this summit, just by the fact that he has comprehended and thus resolved this category, just by this fact is he also the beginning of a necessary self-resolution of modern cultural formation: as this summit he has already gone above theory – granted that at the same time he is still within theory – and has postulated a new, practical world which will bring itself to completion by no means through a formal application and diffusion of theories already worked out, but only through an original act of the practical autonomous Spirit. Contradiction is the essence not only of every specific, particular theory, but also of theory in general, and so the dialectical phase of its comprehension is simultaneously the phase of the fulfilment of theory; but its

---

Burlington: Ashgate, 2007) (*Kierkegaard Research: Sources, Reception and Resources*, vol. 6), pp. 335–371.

[8] This is the thesis of Martine Del Giudice in her dissertation, *The Young Bakunin and Left Hegelianism: Origins of Russian Radicalism and the Theory of Praxis, 1814–1842*, PhD thesis, McGill University (1981).

fulfilment is its self-resolution into an original and new, practical world, into the real presence of freedom.[9]

Here Bakunin refers to Hegel's dialectical methodology in *The Phenomenology of Spirit*, where the analysis moves to ever higher and more complex stages of development by means of the contradictions found in the different views along the way. The "immanent development" thus refers to the ways in which theories or systems of thought contain their own contradictions, which prove to be their ruin. The development of these theories is thus immanent since nothing external needs to be imported in order to undermine them. Bakunin clearly regards Hegel's philosophy as having great historical importance. Moreover, he sees it as marking a transition from thought to action in the world. He appeals to Hegel's dialectical theory of negativity and contradiction in his call for rebellion against the repressive social order of the day.

When the government outlawed the *Deutsche Jahrbücher* at the beginning of 1844, both Ruge and Bakunin relocated to Paris. There Bakunin came into contact with Marx, who became Ruge's new collaborator. He also met Proudhon, who decisively influenced his thinking on anarchism. At the same time the Russian government ordered him to return to Russia. When he failed to comply, he was given a sentence *in absentia*. In 1847 he was expelled from France when he criticized the Russian government publicly in a speech on the occasion of the Polish insurrection of 1830. Like Marx before him, he fled from Paris to Brussels. After the Revolution of 1848, Bakunin was able to return to Paris. Around this time a rift began to arise between Marx and Bakunin, which became quite bitter. Attempting to discredit Bakunin, Marx circulated the claim that Bakunin was a spy in the pay of the Russian government, a rumor that the Russian ambassador in Paris had also tried to disseminate.

Bakunin actively tried to foment revolutions at this time. He was ultimately arrested in 1849 and sent back to Russia, where he escaped two death sentences, which were both commuted. He languished in a Russian prison until 1857, when he was allowed to go into exile in Siberia by the grace of the new Czar Alexander II. After escaping exile in 1864, he returned to Western Europe, living in a number of different places. During this period he was active in organizing radical political movements and won a following for his theory of anarchism as an alternative to socialism and communism. His exciting and turbulent life ended in Bern in 1876.

---

[9] Jules Elysard [Bakunin], "Die Reaction in Deutschland. Ein Fragment von einem Franzosen," *Deutsche Jahrbücher für Wissenschaft und Kunst* (ed. by Arnold Ruge), nos. 247–251, October 17–21, 1842, pp. 985–987, pp. 989–991, pp. 993–995, pp. 997–999, pp. 1001–1002; p. 993. (English translation: "The Reaction in Germany: A Fragment from a Frenchman," in *Michael Bakunin: Selected Writings*, ed. by Arthur Lehning [London: Jonathan Cape, 1973], pp. 37–58; p. 47.)

## 9.1   The Interpretation of the Fall and the Criticism of Idealism

In his work *God and the State*, written in 1871, Bakunin develops his theory of individual freedom. He never completed this text in his lifetime, and it was only published posthumously initially in a French translation in 1882, when the manuscript was discovered after his death by his friends and fellow anarchists Carlo Cafiero (1846–1892) and Jacques Élisée Reclus (1830–1905). In time it became perhaps his best-known work and was translated into many languages.[10]

Bakunin begins the text with a criticism of idealism and a praise of materialism. The materialist view had gained increasing popularity in the second half of the nineteenth century through the rapid advances in the natural sciences and not least of all Darwin's theory of evolution. These developments seemed to imply that the physical side of human beings played a far greater role than had been previously recognized. Bakunin sides with the materialists. He argues with Marx that "the whole history of humanity, intellectual and moral, political and social, is but a reflection of its economic history."[11] Humans are simply the highest form of the development of nature at the moment.

Yet, he acknowledges, the story of human development represents a separation from nature or, as he says, "the deliberate and gradual negation of the animal element."[12] He follows Hegel here in his understanding of the way in which humans develop from nature and become, to use Hegel's language, spirit. Like Hegel,[13] he has recourse to the myth of the Fall in order to understand the fundamental shift from nature to spirit. Also like Hegel, Bakunin believes that the biblical story captures some important truths about human nature, although it must be divested of its mythological elements. He agrees with Hegel in the idea that the story of the Fall illustrates the shift from animal life to true self-consciousness and the ability to think and reason. But he focuses on an element in the story that Hegel does not make much of, specifically the desire of humans to rebel. Indeed, the story of the Fall is the story of the rebellion of the first humans against God, and this is why the traditional theological interpretation has been that this was the first sin. Bakunin points out that, according to the way in which the story is told, it is clear that God's intention was for humans to remain as animals since this is what lies behind the prohibition to eat from the tree of knowledge: "man destitute of all understanding of himself, should remain an eternal beast, ever

---

[10]   Michel Bakounine, *Dieu et l'État*, trans. by Carlo Cafiero and Élisée Reclus (Geneva: Imprimerie Jurasienne, 1882). In what follows I quote from the edition *Dieu et l'État* (no place of publication given: L'Altiplano, 2008). (English translation: *God and the State*, ed. by Paul Avrich [New York: Dover, 1970].)

[11]   Bakunin, *Dieu et l'État*, pp. 15f.; *God and the State*, p. 9.

[12]   Bakunin, *Dieu et l'État*, p. 16; *God and the State*, p. 9.

[13]   See Chapter 3, Section 3.2.

on all-fours before the eternal God, his creator and his master."[14] By urging Eve to eat the apple, the serpent – or, if one will, the devil – is, according to Bakunin, not the source of sin but rather the great liberator of humanity. Bakunin makes the same point as Hegel in his interpretation, namely that, contrary to the theological interpretation, the serpent is no liar or deceiver since God in fact confirms the truth of what the serpent said when he urged Adam and Eve with the lure that they would become like God. After they do so and become self-conscious, God himself confirms this by acknowledging, apparently with some anxiety, that the humans have become like the gods.[15]

For Bakunin, the important thing about the biblical account is the element of rebellion. He explains, "Man has emancipated himself; he has separated himself from animality and constituted himself a man; he has begun his distinctively human history and development by an act of disobedience and science – that is, by *rebellion* and by *thought*."[16] He thus identifies three elements in human nature. The first is the physical part, which he refers to as *animality*. This is the material aspect of human beings, and from this stem all of the material conditions of human social and economic life. Then comes the element of *thought*, which is the key for Hegel. Thought separates us from nature and marks the beginning of science and what we might regard as human culture generally. Finally, there is the element of *rebellion*, which is the source of human freedom. In order to be free, humans, according to Bakunin, must rebel against all forms of external authority and coercion. This is the foundation of his theory of anarchism. Humans separate themselves from nature by their ability to rebel and act of their own volition, free from external constraint.

This third element of rebellion is absent in Hegel since his theory of freedom is limited to what Bakunin designated the second element, namely thought. For Hegel, freedom does not mean being free from external coercion but rather autonomy or the ability to determine one's actions for oneself as a result of one's rationality. Hegel would argue that rebellion cannot be one of the defining features of human nature that mark the separation of the human from the animal and the beginning of human history. Animals also rebel. When taken from nature and put in a cage or in confinement, animals resist and use any means to escape. Only a relatively small number of species are able to be domesticated, and this process of domestication has taken place over a long period of time. Given this, it is difficult to see how rebellion can be understood as what is specifically human.

Bakunin returns to press his case for materialism, which he argues is the only way to make sense of the world around us. Science has demonstrated this

[14] Bakunin, *Dieu et l'État*, p. 18; *God and the State*, p. 10.
[15] See Chapter 2, Section 2.2.
[16] Bakunin, *Dieu et l'État*, p. 21; *God and the State*, p. 12.

with principles that are readily comprehensible. He writes, "The gradual development of the material world, as well as of organic animal life and of the historically progressive intelligence of man, individually or socially, is perfectly conceivable. It is a wholly natural movement from the simple to the complex, from the lower to the higher, from the inferior to the superior."[17] Science, so to speak, starts from the bottom and works up, showing how certain simple structures in time develop into more complex ones. By contrast, Bakunin argues, the idealists and the theologians start at the other end, from the top, and try from there to work down:

> They go from the higher to the lower, from the superior to the inferior, from the complex to the simple. They begin with God, either as a person or as divine substance or idea, and the first step that they take is a terrible fall from the sublime heights of the eternal ideal into the mire of the material world; from absolute perfection into absolute imperfection; from thought to being, or rather, from supreme being to nothing.[18]

This form of explanation is, according to Bakunin, contrary to all reason and experience.

Bakunin's fundamental point is about where the focus should be placed. The idealists start with ideas and from them try to derive the material world, which is, he thinks, an absurdity. By contrast, the materialists start with the physical world around us and then try to understand how human society and thinking have developed. While not everything has yet been explained by this, he believes the natural scientific approach has been far more effective as an explanatory tool than the appeal to God or other abstractions.

## 9.2   The Criticism of Religion

According to Bakunin, no religious or philosophical system can explain why God would occupy himself by creating a material world and entering into it. Despite all of the grand theories of philosophers and pious words of theologians, no adequate explanation for this has ever been given: "It is evident that this terrible mystery is inexplicable – that is, absurd, because only the absurd admits of no explanation."[19] The problem is in a sense a psychological one – people feel a need to believe in this because it gives them a feeling of security. But this, claims Bakunin, is irrational:

> It is evident that whoever finds it essential to his happiness and life must renounce his reason, and return, if he can, to naive, blind, stupid faith, to repeat with Tertullian and all sincere believers these words, which sum up

---

[17] Bakunin, *Dieu et l'État*, p. 22; *God and the State*, p. 13.
[18] Bakunin, *Dieu et l'État*, p. 23; *God and the State*, p. 14.
[19] Bakunin, *Dieu et l'État*, p. 25; *God and the State*, p. 15.

the very quintessence of theology: *Credo quia absurdum*. Then all discussion ceases, and nothing remains but the triumphant stupidity of faith.[20]

Thus, like Bruno Bauer, Bakunin believes that religion renders people stupid by depriving them of their capacity for critical thinking.

We recall Marx's famous claim that religion "is the *opium* of the people."[21] Bakunin agrees with this diagnosis that it is the suffering of people in the context of their oppressed condition that makes religion flourish. He writes, "There is another reason which explains and in some sort justifies the absurd beliefs of the people – namely, the wretched situation to which they find themselves fatally condemned by the economic organization of society in the most civilized countries of Europe."[22] Given their miserable and hopeless condition, it makes sense that people will seek solace and comfort in religion. Bakunin points out that while the masses still believe in religion, the educated people have abandoned it, recognizing it as superstition. According to Bakunin, this is the class of people that, including the priests, represents "all the tormentors, all the oppressors, and all the exploiters of humanity."[23]

Bakunin returns to his Hegelian idea of history, according to which humans emerge from nature and slowly struggle to cultivate the rational element in themselves in order to be free. After liberating themselves from the oppression of nature, they must free themselves of the belief in God, which also stands in the way of human self-fulfillment and freedom. Only with the negation of nature and the errors and superstitions of the past is true human flourishing possible: Human beings are

> now marching on to the conquest and realization of human liberty . . . . For behind us is our animality and before us our humanity; human light, the only thing that can warm and enlighten us, the only thing that can emancipate us, give us dignity, freedom, and happiness, and realize fraternity among us, is never at the beginning, but, relatively to the epoch in which we live, always at the end of history.[24]

While for Hegel this realization comes with the realization of Christianity as the absolute religion and the culmination of the process of the development of

---

[20] Bakunin, *Dieu et l'État*, pp. 25f.; *God and the State*, p. 15.

[21] Karl Marx, "Zur Kritik der Hegel'schen Rechts-Philosophie. Einleitung," *Deutsch-Französische Jahrbücher*, 1–2 (1844), 71f.; "Contribution to the Critique of Hegel's *Philosophy of Right*: Introduction," in *The Marx-Engels Reader*, ed. by Robert C. Tucker (New York and London: W. W. Norton & Company, 1978), p. 54.

[22] Bakunin, *Dieu et l'État*, p. 27; *God and the State*, p. 16. See also *Dieu et l'État*, p. 43; *God and the State*, p. 23: religious beliefs "do not signify in man so much an aberration of mind as a deep discontent at heart. They are the instinctive and passionate protest of the human being against the narrowness, the platitudes, the sorrows, and the shame of a wretched existence."

[23] Bakunin, *Dieu et l'État*, p. 28; *God and the State*, p. 17.

[24] Bakunin, *Dieu et l'État*, pp. 38f.; *God and the State*, p. 21.

the religions of the world, for Bakunin, this is precisely what is preventing humans from becoming free.

Bakunin attempts to give an account of the origin of religious belief in order to debunk it. Here he clearly follows Feuerbach's account:

> [Religion] is nothing but a mirage in which man, exalted by ignorance and faith, discovers his own image, but enlarged and reversed – that is, divinized .... As fast as [human beings] discovered, in the course of their historically progressive advance, either in themselves or in external nature, a power, a quality, or even any great defect whatever, they attributed them to their gods, after having exaggerated and enlarged them beyond measure.[25]

Bakunin continues by giving the following account, which could be taken directly from Feuerbach's *The Essence of Christianity*:

> Not having yet the consciousness of his own intelligent action, not knowing yet that he himself has produced and continues to produce these imaginations, these concepts, these ideas, ignoring their wholly *subjective* – that is, human – origin, he [i.e., the human being] must naturally consider them as *objective* beings, as real beings, wholly independent of him, existing by themselves and in themselves.[26]

These ideas develop over time into the collective delusion that we know as religion. Again following Feuerbach, Bakunin claims that while humans project these qualities onto God, they simultaneously deprive themselves: "the richer heaven became, the more wretched became humanity and the earth .... the world thenceforth was nothing, God was all."[27] In this process humans deprived themselves of their own freedom and made themselves the slaves to God. Christianity, he claims, "is the impoverishment, enslavement, and annihilation of humanity for the benefit of divinity."[28] For Bakunin, like Feuerbach, humans are alienated from their essential being by placing this in the divine.

Bakunin argues that when people are unable to find truth and justice in this world, it is natural for them to ascribe these things to the sole purview of God in another realm. The result is that any form of human truth and justice appears impoverished and dubious in comparison to the divine standard. The next step is the entry of messiahs, prophets, and priests who claim to speak in God's name. They thus become oppressors since it is impossible to argue against God's word with only human truths. As Bauer claimed, humans then become slaves since they are forbidden from using their critical reason. They are obliged simply to go along with whatever the religious leaders

[25] Bakunin, *Dieu et l'État*, p. 44; *God and the State*, p. 23.
[26] Bakunin, *Dieu et l'État*, p. 140; *God and the State*, p. 67.
[27] Bakunin, *Dieu et l'État*, p. 45; *God and the State*, p. 24.
[28] Bakunin, *Dieu et l'État*, p. 45; *God and the State*, p. 24.

proclaim in the name of God. In this way humans become "slaves of God" as well as "slaves of Church and State."[29] Bakunin seems to echo Bauer's argument when he claims, "The idea of God implies the abdication of human reason and justice; it is the most decisive negation of human liberty, and necessarily ends in the enslavement of mankind, both in theory and practice."[30] As long as the belief in God exists, humans will always be slaves.

It might be argued here that both Bauer and Bakunin take as their point of departure Hegel's criticism of Judaism, which we examined briefly in Chapter 2, Section 2.3.[31] As will be recalled, Hegel characterizes the God of Judaism as demanding absolute obedience without recognizing the inward rational nature of the people. For Hegel, the point of this analysis was to contrast this conception of the God of the Old Testament with the God of Christianity, who appeals to the rational consent of the believers, thus recognizing their inwardness and reason. By contrast, Bauer and Bakunin seem to generalize Hegel's account of Judaism to include all forms of religious belief, including Christianity. It is not just a single religion that is oppressive but all of them.

Bakunin discusses Hegel's theory of religion directly and gives it a generally secular reading. He claims that Hegel tried to restore the ideas of religion: "Hegel went about his work of restoration in so impolite a manner that he killed the good God for ever. He took away from these ideas their divine halo, by showing to whoever will read him that they were never anything more than a creation of the human mind running through history in search of itself."[32] He then sees Feuerbach as "the disciple and demolisher of Hegel,"[33] who developed and stated explicitly the secular implications of Hegel's philosophy of religion.

While Bakunin is known primarily for his social-political theory, we see here the absolutely central role that religion plays for him. He is not usually counted among the major philosophers of religion, but his views on religion are important in the development of philosophy in the nineteenth century. As was the case with Marx, Bakunin sees religious oppression as being closely bound up with political-economic oppression. They agree that it is meaningless to combat the latter without at the same time combatting the former. For Bakunin, the question of God and state power are thus intimately connected, as the title of his work suggests. Bakunin, like Marx, thus believes the elimination of religious superstition to be a necessary condition for human liberation. Bakunin cites Voltaire's famous one-liner, "If God did not exist, it would be necessary to invent him."[34] He then modifies it to read: "if God really existed, it

[29]  Bakunin, *Dieu et l'État*, p. 46; *God and the State*, p. 24.
[30]  Bakunin, *Dieu et l'État*, p. 47; *God and the State*, p. 25.
[31]  See Chapter 2, Section 2.3.
[32]  Bakunin, *Dieu et l'État*, p. 148; *God and the State*, pp. 71f.
[33]  Bakunin, *Dieu et l'État*, p. 149; *God and the State*, p. 72.
[34]  Bakunin, *Dieu et l'État*, p. 29; *God and the State*, p. 17.

would be necessary to abolish him."[35] The idea is that God (or religion) represents a form of authority that must be undermined before people can truly be free. As long as this authority exists, humans will always live in oppression. This is an instructive lesson about the nature of philosophy in the nineteenth century, where the important role of the debates about religion are often overlooked, while the questions of politics or metaphysics are given center stage.

## 9.3   Bakunin's Theory of Anarchism

At the heart of Bakunin's theory of anarchism is an analysis of the nature of authority and power. He notes that nature is one kind of power to which we are subject. It has basic laws that we are necessarily bound to comply with. However, this is not a nefarious form of authority since it constitutes the very conditions of our existence. There is nothing demeaning about this. The laws and conditions of nature are not imposed on us by some external authority, but rather they constitute in a sense who we are.[36] When we become educated and grow, we know and understand natural laws and their power over us. In this way we come to recognize them ourselves.

Human authority and power are different from that of nature. Some people exercise authority over others. Here the power is something foreign and is imposed by something external to the individual, namely another person or group of people. Bakunin believes that it is a natural feature of power that it corrupts those who exercise it. Once people come into positions of authority by occupying privileged positions in society, they become corrupt and morally depraved. This is the nature, he believes, of all forms of government, which quickly develop their own nefarious ruling classes and political aristocracy.[37]

Bakunin is often criticized for rejecting any form of authority. However, he anticipates this with the following clarification:

> Does it follow that I reject all authority? Far from me such a thought. In the matter of boots, I refer to the authority of the bootmaker; concerning houses, canals, or railroads, I consult that of the architect or engineer. For such or such special knowledge I apply to such or such a *savant*. But I allow neither the bootmaker nor the architect nor the *savant* to impose his authority upon me.[38]

His point is that although it is true that we need to recognize the special expertise of other people, this does not mean that we thereby surrender to them our own critical reason and faculty of understanding. We can carefully

---

[35] Bakunin, *Dieu et l'État*, p. 54; *God and the State*, p. 28.
[36] Bakunin, *Dieu et l'État*, p. 54; *God and the State*, pp. 28f.
[37] Bakunin, *Dieu et l'État*, pp. 63f.; *God and the State*, p. 32.
[38] Bakunin, *Dieu et l'État*, p. 64; *God and the State*, p. 32.

listen to what they say and try to understand their expert opinion, but this is not to say that we make ourselves slaves to their views. As rational adults, we have the right to form our own opinions based on the best information available. We should not have to give up our freedom and subject ourselves to the authority of others, regardless of how great their knowledge, experience, and expertise are.

In the end Bakunin declares, "I recognize no infallible authority."[39] Even expert opinions can be wrong, and the standard views in the different fields of expertise can change over time. There can be disputes among experts about certain things. Given this, it would be absurd to defer to expert opinion blindly and to give up one's freedom. He argues, "there is no fixed and constant authority, but a continual exchange of mutual, temporary, and above all, voluntary authority and subordination."[40] This is a fluid situation, as I respect the authority of specific experts or people who know more than I do, but I do so with my own consent and after examining their views with my own reason. Thus expertise is no argument for the legitimation of the exercise of power or authority. While we can recognize the authority of science as the road to the truth as such, it would be absurd to accept blindly the authority of any specific scientist or expert.[41]

If we surrender our freedom to the opinions of experts without evaluating their views critically, we would inevitably not only undermine our own freedom but also render ourselves stupid. We reduce ourselves to the role of children who must accept the views of their parents, teachers, and other figures of authority without being able to have their own opinion on the matter. Bakunin believes that the nefarious forms of state power have a vested interest in keeping people ignorant in this way, and he points to the shortcomings of the educational system as a demonstration of this. Young people are not taught to think critically. They are fed complete absurdities with regard to, for example, religious education. In this way their freedom is undermined, and their personal growth and development are stunted. It will be noted that this is a variant of Bruno Bauer's argument that Christianity and religion in general rob people of their freedom by demanding that they uncritically accept religious dogma. In this way, religious leaders make it a sin to use one's faculty of critical reason, the very thing that makes us human and separates us from the animals. Bakunin argues that this same phenomenon takes place in the sphere of politics when governments, just like the church and the clergy, impose their power on others and demand uncritical respect and blind obedience. This too necessarily undermines human freedom and reason, reducing people to "slavery and imbecility."[42]

---

[39]  Bakunin, *Dieu et l'État*, p. 64; *God and the State*, p. 32.
[40]  Bakunin, *Dieu et l'État*, p. 66; *God and the State*, p. 33.
[41]  Bakunin, *Dieu et l'État*, p. 68; *God and the State*, p. 34.
[42]  Bakunin, *Dieu et l'État*, p. 67; *God and the State*, p. 33.

The problem comes when authority becomes something fixed and static with a specific group always exercising it as if by right. It would be irrational for me "to recognize a fixed, constant, and universal authority, because there is no universal man, no man capable of grasping in that wealth of detail, without which the application of science to life is impossible, all the sciences, all the branches of social life."[43] Authority should thus never be unwaveringly fixed on a specific individual or group. But, alas, this is precisely what happens in the case of governments. They are granted authority as if they were infallible.

Bakunin urges his readers to reject all other authorities apart from that of science itself as "false, arbitrary and fatal."[44] He locates the key to social ills in the fixed power structures that are found in every state and every society. His definition of anarchism is the rejection of "all legislation, all authority, and all privileged, licensed, official, and legal influence, even though arising from universal suffrage," since "it can turn only to the advantage of a dominant minority of exploiters against the interests of the immense majority in subjection to them."[45] These fixed power structures are what is standing in the way of true human development and freedom. As long as we are subject to the arbitrary authority of others, we will never be free. However, there is a legitimate use of power, but it is always tempered by our insight and consent and is never imposed on us by appeal to some external authority.

## 9.4   Bakunin's Hegelian Theory of Freedom and Recognition

A part of Bakunin's manuscript of *God and the State* was omitted from the original publication and published separately in the first volume of the French edition of his collected works in 1895.[46] This is an insightful text, in which he argues against the hypocrisy of liberals who claim to be against state power but then, once their own wealth and property is endangered, become the most virulent defenders of the state. He traces this back to the liberal conception of what a human being is. He explains, "According to them [i.e., the liberals], individual freedom is not a creation, a historic product of society. They maintain, on the contrary, that individual freedom is anterior to all society .... man is accordingly a complete being, absolutely independent

[43] Bakunin, *Dieu et l'État*, p. 66; *God and the State*, p. 33.
[44] Bakunin, *Dieu et l'État*, p. 68; *God and the State*, p. 34.
[45] Bakunin, *Dieu et l'État*, p. 70; *God and the State*, p. 35.
[46] Michel Bakounine, *Oeuvres*, vols. 1-6, ed. by Max Nettlau (vol. 1) and James Guillaume (vols. 2-6) (Paris: P. V. Stock, 1895-1913). The text appears as "Dieu et l'État (extrait du manuscrit inédit)," in *Oeuvres*, vol. 1, pp. 264-320. A part of this text has been translated into English as "Man, Society and Freedom," in *Bakunin on Anarchy*, ed. and trans. by Sam Dolgoff (New York: Random House, 1971), pp. 234-242.

apart from and outside society."[47] Bakunin refers here to thinkers such as Locke and Hobbes and the tradition of contract theory. He argues that since these thinkers begin with a conception of humans as completely isolated and atomistic individuals, they have no meaningful conception of society or social life. We often tend to think that we as individuals are wholly free on our own and that we are solely responsible for our achievements in the world. But Bakunin argues that we are subtly interconnected with everyone else, and that none of us is an atomic individual who alone can realize themselves. He argues that no matter what high or esteemed position one holds in society, one will never be truly free until everyone is free. The fate of every individual is bound up with that of every other individual. Bakunin thus argues for the necessary interconnections and dependence of everyone in society. No one is an island.

Here it is important to keep in mind the positive model that Bakunin is clearly thinking of, namely Hegel's theory. As we have seen, for Hegel, it is an illusion to think of oneself as being a fully developed human apart from all human interactions. We become self-conscious by means of our relations to other human beings. Moreover, true freedom involves the development and use of rationality, and this only takes place collectively in the long process of history. Bakunin writes,

> Emerging from the state of the gorilla, man has only with great difficulty attained the consciousness of his humanity and liberty . . . . He was born a ferocious beast and a slave, and has gradually humanized and emancipated himself only in society . . . . He can achieve this emancipation only through the collective effort of all the members, past and present, of society, which is the source, the natural beginning of his human existence.[48]

We therefore need each other in order to develop our full human potential and, indeed, to be truly human. It is impossible to talk about human freedom, as is done in the liberal tradition, in a state of nature prior to the creation of human societies. Therefore, "Society, far from decreasing his freedom, on the contrary creates the individual freedom of all human beings."[49] Again, following Hegel's conception of history, he claims, "It can be said that the real and complete emancipation of every individual is the true, the great, the supreme aim of history."[50] As noted earlier, in his *Lectures on the Philosophy of History*, Hegel

---

[47] Bakunin, "Dieu et l'État (extrait du manuscrit inédit)," in *Oeuvres*, vol. 1, pp. 265f.; "Man, Society and Freedom," p. 235.

[48] Bakunin, "Dieu et l'État (extrait du manuscrit inédit)," in *Oeuvres*, vol. 1, p. 275; "Man, Society and Freedom," p. 236.

[49] Bakunin, "Dieu et l'État (extrait du manuscrit inédit)," in *Oeuvres*, vol. 1, p. 275; "Man, Society and Freedom," p. 236.

[50] Bakunin, "Dieu et l'État (extrait du manuscrit inédit)," in *Oeuvres*, vol. 1, p. 275; "Man, Society and Freedom," p. 236.

claims that the march of history is about the increasing development of human freedom, which is extended to wider and wider circles. Complete freedom is only realized when it is granted not to a king or a class of rulers but to everyone as an individual. But despite this clear debt to Hegel, Bakunin is keen to designate his view "materialist" and distinguish it from all forms of idealism. In agreement with Marx, he claims that the fundamental element in the development of freedom is not ideas or concepts but rather the basic material conditions of human existence.[51]

Bakunin appeals to a Hegelian theory of recognition. He describes as follows what is constitutive of human beings:

> To be free means to be *acknowledged* and treated as such by all his fellowmen. The liberty of every individual is only the reflection of his own humanity, or his human right through the conscience of all free men, his brothers and his equals. I can feel free only in the presence of and in relation with other men. In the presence of an inferior species of animal I am neither free nor a man, because this animal is incapable of conceiving and consequently *recognizing* my humanity. I am not myself free or human until I *recognize* the freedom and humanity of all my fellowmen.[52]

From this passage it is obvious that Bakunin is influenced by Hegel's analysis of the lord and the bondsman. The lord does not receive meaningful recognition from the bondsman since that recognition comes from an inferior being. The lord must grant the bondsman his freedom in order for the bondsman's recognition to be valid. This connection to Hegel's analysis could hardly be made clearer than when Bakunin writes, "A slave owner is not a man but a master. By denying the humanity of his slaves, he also abrogates his own humanity."[53] He concludes, "I am truly free only when all human beings, men and women, are equally free. The freedom of other men, far from negating or limiting my freedom, is, on the contrary, its necessary premise and confirmation."[54] As Hegel's master-slave dialectic showed, despite his apparent superiority, the master cannot be free because he does not receive the freely

---

[51] Bakunin, "Dieu et l'État (extrait du manuscrit inédit)," in *Oeuvres*, vol. 1, pp. 277f.; "Man, Society and Freedom," pp. 236f.: "Man becomes conscious of himself and his humanity only in society and only by the collective action of the whole society. He frees himself from the yoke of external nature only by collective and social labor, which alone can transform the earth into an abode favorable to the development of humanity. Without such material emancipation the intellectual and moral emancipation of the individual is impossible."

[52] Bakunin, "Dieu et l'État (extrait du manuscrit inédit)," in *Oeuvres*, vol. 1, pp. 278f.; "Man, Society and Freedom," p. 237. My italics.

[53] Bakunin, "Dieu et l'État (extrait du manuscrit inédit)," in *Oeuvres*, vol. 1, p. 279; "Man, Society and Freedom," p. 237.

[54] Bakunin, "Dieu et l'État (extrait du manuscrit inédit)," in *Oeuvres*, vol. 1, p. 281; "Man, Society and Freedom," p. 237.

given recognition of the slave. So long as the master continues to oppress and coerce the slave, he himself will not be free.

Bakunin's Hegelianism is undeniable in these passages. There is something striking about this since one of the traditional criticisms of Hegel's social-political philosophy is that he reifies or divinizes the state and does not have any sensitivity to the rights of the individual. On the traditional reading, Hegel should by all accounts be a great enemy of Bakunin, whose entire theory is aimed at undermining all forms of authority and especially that of the state. But instead, Bakunin is profoundly receptive to key aspects of Hegel's theory of human freedom and philosophical anthropology, which he coopts for his own purposes. Here we can see the long shadow that Hegel cast over the development of philosophy in the nineteenth century, even in areas where it is not expected.

Bakunin identifies what he regards as the positive and negative elements of freedom. The positive element of freedom involves the ways in which humans develop themselves as fully human by means of their upbringing and education in society. This makes it possible for them to flourish and fully develop their potential. Evidence of this can be found in the example of feral children whose development is clearly irreversibly stunted by their isolation from society. Contrary to the liberal view, they are not fully formed humans apart from and prior to their social relations.

Bakunin also takes up what he designates the negative elements of freedom, which are characterized by a rejection of external authority. The first of these to be cast off is religion. Here he clearly follows in the tradition of Feuerbach and Bauer when he writes, "The first revolt is against the supreme tyranny of theology, of the phantom of God. As long as we have a master in heaven, we will be slaves on earth. Our reason and our will will be equally annulled."[55] As was seen, Bauer claims that the belief in Christianity demands that people put aside their critical reason and instead blindly accept the dogmas of religion. By doing so, according to Bauer, Christianity inhibits historical development and deprives people of their very humanity, which is fundamentally connected with their rationality. Bakunin seems to be wholly in agreement: "God, or rather the fiction of God, is the consecration and the intellectual and moral source of all slavery on earth, and the freedom of mankind will never be complete until the disastrous and insidious fiction of a heavenly master is annihilated."[56]

The second form of revolt that is required for the development of freedom is that against "the tyranny of men,"[57] which takes two forms: social tyranny and

---

[55] Bakunin, "Dieu et l'État (extrait du manuscrit inédit)," in *Oeuvres*, vol. 1, p. 282; "Man, Society and Freedom," p. 238.

[56] Bakunin, "Dieu et l'État (extrait du manuscrit inédit)," in *Oeuvres*, vol. 1, p. 283; "Man, Society and Freedom," p. 238.

[57] Bakunin, "Dieu et l'État (extrait du manuscrit inédit)," in *Oeuvres*, vol. 1, p. 283; "Man, Society and Freedom," p. 239.

the tyranny of the state. By "social tyranny," Bakunin means what Hegel generally refers to as "Sittlichkeit," that is, the sphere of customs, traditions, and beliefs that are found in every culture. These are inculcated in us from an early age, and thus we unconsciously come to take over the general beliefs and worldview of our society. But unfortunately this involves many myths, illusions, and prejudices that the rational individual must strive to reject. It is necessary as an individual to wage a revolt against these inherited views and prejudices, even though this means in part a revolt against oneself insofar as these views constitute a part of who one is. This is a difficult form of revolt to realize because, as members of society, we are all subject to a tremendous amount of peer pressure to conform. It is thus not easy to reject the views that everyone else holds as sacred and to stand alone as an iconoclast.[58] The tyranny of the state is more clear-cut since the power of the state is obvious for all to see. It is not something that one has inherited from the collective consciousness of one's society from the earliest childhood. Bakunin's criticism of state power constitutes a central part of his theory of anarchism, and it is to this that we now turn.

## 9.5   The Criticism of Hegel and His Followers

Bakunin published his last book, *Statism and Anarchy*, in Russian in 1873.[59] In this work he gives a criticism of the role that Hegel's philosophy has played in politics in Germany. While he acknowledges the importance of Hegel's thinking, he claims that its high level of abstraction led to a sense of alienation with the real world:

> In the history of the development of human thought, Hegel's philosophy was in fact a significant phenomenon. It was the last and definitive word of the pantheistic and abstractly humanistic movement of the German spirit which began with the works of Lessing and achieved comprehensive development in the works of Goethe. This movement created a world that was infinitely broad, rich, lofty, and ostensibly perfectly rational, but that remained as alien to earthly life and reality as it was to the heaven of Christian theology.[60]

Bakunin claims that Hegel's philosophy was overly focused on ideas and thus neglected the material world. It led Hegel's followers to a blind introspection that made them unaware of the realities taking place around them. Moreover, this split between high ideas and concrete realities made it possible for the

---

[58]   Bakunin, "Dieu et l'État (extrait du manuscrit inédit)," in *Oeuvres*, vol. 1, p. 295; "Man, Society and Freedom," pp. 241f.
[59]   In English as Bakunin, *Statism and Anarchy*.
[60]   Bakunin, *Statism and Anarchy*, pp. 130f.

adherents of Hegel to support the repressive forces of the Restoration since it made them blind to the injustices of the real world.

Bakunin then sketches the character of the right and left Hegelian schools, which developed after Hegel's death. Of the former, he writes, "the conservative party, found in the new philosophy the justification and legitimization of everything that exists, seizing upon Hegel's famous dictum 'all that is real is rational.' This party created the so-called official philosophy of the Prussian monarchy, which had been upheld by Hegel himself as the ideal political organization."[61] Bakunin refers to Hegel's statement about the unity of the actual and the rational in the *Philosophy of Right*,[62] which we discussed before.[63] Despite the openly hostile position of the Prussian state toward the Hegelians, Bakunin claims that they adopted Hegel's system as their own, and thus that Hegel inadvertently served to justify the abuses of the reactionary Prussian state.

Bakunin then characterizes the left Hegelian school. Although he acknowledges their merits, he claims that they too remain overly abstract and wallow in metaphysics:

> The other party, the so-called *revolutionary* Hegelians, proved more consistent than Hegel himself, and incomparably bolder. It tore away the conservative mask from his doctrines and revealed in all its nakedness the merciless negation that constitutes their essence. At the head of this party stood the illustrious Feuerbach, who pressed logical consistency not only to the utter negation of the whole divine world but to the negation of metaphysics itself.[64]

Bakunin explains the great hope that was attached to Hegel's philosophy among the left Hegelians, who believed that it would be the basis for a radical revolution:

> In the 1830s and 1840s the prevailing opinion was that a revolution which followed the dissemination of a Hegelianism developed in the direction of utter negation would be incomparably more radical, profound, merciless, and sweeping in its destructiveness than the revolution of 1793. That was because the philosophy worked out by Hegel and taken to its most extreme conclusions by his students was actually more complete, more comprehensive, and more profound than the thinking of Voltaire and Rousseau.[65]

[61] Bakunin, *Statism and Anarchy*, p. 131.
[62] G. W. F. Hegel, *Naturrecht und Staatswissenschaft im Grundrisse. Grundlinien der Philosophie des Rechts* (Berlin: Nicolaische Buchhandlung, 1821), p. xix. (English translation: *Elements of the Philosophy of Right*, trans. by H. B. Nisbet, ed. by Allen Wood [Cambridge and New York: Cambridge University Press, 1991], p. 20.)
[63] See Chapter 4, Section 4.4.
[64] Bakunin, *Statism and Anarchy*, p. 131.
[65] Bakunin, *Statism and Anarchy*, p. 132.

This fits well with Bruno Bauer, who, as we have seen, developed the principle of "criticism" from Hegel's philosophy and who also found inspiration in the atheism of the eighteenth century. It was believed that the Hegelians would lead the future revolution. This also accords with Heine's prophesy of a German revolution where philosophy would play a central role.

Unfortunately, according to Bakunin, the optimistic view of the beneficial role of the Hegelians in the coming political reforms was disappointed by the Revolution of 1848. The reason for this, he claims, is that they remained overly metaphysical and abstract, approaching the issue from the realm of ideas and not concrete material conditions. He claims, "anyone who takes abstract thought as his starting-point will never make it to life, for there is no road leading from metaphysics to life. An abyss separates them."[66] Bakunin explicitly contrasts this Hegelian approach with his own view of "the *anarchist* social revolution," which he claims begins from the grassroots and the concrete conditions of everyday people.[67]

Bakunin argues that the Hegelians and the other "metaphysicians" begin with an idea and then try to make the state and the social order conform to it. At bottom lies the idea that it is the experts or scholars who understand best the fundamental laws of justice, and thus they are best qualified to create the state and the institutions that can realize it in the world. This idea goes back to Plato's *Republic* and the idea of the philosopher king. Socrates argues that since it makes sense for specialists in different areas, such as horse training or military affairs, to be consulted when these areas are what is at issue, so also it makes sense for those who are experts in matters of justice and the state to be consulted in such contexts where this is relevant. And it is the philosophers or those specialized in justice and political theory who are most fit to rule since the others do not share their training and expertise. The assumption is that the people as such are ignorant of such complicated things, and thus it would be ill advised to allow them to organize political affairs. Instead, these matters are best left in the hands of experts qualified to do the job.

Bakunin radically rejects this view. He could see in his own time the rise of technocrats and was suspicious of this development. He reasons that there would only be a small number of people specialized in the field of sociology who think themselves to have the special knowledge required to construct a society and a state according to rational principles.[68] But he argues that it would be absurd to allow these people to control everyone else. The natural result would be that such a system would quickly become repressive since they would justify any action at all with their alleged superior specialized knowledge. Such a cadre of scholars would become tyrants. Despite their learning,

---

[66] Bakunin, *Statism and Anarchy*, p. 133.
[67] Bakunin, *Statism and Anarchy*, p. 133.
[68] Bakunin, *Statism and Anarchy*, p. 134.

such scholars would be subject to the fundamental human weakness of abuse of power once it is bestowed upon them. This is not just a criticism of scholars but indeed of everyone. Like Dostoevsky, Bakunin is suspicious of the rise of the social sciences and the belief that they will lead the way toward a new rational social order based on scientific principles. Both thinkers are convinced that this is a recipe for oppression and tyranny.

This leads Bakunin to his more radical claims. He thus rejects any form of authority in the social order since he believes that "anyone who is invested with power by an invariable social law will inevitably become the oppressor and exploiter of society."[69] He declares that he rejects any form of state since this inevitably leads to repression. He returns to contrast his view with that of the Hegelians and the metaphysicians. While the latter begin with an abstract idea or thought and try to impose it on everyone, he and the revolutionary anarchist movement begin with "natural and social life," which "always precedes thought."[70] He starts with real life and not ideas. All the great ideologies of the world are built on certain abstract ideas that they try to universalize. At some point this always leads to violence and tyranny when the ideologues perceive certain people or institutions that fail to conform to their ideas. The only way to avoid this is to reject these abstractions at the outset and focus on the real lives of people as individuals. He believes that people already have everything that is required for them to function as social beings without the imposition of an oppressive state apparatus. Bakunin thus lays at the doorstep of idealism the responsibility for all fundamental forms of oppression. It is *ideas* that, when insisted upon and imposed on others, become dangerous.

Any kind of state power is a form of alienation since it imposes on people some abstract idea or principle that is at bottom foreign to their nature. Therefore the only way to eliminate this alienation is to get rid of the state itself and all other forms of authority that impose themselves on individuals. For Hegel, while there are indeed repressive states and institutions, this is just an unfortunate fact of history. There can, however, also be just states and institutions that are organized in accordance with the true idea of justice or right. When the individual sees their own rational will reflected in the laws or institutions of the states, they have a sense of identification. In such a state, individuals can flourish and develop themselves fully. Bakunin rejects Hegel's view as naively optimistic. The oppression of individual states is not simply a historical accident that sometimes appears and sometimes does not. Instead, it is a fundamental and necessary feature of all forms of state power. According to Bakunin's anarchist view, wherever there is a state, there will be repression and alienation. He argues

[69] Bakunin, *Statism and Anarchy*, p. 134.
[70] Bakunin, *Statism and Anarchy*, p. 135.

that this lies in the very nature of any form of authority: "power corrupts those invested with it just as much as those compelled to submit to it. Under its pernicious influence the former become ambitious and avaricious despots, exploiters of society for their own personal or class advantage, and the latter become slaves."[71]

Bakunin's vision is that instead of starting with ideas and proceeding to social life, one must start the other way around. Power should be granted to individuals at the grassroots level, who are perfectly capable of organizing the key elements of social life among themselves without any external ideological imposition. Power should proceed not from the top down but rather from the ground up. Only in this way will the true rationality of humans be properly recognized and validated. Bakunin thus believes that the followers of Hegel have failed to realize their high ideals and hopes for a Hegelian-led revolution. Instead, the very principle of Hegel's idealism leads to repression and plays into the hands of the reactionaries.

Hegel would, of course, argue that there is a dialectical relation between ideas and the material world – what he would call universals and particulars. While it is true that there are ideas that are oppressive, this is no reason to reject all ideas simply as such. We operate with ideas in our daily lives, and this is a beneficial thing since we like to think that when we act in the real world we do so in accordance with certain basic principles of ethics or reason. To act without thinking is regarded as something negative. Hegel would be quick to point out that there are cases when ideas have played a positive and liberating effect in politics. For example, after the French Revolution the Jews were granted civil rights and allowed to pursue professions of their own choosing. These rights also came into effect in the German states under the empire of Napoleon. Although these ideas were imposed by force, they were just and socially beneficial. Bakunin's theory would be compelled also to reject these kinds of ideas that play a positive role along with all of the oppressive ones that he dismisses as ideological. One might also claim that the emancipation of the Jews is an ideological view, but at some point we are compelled to return to our basic intuitions in such matters, and these are based on ideas. So Hegel would argue for a dialectical relation between ideas and the material world, which allows for some space for ideas in politics since these can play a positive role.

## 9.6   The Criticism of Marx

Bakunin gives a brief portrait of his former friend Karl Marx[72] before entering into an extended criticism of Marx's proposed communist revolution. Despite

---

[71] Bakunin, *Statism and Anarchy*, p. 136.
[72] Bakunin, *Statism and Anarchy*, pp. 141–143. For the relation between Bakunin and Marx, see Paul Thomas, *Karl Marx and the Anarchists* (London and Boston: Routledge & Kegan

their bitter personal history, Bakunin's description is surprisingly balanced. Bakunin agrees with Marx's interpretation of history as being fueled by class struggle: "Marx . . . advanced and proved the inconvertible truth, confirmed by the entire past and present history of human society, nations, and states, that economic fact has always preceded legal and political right. The exposition and demonstration of that truth constitutes one of Marx's principal contributions to science."[73] While they agree on this, Bakunin parts company with Marx on the fundamental question of state power.

By this time in 1873, Marx's theory had grown in popularity. Bakunin refers to Marx as one of the many "doctrinaire revolutionaries" who virulently argue for the overthrow of the state but in the end wish to replace it with a new political order that is no less repressive.[74] Marx's criticism is not of repressive state power as such but rather of the fact that at the moment this power lies in the hands of others. His calls for revolution are simply pleas to deliver this power into the hands of the communists while leaving the ills of state power in place. Bakunin raises the critical question, "If the proletariat is to be the ruling class, it may be asked, then whom will it rule?"[75] He argues that as soon as the proletariat, the formerly oppressed and exploited class, comes to power, they would in turn simply subject another group to the same kind of oppression that they suffered. The groups would be different, but the fundamentals of power would remain the same. Bakunin claims, "If there is a state, then necessarily there is domination and consequently slavery. A state without slavery, open or camouflaged, is inconceivable."[76] Thus, instead of liberating humanity, Marx's theory would simply perpetuate the same injustices that have always existed.

Bakunin also critically examines Marx's claim that the proletariat will be the governing class. What exactly does this mean? It is clear that since the proletariat are so numerous, they cannot all be rulers. Marx's solution is, of course, that the proletariat would choose people from among their own ranks to represent them, so it would be an elected group who would rule and not the entire class as such. Bakunin argues that although, on Marx's theory, the leaders would be chosen from among the workers, they would not represent the interests of the workers since from the moment they came into power, they would have different interests. Bakunin argues as follows:

> it always comes down to the same dismal result: government of the vast majority of the people by a privileged minority. But this minority, the

Paul, 1980); K. J. Kenafick, *Michael Bakunin and Karl Marx* (Melbourne: A. Mailer, 1948); Alvin Gouldner, *Against Fragmentation: The Origins of Marxism and the Sociology of Intellectuals* (Oxford: Oxford University Press, 1985).

[73]  Bakunin, *Statism and Anarchy*, p. 142.
[74]  Bakunin, *Statism and Anarchy*, p. 137.
[75]  Bakunin, *Statism and Anarchy*, p. 177.
[76]  Bakunin, *Statism and Anarchy*, p. 178.

Marxists say, will consist of workers. Yes, perhaps of former workers, who, as soon as they become rulers or representatives of the people will cease to be workers and will begin to look upon the whole workers' world from the heights of the state. They will no longer represent the people but themselves and their own pretensions to govern the people. Anyone who doubts this is not at all familiar with human nature.[77]

It must be said that the subsequent history of communist states seems to bear out Bakunin's criticism with remarkable consistency.

We saw that Bakunin was critical of allowing any group of alleged experts to govern while excluding everyone else who is presumed to be unqualified. He believes that Marx's view fits into this pattern well since it will require that only those who have mastered Marx's theory will be allowed into the ruling elite. He reasons, "The words 'learned socialist' and 'scientific socialism,' which recur constantly in the writings and speeches of the ... Marxists, are proof in themselves that the pseudo-popular state will be nothing but the highly despotic government of the masses by a new and very small aristocracy of real or pretended scholars."[78] Once again Bakunin's criticism seems entirely accurate when one considers the pseudo-discipline of Marxism-Leninism that used to exist as a field of study in all of the Soviet-bloc countries.

Bakunin then turns to a counterargument offered by the Marxists, namely that the state apparatus is just a temporary necessity that is required in order to set up communism as a system. But once this is well established, they argue, there will no longer be any need for a state, and it will gradually fade away. But Bakunin objects that there is an absurdity in claiming that in order for people to achieve freedom, they must first be made slaves. Moreover, it is an illusion to believe that such a state, once established, will simply fade away. People do not give up power willingly, and it is impossible to imagine them doing so once they have established themselves in a privileged position in society with all of the advantages that come with this. Bakunin writes that the Marxists "claim that only a dictatorship (theirs, of course) can create popular freedom. We reply that no dictatorship can have any other objective than to perpetuate itself, and that it can engender and nurture only slavery in the people who endure it."[79] Once again, history seems to accord with Bakunin's assessment since the administrative apparatus of the communist states seems simply to grow and grow as the years go by, and there is no evidence that it gradually diminishes and ultimately disappears.

Bakunin emphasizes the main difference between his view and that of Marx. He believes that a key source of human oppression is the state, and thus the only way to achieve true human liberation is to eliminate state power. Marx, by

---

[77] Bakunin, *Statism and Anarchy*, p. 178.
[78] Bakunin, *Statism and Anarchy*, pp. 178f.
[79] Bakunin, *Statism and Anarchy*, p. 179.

contrast, argues that only with the state is it possible for the proletariat to be liberated. Thus, after the communist revolution, the goal is not to get rid of the state, but instead simply to rebuild it in a different form to serve the interests of the revolutionaries and not the former rulers. But once again, the same basic categories of oppressors and oppressed remain in place. Bakunin illustrates the difference between his view and the Marxists as follows:

> According to Marx's theory . . . the people not only must not destroy [the state], they must fortify it and strengthen it, and in this form place it at the complete disposal of their benefactors, guardians, and teachers – the leaders of the communist party, in a word, Marx and his friends, who will begin to liberate them in their own way. They will concentrate the reins of government in a strong hand, because the ignorant people require strong supervision.[80]

Bakunin sees Marxism as another blueprint for human oppression perniciously hiding under the veneer of a call for liberation. He prophetically saw the rise of the dictatorship of the communist party and its leaders in numerous states.

## 9.7    Marx's Response

Marx read Bakunin's *Statism and Anarchy* and was keen to respond to the criticisms of his theory that it issued. Between April 1874 and January 1875, he worked on a text that remained unpublished at his death. This work appears under the title "Notes on Bakunin's Book *Statehood and Anarchy*" in the collected works edition of Marx and Engels.[81] Marx excerpts individual passages from Bakunin's work and then attempts to respond with corrections and, where necessary, counterarguments. The tone of Marx's comments displays the bitterness of an old friendship gone sour. His remarks are full of sarcasm and ad hominem arguments.

Marx excerpts Bakunin's critical question of whom the proletariat will rule once they gain power. As we have seen, Bakunin believes that this will simply lead to replacing one oppressive group with another. Marx's response to this does not address the point. He simply emphasizes that as long as the capitalist class still exists, the proletariat will need to use force against it.[82] But Bakunin's

---

[80] Bakunin, *Statism and Anarchy*, p. 181.

[81] Karl Marx, "Konspekt von Bakunins Buch *Staatlichkeit und Anarchie*," in *Marx-Engels-Werke*, vols. 1–46, ed. by the Institut für Marxismus-Leninismus (Berlin: Dietz, 1956–2018), vol. 18, pp. 597–642. (English translation: "Notes on Bakunin's Book *Statehood and Anarchy*," in *Marx/Engels Collected Works*, vols. 1–50 [Moscow: Progress Publishers, 1975–2004], vol. 24, pp. 485–526.)

[82] Marx, "Konspekt von Bakunins Buch *Staatlichkeit und Anarchie*," p. 630; "Notes on Bakunin's Book *Statehood and Anarchy*," p. 517.

argument is clearly that the whole point of the communist revolution is the overthrow of the capitalist class, and so after the revolution the proletariat will not need to struggle against it. Instead, according to Bakunin, the natural logic of power will create a new class that the proletariat will in turn oppress. Marx could argue that the embittered capitalists will still be a threat after the revolution, so the proletariat must continue to struggle against them. However, at that point they will no longer be capitalists since they will be deprived of the ownership of the means of production that they once enjoyed.

Marx also responds to Bakunin's criticism of the imagined rule of the proletariat. To Bakunin's critical question of whether the entire proletariat class will form the government, Marx responds by asking, "In a trade union, for example, does the entire union form its executive committee?"[83] Since this is not the case, does this rule out the legitimacy of trade unions? Marx sticks by his principle of representation, which Bakunin believed was a sham that only led to further oppression.

Along the same lines, Bakunin also criticized Marx's view for leading to a dictatorship of a small minority, who, whether elected or not, will still constitute an oppressive force. On this point Marx sticks with his claim that collective ownership is the solution. With this, "the so-called will of the people disappears and makes way for the genuine will of the cooperative."[84] Clearly, Bakunin thinks that this is pure fantasy. Those who are in charge will work for their interests and not for those of the whole. In response to Bakunin's charge that once workers are put in charge, they cease to be workers and start operating with a different set of interests, Marx has no convincing response. He can only appeal to the positive examples he is familiar with of managers in cooperative factories. Marx takes Bakunin to have a mistaken and overly pessimistic view of human nature in this regard.

Likewise, Bakunin's claim that such a power structure led by a small elite will simply perpetuate itself is met with disapproval by Marx, who seems simply to repeat what Bakunin mentioned on his behalf, namely that this is only a temporary measure and that the government will gradually fall away as the communist society develops. Marx claims, "The class rule of the workers over the strata of the old world who are struggling against them can only last as long as the economic basis of class society has not been destroyed."[85] This, however, clearly does not answer the objection and seems to be disproved historically. Bakunin points out the absurdity of arguing that the state, although an oppressive tool, is a necessary means to achieve human liberty, and we must

---

[83] Marx, "Konspekt von Bakunins Buch *Staatlichkeit und Anarchie*," p. 634; "Notes on Bakunin's Book *Statehood and Anarchy*," p. 519.

[84] Marx, "Konspekt von Bakunins Buch *Staatlichkeit und Anarchie*," p. 635; "Notes on Bakunin's Book *Statehood and Anarchy*," p. 520.

[85] Marx, "Konspekt von Bakunins Buch *Staatlichkeit und Anarchie*," p. 636; "Notes on Bakunin's Book *Statehood and Anarchy*," p. 521.

take it as a promissory note that it will disappear in time. In response, Marx makes a utilitarian argument for his position, saying that as the proletariat works toward the revolution and the creation of a communist society, it is legitimate to have "recourse to methods which will be discarded once the liberation has been attained."[86] Marx's counterargument is to reproach Bakunin of quietism: "Bakunin deduces that the proletariat should rather do nothing at all ... and just wait for the day of universal liquidation – the Last Judgment."[87]

Engels also discusses Bakunin's anarchism in a letter to Theodor Cuno (1846–1934) from 1872. The letter was written prior to the publication of *Statism and Anarchy* and thus is not a response to Bakunin's criticism of communism in that context. However, it does contain some interesting objections to Bakunin's anarchism in general. Engels describes the difference between Bakunin's position and his own as follows: "Bakunin has a singular theory, a potpourri of Proudhonism and communism, the chief point of which is first of all, that he does not regard capital, and hence the class antagonism between capitalists and wage workers which has arisen through the development of society, as the main evil to be abolished, but instead the *state*."[88] The key question is what is the real root of oppression and social evil: the capitalist economic system or government power as such. Engels continues,

> Bakunin maintains that the *state* has created capital, that the capitalist has his capital only *by the grace of the state*. And since the state is the chief evil, the state above all must be abolished; then capital will go to hell of itself. We, on the contrary, say: Abolish capital, the appropriation of all the means of production by the few, and the state will fall of itself.[89]

Engels says that since Bakunin wants to do away with any form of state power, he is effectively calling for a "complete abstention from all politics."[90] Engels claims that it is dangerous to tell the workers not to engage in politics since this will undermine the revolutionary movement. This objection seems exaggerated since not all politics concerns state power strictly speaking. Bakunin's point is clearly not that he wants to forbid people from having political discussions. It is easy to talk about questions of justice or social politics

---

[86] Marx, "Konspekt von Bakunins Buch *Staatlichkeit und Anarchie*," p. 636; "Notes on Bakunin's Book *Statehood and Anarchy*," p. 521.

[87] Marx, "Konspekt von Bakunins Buch *Staatlichkeit und Anarchie*," p. 636; "Notes on Bakunin's Book *Statehood and Anarchy*," p. 521.

[88] Friedrich Engels, "Engels an Theodor Cuno in Mailand," in *Marx-Engels-Werke*, vol. 33, p. 388. (English translation, "Letter to Theodor Cuno, 24 January 1872," in *Marx/Engels Collected Works*, vol. 44, p. 306.)

[89] Engels, "Engels an Theodor Cuno in Mailand," p. 388; "Letter to Theodor Cuno, 24 January 1872," pp. 306f.

[90] Engels, "Engels an Theodor Cuno in Mailand," p. 388; "Letter to Theodor Cuno, 24 January 1872," p. 307.

without the question of state power being the central issue. Engels raises a more serious objection as follows: in the society proposed by Bakunin,

> there will above all be no authority, for authority = state = evil in the absolute. (How these people propose to operate a factory, run a railway, or steer a ship without one will that decides in the last resort, without unified direction, they do not, of course, tell us.) ... Every individual, every community, is autonomous, but how a society of even two people is possible unless each gives up some of his autonomy, Bakunin again keeps to himself.[91]

Engels thus calls into question whether Bakunin's model is even possible. As we have seen, Bakunin wants to see power disseminate from the bottom up and not the top down. But even if power is given to individuals, they will naturally organize into private groups for special purposes, and as these groups grow, some form of structure must be created for them to be effective in meeting the ends for which they were created. This inevitably involves putting some person or a group of people in charge. It is difficult to imagine how this can be avoided in Bakunin's model. Some minimal form of hierarchy and some basic power structure seems to be a fundamental element in any form of organization. Without this, it would be impossible for any organization, private or public, to function at all.

## 9.8   Bakunin's Message of Rebellion

Bakunin's theory of anarchism has long been criticized as unfeasible. Following the objection of Engels, critics have doubted the possibility of a form of social organization that allows for no form of authority or hierarchy. But despite this, Bakunin still has many valuable insights and ideas. His consistent objection to all forms of authority gives voice to the sense of injustice and repression that many people felt during his time. For Bakunin, people are alienated from the many instances of power and coercion that govern virtually every aspect of their lives. As long as these exist, we can never realize our freedom or feel any deeper sense of satisfaction.

There is a deep philosophical idea in Bakunin's philosophical anthropology. As we have seen, he regards humans as a combination of (1) the physical aspect, which we share in common with the animals, and (2) the mental aspect or thought.[92] There is, of course, nothing new in this idea that humans have these two sides, but what Bakunin adds to the traditional picture is the idea that

---

[91] Engels, "Engels an Theodor Cuno in Mailand," p. 389; "Letter to Theodor Cuno, 24 January 1872," p. 307.
[92] Bakunin, *Dieu et l'État*, p. 21; *God and the State*, p. 12. See Section 9.1.

(3) rebellion also constitutes a part of human nature. His idea is that in order for us to realize our freedom and humanity, we must at some point rebel.

When we are young, we learn about the world from our parents, our teachers, and others. Children are taught to obey, and this is a fundamental aspect of their social competence, which makes it possible for them to participate in society as adults. As children grow into their teenage years, they often experience some phase of rebellion, which can be more or less radical and can last for a longer or shorter period of time. This period arises as young people begin to think for themselves and make their first critical reflections about the world around them. In this process they come to realize that some or even much of what they have been taught by their parents and teachers is mistaken or contradictory. This then leads to the desire to rebel against these ways of thinking and to explore new ones. This observation might seem banal given the fact that youthful rebellion is a well-known phenomenon, but Bakunin's point is a deeper one. His claim is that we must rebel in order truly to realize our humanity. Children learn to walk and to speak, and these faculties are necessary for their full growth and development. Bakunin's claim is that no less important for human development is learning how to rebel. Only when we learn to think for ourselves and to rebel against the errors, lies, and injustices of the world can we be said to be fully free. Those who simply blindly accept everything that they are told by their families or cultures and live following the customs and traditions that they were born into fail to realize their true human potential. Those who live their lives following the preset patterns of their parents or society cannot be said to be autonomous. They are unable to decide for themselves and to dictate the terms of their own lives. They are in a sense immature as human beings in the way children are immature who have not yet learned how to speak. Not to rebel is to remain a child forever.

This idea in Bakunin can be seen as an extension and radicalization of Hegel's idea of spirit becoming aware of itself over the course of history. According to Hegel's philosophy of history, in the past humans were dominated by time-honored tradition and custom. This was taken to be absolute, and people generally did not consider any alternative ways of doing things. At some point in the Greek world, there arose a new spirit that began to call into question these traditional customs and beliefs. This new spirit appeared as a result of the emergence of scientific thinking, which undermined traditional Greek religion. A key figure in this movement was Socrates, who represented critical reason. He went around Athens questioning people about their beliefs, and when he was given traditional answers, he politely pointed out the contradictions in the answers given. He demanded rational explanations for things that had been uncritically accepted. This was regarded as a threat to traditional society, and, as is well known, Socrates was prosecuted and condemned for this. Hegel's point is that this principle of critical reflection that began with Socrates is one that in time spread throughout the Western world.

In modernity it becomes the dominant principle, at which time people collect-ively can be said to become aware of themselves for the first time, as people realize that they have within themselves an inward side that can think for itself.

As we have seen, Heine was a serious social critic who called for political revolt in his works.[93] Like Bakunin, he goes back to the figure of Adam as the first human to assert his freedom, which was made possible by an initial act of rebellion.[94] A variant of this idea was also developed by Bruno Bauer.[95] Inspired by Hegel, Bauer spoke of the idea of modern criticism that began in the eighteenth century in the thought of the Enlightenment. In that context the criticism was aimed largely at religious thinking. Bauer adopts this and makes it into his own methodological principle, extending this critical thinking to all other areas as well. Despite Marx's satirical criticism of Bauer, he seems in principle to be in agreement with him on this point. We saw his praise of the critique of religion that took place in post-Hegelian philosophy, which he believed paved the way for his own criticism of the social-political order of the day.[96] For Marx, criticism of the social-political order of the present is fundamental, and an important goal is to create class consciousness that educates people by making them aware of their own common exploitation, which in turn will lead them to stage a revolution.

Thus with the concept of rebellion, Bakunin has clearly identified and further developed a central motif of the age. His profound insight is that rebellion is not just something contingent that is dictated by chance political circumstances that one finds oneself in. Rather, it is a fundamental feature of human growth and development that is absolutely necessary for the full realization of our highest faculties and indeed our very humanity.

[93] See Chapter 3, Sections 3.5–3.6.
[94] See Chapter 3, Section 3.4.
[95] See Chapter 5, Section 5.2.
[96] See Chapter 6, Section 6.1.

# 10

## Engels' Criticism of Feuerbach and Classical German Philosophy

The forty-year collaboration of Friedrich Engels with Marx was essential for the development of Marx's influential theory of communism. Engels became an increasingly important figure toward the end of the nineteenth century as Marxism began to catch on and win adherents internationally. He was instrumental in the dissemination of the work of Marx after the latter's death.

Engels was born in 1820 in the growing industrial town of Barmen, Prussia (today Wuppertal).[1] His father was a wealthy textile manufacturer, and his parents had planned for him, as their eldest son, to continue the family textile business run by his father. In his early education he became interested in German national literature in the context of the Romantic revival of folk tales and legends. In 1837, still a young man, he was taken from school in order to learn the family business. The next year the young Engels accompanied his father on a business trip to England, where they met with suppliers and customers. Upon their return, he was sent to Bremen, where he worked as

---

[1] For Engels' biography, see Gustav Mayer, *Friedrich Engels. Eine Biographie*, vol. 1, *Friedrich Engels in seiner Frühzeit 1820 bis 1851* (Berlin and Heidelberg: Springer, 1920). The second volume of Mayer's biography only appeared in 1934, when it was printed along with a revised edition of the first volume: *Friedrich Engels. Eine Biographie*, vol. 1, *Friedrich Engels in seiner Frühzeit 1820 bis 1851*, and vol. 2, *Engels und der Aufstieg der Arbeiterbewegung in Europa*, 2nd ed. (The Hague: Martinus Nijhoff, 1934). (English translation: *Friedrich Engels: A Biography*, trans. by Gilbert Highet and Helen Highet, ed. by Richard Howard Stafford Crossman [London: Chapman & Hall, 1936].) See also Tristram Hunt, *The Frock-Coated Communist: The Revolutionary Life of Friedrich Engels* (London: Penguin, 2009) (published in the USA as *Marx's General: The Revolutionary Life of Friedrich Engels* [New York: Henry Holt, 2009]); Evgeniia Akimovna Stepanova, *Engels: A Short Biography* (Moscow: Progress Publishers, 1988); John Green, *A Revolutionary Life: Biography of Friedrich Engels* (London: Artery Publications, 2008); Terrell Carver, *Friedrich Engels: His Life and Thought* (London: Macmillan, 1989); David McLellan, *Engels* (Glasgow: Fontana/Collins, 1977); W. O. Henderson, *The Life of Friedrich Engels*, vols. 1–2 (London: Frank Cass, 1976); Steven Marcus, *Engels, Manchester and the Working Class* (New York: Random House, 1974); Reinhart Seeger, *Friedrich Engels. Die religiöse Entwicklung eines Spätpietisten und Frühsozialisten* (Halle: Akademischer Verlag, 1935); Karl Kupisch, *Vom Pietismus zum Kommunismus* (Berlin: Lettner-Verlag, 1953); Horst Ullrich, *Der junge Engels*, vols. 1–2 (Berlin: Deutscher Verlag der Wissenschaften, 1961–1966). See also Manfred Kliem (ed.), *Friedrich Engels: Dokumente seines Lebens* (Frankfurt am Main: Röderberg-Verlag, 1977).

an office clerk in the family business, dealing mostly with international correspondence. Since he was bored with his job, his interests turned to the key
authors of the Young Germany movement, Heinrich Heine, Heinrich Laube,
and Karl Gutzkow. This was his first step toward radical politics. During this
time he also discovered the works of Hegel and David Friedrich Strauss and
quickly became an enthusiast about both. To the alarm of his parents, his views
became more and more radical. He soon began publishing articles that criticized the ills of industrialization.

In 1841 he was obliged to perform his military service, so he joined the
Prussian army on a one-year commission. This brought him to Berlin and gave
him the opportunity to attend lectures at the university, where Hegel's philosophy was still very much the object of discussion. Along with Kierkegaard,
Bakunin, and many others, he attended Schelling's famous course entitled the
"Philosophy of Revelation" that began in that year. As has been noted,
Schelling's task was to criticize Hegel's philosophy, which the Prussian authorities were increasingly concerned about. Engels was keen to defend Hegel
against these attacks. By attending lectures like this, he was immediately
catapulted into the exhilarating academic life of the capital. Although officially
performing his military service, he spent most of his time at the university. He
became a part of a radical group of intellectuals known as *Die Freien* ("The
Free"), which met regularly at the local cafes and wine bars. This group
included, among others, Bruno Bauer, Max Stirner, Karl Köppen, Karl
Nauwerck, Eduard Meyen, and Arnold Ruge. In Berlin, Engels began writing
critical articles about the poor conditions of factory workers for the *Rheinische
Zeitung*, of which Marx was the editor.

After he had completed his military service in 1842, Engels was sent by his
father to work in the family's textile mills in Manchester. He met Marx for the
first time in Cologne in November 1842, when he was on his way to England.
During his time at his father's mills in England, Engels wrote "Outline of
a Critique of Political Economy," which he published in 1844 in the *Deutsch-
Französische Jahrbücher*, another journal edited by Marx.[2] He also penned
a series of articles outlining the poor conditions for English laborers, which
eventually formed the basis of his book *The Condition of the Working Class in
England*, which appeared in 1845.[3] He gradually became active in the British
labor movement. Engels' guide to the sobering truths about the condition of

---

[2] Friedrich Engels, "Umrisse zu einer Kritik der Nationaloekonomie," *Deutsch-Französische
Jahrbücher*, 1–2 (1844), 86–114. (English translation: "Outlines of a Critique of Political
Economy," in *Marx/Engels Collected Works*, vols. 1–50 [Moscow: Progress Publishers,
1975–2004], vol. 3, pp. 418–443.)
[3] Friedrich Engels, *Die Lage der arbeitenden Klasse in England. Nach eigner Anschauung und
authentischen Quellen* (Leipzig: Otto Wigand, 1845). (English translation: *The Condition
of the Working Class in England*, ed. by David McLellan [Oxford: Oxford University Press,
1993].)

laborers was an Irish woman named Mary Burns (1821–1863), with whom he had a stable relationship that ended only with her death.

After the completion of his apprenticeship in Manchester, Engels returned to his parents' house in Prussia in 1844. On the way back he stopped in Paris, where he stayed for ten days in order to visit Marx, who had fled to France after the closure of his journal in Cologne. This short visit sealed their lifelong friendship and initiated a close collaboration. The two immediately found that they had similar political intuitions. Their first collaborative work was the criticism mentioned in Chapter 6, Sections 6.4–6.5 of Bruno Bauer and his Berlin group, entitled *The Holy Family*.[4] Engels returned briefly to his parents' home in Barmen, but then in April of 1845 he relocated to Brussels, where Marx had fled after he was obliged to leave France. There the two collaborated on *The German Ideology*. They lived in Brussels for the next three years and became members of a group called the Communist League. It was for this organization that they wrote the *Communist Manifesto*, which was published in 1848.

After the Revolution of 1848, Marx and Engels returned to Prussia and started a new newspaper, the *Neue Rheinische Zeitung*, based in Cologne. After Marx was expelled from Prussia once again, Engels took part in revolutionary uprisings, which were suppressed by the Prussian military. He fled to Switzerland and from there via Italy to England, where he arrived in November of 1849. Back in England, he resumed work for his father's company in Manchester, where he was in close contact with Marx, who was living in exile in London. He continued his work with Marx, and they jointly edited the *Neue Rheinische Zeitung Politisch-ökonomische Revue*. In addition to a number of newspaper articles, Engels published in 1850 a book entitled *The Peasant War in Germany*.[5]

Engels eventually retired from the family business and dedicated himself fully to writing and political activity. In 1870 he moved to London, where he published *Herr Eugen Dühring's Revolution in Science* in 1878.[6] Two years later followed his *Socialism Utopian and Scientific*, which first appeared in

[4] Friedrich Engels and Karl Marx, *Die heilige Familie, oder Kritik der kritischen Kritik. Gegen Bruno Bauer & Consorten* (Frankfurt am Main: Literarische Anstalt, 1845). (English translation: *The Holy Family or Critique of Critical Critique*, trans. by Richard Dixon [Moscow: Foreign Languages Publishing House, 1956].)

[5] Friedrich Engels, "Der deutsche Bauernkrieg," *Neue Rheinische Zeitung. Politisch-ökonomische Revue*, 5–6 (1850), 1–99. This work was then published as a monograph: *Der deutsche Bauernkrieg* (Leipzig: Verlag der Expedition des *Volksstaat*, 1870). (English translation: *The Peasant War in Germany*, trans. by Moissaye J. Olgin [New York: International Publishers, 1926].)

[6] Friedrich Engels, "Herrn Eugen Dühring's Umwälzung der Wissenschaft. Philosophie, Politische Oekonomie. Sozialismus," *Vorwärts*, January 3–July 7 (1878). This work was then published as a monograph: *Herrn Eugen Dühring's Umwälzung der Wissenschaft. Philosophie, Politische Oekonomie. Sozialismus* (Leipzig: Druck und Verlag der Genossenschafts Buchdruckerei, 1878). (English translation: *Anti-Dühring. Herr Eugen*

French.[7] In 1884 he published his last important work, *The Origin of the Family, Private Property and the State*.[8] After Marx's death in 1883, he dedicated himself to editing *Capital* for publication. Engels died on August 5, 1895.

## 10.1 The Occasion and Context of Engels' Book on Feuerbach and German Philosophy

In 1888 Engels published a short monograph entitled *Ludwig Feuerbach and the Outcome of Classical German Philosophy*.[9] This work was a revised version of an article he had published two years earlier in the journal *Die Neue Zeit*[10] on occasion of the publication of a new book on Feuerbach by the Danish sociologist and philosopher Carl Nicolai Starcke (1858–1926).[11] In his foreword to the work, Engels explains that many years earlier, in 1845, he, together with Marx, wrote *The German Ideology*, in which they tried to give a critical evaluation of German philosophy and develop their own position of historical materialism in contrast to this. This was important for their own self-understanding since in their youth they had both been enthusiastic about Hegel's philosophy and only in time came to distance themselves from it as their own ideas began to take shape. Moreover, the important role of Feuerbach, who, Engels claims, constituted "an intermediate link" between Hegel and the view he and Marx were trying to develop, had never been adequately explored.[12] However, *The German Ideology* remained

*Dühring's Revolution in Science*, trans. by Emile Burns [Moscow: Progress Publishers, 1947].)

[7] Friedrich Engels, *Socialisme utopique et socialisme scientifique*, trans. by Paul Lafargue (Paris: Derveaux Libraire-Éditor, 1880). In German: *Die Entwicklung des Sozialismus von der Utopie zur Wissenschaft* (Hottigen-Zürich: Verlag der Schweizerischen Volksbuchhandlung, 1882). (English translation: *Socialism Utopian and Scientific*, trans. by Edward Aveling [London: Swan Sonnenschein & Co.; New York: Charles Scribner's Sons, 1892].)

[8] Friedrich Engels, *Der Ursprung der Familie, des Privateigenthums und des Staats. Im Anschluss an Lewis H. Morgan's Forschungen* (Hottigen-Zürich: Verlag der Schweizerischen Volksbuchhandlung, 1884). (English translation: *The Origin of the Family, Private Property and the State*, ed. by Tristram Hunt [London: Penguin, 2010].)

[9] Friedrich Engels, *Ludwig Feuerbach und der Ausgang der klassischen deutschen Philosophie. Mit Anhang: Karl Marx über Feuerbach vom Jahre 1845* (Stuttgart: J. H. W. Dietz, 1888). (English translation: *Ludwig Feuerbach and the Outcome of Classical German Philosophy*, ed. by C. P. Dutt [New York: International Publishers, 1941].)

[10] Friedrich Engels, "Ludwig Feuerbach und der Ausgang der klassischen deutschen Philosophie," *Die neue Zeit: Revue des geistigen und öffentlichen Lebens*, 4(4) (1886), 145–157 (Parts I–II), (5), 193–209 (Parts III–IV).

[11] C. N. Starcke, *Ludwig Feuerbach* (Stuttgart: Ferdinand Enke, 1885).

[12] Engels, "Ludwig Feuerbach und der Ausgang der klassischen deutschen Philosophie," cited from *Marx-Engels-Werke*, vols. 1–46, ed. by the Institut für Marxismus-Leninismus (Berlin: Dietz, 1956–2018), vol. 21, p. 263 (the following references all refer to this edition); *Ludwig Feuerbach and the Outcome of Classical German Philosophy*, p. 7.

unpublished, and neither Marx nor Engels had published an extensive statement on this topic. (It will be recalled that the "Economic and Philosophic
Manuscripts of 1844" were also published posthumously.) So Engels takes
the opportunity provided by Starcke's book to return to the topic. He writes,
"We have expressed ourselves in various places regarding our relation to
Hegel, but nowhere in a comprehensive, connected account."[13] Engels thus
feels a need for a thorough reckoning with Hegel, who was important for the
development of his thought and that of Marx. This provides him with an
occasion to identify the points of commonality with Hegel and the points
where he and Marx depart from him. Moreover, he reflects generally on the
development of post-Hegelian philosophy in the German-speaking world. As
the title indicates, the work reserves a special role for Feuerbach, who was
a great source of inspiration to both Marx and Engels when they were young.
Engels says that he regards it as "an undischarged debt of honor" to give an
account of Feuerbach's importance for them.[14]

By this time Marx's philosophy was beginning to have a wide international
reception. At the same time German Idealism was enjoying a revival, and
therefore Engels believed that his monograph would be of interest to the
reading public. Marx had died five years earlier, and Engels was an old man
by this time. One can hear a tone of nostalgia in the account he gives of the
development of German philosophy as experienced it in their youth.
Engels' monograph can thus be seen as a combination of a brief history of
German philosophy and a personal memoir.

Engels explains that he still had the original manuscript of *The German
Ideology*, but after consulting it, he found that it was irrelevant for the
task of presenting the development of his and Marx's relation to German
philosophy since it contained no real criticism of Feuerbach and the
section on him remained incomplete.[15] However, in rummaging through
his old papers, Engels did find one of Marx's old notebooks, where the
famous "Theses on Feuerbach" were written. Recognizing the importance
of this short text, he decided to include it as an appendix to *Ludwig
Feuerbach and the Outcome of Classical German Philosophy*. Although the
theses were often anthologized later, this was the first time that they
appeared in print. Interestingly, Engels implies that these few pages
represent the beginning of Marx's mature theory and thus ascribes to
them a surprising importance. Engels' assessment fits with the fact that, as

---

[13] Engels, "Ludwig Feuerbach und der Ausgang der klassischen deutschen Philosophie,"
p. 263; *Ludwig Feuerbach and the Outcome of Classical German Philosophy*, p. 7.

[14] Engels, "Ludwig Feuerbach und der Ausgang der klassischen deutschen Philosophie," p. 264;
*Ludwig Feuerbach and the Outcome of Classical German Philosophy*, p. 8.

[15] Engels, "Ludwig Feuerbach und der Ausgang der klassischen deutschen Philosophie,"
p. 264; *Ludwig Feuerbach and the Outcome of Classical German Philosophy*, p. 8.

noted earlier,[16] the "Theses" are more critical of Feuerbach than Marx's earlier statements.

Engels' book is divided into four sections or chapters. The first provides the overview of the development of German philosophy from Hegel to Feuerbach. In the second chapter, he contrasts Hegelian idealism with Marxist dialectical materialism. Chapter 3 is dedicated to a critical assessment of Feuerbach's philosophy, which, for Engels, is appropriate given its importance in the development of Marxist thought. Finally, the fourth chapter presents the view of dialectical materialism that Marx and Engels reached after they had parted ways with Hegel and Feuerbach. Due to its clear presentation, this text played an important role in the reception of Hegel's philosophy on key points, such as the relation of Hegel to the Prussian state, the dialectic, or the movement of history. It is possible to see echoes of this text in the accounts of Hegel given by many later authors.

## 10.2   Hegel on the Rational and the Actual

In chapter 1 Engels laments that the philosophy of his youth in the 1830s and '40s has largely been forgotten by the new generation. He explains that the period of German philosophy that he intends to treat should be considered the preparation for the Revolution of 1848. He contrasts this uprising with the French Revolution of 1789. Just as the French Revolution was inspired by the leading French intellectuals of the Enlightenment, so also in Germany the Revolution of 1848 was inspired by the leading German philosophers of the previous generation. Indeed, many of the key figures of the Revolution of 1848 in the different European countries were students of Hegel. However, Engels notes that there is an important difference that should not be overlooked. While the French intellectuals were openly critical of the Church and the government, and suffered persecution for this, in Germany they were professors of philosophy and thus highly respected employees of the state.

In this context he refers specifically to Hegel's philosophy, which, he claims, "was even raised, to some degree, to the rank of a royal Prussian philosophy of state."[17] This statement has led to some misunderstanding and controversy in the literature since, without further explanation or qualification, it can be confusing.[18]

---

[16] See Chapter 6, Section 6.6.

[17] Engels, "Ludwig Feuerbach und der Ausgang der klassischen deutschen Philosophie," p. 265; *Ludwig Feuerbach and the Outcome of Classical German Philosophy*, p. 9.

[18] See M. W. Jackson, "Hegel: The Real and the Rational," in Jon Stewart (ed.), *The Hegel Myths and Legends* (Evanston: Northwestern University Press, 1996), pp. 19–25; Yirmiahu Yovel, "Hegel's Dictum that the Rational is Actual and the Actual is Rational: Its Ontological Content and Its Function in Discourse," in Stewart (ed.) *The Hegel Myths and Legends*, pp. 26–41; Emil L. Fackenheim, "On the Actuality of the Rational and the Rationality of the Actual," in Stewart (ed.) *The Hegel Myths and Legends*, pp. 52–49.

Hegel was, of course, employed at the leading Prussian university in Berlin. As noted previously, his philosophy was supported by the Prussian Minister of Education, Karl Freiherr vom Stein zum Altenstein, who served under the King of Prussia, Friedrich Wilhelm III. However, as we have seen, when Altenstein became ill and retired, he was replaced in 1840 by Johann Albrecht Friedrich von Eichhorn, who, upon seeing the rise of left Hegelianism, was decidedly hostile to Hegel. It was under Eichhorn's influence that the new king, Friedrich Wilhelm IV, appointed Schelling to a professorship at the University of Berlin in 1841 with the explicit purpose of combatting Hegelianism.[19] So when Engels talks about Hegel's philosophy having friendly relations with the Prussian state, he is referring to the period before the beginning of the reign of Friedrich Wilhelm IV in 1840. But even during this period, Hegel's philosophy was never made into any official policy of the Prussia state or formally adopted in any way whatsoever. Indeed, as has often been pointed out (even, by Engels himself),[20] the rational state that Hegel sketches in his political philosophy has many institutions that differ radically from the Prussian state of the time.

Engels claims that Hegel could play a secret revolutionary role by formulating his philosophy in such a difficult way. During the last decade of Hegel's life, there was a great deal of tension about questions of politics and religion, and some of Hegel's colleagues had been fired from their positions for being too outspoken in their views. Hegel could not help but be aware of this, and it can be argued that one of the reasons that he couched his philosophy in such difficult language was that he could in this way make it more difficult for the censors and the authorities to determine his views clearly. If he were ever under suspicion of incendiary and subversive ideas, the enigmatic and ambiguous nature of his statements would always give him plenty of leeway to defend himself by means of an interpretation that was in line with what the Prussian authorities wanted to hear. One might argue that precisely this ambiguity, which was intended as a kind of protective measure, was what gave rise to the schools of right and left Hegelianism subsequently since the right Hegelians took his statements at face value, whereas the left Hegelians, like Engels, claimed that in fact they were subversive if one read between the lines.

Engels gives a famous example of this ambiguity from the preface of Hegel's *The Philosophy of Right*.[21] As discussed,[22] Feuerbach refers to Hegel's controversial claim that the rational is the actual and the actual is the rational.[23]

---

[19] See Chapter 3, Section 3.2.

[20] Engels, "Ludwig Feuerbach und der Ausgang der klassischen deutschen Philosophie," p. 269; *Ludwig Feuerbach and the Outcome of Classical German Philosophy*, p. 13.

[21] Engels, "Ludwig Feuerbach und der Ausgang der klassischen deutschen Philosophie," p. 266; *Ludwig Feuerbach and the Outcome of Classical German Philosophy*, p. 10.

[22] See Chapter 4, Section 4.4, and Chapter 9, Section 9.5.

[23] G. W. F. Hegel, *Naturrecht und Staatswissenschaft im Grundrisse. Grundlinien der Philosophie des Rechts* (Berlin: Nicolaische Buchhandlung, 1821), p. xix. (English

Engels takes this claim to have functioned as a legitimation and sanction for the reactionary Prussian government and its repression. But Engels is aware that this was never Hegel's meaning or intention: "But according to Hegel everything that exists is certainly not *real*, without further qualification. For Hegel the attribute of reality belongs only to that which at the same time is necessary."[24] Thus not every given law or act of government is rational for Hegel – only those that are necessary in the sense of being in accordance with the development of freedom in history. Nonetheless, at the time, Engels explains, Hegel's statement was taken to mean that the existing Prussian state was ipso facto rational.

But, Engels argues, Hegel's theory can also be taken to mean exactly the opposite. It is, according to Hegel, the irrational elements of existing reality that are not actual and which therefore fall away. He notes that Hegel was always positively disposed toward the French Revolution of 1789 because "the French monarchy had become so unreal" and "had been so robbed of all necessity."[25] In this sense Hegel's theory can be seen to support the idea of revolution, which plays an important role in history by getting rid of the irrational elements of society or the government that have accrued over time. When people begin to feel alienated from the existing conditions, there arises an impulse for change. So in this case, contrary to the interpretation of Hegel as a blind supporter of the Prussian state, his view vindicates revolution as something necessary and rational. Revolution is the mechanism that replaces the old repressive system with a new one that is more just and conducive to the development of human freedom. Only in this way can alienation be overcome in the historical process.

## 10.3   The Importance of Hegel's Dialectical Methodology

Engels thus argues that the radical nature of Hegel's philosophy lies in its dialectical methodology. While it might at first glance look like Hegel is attempting to glorify the actual, in fact his theory shows that everything that arises in history appears at a specific place and under specific circumstances, and in time everything grows old and decays, at which point it is replaced by something new that is better suited to the new situation. Engels thus claims, "In

translation: *Elements of the Philosophy of Right*, trans. by H. B. Nisbet, ed. by Allen Wood [Cambridge and New York: Cambridge University Press, 1991], p. 20.) See Ludwig Feuerbach, *Das Wesen des Christenthums*, 2nd ed. (Leipzig: Otto Wigand, 1843), p. 55; *The Essence of Christianity*, trans. by Marian Evans (New York: Calvin Blanchard, 1855), p. 61.
[24] Engels, "Ludwig Feuerbach und der Ausgang der klassischen deutschen Philosophie," p. 266; *Ludwig Feuerbach and the Outcome of Classical German Philosophy*, p. 10.
[25] Engels, "Ludwig Feuerbach und der Ausgang der klassischen deutschen Philosophie," p. 266; *Ludwig Feuerbach and the Outcome of Classical German Philosophy*, p. 10.

accordance with all the rules of the Hegelian method of thought, the proposition of the rationality of everything which is real resolves itself into the other
proposition: All that exists deserves to perish."[26] Here he quotes the words of
Mephistopheles from Goethe's *Faust*.[27] Engels thus praises Hegel's theory for
its understanding of truth not as something static but rather as a dynamic
movement from one stage to the next. With each new stage of history, a feeling
of alienation arises anew and provokes a new crisis that ends in revolution.
Alienation is therefore a fixed and recurring element in history.

His interpretation of Hegel's system thus focuses on the dialectical movement, which he claims never comes to an end. He explains,

> Truth now lay in the process of cognition itself, in the long historical
> development of science, which mounts from lower to ever higher levels of
> knowledge without ever reaching, by discovering so-called absolute truth,
> a point at which it can proceed no further, and where it would have
> nothing more to do than to fold its hands and admire the absolute truth
> to which it had attained.[28]

This is a controversial point in Hegel. While Engels chooses to focus on the
dynamic, dialectical aspect of his thought, there is also another side of Hegel.
*The Phenomenology of Spirit*, the *Encyclopedia of the Philosophical Sciences*,
and the *Science of Logic* end with an idea of some kind of absolute truth, which
encompasses everything that has come before it. This seems to be an important
part of Hegel's understanding of systems, according to which a thing has its
truth and meaning based on its specific role in the system. But if there is no
final stage or closure, then this will always remain indeterminate. The result
would be what Hegel calls the bad infinity, which continues indefinitely.
Despite this, Engels' interpretation does, however, capture one side of
Hegel's thought.

Of special interest is Engels' extension of this idea to the sphere of politics.
He explains, "Just as knowledge is unable to reach a perfected termination in
a perfect, ideal condition of humanity, so is history unable to do so; a perfect
society, a perfect 'state,' are things which can only exist in imagination."[29] This

---

[26] Engels, "Ludwig Feuerbach und der Ausgang der klassischen deutschen Philosophie,"
p. 267; *Ludwig Feuerbach and the Outcome of Classical German Philosophy*, p. 11.

[27] Johann Wolfgang von Goethe, *Faust. Eine Tragödie* in *Goethe's Werke. Vollständige Ausgabe
letzter Hand*, vols. 1–55 (Stuttgart and Tübingen: J. G. Cotta'sche Buchhandlung,
1828–1833), vol. 12 (1828), p. 70: "Und das mit Recht; denn alles, was entsteht, / Ist wert,
daß es zu Grunde geht." (English translation: Goethe, *Faust I & II*, trans. by Stuart Atkins
[Princeton: Princeton University Press, 1994], p. 36: "and rightly so, since all that gains
existence / is only fit to be destroyed …")

[28] Engels, "Ludwig Feuerbach und der Ausgang der klassischen deutschen Philosophie,"
p. 267; *Ludwig Feuerbach and the Outcome of Classical German Philosophy*, p. 11.

[29] Engels, "Ludwig Feuerbach und der Ausgang der klassischen deutschen Philosophie,"
p. 267; *Ludwig Feuerbach and the Outcome of Classical German Philosophy*, pp. 11f.

is striking when one recalls the later claims by Marxists that the classless society is indeed the final stage of history and the perfect state. With this interpretation of a more mutable and dynamic understanding of history, Engels appears to be much less dogmatic than he is usually portrayed to be. While every given stage of history has its own necessity and justification, there is no finality. Hegel's philosophy thus "reveals the transitory character of everything and in everything; nothing can endure before it except the uninterrupted process of becoming and passing away, of endless ascendency from the lower to the higher."[30] Therefore what was originally taken to be a conservative streak in Hegel's philosophy that purportedly wanted to justify the existing, in fact, is something radical and revolutionary. It seems obvious here that Engels emphasizes this in order to demonstrate that it was an important point of agreement for him and Marx with Hegel's philosophy, and one which they developed further in their own theory.

Engels grants that the issue that he has emphasized does not appear so straightforwardly in Hegel himself. But instead it is a natural consequence of his method,[31] which Hegel himself never fully developed but which Marx and Engels were attentive to. Engels thus concedes that Hegel, due to his systematic intent, felt obliged to end his system with some kind of finality, specifically with the so-called "Absolute Idea."[32] This even takes on a degree of academic arrogance when the end of history is thought to be "the arrival of all mankind at the cognition of this self-same Absolute Idea" and that "this cognition of the Absolute Idea is reached in Hegelian philosophy."[33] But he claims that this notion in Hegel of an Absolute Idea stands in marked contradiction to his own method. The notion of closure and completeness represents the conservative side of Hegel. Engels expresses his disappointment with this aspect of Hegel, noting that the *Philosophy of Right* ends with the Absolute Idea being realized in the form of a constitutional monarchy and specifically, he claims, that of Frederick William III of Prussia.

Engels thus indicates that there is a genuine ambiguity in Hegel's thought between the revolutionary aspect, which is found in the dialectical method, and the conservative aspect, which is found in the dogmatic systematic aspect. The ambiguity helps to explain the complex reception of Hegel's philosophy that divided thinkers with very different political intuitions. Engels rightly shows that there are elements in Hegel's thought that support two radically differing

---

[30] Engels, "Ludwig Feuerbach und der Ausgang der klassischen deutschen Philosophie," p. 267; *Ludwig Feuerbach and the Outcome of Classical German Philosophy*, p. 12.

[31] Engels, "Ludwig Feuerbach und der Ausgang der klassischen deutschen Philosophie," p. 268; *Ludwig Feuerbach and the Outcome of Classical German Philosophy*, pp. 12f.

[32] Engels, "Ludwig Feuerbach und der Ausgang der klassischen deutschen Philosophie," p. 268; *Ludwig Feuerbach and the Outcome of Classical German Philosophy*, p. 13.

[33] Engels, "Ludwig Feuerbach und der Ausgang der klassischen deutschen Philosophie," p. 268; *Ludwig Feuerbach and the Outcome of Classical German Philosophy*, p. 13.

conclusions with regard to the key issues of philosophical truth, history, and politics. Clearly, he and Marx were inspired by the former. Hegel's theory of historical development fit well with their idea that the new industrial capitalism was a system that displaced the previous outdated one inherited from the feudalism of the Middle Ages, which had been destroyed by its own contradictions. In turn, capitalism too will suffer the same fate in time as its contradictions become evident.

It is interesting, however, that the mature theory of Marx and Engels also needs the conservative element in Hegel's philosophy since their account of historical development also has a clear *telos*, namely the classless communist society. This is not just one of the many contradictory forms of social organization that come and go in history. Instead, this is the sole true and correct one, which can lead to human freedom and flourishing. Only with communism can the long cycle of class struggle be broken and exploitation finally be overcome. This is the element in Marxism that represents the pendant to Absolute Knowing in Hegel. The interesting contradiction here is that Engels hails Hegel's method as a useful critical tool that can be used to criticize the capitalist system or indeed any existing institution that one finds contradictory. However, this critical tool is then put aside to the advantage of the conservative aspect of Hegel's thought when it comes to the theory of communism itself. Here Bakunin's view seems to be more consistent since it insists on maintaining a critical disposition toward any form of authority and state power. Despite his criticisms of Hegel, Engels acknowledges "all of this did not prevent the Hegelian system from covering an incomparably greater domain than any earlier system; nor from developing in this domain a wealth of thought which is astounding even today."[34] He notes that Hegel's system had an influence in a large number of different disciplines and was by no means confined to philosophy.

Engels in a sense echoes one of the criticisms that Kierkegaard issued. The shortcoming of any form of systematic thought is the need to resolve all contradictions.[35] Once this happens, then all real thinking comes to an end, and the system itself becomes a mere museum piece to be admired under glass. The key is instead to realize that the contradictions will always be present and to acknowledge that this is not a negative thing to be fled but rather a positive and constructive thing. We should abandon the idea of Absolute Knowing or complete closure and rather celebrate the struggle along the path to it, knowing all the while that we will never reach it. Engels takes this realization to mean the "end of all philosophy in the hitherto accepted sense of the word,"[36] that is,

[34] Engels, "Ludwig Feuerbach und der Ausgang der klassischen deutschen Philosophie," p. 269; *Ludwig Feuerbach and the Outcome of Classical German Philosophy*, p. 14.
[35] Engels, "Ludwig Feuerbach und der Ausgang der klassischen deutschen Philosophie," p. 270; *Ludwig Feuerbach and the Outcome of Classical German Philosophy*, p. 14.
[36] Engels, "Ludwig Feuerbach und der Ausgang der klassischen deutschen Philosophie," p. 270; *Ludwig Feuerbach and the Outcome of Classical German Philosophy*, p. 15.

taken as the determination of some eternal, fixed truth about the world. In this sense Hegel was the last philosopher. But it was Hegel's dialectical methodology that showed us the way out of this traditional form of thinking. The task of the new age is to attain not the absolute truth about everything but rather smaller, mutable insights or relative truths that form a part of equally mutable theories and ways of thinking that constitute all thinking in the sciences.

Engels then recalls the profound impact that Hegel's philosophy had during the 1830s. He begins his brief sketch of the development of the Hegel schools by noting that the two main fields where the battles were fought were religion and politics.[37] Those who were impressed by Hegel's system represented the conservative party, while those who emphasized his dialectical methodology constituted the more progressive group. He states that ultimately Hegel himself was presumably more in line with the conservative interpretation.

In his account of the Hegelian schools, Engels makes an observation that while the arguments began in the context of academic issues in the classroom, they developed into something much more important. He notes that when the reactionary King Frederick William IV ascended to the throne of Prussia and inaugurated an anti-Hegelian campaign, this created a new atmosphere, which was a call to action for the left Hegelians. He writes, "The fight was still carried on with philosophical weapons, but no longer for abstract philosophical aims. It turned directly on the destruction of traditional religion and of the existing state."[38] Hegel's philosophy was no longer just a theoretical issue as it had once been. Now it was a revolutionary way of thinking that had concrete goals in the real world. In short, it moved from thoughts and ideas to action. This is a radical claim that explains something of the electric atmosphere that surrounded discussions about Hegel's philosophy during Engels' youth.

Engels notes the beginnings of the discussion in the sphere of religion with the works of Strauss and Bauer, which was then further developed in the social theories of Stirner and Bakunin. He then hails Feuerbach's *The Essence of Christianity* as the revolutionary work that decidedly broke with Hegel's idealism by claiming the priority and irreducibility of nature.[39] Feuerbach's theory, being grounded firmly in materialism, he claims, reduced religious belief to fantasy once and for all. Engels recalls, "One must himself have experienced the liberating effect of this book to get an idea of it. Enthusiasm was general; we all became at once Feuerbachians."[40] As we will see, Engels

---

[37] Engels, "Ludwig Feuerbach und der Ausgang der klassischen deutschen Philosophie," p. 270; *Ludwig Feuerbach and the Outcome of Classical German Philosophy*, p. 15.

[38] Engels, "Ludwig Feuerbach und der Ausgang der klassischen deutschen Philosophie," p. 271; *Ludwig Feuerbach and the Outcome of Classical German Philosophy*, p. 16.

[39] Engels, "Ludwig Feuerbach und der Ausgang der klassischen deutschen Philosophie," p. 272; *Ludwig Feuerbach and the Outcome of Classical German Philosophy*, p. 18.

[40] Engels, "Ludwig Feuerbach und der Ausgang der klassischen deutschen Philosophie," p. 272; *Ludwig Feuerbach and the Outcome of Classical German Philosophy*, p. 18.

takes a considerably more critical view of Feuerbach on this point in chapter 3 of the work, where Feuerbach is criticized as an idealist, despite his claims to the contrary.

Engels astutely observes that while the figures mentioned were in many ways critical of Hegel's philosophy, it would be a mistake to think that Hegel was simply forgotten or left behind. Instead, he claims, Hegel's philosophy was in his own sense *aufgehoben* in the works of the new generation of thinkers. Although they criticized his work, they appropriated many aspects of it, not least of all his methodology, which they put to productive use in their own contexts. Thus Hegel inspired the young scholars, who took his work in different directions.

## 10.4   The Relation of Idealism and Materialism

The second chapter of Engels' work concerns a fundamental divide between Hegel and his left Hegelian successors, namely the issue of idealism versus materialism. Engels explains that this basic philosophical question has split philosophers in the modern age. Hegel belongs to the idealists, "who asserted the primacy of spirit to nature."[41] This view is opposed to that of the materialists, "who regarded nature as primary."[42] We have already seen the repeated criticism of Hegel in Feuerbach, Marx, and others for being overly abstract and for failing to recognize the degree to which we are physical beings, the products of nature. The intervening period in the second half of the nineteenth century saw a profound rise in the authority of the natural sciences with a number of important advances in the different fields. These included Darwin's theory of evolution by natural selection, made famous by the publication of *On The Origin of Species* in 1859, Hermann von Helmholtz's law of the conservation of energy in 1847, and the development of cell theory by scientists Theodor Schwann (1810–1882) and Matthias Jakob Schleiden (1804–1881) in 1839 and by Robert Remak (1815–1865), Rudolf Virchow (1821–1902), and Albert Kolliker (1817–1905) in the 1850s.[43] Running parallel to this was a new movement of materialism in philosophy in the work of thinkers such as Ludwig Büchner (1824–1899), Jacob Moleschott (1822–1893), and Karl Vogt (1817–1895), who are all mentioned by Engels.[44] This materialist

---

[41]  Engels, "Ludwig Feuerbach und der Ausgang der klassischen deutschen Philosophie," p. 275; *Ludwig Feuerbach and the Outcome of Classical German Philosophy*, p. 21.

[42]  Engels, "Ludwig Feuerbach und der Ausgang der klassischen deutschen Philosophie," p. 275; *Ludwig Feuerbach and the Outcome of Classical German Philosophy*, p. 21.

[43]  See Engels, "Ludwig Feuerbach und der Ausgang der klassischen deutschen Philosophie," p. 280, pp. 294f.; *Ludwig Feuerbach and the Outcome of Classical German Philosophy*, p. 29, p. 46.

[44]  Engels, "Ludwig Feuerbach und der Ausgang der klassischen deutschen Philosophie," p. 278; *Ludwig Feuerbach and the Outcome of Classical German Philosophy*, p. 25.

movement was in part a reaction against and rejection of German Idealism. Thus by the time that Engels wrote his piece on Feuerbach, this seemed more than ever to be a foregone conclusion.

Engels goes on to note that this issue also concerns epistemology since we are interested in whether our ideas about the world are in fact veridical representations of that world. In other words, can the human mind grasp the world in thought? Engels notes that this is often referred to as the issue of "the identity of thinking and being."[45] This is thematized by Kierkegaard in the *Concluding Unscientific Postscript*,[46] and it is taken up by Feuerbach in his *Principles of the Philosophy of the Future*.[47] The claim of the unity of thought and being is one that Hegel was known for since he believed that the world consisted of a content of thought that was continually developing. This is something that the human mind can grasp since the mind can understand its own thoughts. What is most true for Hegel is the Absolute Idea that exists for all time.

In contrast to this view is that of the materialists, among whom Engels counts Hume and, more controversially, Kant.[48] Engels recounts a number of scientific discoveries that in effect refuted the Kantian view that nature represented a "thing-in-itself" that ultimately could not be known. While this might at first glance appear intuitive, in fact scientific discovery uncovers these things and shows them to us. Engels seems to associate Kant's agnosticism about things-in-themselves with materialism, which is somewhat misleading.

Engels also praises Feuerbach's materialism in this context and traces his development from a Hegelian idealist to a materialist. Hegel's notion of the Absolute Idea that exists for all time is a mere holdover from the earlier religious conceptions of a creator God who existed before the creation of the universe. According to Engels, Feuerbach realized that the only true reality is the real material one that we are familiar with from our everyday life. Consciousness and thought are the product of a physical organ, the brain. But Feuerbach, claims Engels, did not fully embrace materialism since he

---

[45] Engels, "Ludwig Feuerbach und der Ausgang der klassischen deutschen Philosophie," p. 275; *Ludwig Feuerbach and the Outcome of Classical German Philosophy*, p. 21.

[46] Søren Kierkegaard, *Søren Kierkegaards Skrifter*, vols. 1–28, K1–K28, ed. by Niels Jørgen Cappelørn, Joakim Garff, Jette Knudsen, Johnny Kondrup, and Alastair McKinnon (Copenhagen: Gad Publishers, 1997–2012), vol. 7, pp. 173–182, pp. 300–306. (English translation: Søren Kierkegaard, *Concluding Unscientific Postscript*, vols. 1–2, trans. by Howard V. Hong and Edna H. Hong [Princeton: Princeton University Press, 1992], vol. 1, pp. 189–199, pp. 329–335.)

[47] Ludwig Feuerbach, *Grundsätze der Philosophie der Zukunft* (Zürich and Winterthur: Verlag des literarischen Comptoirs, 1843), §§ 24–29, pp. 42–55; § 51, p. 77. (English translation: *Principles of the Philosophy of the Future*, trans. by Manfred Vogel [Indianapolis and Cambridge: Hackett, 1986], §§ 24–29, pp. 38–48; § 51, pp. 67–68.)

[48] Engels, "Ludwig Feuerbach und der Ausgang der klassischen deutschen Philosophie," p. 276; *Ludwig Feuerbach and the Outcome of Classical German Philosophy*, p. 22.

confused it with the crude versions of it that arose in the wake of the Enlightenment. This earlier form of materialism conceived of nature as mechanical in the context of the rise of mechanics. This was, according to Engels, its first limitation. The second was its inability to understand nature as a changing, developing process. Natural science in the eighteenth century saw in nature only simple repetitions but not development. This only arose later in Engels' own time with, for example, Darwin's theory of evolution. Engels reproaches Hegel for adhering to the older view of nature, despite his own insistence on dialectical development.[49]

Engels explains why Feuerbach did not fully embrace materialism as he should have. Although Feuerbach lived to see the key scientific discoveries of the age, it was impossible for him to appreciate their true significance because he was marginalized from university life and forced to pursue his research in relative seclusion.[50] Moreover, Feuerbach rejected the idea that the natural sciences were the key to explaining everything. Instead, he wanted to bring the human sciences into harmony with the foundation created by the natural sciences.[51]

### 10.5  Engels' Criticism of Feuerbach's Theory of Religion and Ethics

Engels continues his account of Feuerbach's thought in chapter 3, where he begins with a discussion of religion. Contrary to what is often claimed, Feuerbach "by no means wishes to abolish religion: he wants to perfect it."[52] While it is true that Feuerbach criticizes the idea of a transcendent God, which he believes is a projection of the human mind, he wants to find the source of religious truth elsewhere, specifically in the concept of love. According to Feuerbach's theory, we think of the Christian God as a God of love, but once again reflection tells us that love is a human quality that has been projected onto the divine. Thus Feuerbach's solution is that instead of extending our love to some fiction of the human mind, we should instead bestow it on other human beings. With the idea of human love for another human being, the problem of alienation from a transcendent entity is eliminated and the true anthropological nature of religion is revealed. Feuerbach "does not simply accept mutual relations based on reciprocal inclination between human beings, such as sex love, friendship, compassion, self-sacrifice, etc., as what

---

[49] Engels, "Ludwig Feuerbach und der Ausgang der klassischen deutschen Philosophie," p. 279; *Ludwig Feuerbach and the Outcome of Classical German Philosophy*, p. 27.

[50] Engels, "Ludwig Feuerbach und der Ausgang der klassischen deutschen Philosophie," p. 280; *Ludwig Feuerbach and the Outcome of Classical German Philosophy*, pp. 28f.

[51] Engels, "Ludwig Feuerbach und der Ausgang der klassischen deutschen Philosophie," pp. 280f.; *Ludwig Feuerbach and the Outcome of Classical German Philosophy*, p. 29.

[52] Engels, "Ludwig Feuerbach und der Ausgang der klassischen deutschen Philosophie," p. 283; *Ludwig Feuerbach and the Outcome of Classical German Philosophy*, p. 33.

they are in themselves . . . but instead he asserts that they will come to their full realization for the first time as soon as they are consecrated by the name of religion."[53] Engels finds it contradictory that Feuerbach still wishes to maintain religion in a wholly secular fashion, propping it up with the idea of human love in order to try to compensate for the loss of God. It is as if Feuerbach cannot recognize that love between people can take place wholly independent of religion. It is absurd to think of all human love as being the result of a retraction of one's love of God.

Engels objects to Feuerbach's theory of history, which claims that the great changes in history have been determined by religion.[54] Feuerbach, according to this view, has failed to recognize that the real stimulant of historical change is class struggle. This is relevant for the previous discussion since Engels believes that class divisions stand in the way of the full realization of human love that Feuerbach wanted to develop. Engels explains, "The possibility of purely human sentiments in the intercourse with other human beings has nowadays been sufficiently curtailed by the society in which we live, which is based upon class antagonism and class rule."[55]

While Feuerbach claims to be eliminating the abstractions that have plagued religion and human relations historically, he is in fact continuing to reify them, according to Engels. Feuerbach demonstrates well that God is simply an abstraction from the human mind. But then it becomes clear that the image of human beings that he has is equally an abstraction:

> man, whose image this god is, is therefore also not a real man, but likewise the quintessence of the numerous real men, man in the abstract, therefore himself again a mental image. The same Feuerbach who, on every page, preaches sensuousness, absorption in the concrete, in actuality, becomes thoroughly abstract as soon as he begins to talk of any other than mere sex relations between human beings.[56]

Feuerbach himself thus falls victim to exactly the kind of abstraction that he is trying to criticize and eliminate. Likewise, when Feuerbach talks about ethics, his theory fails to understand the human being as embedded in a surrounding world. In contrast to Hegel's theory of ethics, which is closely connected to a theory of history, law, and politics, Feuerbach's views are abstract and sterile. Feuerbach's human being "does not live in a real world historically created and

---

[53] Engels, "Ludwig Feuerbach und der Ausgang der klassischen deutschen Philosophie," p. 284; *Ludwig Feuerbach and the Outcome of Classical German Philosophy*, p. 34.

[54] Engels, "Ludwig Feuerbach und der Ausgang der klassischen deutschen Philosophie," pp. 284f.; *Ludwig Feuerbach and the Outcome of Classical German Philosophy*, p. 35.

[55] Engels, "Ludwig Feuerbach und der Ausgang der klassischen deutschen Philosophie," p. 285; *Ludwig Feuerbach and the Outcome of Classical German Philosophy*, p. 35.

[56] Engels, "Ludwig Feuerbach und der Ausgang der klassischen deutschen Philosophie," p. 286; *Ludwig Feuerbach and the Outcome of Classical German Philosophy*, p. 36.

historically determined. It is true he has intercourse with other men, but each one of them is, however, just as much an abstraction as he himself is."[57] It is precisely in this point that Engels identifies a residual idealist element in Feuerbach's thought. Feuerbach does not give an account of concrete human beings living in their specific historical and socio-economic situations. Instead, he analyzes a purely abstract idea of a human being that does not exist anywhere.

Engels recalls Hegel's theory of the Fall, according to which original sin, although traditionally lamented, was in fact essential for the development of humanity because it meant the arrival of self-consciousness. Engels sees this to be in harmony with the theory of history that he championed together with Marx: "it is precisely the wicked passions of man – greed and lust for power – which, since the emergence of class antagonisms, serve as levers of historical development."[58] Engels thus reproaches Feuerbach for having a naive and undeveloped view of history: "It does not occur to Feuerbach to investigate the historical role of moral evil."[59] For all that Feuerbach says about the mechanism of the creation of the divine by means of the projection of the human mind, he never gives any meaningful historical account of the different religions of the world in the way that Hegel does. He never offers any historical evidence about exactly how and when this projection took place.

Engels claims that Feuerbach's ethics can be reduced to two basic principles that are derived from the idea that all human beings naturally seek their own happiness. First, with regard to the pursuit of our own happiness, we must exercise a degree of self-restraint since without this we can be led to excess and debauchery.[60] With regard to this point, Engels criticizes Feuerbach for considering these matters from a purely individualistic perspective. Feuerbach fails to understand that when we seek our happiness, we are constantly dependent on the conditions in the world around us. No one can do this only on their own. It is impossible to flourish and be happy if one is compelled to live under oppressive work conditions in a situation of exploitation and alienation. There are thus deeper factors involved in the determination of the happiness of the individual than Feuerbach realizes.

Second, with regard to others, we must recognize that just like ourselves, other people are also seeking their own happiness. Feuerbach thus has a theory of mutual recognition since he believes that individuals must respect the rights

[57] Engels, "Ludwig Feuerbach und der Ausgang der klassischen deutschen Philosophie," p. 286; *Ludwig Feuerbach and the Outcome of Classical German Philosophy*, pp. 36f.
[58] Engels, "Ludwig Feuerbach und der Ausgang der klassischen deutschen Philosophie," p. 287; *Ludwig Feuerbach and the Outcome of Classical German Philosophy*, p. 37.
[59] Engels, "Ludwig Feuerbach und der Ausgang der klassischen deutschen Philosophie," p. 287; *Ludwig Feuerbach and the Outcome of Classical German Philosophy*, p. 37.
[60] Engels, "Ludwig Feuerbach und der Ausgang der klassischen deutschen Philosophie," p. 287; *Ludwig Feuerbach and the Outcome of Classical German Philosophy*, p. 38.

of each other to pursue happiness; this recognition prevents them from interfering with each other in this regard.[61] This seems to be an echo or a variant of Fichte's and Hegel's notion of recognition. Engels criticizes this as an empty moral imperative that has never been recognized historically:

> But since when has it been valid? Was there ever in antiquity between slaves and masters, or in the Middle Ages between serfs and barons, any talk about an equal right to the pursuit of happiness? Was not the urge towards happiness of the oppressed class sacrificed ruthlessly "by right of law" to the interests of the ruling class?[62]

Even though today equal rights are something that is generally recognized, this is an illusion in practice. In order for people to pursue their happiness, they need certain basic material means, of which they are often deprived. Thus to talk about equal rights from a purely legal perspective rings hollow if the economic conditions prevent people from ever truly realizing them.

Engels finds Feuerbach's mantra about love to be naive because, despite its noble and high-sounding tone, it will never be able to resolve the deeper social problems that are based on fundamental economic conditions: "But love! – yes, with Feuerbach, love is everywhere and at all times the wonder-working god who should help to surmount all difficulties of practical life – and at that in a society which is split into classes with diametrically opposite interests."[63] Despite the cliché, love does not conquer all and will not right the basic wrongs of society, which need to be addressed in a more sober fashion. When seen in this way, Feuerbach's theory loses much of its revolutionary character and instead looks rather lukewarm. Indeed, it can be used to support the status quo. Like Kant's ethics, Feuerbach's view is overly abstract and as a result is meaningless for the problems of the real world.

Despite his polemic against the abstract nature of Hegel's system, Feuerbach himself falls into precisely the same kind of abstraction that renders his theory tame. For all of his talk of anthropology and a return to the human, Feuerbach's conception of human beings remains sadly distant. Engels disdainfully refers to Feuerbach's idea of a new religion as the "cult of abstract man."[64] Real human beings, for Engels, can only be understood in a clear historical context. Feuerbach failed to grasp the meaning of the Revolution of 1848 because he had no clear understanding of history. The true understanding of the human

---

[61] Engels, "Ludwig Feuerbach und der Ausgang der klassischen deutschen Philosophie," p. 287; *Ludwig Feuerbach and the Outcome of Classical German Philosophy*, p. 38.

[62] Engels, "Ludwig Feuerbach und der Ausgang der klassischen deutschen Philosophie," p. 288; *Ludwig Feuerbach and the Outcome of Classical German Philosophy*, pp. 38f.

[63] Engels, "Ludwig Feuerbach und der Ausgang der klassischen deutschen Philosophie," p. 289; *Ludwig Feuerbach and the Outcome of Classical German Philosophy*, p. 40.

[64] Engels, "Ludwig Feuerbach und der Ausgang der klassischen deutschen Philosophie," p. 290; *Ludwig Feuerbach and the Outcome of Classical German Philosophy*, p. 41.

and history was only developed subsequently by Marx, and it is to this that
Engels turns in the final chapter of his work.

## 10.6   Marx's Contribution

Engels begins chapter 4 with an overview of the previous results of his study,
mentioning the leading figures in post-Hegelian thinking: Strauss, Bauer,
Stirner, Feuerbach, and Bakunin. Of these figures, "Feuerbach alone was of
significance as a philosopher,"[65] but, Engels claims, unfortunately he did not
go far enough beyond Hegel, and his philosophy still displays vestiges of
idealism. Here Engels refers to his previous criticism of Feuerbach for having
only an abstract conception of the human being with no account of the
historical or socio-economic context in which we live. Engels then declares
the topic of the chapter by asserting that in the end it was only Marx who
emerged from Hegelian thinking with an enduring philosophical approach. In
a famous footnote Engels explains his role in the development of Marxist
theory and humbly acknowledges Marx's broad vision and great genius.[66]
Engels thus gives to Marx the lion's share of the credit for the creation of the
communist theory that resulted from their long collaboration. It seems clear
that an important element in this chapter, and indeed in the work as a whole, is
to acknowledge the legacy of Marx after his death.

Engels claims that Marx was able to achieve his monumental results due to
the fact that, in contrast to Feuerbach, he was able to emancipate himself fully
from idealism and embrace a consistent materialism. Marx did not wholly
abandon Hegel but instead seized upon the dialectical method and transformed it. For Hegel, the dialectic concerned conceptual analysis, that is,
ideas. For example, his *Science of Logic* examined the nature of the individual
categories or concepts and traced their development through a long series.
This struck Marx as overly abstract, so he applied the dialectic to history and
the social order; in short, the phenomena of the real world itself. The dialectic
was concerned with demonstrating movement. In the case of Hegel, this was
the movement of one concept to another, for example, being, nothing, and
becoming. Marx realized, according to Engels, that this was not what was
primary. Rather, there was a more fundamental dialectical movement in the
real world, and the abstract concepts, instead of being the foundation for this,
were a reflection of it. While, for Hegel, the dialectic traces the movement from
one category to the next, for Marx, it traced the necessary movement of one

[65] Engels, "Ludwig Feuerbach und der Ausgang der klassischen deutschen Philosophie,"
p. 291; *Ludwig Feuerbach and the Outcome of Classical German Philosophy*, p. 42.
[66] Engels, "Ludwig Feuerbach und der Ausgang der klassischen deutschen Philosophie,"
pp. 291n–292n; *Ludwig Feuerbach and the Outcome of Classical German Philosophy*,
pp. 42n–43n.

social-economic order to the next as these developed historically. With Marx's insight of applying Hegel's methodology to the real social-political phenomena, "the dialectic of Hegel was placed upon his head."[67] More importantly, it was given a firm grounding in the real world. Engels refers to this as the "materialist dialectic,"[68] presumably in contrast to Hegel's idealist dialectic. This analysis makes clear the ambivalent relationship that Marx and Engels had toward Hegel. While they rejected his idealism, they happily coopted his dialectical method for their own purposes.

Marx understood history as a "complex of *processes*," which had a progressive character.[69] Instead of focusing ahead of time on an abstract idea in history like Hegel, Marx focused on the empirical facts and found the *logos* in them themselves. In a surprising passage, Engels indicates that this approach in effect gives up the old idea of an absolute metaphysical truth: "If, however, investigation always proceeds from [the dialectical] standpoint, the demand for final solutions and eternal truths ceases once for all; one is always conscious of the necessary limitation of all acquired knowledge."[70] This statement stands in striking contrast to the dogmatic picture of Marx that is usually presented. One cannot help but wonder whether Engels means for this also to apply to Marx's theory itself. Is it also just one finite, flawed theory in the sequence, or does it represent an absolute that, once attained, will end the course of development?

Engels notes that the recent advancements in the natural sciences contributed to understanding things in terms of developmental processes, thus getting away from the older metaphysical view of things as fixed and determined entities. Modern natural science thus demonstrates the complex interconnection of things in the different spheres. The point of these observations about the natural sciences is presumably to demonstrate that Marx's theory is in line with these developments in its focus on empirical processes. In the absence of clear empirical data, scientists and scholars in the past tended to invent their own ideas in order to explain things. This is what modern natural science has radically improved upon with its new discoveries about the interconnections of natural phenomena. Now there is no longer any need to appeal to abstract, somewhat arbitrary ideas to explain observed phenomena. Modern science has removed the guesswork that was typical of earlier times.

---

[67] Engels, "Ludwig Feuerbach und der Ausgang der klassischen deutschen Philosophie," p. 293; *Ludwig Feuerbach and the Outcome of Classical German Philosophy*, p. 44.

[68] Engels, "Ludwig Feuerbach und der Ausgang der klassischen deutschen Philosophie," p. 293; *Ludwig Feuerbach and the Outcome of Classical German Philosophy*, p. 44.

[69] Engels, "Ludwig Feuerbach und der Ausgang der klassischen deutschen Philosophie," p. 293; *Ludwig Feuerbach and the Outcome of Classical German Philosophy*, p. 44.

[70] Engels, "Ludwig Feuerbach und der Ausgang der klassischen deutschen Philosophie," p. 293; *Ludwig Feuerbach and the Outcome of Classical German Philosophy*, p. 45.

Engels then claims that the new understanding of the natural sciences is also relevant for the human sphere as well. Far from being a chaotic series of more or less random events, history can be understood as a dialectical, developmental process. While it is true that in contrast to the objects of nature, which are not conscious, history and the human sphere are the result of human goals and intentions, nonetheless these are rarely realized in the way in which they are originally conceived. But this does not mean that the human sphere is purely random or chaotic, as is sometimes thought. There is a higher order of law that governs this sphere in which humans act and interact in the world. In this way the human sphere is similar to nature in that there is an unconscious tendency or *logos* to be found in the midst of apparently chaotic events and actions.[71] The goal of the scholar is to discover these hidden laws.

The earlier view was that history was created by the good or bad intentions of powerful individuals such as kings or generals. Through their actions they realized their goals, thus shaping the course of events. This kind of philosophy of history had a moralizing tone since the focus was on the nature of the intentions of these individuals. However, Hegel's philosophy of history, according to Engels, rightly saw that these goals and intentions were not the true driving forces of history. Instead, there was something higher: what Hegel called the idea of human freedom, which he believed developed historically.[72] Engels acknowledges that this is an improvement over the older conception of history, but he nonetheless still objects to Hegel's view. Hegel imposed a concept on history from his own ideas instead of seeking it in history itself. Engels refers to this as "ideological."[73] In the absence of sufficient data, Hegel, ever the idealist, was obliged to posit *an idea* to explain history. The intended contrast is Marx, who rightly recognized that the true driving force in history is class struggle.

The developments in the Industrial Revolution in England made this historical mechanism clear for the first time. Instead of appealing to some abstract idea, Marx located the motor of history in actual, documentable historical events – the repeated cycles of class conflict that are found at regular intervals throughout all of recorded history. Engels believes that the struggles between the landed aristocracy, the bourgeoisie, and the proletariat have in his time become so obvious that one need not be a scholar to recognize them. This is the key to the correct understanding of both history and the current social and political order of things. By concentrating on the key economic factors that were at the heart of class conflict, Marx was able to understand the true nature of historical development. While traditional theories highlighted the power of

---

[71] Engels, "Ludwig Feuerbach und der Ausgang der klassischen deutschen Philosophie," p. 296; *Ludwig Feuerbach and the Outcome of Classical German Philosophy*, p. 48.

[72] Engels, "Ludwig Feuerbach und der Ausgang der klassischen deutschen Philosophie," p. 298; *Ludwig Feuerbach and the Outcome of Classical German Philosophy*, p. 49.

[73] Engels, "Ludwig Feuerbach und der Ausgang der klassischen deutschen Philosophie," p. 298; *Ludwig Feuerbach and the Outcome of Classical German Philosophy*, p. 50.

the state as the determining force in human events, Marx perceived that this was ultimately subordinated to the economic foundation of the class struggle, which used politics toward its own ends. In other words, the laws and the political institutions are created and developed to serve the interests of the class of owners. For this reason, Marx and Engels believe that economic reform is the key to everything. Without this, all pious talk about, for example, human rights and progressive legislation is meaningless. It is the economic order that steers politics and not the other way around.

Engels' position is somewhat dogmatic or foundationalist. He seems to imply that while Hegel and everyone else were tapping in the dark with regard to history, he and Marx reached the final, definitive truth of the matter. Engels concludes by stating that with the discovery of the true principle of history, the discipline of the philosophy of history is rendered superfluous.[74] Now there is no longer any need to speculate about the forces of history and to try to come up with bright ideas to explain historical change and movement. After Marx there is no point in this kind of thing since historical development has now been laid bare and empirically established by straightforward material conditions or facts. The earlier theories of history, including that of Hegel, had appealed to abstract ideas that they imposed on the subject matter from the outside. By contrast, Engels seems to believe that the Marxist theory escapes this problem by strictly sticking to the material side of things. He seems to want to claim that their notion of class struggle as the key to history is a true reflection of reality itself. But, of course, he cannot escape the fact that this is also an *idea* and that the Marxist view of society and history is also a *theory* based on ideas. It thus seems absurd to dismiss Hegel's idealism and claim a more materialist approach while Marx and Engels themselves also simply propose *ideas*, which they try to hide under the name of material facts. It is, of course, impossible to grasp the naked reality immediately, and this is why we have theories in the first place. We observe reality and look for patterns and consistencies, which we then use to create ideas, laws, or theories that try to explain the given phenomenon. But, as Hegel noted with his doctrine of the Concept, there are always two sides to this – the idea and the empirically perceived phenomenon. The trick is, of course, how they relate to one another. But it is clear that it is absurd to think of either the one or the other in isolation. The two sides naturally and necessarily belong together.

## 10.7   The Legacy of Classical German Philosophy

Engels marks the end of post-Hegelian philosophy with the Revolution of 1848. He claims that with this event, "'educated' Germany said farewell to

---

[74] Engels, "Ludwig Feuerbach und der Ausgang der klassischen deutschen Philosophie," p. 306; *Ludwig Feuerbach and the Outcome of Classical German Philosophy*, p. 59.

theory and went over to the field of practice."[75] He laments the fact that German philosophy has now descended into "empty eclecticism and an anxious concern for career and income."[76] The increasing professionalism of philosophy meant that those who held prestigious positions at universities were in effect mere puppets or ideologues for the state, a trend that began with Schelling's appointment at the University of Berlin. The old mission of philosophy as the critical search for truth has thus been thoroughly betrayed. For Engels, this was a sad commentary on the state of philosophical inquiry at the time.

One might say that, for Engels, this represents a kind of crisis of the age since philosophy, history, and the other humanities disciplines were completely meaningless in the form in which they were taught at universities. There was a yearning among the students for something more meaningful and relevant. He claims that in fact there are outstanding philosophers in his own time interested in theory in his day, but these are not to be found at the university. Instead, they come from the working class. They have realized that "the key to the understanding of the whole history of society lies in the historical development of labor."[77] Using this explanatory principle as their point of departure, they continue in the true spirit of philosophy. He thus concludes the work with the striking claim, "The German working class is the inheritor of German classical philosophy."[78] The idea seems to be that the workers have understood Marx's theory and thus represent the real theoreticians of the day. This is a surprising and powerful pronouncement.

We have explored Hegel's theory about how self-consciousness emerged from the violent conflict of one individual with another in the master-slave dialectic. Humans become conscious of themselves by means of the reflection that they see of themselves in the eyes of the other. As we have seen, this idea of self-consciousness has been an influential idea in the development of philosophy in the nineteenth century. Marx and Engels take the idea of the necessary conflict of the master and the slave and apply it to history and society. As we have seen, what emerges is the theory of class struggle. The bourgeoisie is the master and the proletariat the slave. Marx and Engels also further develop the idea of self-conscious into a theory of class consciousness. Individuals come to realize that they are not primarily members of a specific religion, country, or race. Instead, their fundamental point of orientation with regard to their

---

[75] Engels, "Ludwig Feuerbach und der Ausgang der klassischen deutschen Philosophie," p. 306; *Ludwig Feuerbach and the Outcome of Classical German Philosophy*, p. 60.
[76] Engels, "Ludwig Feuerbach und der Ausgang der klassischen deutschen Philosophie," p. 306; *Ludwig Feuerbach and the Outcome of Classical German Philosophy*, p. 60.
[77] Engels, "Ludwig Feuerbach und der Ausgang der klassischen deutschen Philosophie," p. 307; *Ludwig Feuerbach and the Outcome of Classical German Philosophy*, pp. 60f.
[78] Engels, "Ludwig Feuerbach und der Ausgang der klassischen deutschen Philosophie," p. 307; *Ludwig Feuerbach and the Outcome of Classical German Philosophy*, p. 61.

self-identity is that of their class. They are workers, and as such they share with other workers a series of vested interests. The dialectic of recognition is also relevant here since one class is always necessarily pitted against another. As the workers feel a sense of self-identification with their own class, the proletariat, they likewise feel a sense of alienation from the owners who disdain and exploit them. The theory of class consciousness can thus be seen as an extension of Hegel's theory of self-consciousness. In both cases, the dawning awareness of oneself is the key to the realization of human freedom. It is perhaps in this sense that Engels means that the workers are the true philosophers of the day. In other words, following Marx's theory, they have realized their class consciousness and thus come to a clear understanding of history and the social-economic order of the day.

   Despite all of his criticism of Hegel and classical German philosophy, Engels clearly maintains a deep respect for this tradition and portrays Marx himself as an heir to it. His idea here seems to be that the true philosophers are those thinkers, such as Marx, who have understood the truth of history and are now working to apply this to other areas. It is true that this sounds rather dogmatic since it reduces philosophy just to Marxist philosophy. But there is nonetheless something powerful in the idea that something important was lost in the practice of philosophy once it became institutionalized. The true spirit of philosophy can only exist outside these structures in the spirit of free inquiry.

# 11

# Hegel's Long Shadow in the History of Nineteenth-Century Philosophy

This study has shown the long shadow cast by Hegel in the history of nineteenth-century philosophy. It is usually thought that Hegel's philosophy died out in the first half of the century, to be replaced by materialism and positivism. This view emphasizes how thinkers such as Feuerbach, Marx, and Kierkegaard polemically reacted to Hegel and attempted to distance themselves from his idealism and abstraction. This criticism, it is thought, continued in the works of thinkers such as Dostoevsky, Bakunin, and Nietzsche, who represent a radical break from the first half of the century. Their rejection of Hegel's idealism was thought to be in part fueled by a growing awareness of the rise of the natural sciences, including Darwin's theory of evolution, which radically challenged long-accepted intuitions about the nature of human beings and society during this later period.

While all of this is true on some level, it is one-sided. Although these thinkers rejected Hegel's idealism and what they regarded as its abstraction, there were, as we have seen, several aspects of his philosophy that they embraced and used as rich sources of inspiration. There is a natural tendency in histories of philosophy to underscore the differences in the various thinkers so that their individual profiles and contributions can come out more clearly. One wants to see things as black and white and characterize the different schools of thought with clear contours and sharp edges. However, it can also be insightful to emphasize their continuities since in this way it is possible to see how the key ideas arose and developed in different mutations over time. The history of philosophy is not simply about one thinker wholeheartedly and completely rejecting the thought of their predecessor. If this were the case, it would be numbingly uninteresting. Instead, it is about how thinkers struggle with the ideas of their forerunners and try to revise the ones that they find problematic. The movement of thought is rarely one of simple replacement changes but rather of constant modifications and revisions. While differences, of course, do exist, they can be understood in a broader context of identity. While it might appear that a later thinker is rejecting a specific idea of an earlier one, this obscures the fact that they might well share a common methodology, a set of perceived problems, and a general view of philosophical inquiry. Thus the criticism or rejection of any given idea or theory only makes sense against a broader background of identity and commonality. As Hegel himself demonstrated, the concepts of identity and difference are dialectically related, and there exists what he calls an identity of identity and difference.

Too often historians of ideas have been seduced by polemical statements made by philosophers that seem to imply a radical break with another thinker. But anyone who has ever been to a professional conference in philosophy knows how philosophers love to posture and exaggerate the importance and originality of their own views. This usually comes out in the form of polemics, by which they attempt to belittle rival views so that the purported merits of their own position can be appreciated and appropriately celebrated. While these kinds of exchanges can be entertaining to young scholars, after one has been in the field for a few years it becomes increasingly difficult to take them seriously. If we have learned anything from logic, we know that we should keep our focus on the actual arguments and evidence presented and ignore all of the rhetorical bluff and bluster that surrounds them.

Moreover, as the theory of the anxiety of influence suggests, such polemics might well be an indication of a deep intellectual debt.[1] This can be seen in many of the thinkers examined in this study, whose thought gradually developed and who can be characterized by their changing views towards their predecessors. For example, as we have seen, Marx was initially quite positively disposed toward Feuerbach, regarding *The Essence of Christianity* as a revolutionary criticism of religion and a key first step in a general criticism that Marx himself wished to extend to the social-political sphere. Marx thus at first clearly saw his own work as an extension of a more specific academic program that Feuerbach began. But then, only a fairly short time later, Marx's tone turns much more critical, and he rebukes Feuerbach for not going far enough and for being stranded in a lukewarm materialism that maintains the abstractions of Hegelian idealism. While Marx turned polemical against his former intellectual hero, it would be a mistake to think that he simply rejected his former positive analysis of Feuerbach's criticism of religion as paving the way for a criticism of the social sphere. This shift in tone is not unique and can be seen in the work of a number of thinkers of this generation. Similarly, the young Kierkegaard actively and openly appropriates many aspects of Hegel's thought but then later turns polemical especially against Hegel's followers. He himself clearly recognizes this change in view when, in 1850, he looks back at his dissertation from 1841 and criticizes himself for being a "Hegelian fool" at the time.[2] The young Bakunin was likewise zealous in his praise of Hegel's

---

[1] Harold Bloom, *The Anxiety of Influence: A Theory of Poetry* (New York: Oxford University Press, 1973). See also Ronald M. Green, *Kierkegaard and Kant: The Hidden Debt* (Albany: State University of New York Press, 1992).

[2] Søren Kierkegaard, *Søren Kierkegaards Skrifter*, vols. 1–28, K1–K28, ed. by Niels Jørgen Cappelørn, Joakim Garff, Jette Knudsen, Johnny Kondrup, and Alastair McKinnon

thought, but as he grew older his tone became much more detached. As we have seen in Chapter 10, Engels directly emphasizes the ambiguity in the reception of Hegel's thought by his generation, identifying a conservative element that was criticized and a progressive one that was praised and coopted. These examples should suffice to show that the conception of the history of philosophy as one primarily of difference and the straightforward rejection of earlier ideas is misleading. This underestimates the complexities and ambiguities of the development of ideas.

We began this study with a question about what it was about Hegel's thought that was able to cause such a stir among so many highly talented thinkers coming from different backgrounds. A number of answers have been given to this question: Hegel's theory of historical development, his dialectical method, his criticism of religion, his interpretation of the Fall, his philosophical anthropology, his analysis of the crisis of the age, his understanding of the nature of the philosophical enterprise, and his account of subjective freedom. These are all important ideas that were taken up by later thinkers. However, the present study has tried to focus specifically on tracing the development of his ideas of alienation and recognition. Variations of these ideas can be found explicitly or implicitly in all of the thinkers examined here and appear in a number of different contexts in addition to philosophy: religion, history, politics, literature, poetry, etc. This shows that the seed that Hegel planted in *The Phenomenology of Spirit* and later in his Berlin lectures in the 1820s continued to grow through the subsequent decades.

## 11.1   The Nature of the Crisis and the Causes of Alienation

We saw how Hegel began with a theory of alienation in the lordship and bondage dialectic in *The Phenomenology of Spirit*. This notion of alienation was further developed in his *Lectures on the Philosophy of Religion*, where he sketched a form of religious alienation in Judaism, and in his *Lectures on the Philosophy of History*, where he characterized the early Roman Empire as a period of alienation. He gives many reasons for the causes of alienation. In the case of the unhappy consciousness, this was the result of the feeling of separation from the divine. In Judaism there was no developed conception of inwardness or subjective freedom, so the ancient Jews regarded themselves as

(Copenhagen: Gad Publishers, 1997–2012), vol. 24, p. 32, NB21:35. (English translation: *Kierkegaard's Journals and Notebooks*, vols. 1-11, ed. by Niels Jørgen Cappelørn, Alastair Hannay, David Kangas, Bruce H. Kirmmse, George Pattison, Vanessa Rumble, and K. Brian Söderquist [Princeton and Oxford: Princeton University Press, 2007–2020], vol. 8, p. 29.) "Influenced as I was by Hegel and by everything modern, lacking the maturity to comprehend greatness, I was unable to resist pointing out in a passage somewhere in my dissertation that it was a shortcoming in Socrates that he had no eye for the totality but only paid attention, numerically, to the individuals. Oh, what a Hegelian fool I was."

subject to the absolute commands and threats of their God. In the Roman world there was only an abstract sense of the self that was reflected in Roman law in the notion of citizenship rights, but there was no full recognition of the individual as inwardly and subjectively free. The rights of the individual were at the mercy of the arbitrary whims of the emperor, from whom the people were alienated.

In the modern world the breakdown of traditional customs and values leads to new forms of alienation that Hegel perceives as arising in his own time in the wake of the French Revolution. As we have seen,[3] Hegel ends his *Lectures on the Philosophy of Religion* on what he calls a "discordant note," claiming that the modern world is, like ancient Rome, characterized by alienation. From this sense of alienation arises the crisis of modernity. These motifs of alienation and crisis are echoed throughout the century in the works of many subsequent thinkers, who all explore the root causes of alienation and crisis in the areas of their specific interest and expertise. This evidences the fact that Hegel put his finger on something that was felt by others at the time.

For the poet Heine, the crisis is not so much cultural as political. The conservative forces of the Restoration deprive people of their basic rights. They are not permitted to speak freely, to publish their views, or to pursue the professions of their choice. Human development has thus been stifled. A mindless nationalism, anti-Semitism, and rigid class system separate people from one another and prevent them from seeing their common humanity. This leads to a sense of alienation from the political order in general. But it also results in a sense of self-alienation since the individual is prevented from being who they want to be and is forced to live in lies and hypocrisy in order to avoid being punished by the authorities.

For Feuerbach, the crisis is to be found in the religious sphere. The cause of alienation can be traced back to the idea of a transcendent God, who is conceived to be radically different from the human. But this is simply a projection of specific human qualities onto a fictional external other. This results in an alienation of these qualities from the human sphere. People thus live like Hegel's unhappy consciousness, suffering from a feeling of division from the divine. They put all of their focus and attention into this God of their own making, thus impoverishing themselves.

Bauer also believes that the great crisis of the day is to be found in the sphere of religion, but his focus is different from that of Feuerbach. For Bauer, the root cause of alienation is not the specific idea of a transcendent God on its own but rather the whole complex realm of organized religion and religious belief. For this reason Bauer's account is much more contextually oriented in the long history of religion than was the case with Feuerbach. Bauer targets specifically Christianity, which he holds responsible for the ills of the day. Following in the

[3] In Chapter 2, Section 2.8.

footsteps of the Enlightenment thinkers, Bauer believes that religion has produced great suffering through its intolerance, which has resulted in persecutions and wars. The terrible history of such things is not accidental but rather lies in the very nature of religious belief, which Bauer believes to be fundamentally intolerant. By making an absolute claim for its own truth, each religious group must condemn all the others. Moreover, Christianity undermines the development of the individual by forbidding people from using their intelligence and critical capacity to think for themselves. This discourages all scientific inquiry and stunts the growth of human beings in their very essence.

For Marx and Engels, the crisis of the age can clearly be seen in the economic sphere. The root cause of alienation is the capitalist economic system that alienates individuals from the objects of their labor, from each other, and from themselves and their basic human nature. The situation, they believe, has become acute with the Industrial Revolution and the increasing exploitation of the working class. These problems are entrenched in the capitalist system itself, which determines all of the spheres of society, including both religion and politics. Workers live in daily oppression because they are at the mercy of the owners of the means of production, who are completely indifferent to their suffering. This is not something that is accidental, with some owners simply being insensitive or unfeeling, but rather it lies in the nature of the system itself, which dictates that the owners maximize profits, an important part of which is minimizing production costs. A central part of this involves keeping the wages as low as possible, and there is no motivation for the owners to improve the working conditions of their employees.

For Kierkegaard, the crisis of the day is not in politics, economics, or culture; indeed, it is not to be found in the external sphere at all. Instead, it is a crisis that takes place in the inwardness of each individual. The cause of alienation is different forms of despair that divide the self. With his focus on the individual, Kierkegaard is thus known as an important philosophical psychologist. Toward the end of his life he saw a religious crisis in the way in which the Danish State Church in its teachings departed from what he regarded as the radicality of original Christianity. The Church had turned Christian belief into something obvious and taken for granted. Kierkegaard was at pains to point out how the early Christians were subjected to terrible persecution and sufferings of which the complacent clergy of his day knew nothing. This distortion of Christianity is a major issue for him in his later work and can be regarded as a crisis because it misleads many people. He explicitly highlights what he takes to be the absurd and contradictory nature of Christian faith in order to indicate to his contemporaries the rigors of belief.

Dostoevsky identifies a number of modern trends that lead to alienation and a sense of crisis. The rise of the natural sciences and new technological innovations have given people an unshaking belief in the laws of nature and the value of scientific research. With this evidence, people believe in the idea of historical progress and have an optimistic view of the future, with the naive idea that a utopian society is right around the next corner. Seduced by these trends, people believe that science holds the magic key to human happiness. But the modern scientific worldview reduces human beings to their physical aspect. It fails to take into account the irrational side of human nature that is tied to human freedom. Dostoevsky is concerned about the one-sided, reductionistic materialism of the modern worldview, which he believes can be an oppressive force. The modern scientific world is a godless one that opens the door to relativism and nihilism. While science presumptuously pretends to have all of the answers, it is utterly mute when it comes to questions of meaning. This is the cause of the modern crisis of values.

For Bakunin, the true source of alienation is primarily state power or indeed any form of external authority. Throughout history people have been prevented from developing their natural capacities since they have always been subject to some higher authority that dictated what they were supposed to do. There was always an argument that these higher authorities, such as the state or the Church, knew what was best and were acting in the interests of everyone. But Bakunin argues that power, by its very nature, has a corrupting influence, and those who possess it invariably act in their own self-interest at the expense of others. The problem does not lie in the specific power structure of the capitalist system, as Marx argues, but in any form of state power that imposes its will on individuals. Humans will never be free until they can shake off the shackles of this subjugation and oppression that come from all hierarchically organized forms of society.

## 11.2   The Proposed Solutions to the Crisis and Alienation

Just as the different thinkers of the period had very different diagnoses of the nature of the crisis of the age, so also they had different proposals for its solution. Heine's solution to the crisis of the age is political reform. He urges a spirit of rebellion against these forces of oppression and sees poetry as playing an important role in awakening people to this. Poetry can encourage people to see their common interests and pursue the cause of freedom. The struggle for freedom must continue until it is possible for people to fulfill the true human potential. Heine's goal was in part realized in the Revolution of 1848, which saw the overthrow of the reactionary forces that were set up after Napoleon's defeat.

Feuerbach's revolutionary message is that we must reject the idea of the divine as something separate and other; instead, we should try to recapture the lost energy and focus spent on this conception and return it to human beings. When we regain this, humans will have a radically different, positive conception of themselves and will be able to approach the real issues of the mundane world with new energy. The key to this is, of course, the realization that God is a projection, which Feuerbach's philosophy purports to demonstrate. Thus Feuerbach takes his work to have historical importance since he believes it will mark a radical change in the way people think about religion and themselves. By realizing that God is just a projection of human qualities, human beings will be infinitely raised in their own eyes. They will feel a new sense of autonomy and empowerment as they eliminate the feeling of separation and alienation.

The goal of Bauer's revolution is the overthrow of the hegemony of Christianity, which, he believes, is the only possible way for humanity to recover its natural freedom and develop its rationality. Since Christianity serves to buttress political power, undermining it will also lead to political reform. Only when the Church loses its power will religious wars and persecutions stop. At the end of *Christianity Exposed*, Bauer imagines a situation where Christianity has been defeated and a more enlightened and humane social order will appear. He raises the question about whether the leaders in this new world would permit the remaining Christians to continue in their erroneous worship. He suggests that they can be allowed to do so since they will only be hurting themselves and will no longer be a threat to others.[4]

With Marx and Engels, the solution to the problem of alienation is a political revolution. Only the complete abolishment of the system of capitalism can put an end to the suffering and injustices that they believe are so widespread. Any attempt to work on the problem by means of piecemeal reforms is misguided and doomed to failure. The problem lies not with some specific issue such as concrete wages or working conditions, but rather with the capitalist system as a whole, which by its very nature necessarily creates poverty, injustice, and suffering. Marx and Engels were thus both actively involved in the workers' movement and were constantly agitating for revolution.

For Kierkegaard, the cause of alienation is despair that divides the self. His solution to the problem is in a sense to help religious believers to actualize their own individual reforms. He would disdain the ideas of Marx or Bakunin about the importance of the political sphere and social reform. In fact, he regularly ridiculed Johan Ludvig Heiberg's urgent call to action to meet the demands of the times.[5] Kierkegaard takes this kind of talk to be pretentious in the sense

---

[4] Bruno Bauer, *Das entdeckte Christenthum. Eine Erinnerung an das 18. Jahrhundert und ein Beitrag zur Krisis des 19.* (Zürich and Winterthur: Verlag des literarischen Comptoirs, 1843), p. 119. (English translation: *An English Edition of Bruno Bauer's 1843 Christianity Exposed: A Recollection of the Eighteenth Century and a Contribution to the Crisis of the Nineteenth Century*, ed. by Paul Trejo, trans. by Esther Ziegler and Jutta Hamm [Lewiston, NY: Edwin Mellon Press, 2002] [*Studies in German Thought and History*, vol. 23], p. 117.)

[5] See Jon Stewart, *The Cultural Crisis of the Danish Golden Age: Heiberg, Martensen and Kierkegaard* (Copenhagen: Museum Tusculanum Press, 2015) (*Danish Golden Age Studies*, vol. 9), p. 28, pp. 51–53, p. 74, pp. 114–115, p. 210, p. 257; *Heiberg's Introductory Lecture to the Logic Course and Other Texts*, ed. and trans. by Jon Stewart, Copenhagen: C. A. Reitzel 2007 (*Texts from Golden Age Denmark*, vol. 3), pp. 168–170.

that one ascribes to oneself the knowledge of what the age needs and then takes it upon oneself to work toward it. For Kierkegaard, the more important struggle is the inward one that takes place in each and every individual. Political causes and parties will come and go, but they will never have more than a limited, finite importance. By contrast, one's religious disposition and relation to God is both unique and infinite. This should be something that each individual has as their highest interest. Kierkegaard does not presume to tell his readers what they should do or to dictate some plan of action for their inward religious reform. His works are rather designed to motivate his readers to think and to do this on their own. He further believes that there is ultimately no solution to the problem of alienation and despair, which is simply a part of our modern condition. Christian faith will always by its very nature be a difficult struggle.

For Dostoevsky the solution to the crisis of nihilism caused by modern scientific rationalism and materialism is a return to our basic moral instincts. Our natural moral conscience is a good guide if we can prevent it from being distorted by modern ideological tendencies of thought. A part of this means a return to Christianity. While it is no easy task to accept the full burden of human freedom as Jesus demanded, this is what is required. We should resist the simplistic solutions offered to us by modern social and political programs that prescribe different ways in which we can achieve happiness if only we surrender our freedom. Like Kierkegaard, Dostoevsky believes that the way forward is not an easy one; indeed, it involves a constant struggle. But it is infinitely better than the seductive solutions that would deprive us of our freedom and ultimately destroy our very humanity.

For Bakunin, the solution to the problem of the age is quite simple: It is necessary to eliminate the different forms of state power. Like Marx and Engels, he too advocates revolutionary change. It lies in the nature of human beings to rebel; indeed, in order to become fully human and to actualize our freedom, we must do so. Only when we take responsibility for ourselves and throw off the yoke of external oppression can we be said to realize fully our human capacity. This also means rejecting the pressure exerted on us by our family, culture, and society to follow tradition and custom. We must stage our own individual rebellion and insist on making our own decisions. Also like Marx and Engels, Bakunin spent most of his life as a political agitator working for these goals and advocating anarchy.

## 11.3   The Nature and Task of Philosophy

In the different responses to the fundamental problem of alienation and the perceived crisis of the age, we can discern implicitly an ongoing debate about the very nature and task of philosophy. On this topic it is possible to see a general dissatisfaction with Hegel and a desire to move beyond him. The new generation of thinkers was concerned not just with abstract concepts but with philosophy's actual relation to the world. As a result they developed different views of the mission of philosophy that were all in some way praxis-oriented. The issue of alienation provided a perfect vehicle for them to develop their theories since the feeling of alienation is something that comes from our immediate experience with the world.

Hegel's view of the office of philosophy is primarily one of understanding. The goal is to grasp the world in all of its complexity. In the *Science of Logic* and the *Encyclopedia of the Philosophical Sciences*, he develops an elaborate theory of categories that he takes to be the basic structure of both thought and the world. But little is said about the use to which this understanding can be put. As we have seen, at the end of his *Lectures on the Philosophy of Religion*, Hegel explicitly uses the metaphor of a cloister, where philosophers, distanced from the mundane concerns of the world, can dedicate themselves to the task of learning and understanding.[6] For Hegel, philosophers are different from politicians, sociologists, or social workers, and it is a mistake to think of them as great reformers. Such attempts rarely end well. Philosophy is the search for knowledge for its own sake, and this is the task to which Hegel dedicates himself. Philosophy can help us to diagnose and understand the crisis of the day, but it is up to others to do something about it.

For Heine, the task of philosophy was also something primarily practical. Together with poetry and literature, it could help to lead the way to political reform and the general advancement of human freedom. While the earlier revolution of thought in German philosophy was important, the more important event will be when this philosophical thinking turns into a real political revolution. Heine seems to recognize the importance of philosophical thinking on its own terms, but he also thinks that its full force can only be felt when it breaks away from thought and is transformed into a force of reform in the world. It is, of course, important that philosophers can debate the nature of human freedom, but the goal should be to realize this in the real world in one's own life.

Feuerbach was quick to criticize Hegel for sterile abstraction and insisted that his own view was one of hard-headed materialism. His conception of the goal of philosophy is also practical on some level, although he is vague about the specific details. He clearly believes that philosophical ideas can have a radical effect on people and that changing ways of thinking is profoundly important. He seems to believe that disabusing people of the mistaken idea of a transcendent God will be enough to start a revolution. But Marx criticizes him on this point. For however important this insight might be, it remains empty if there is no corresponding change in the actual material conditions of people. Feuerbach has nothing to say about work conditions, labor practices,

---

[6] In Chapter 2, Section 2.8.

or other such concrete issues that are formative for life in the real world. Thus Marx claims that Feuerbach falls victim to abstraction in the sense that he takes people out of their actual context and regards them merely from the perspective of thinking beings who have erroneous beliefs about the nature of God. So while Feuerbach sees the nature of philosophy as also being in part practical and having the potential to lead to reform, it is not clear exactly how he conceives of this or how deep such a reform can really go if, in the end, it is just about disabusing people of their mistaken religious ideas.

Bauer's conception of the goal of philosophy also seems to contain both a theoretical and a practical element. He is concerned with real reform in the world, so it is not just about changing people's minds about a specific theological point. Rather it is about the much more urgent issue of putting a stop to intolerance and the forms of oppression that come with organized religion and its belief system. But with this said, Bauer was not a political activist in the way that Marx, Engels, and Bakunin were. In his later life he remained above all a scholar, interested primarily in the origins of Christian thinking. He too was criticized by Marx and Engels for abstraction and quietism. Bauer presumably believed that his program of criticism was important in undermining the repressive forces of the day and leading to liberation. But Marx and Engels saw this rather as simply a descent into endless arid philosophical discussions that had nothing to do with the problems of the real world.

Marx offers a clear statement about the nature and goal of philosophy. As we have seen in his eleventh thesis on Feuerbach,[7] he rebukes the philosophers of the past, presumably Hegel among them, for confining themselves to merely understanding the world. The goal, he claims, is to change the world. Perhaps more than any of the other thinkers explored here, he takes the practical element to be a central point in the philosophical enterprise itself. He has contempt for any philosophy from which no clear practical consequences follow. He is especially critical of what he regards as self-indulgent abstraction. It would not be unfair to say that Marx in a sense politicizes philosophy. He regards the classical German idealists, including Hegel, as bourgeois philosophers who are beholden to the larger capitalist system that employs them at universities, a fact which compromises their work. They are products of bourgeois culture and thus invariably reflect the class interests of those who enjoy the privileges in this system. Schelling's appointment to the University of Berlin by the King of Prussia was a clear demonstration of how classical German philosophy had sold out to the reactionary forces of the Restoration.[8] For Marx, true philosophers are reflective enough to think for themselves and thus are not ideologues for an oppressive system.

---

[7] See Chapter 6, Section 6.6.
[8] See Chapter 3, Section 3.2.

Kierkegaard joins the chorus of criticism against Hegel's philosophy for abstraction. However, he rejects the label of philosopher for himself, and this tells us something about both his conception of philosophy and his view of his own project.[9] To his mind the awakening of the inward religious awareness of the individual reader has nothing whatsoever to do with philosophy. Compared to this, the task of philosophy is completely irrelevant and even trivial. Thus Kierkegaard denies the idea that philosophy can play any important role in what really matters. For however interesting or insightful it might be on different topics, philosophy by its very nature as objective knowing is not suited to treat the most important issue of the religious faith of the individual. With this said, however, Kierkegaard distinguishes between the ancient philosopher and the modern German philosopher.[10] While he characterizes the latter as lost in meaningless abstractions, the former is engaged with the important existential issues of life. Kierkegaard emulates Socrates as a model in this regard.[11] In this sense he can perhaps be seen as trying to revive a certain conception of ancient philosophy that he believes is completely antithetical to the then current practice of the field.

Dostoevsky presumably did not regard himself as a philosopher and was thus probably less invested in the issue of the nature of philosophy than some of the other thinkers examined here. However, it should be noted that under the reactionary and repressive political regime of Russia in the nineteenth century, where philosophy was for long periods forbidden at universities and philosophers were persecuted, it was natural for many thinkers with philosophical proclivities to turn to literature as their forum for expression. While literary works were also regularly banned, it was nonetheless easier to conceal radical and seditious views in this genre. Dostoevsky is concerned with key issues in the fields of religion, psychology, and social-political thinking. His work can be understood as social criticism, which clearly has some practical implications even if it is not a fully worked-out political platform. However, we should not forget that his social-political views were important enough to the authorities to earn him several years in prison and to subject him to police surveillance.

Bakunin himself is usually regarded more as a political thinker and activist than as a philosopher per se. However, we have seen that he clearly also had developed views in the areas of philosophy of religion and philosophical psychology. His work has very much the same urgent tone of that of Marx, and he seems primarily oriented to the cause of revolutionary social and

---

[9] See Jon Stewart, *Kierkegaard's Relations to Hegel Reconsidered* (New York: Cambridge University Press, 2003), pp. 632–650.

[10] Stewart, *Kierkegaard's Relations to Hegel Reconsidered*, pp. 641–645.

[11] See Jon Stewart, *Søren Kierkegaard: Subjectivity, Irony and the Crisis of Modernity* (Oxford: Oxford University Press, 2015).

political change. Despite his early enthusiasm for Hegel, he thinks that Hegel's philosophy did not go far enough and dwelled in abstractions, remaining "alien to earthy life and reality."[12] He expresses astonishment that some of Hegel's students ended with conservative views and supported "the inhumane and illiberal measures" prescribed by the Prussian government and those of the other German-speaking states.[13] However, Bakunin acknowledges that Hegel, to his credit, inspired a group of revolutionary thinkers who tried to apply his principles in the service of progressive social change. Thus Bakunin sees the true philosophical enterprise as something where theory and practice go hand in hand.

Engels is critical of academic philosophy in his own day, which he claims is dominated by careerism and bourgeois values. Nothing new or interesting can be expected to come from this. In his *Ludwig Feuerbach and the Outcome of Classical German Philosophy*, he suggests that the true philosophers of his own time can be found not at the university but rather among the class of workers.[14] Despite the fact that they have less formal training than academic philosophers, the workers are better thinkers since they are free from the ideology and vested interests of the status quo. Such thinkers are in a better position to see the ills of modern society and work for constructive changes to ameliorate them. Engels thus still has faith in philosophy as a discipline, but he thinks that universities have abandoned it because they are controlled by conservative forces that cannot allow true freedom of thought. Like Marx, he clearly sees the key mission of philosophy as intimately connected to social-political reform.

Given all of this, it seems clear that as philosophical thinking developed in the course of the nineteenth century, so also did the very conception of what philosophy is and should be. The present study has also shown that the most interesting and influential works in philosophy of the nineteenth century came, generally speaking, from people who were not university professors. Hegel also had a number of students and followers, such as Rosenkranz, Erdmann, Marheineke, and Cousin, who had great careers at the university. But ultimately they never exercised the same long-term influence as the radicals, who were excluded from university life. Apart from Hegel, none of the thinkers discussed here was a university philosopher. Some of the leading figures of the age were fired from their positions at the university (Strauss, Feuerbach, Bauer), and others were prevented from pursuing a university

---

[12] Mikhail Bakunin, *Statism and Anarchy*, trans. by Marshall S. Shatz (Cambridge: Cambridge University Press, 2005), p. 131.

[13] Bakunin, *Statism and Anarchy*.

[14] Friedrich Engels, "Ludwig Feuerbach und der Ausgang der klassischen deutschen Philosophie," in *Marx-Engels-Werke*, vols. 1–46, ed. by the Institut für Marxismus-Leninismus (Berlin: Dietz, 1956–2018), vol. 21, p. 307. (English translation: *Ludwig Feuerbach and the Outcome of Classical German Philosophy*, ed. by C. P. Dutt [New York: International Publishers, 1941], pp. 60f.). See Chapter 10, Section 10.7.

career (Heine, Marx, Bakunin). Engels' ridicule of the philosophy that was presented at the universities in his day seems at least in part justified. It might be added that Engels was not alone in his critique, and Schopenhauer had railed against the evils of university philosophy as well.[15]

The discussion about the nature of philosophy continued into the twentieth century and our own day. When we think about the vast heterogenous world of modern academic philosophy, these debates can serve as useful guides. Today we are long since used to hearing doctrinaire arguments from professors of philosophy who claim that what they are doing is true philosophy, whereas what their colleagues are doing is charlatanry. The conflict between analytic philosophy and Continental philosophy is full of acrimonious exchanges of this kind.[16] The discussions about this issue in the nineteenth century show that the nature of philosophy was always something in flux. They remind us that occasionally it is good to ask the question of whether our professional world of philosophy is conducive to genuine philosophical thought or instead stands in the way of it.[17]

## 11.4   The Transition to the Twentieth Century

When we look at the development of the many different directions of philosophy in the twentieth century, it is clear that Hegel's thought has in many ways had a formative influence. This can be seen perhaps most obviously when we examine how the concepts of alienation and recognition were taken up by later thinkers and used in new contexts. It is often thought that the school of existentialism marked an important break from Hegel and that Husserl's phenomenology struck out in a new direction having, despite the name, little to do with *The Phenomenology of Spirit*. Both of these key movements in Continental philosophy rejected what they regarded as the abstraction of pure conceptual analysis and tried to pioneer new approaches that would return philosophy to the lived experience. While there are, of course, important differences between these traditions and Hegel's philosophy, there are once again also equally important continuities, especially when we look at the key issues traced in this study.[18] We should take our cue from Merleau-Ponty, who

---

[15] See Jon Stewart, "Schopenhauer's Charge and Modern Academic Philosophy: Some Problems Facing Philosophical Pedagogy," *Metaphilosophy*, 26(3) (1995), 270–278.

[16] See Richard Rorty's insightful analysis, "Philosophy in America Today," in his *Consequences of Pragmatism* (Minneapolis: University of Minnesota Press, 1982), pp. 211–230, especially pp. 223–227.

[17] See Jon Stewart, *The Unity of Content and Form in Philosophical Writing: The Perils of Conformity* (London, New Delhi, New York, and Sydney: Bloomsbury, 2013).

[18] Many of these continuities are traced in the articles in the new collection: Jon Stewart (ed.), *The Palgrave Handbook of German Idealism and Existentialism* (Basingstoke and New York: Palgrave Macmillan, 2020).

openly recognized Hegel's contribution to existentialism and phenomenology in an article dedicated specifically to this topic.[19]

It is well known that Alexandre Kojève's lectures on Hegel in the 1930s played a formative role in the education of the French existentialists. While purportedly a general introduction to Hegel, these lectures in fact focused on a very specific part of Hegel's corpus, namely the lordship and bondage dialectic from *The Phenomenology of Spirit*.[20] It was from this single section that Kojève interpreted the rest of Hegel's thought. Inspired by this, the existentialists developed theories of self-consciousness and intersubjectivity that were in many ways based on Hegel's analysis.

Perhaps most obviously, Sartre's famous analysis of the look of the other in *Being and Nothingness* is clearly modeled on Hegel's account of the master and slave.[21] His thesis that social relations all reduce to sadism or masochism also finds its beginning here.[22] The concept of recognition can be found in Simone de Beauvoir's works such as *The Second Sex* and *The Ethics of Ambiguity*, where she applies it to an analysis of the nature of sex discrimination with explicit reference to the lordship and bondage dialectic.[23] Albert Camus also makes use of Hegel's account of the struggle for recognition in *The Rebel*, where he casts the modern rebel in the role of the slave revolting against his master.[24] More critical than Sartre or de Beauvoir, Camus sees in Hegel's analysis a potentially dangerous view of history that can be used to justify political oppression. However, Camus acknowledges the need for mutual recognition as a necessary element in the development of the individual. Paul Ricoeur made a detailed study of the concept of recognition, in which Hegel plays a central role.[25] Ricoeur's goal is, among other things, to tease out the many different

[19] Maurice Merleau-Ponty, "Hegel's Existentialism," in *Sense and Non-Sense*, trans. by Hubert Dreyfus and Patricia Allen Dreyfus (Evanston: Northwestern University Press, 1964), pp. 63–70.

[20] These lectures were later published as Alexandre Kojève, *Introduction à la lecture de Hegel. Leçons sur la Phénoménologie de l'esprit professées de 1933 à 1939 à l'École des Hautes Études*, ed. by Raymond Queneau (Paris: Gallimard, 1947). (English translation: *Introduction to the Reading of Hegel: Lectures on the Phenomenology of Spirit*, trans. by Allan Bloom [Ithaca: Cornell University Press, 1980].)

[21] Jean-Paul Sartre, "The Look," in his *Being and Nothingness: An Essay on Phenomenological Ontology*, trans. by Hazel E. Barnes (New York: Philosophical Library, 1956), pp. 252–302.

[22] Sartre, "Concrete Relations with Others," in *Being and Nothingness*, pp. 361–430.

[23] Simone de Beauvoir, *The Second Sex*, trans. by H. M. Parshley (New York: Random House, 1952), p. 73, p. 279; Simone de Beauvoir, *The Ethics of Ambiguity*, trans. by Bernard Frechtman (New York: Citadel Press, 1948), p. 62, p. 70, pp. 104f.

[24] See Thomas P. Miles, "The Ethics of Resistance: Camus' Encounter with German Idealism," in Jon Stewart (ed.), *The Palgrave Handbook of German Idealism and Existentialism* (Basingstoke and New York: Palgrave Macmillan, 2020), pp. 439–472.

[25] Paul Ricoeur, *The Course of Recognition*, trans. by David Pellauer (Cambridge, MA: Harvard University Press, 2005); see, for example, pp. 171–186.

meanings of the term and in this way demonstrate the broad impact that it had on philosophy and other fields in the twentieth century.

Although Hegel's concept of recognition was not used explicitly by Freud, it has been subsequently taken up in the field of psychology in the psychoanalytic tradition.[26] Also under the influence of Kojève's lectures, Jacques Lacan made use of the concept in his theory of childhood development. It was also appropriated by Jessica Benjamin in the context of a feminist theory of intersubjectivity.[27] Martin Altmeyer has tried to apply the idea to an understanding of narcissism, claiming that the lack of recognition at an early stage can lead to narcissistic behavior.[28] Melanie Klein makes use of the concept of recognition, albeit with a modified meaning, namely as the acknowledgment of some uncomfortable truth about the world in spite of attempts to repress it.[29] Recognition thus means the opposite of defense mechanisms such as repression or denial. D. W. Winnicott also makes use of the concept of recognition in the context of a theory of childhood development. Specifically, it is understood as the child's cognitive and emotional awareness of the fact that the mother is an entity in her own right, separate from itself.[30]

The concept of recognition took on new importance as the key terms from the lordship and bondage analysis were extended to questions of class, race, and gender. While recognition is regarded as essential for self-development and social life, misrecognition can undermine one's sense of self-esteem and erode social relations. Following in the footsteps of de Beauvoir and Jessica Benjamin, several feminist writers, such as Nancy Fraser, Seyla Benhabib, and Judith Butler, have used the concept of recognition in their theories of intersubjectivity and communication.[31]

---

[26] See Andreas Wildt, "'Recognition' in Psychoanalysis," in Hans-Christoph Schmidt am Busch and Christopher F. Zurn (eds.), *The Philosophy of Recognition: Historical and Contemporary Perspectives* (Lanham: Rowman and Littlefield, 2010), pp. 189–209.

[27] Jessica Benjamin, *The Bonds of Love: Psychoanalysis, Feminism, and the Problem of Domination* (New York: Pantheon, 1988); Jessica Benjamin, *Like Subjects, Love Objects: Essays on Recognition and Sexual Difference* (New Haven: Yale University Press, 1995); Jessica Benjamin, *Shadow of the Other: Intersubjectivity and Gender in Psychoanalysis* (New York and London: Routledge, 1998; Jessica Benjamin, *Beyond Doer and Done To: Recognition Theory, Intersubjectivity and the Third* (New York and London: Routledge, 2018).

[28] Martin Altmeyer, *Narzissmus und Objekt. Ein intersubjektives Verständnis der Selbstbezogenheit* (Gießen: Vandenhoeck & Ruprecht, 2000); Martin Altmeyer, "Narzissmus, Intersubjektivität und Anerkennung," *Psyche*, 54(2) (2000), 143–171; Martin Altmeyer, *Im Spiegel des Anderen. Anwendungen einer relationalen Psychoanalyse* (Gießen: Vandenhoeck & Ruprecht, 2003).

[29] See Wildt, "'Recognition' in Psychoanalysis," pp. 191–195.

[30] D. W. Winnicott, "The Use of an Object and Relating through Identifications," in his *Playing and Reality* (London and New York: Routledge, 2005), p. 120.

[31] Nancy Fraser, "Social Justice in the Age of Identity Politics: Redistribution, Recognition, and Participation," in Nancy Fraser and Axel Honneth, *Redistribution or Recognition?*

Hegel's account of recognition was also important for the tradition of Critical Theory. Jürgen Habermas sees the struggle for recognition in terms of an emancipation from oppressive institutions in the social sphere.[32] In a key chapter in *Theory and Practice*, Habermas ascribes to Hegel an implicit theory of communicative action, which implies a notion of mutual recognition of established norms observed by different speakers.[33] Continuing the Critical Theory tradition, Axel Honneth has developed in great detail a theory of recognition in terms of relations of love, respect, and esteem.[34] He then uses this more broadly as the key concept in the social sphere, governing our relation not just to other individuals but also to institutions. The theory of recognition has also been important in Anglophone philosophy in the work of Charles Taylor and Robert B. Pippin in the context of social-political theory.[35] It can be said that this tradition beginning with Habermas truly established Hegel as a thinker of recognition in a way that was even more explicit and overt than his nineteenth-century reception.

The concept of alienation was also developed and expanded by thinkers in the twentieth century. Inspired again by Hegel's lordship and bondage dialectic, the existentialists were keen to pick up on this concept. They are known for their perceptive analyses of this, which they applied to the malaise of modern life. Heidegger discusses alienation explicitly in *Being and Time*, where he introduces the terms authenticity and inauthenticity to capture the distinction between, on the one hand, a person who is reflective about their existence in the world and critical of inherited values and norms and, on the other, one who is unreflective and conformist. The authentic person takes responsibility for themselves and their own mortality, whereas the inauthentic person does not. For Heidegger, alienation refers to the latter, that is, when the individual is separated from an authentic existence.

*A Political-Philosophical Exchange* (New York: Verso, 2003), pp. 7–109; Seyla Benhabib, *Situating the Self: Gender, Community, and Postmodernism in Contemporary Ethics* (New York: Routledge, 1992); Judith Butler, *The Psychic Life of Power: Theories in Subjection* (Stanford: Stanford University Press, 1997).

32  Jürgen Habermas, "Struggles for Recognition in the Democratic Constitutional State," in Amy Gutmann (ed.), *Multiculturalism: Examining the Politics of Recognition* (Princeton: Princeton University Press, 1994), pp. 107–148.

33  Jürgen Habermas, *Theory and Practice*, trans. by John Viertel (Boston: Beacon Press, 1973), pp. 147–149, p. 157, p. 161.

34  Axel Honneth, *The Struggle for Recognition: The Moral Grammar of Social Conflicts*, trans. by Joel Anderson (Cambridge: Polity Press, 1995); Axel Honneth, *The I in We: Studies in the Theory of Recognition*, trans. by Joseph Ganahl (Cambridge, UK; Malden, MA: Polity Press, 2012).

35  Charles Taylor, "The Politics of Recognition," in Gutmann (ed.), *Multiculturalism: Examining the Politics of Recognition*, pp. 25–73; Robert B. Pippin, *Hegel's Practical Philosophy: Rational Agency as Ethical Life* (Cambridge: Cambridge University Press, 2008), especially pp. 183–238.

The French existentialists draw on this concept from Hegel and Heidegger. Sartre's psychological drama *No Exit* explores the different relations of the master and the slave, and his novel *Nausea* portrays the travails of the protagonist Antoine Roquentin, who experiences an inexplicable sense of estrangement from others and the world itself. Sartre's account of the look of the other in *Being and Nothingness* is also intended to illustrate what he regards as the fundamental sense of alienation from other people: The other reduces me to an object, my body, and separates me from my freedom. Sartre also discusses the idea of alienation in a Marxist context in his *Critique of Dialectical Reason*. Camus' psychological novel *The Stranger* is likewise an exploration of modern alienation. His Meursault has been taken as a case study of a person alienated from society. These existentialist characters feel separated from bourgeois life and values. They are alone and isolated in their search for meaning.

Paul Tillich makes use of alienation in his *Systematic Theology*, where he understands it as a separation of the individual's existence from their true essence. This is, according to Tillich, a fundamental fact of the human condition. He understands this in theological terms, regarding the mission of Jesus as helping us to overcome our alienation and become who we truly are. Tillich's sense of alienation is different from the other existentialists because he operated with an essentialist view of a fixed human nature from which it is possible to be alienated.

In the twentieth century the concept of alienation spread from philosophy to the social sciences, as those fields grew from the turn of the century. In the field of psychology, it was employed extensively by Erich Fromm in his works *Escape from Freedom*, *The Sane Society*, and *Beyond the Chains of Illusion*. Fromm draws explicitly on the use of the term in the Hegelian-Marxist tradition and expands upon it. He explores in detail different forms of alienation from the world, from others, and from oneself. In the psychoanalytic tradition Karen Horney has been perhaps the most influential in her use of the concept of alienation. In her works *New Ways of Psychoanalysis*, *Our Inner Conflicts*, and *Neurosis and Human Growth*, she examines the phenomenon of self-estrangement in the sense of not being prevented from actualizing one's immediate, spontaneous self. This can lead to a sense of being unaware of one's own feelings and beliefs.

While the psychologists focus on different forms of self-alienation, the sociologists understand alienation as a social phenomenon and examine variants of it in the context of different elements or developments of modern society, such as urbanization, globalization, and secularization. They focus on the growing sense of powerlessness and meaninglessness in the face of institutions and social conditions of the modern world that can strike the individual as oppressive. People thus come to perceive the world as something foreign and even hostile or pernicious. At the turn of the century, German sociologist Georg Simmel, in the final chapter of his work *The Philosophy of Money*, developed a theory of alienation based on the results of the increased division of labor. Inspired by Marx, Simmel argues that this leads to an increased number of objects in the world that appear to the individual as foreign or alien. Alienation then represents the ever-widening split between the subject and the object spheres.

In his *Community and Society*, Ferdinand Tönnies developed a theory of alienation, which moved the context of the concept from the economic sphere to that of social relations. He traced the loss of meaning of basic family relations that increasingly gave way to relations in the social sphere dominated by a capitalist work environment. Emile Durkheim, in his study on suicide, discussed social alienation in connection with his analysis of anomie. He describes the fragmentation of society that results from the collapse of traditional norms and values, and which leaves individuals with few links to the broader community. This results in a sense of disorientation and uncertainty with regard to one's social identity. In *White Collar*, a landmark study of the middle class, American sociologist C. Wright Mills explores the concept of social alienation. He argues that capitalism requires a set of skills for marketing and selling products that leads to alienation because individuals feign friendship and concern while they covertly attempt to manipulate each other to their advantage in the marketplace. The concept has been used by Talcott Parsons, who, in his work *The Social System*, takes the concept from its original Marxist context and generalizes it to a theory of human existence as a whole. He claims that there is a dialectical relationship between conformity and alienation that is always present in systems of interaction.

Alienation also plays a role in the work of some of the leading thinkers of Critical Theory. Indeed, Axel Honneth claims, "No concept has been more powerful in defining the character of early Critical Theory than that of alienation."[36] This is unsurprising since the Frankfurt School very self-consciously sees itself as working in the Marxist tradition. In the *Dialectic of Enlightenment*, Max Horkheimer and Theodor Adorno identify the ideals of the Enlightenment as the cause of modern alienation. The goal of the Enlightenment was to purge humanity of superstition and irrationality and to found society on reason. The result of this was, alas, the Holocaust, Stalin's mass killings, and the many other horrors of the twentieth century. The idea of alienation is expanded from being something primarily located in the economic sphere, as with Marx, to being a part of modern mass movements, involving mass communication and forces of political oppression.

Herbert Marcuse began his lifelong study of alienation with his dissertation *The German Artist-Novel*, where he interprets the modern novel as a symptom

---

[36] Axel Honneth, "Foreword," in Rahel Jaeggi, *Alienation*, trans. by Frederick Neuhouser and Alan E. Smith (New York: Columbia University Press, 2014), p. vii.

of alienation in contrast to epic poetry.[37] He portrays the artist as a potentially revolutionary figure with the ability to effect social change and overcome alienation. He also made a careful study of Marx's "Economic and Philosophic Manuscripts" from 1844 when they were first published in 1932. In a review of the new publication, he explicitly acknowledges the importance of Marx's theory of alienation as examined in that work.[38] Then he discusses the concept in his study of Hegel, *Reason and Revolution*, from 1941. Although alienation is not the key concept of the work, he notes the origin of the term in Hegel's thought and its use by Marx in the context of labor relations. He then expands on this and uses the concept in his analysis of the modern condition in his *One-Dimensional Man* from 1964, where he discusses the notion of artistic alienation, which is a rejection of capitalism and bourgeois values from the perspective of a higher level of culture in the form of literature and art.

Habermas gives a critical analysis of alienation in Marx in the second volume of his *Theory of Communicative Action*.[39] He claims that the model that Marx used was too narrow since it focused exclusively on labor relations and excluded a number of other spheres. The Marxist account of alienation is not nuanced enough to capture adequately the complex reality of modern life. Habermas' theory of communicative action can be seen as an attempt to find a way to overcome modern forms of alienation in different contexts. More recently, Rahel Jaeggi has taken up the concept of alienation and attempted to revise it in the service of a critical theory leading to individual emancipation.[40] She argues that theories of alienation implicitly presuppose a fixed human nature and thereby a fixed conception of the good life. She thus attempts to construct a view of alienation that is not dependent on these dubious premises.

This overview is, of course, only a cursory sketch and much more would need to be done to fill out the picture, but it should suffice to demonstrate how the key philosophical concepts from the nineteenth century spilled over into the philosophical debates in the twentieth century, where they were expanded upon and used in a wider range of contexts and fields. These later discussions demonstrate the enduring legacy of Hegel and the tradition that

---

[37] The Introduction to this work can be found in *Art and Liberation*, vol. 4 of *Collected Papers of Herbert Marcuse*, ed. by Douglas Kellner (London and New York: Routledge, 2017), pp. 71–81.

[38] Herbert Marcuse, "New Sources on the Foundation of Historical Materialism," in his *Heideggerian Marxism*, ed. by Richard Wolin and John Abromeit (Lincoln and London: University of Nebraska Press, 2005), pp. 86–121.

[39] Jürgen Habermas, *The Theory of Communicative Action*, vol. 2, *Lifeworld and System: A Critique of Functionalist Reason*, trans. by Thomas McCarthy (Boston: Beacon Press, 1987), pp. 340–342, pp. 349–351.

[40] Jaeggi, *Alienation*.

he inspired. The talented group of thinkers who sat in his classroom and who came to Berlin after his death to study with his students were electrified by the ideas that they heard. They continued to be exercised by these ideas long afterwards as they developed their own theories. These same ideas continue to be a rich source of philosophical inspiration in our day.

# BIBLIOGRAPHY

## Primary Literature

Bakunin, Mikhail [Jules Elysard], "Die Reaction in Deutschland. Ein Fragment von einem Franzosen." *Deutsche Jahrbücher für Wissenschaft und Kunst,* ed. by Arnold Ruge, October 17–21, 1842, nos. 247–251, pp. 985–987, pp. 989–991, pp. 993–995, pp. 997–999, pp. 1001–1002. (English translation: "The Reaction in Germany: A Fragment from a Frenchman," in *Michael Bakunin: Selected Writings,* ed. by Arthur Lehning. London: Jonathan Cape, 1973, pp. 37–58.)

Bakunin, Mikhail [Michel Bakounine], *Dieu et l'État,* trans. by Carlo Cafiero and Élisée Reclus. Geneva: Imprimerie Jurasienne, 1882. (Reprint: *Dieu et l'État.* [No place of publication given]: L'Altiplano, 2008.) (English translation: *God and the State,* ed. by Paul Avrich. New York: Dover, 1970.)

Bakunin, Mikhail [Michel Bakounine], "Dieu et l'État (extrait du manuscrit inédit)." In *Oeuvres,* vols. 1–6, ed. by Max Nettlau (vol. 1) and James Guillaume (vols. 2–6). Paris: P. V. Stock, 1895–1913, vol. 1, pp. 264–320. (Partial English translation: "Man, Society and Freedom," in Sam Dolgoff [ed. and trans.], *Bakunin on Anarchy.* New York: Random House, 1971, pp. 234–242.)

Bakunin, Mikhail [Michel Bakounine], *Oeuvres,* vols. 1–6, ed. by Max Nettlau (vol. 1) and James Guillaume (vols. 2–6). Paris: P. V. Stock, 1895–1913.

Bakunin, Mikhail, *Statism and Anarchy,* trans. by Marshall S. Shatz. Cambridge: Cambridge University Press, 2005.

Bauer, Bruno, ed., *Allgemeine Literatur-Zeitung. Monatsschrift,* 1 (1843), 2–12 (1844). (The journal is reprinted [with no author listed] as *Streit der Kritik mit den modernen Gegensätzen.* Charlottenburg: Verlag von E. Bauer, 1847.)

[Bauer, Bruno], *Briefwechsel zwischen Bruno und Edgar Bauer während der Jahre 1838–1842 aus Bonn und Berlin.* Charlottenburg: Verlag von Egbert Bauer, 1944.

Bauer, Bruno, *Christus und die Cäsaren. Der Ursprung des Christentums aus dem römischen Griechentum.* Berlin: Eugen Grosser, 1877. (English translation: *Christ and the Caesars: The Origin of Christianity from Romanized Greek Culture,* trans. by Frank E. Schacht. Charleston, SC: Charleston House Publishing, 1998.)

Bauer, Bruno, *Das entdeckte Christenthum. Eine Erinnerung an das 18. Jahrhundert und ein Beitrag zur Krisis des 19.* Zürich and Winterthur: Verlag des literarischen Comptoirs, 1843. (Reprint: *Das entdeckte Christentum im Vormärz. Bruno Bauers Kampf gegen Religion und Christentum und Erstausgabe seiner Kampfschrift*, ed. by Ernst Barnikol. Jena: Eugen Diederichs, 1927.) (English translation: *An English Edition of Bruno Bauer's 1843 Christianity Exposed: A Recollection of the Eighteenth Century and a Contribution to the Crisis of the Nineteenth Century*, ed. by Paul Trejo, trans. by Esther Ziegler and Jutta Hamm. Lewiston, NY: Edwin Mellon Press, 2002 [*Studies in German Thought and History*, vol. 23].)

Bauer, Bruno, *Das Urevangelium und die Gegner der Schrift: "Christus und die Caesaren".* Berlin: Eugen Grosser, 1880.

Bauer, Bruno, *Der Untergang des Frankfurter Parlaments. Geschichte der deutschen constituirenden Nationalversammlung.* Berlin: Friedrich Gerhard, 1849.

Bauer, Bruno, *Die bürgerliche Revolution in Deutschland seit dem Anfang der deutsch-katholischen Bewegung bis zur Gegenwart.* Berlin: Gustav Hempel, 1849.

Bauer, Bruno, *Die gute Sache der Freiheit und meine eigene Angelegenheit.* Zürich and Winterthur: Verlag des literarischen Comptoirs, 1842.

Bauer, Bruno, *Die Posaune des jüngsten Gerichts über Hegel den Atheisten und Antichristen. Ein Ultimatum.* Leipzig: Otto Wigand, 1841. (English translation: *The Trumpet of the Last Judgement against Hegel the Atheist and Antichrist: An Ultimatum*, trans. by Laurence Stepelevich. Lewiston, NY: Edwin Mellon Press, 1989.)

Bauer, Bruno, *Disraelis romantischer und Bismarcks socialistischer Imperialismus.* Chemnitz: Schmeitzner, 1882.

Bauer, Bruno, *Geschichte der Politik, Kultur und Aufklärung des 18ten Jahrhunderts*, vols. 1–2. Charlottenburg: Verlag von Egbert Bauer, 1843–1845.

Bauer, Bruno, *Hegels Lehre von der Religion und Kunst von dem Standpuncte des Glaubens aus beurtheilt.* Leipzig: Otto Wigand, 1842.

Bauer, Bruno, *Herr Dr. Hengstenberg. Kritische Briefe über den Gegensatz des Gesetzes und des Evangelium.* Berlin: Ferdinand Dümmler, 1839.

Bauer, Bruno, *Kritik der Evangelien und Geschichte ihres Ursprungs*, vols. 1–4. Berlin: Gustav Hempel, 1850–1852.

Bauer, Bruno, *Kritik der evangelischen Geschichte der Synoptiker*, vols. 1–3. Leipzig: Otto Wigand, 1841–1842.

Bauer, Bruno, *Kritik der evangelischen Geschichte des Johannes.* Bremen: Carl Schünemann, 1840.

Bauer, Bruno, *Kritik der Geschichte der Offenbarung. Die Religion des alten Testaments in der geschichtlichen Entwickelung ihrer Principien dargestellt*, vols. 1–2. Berlin: Ferdinand Dümmler, 1838.

Bauer, Bruno, *Kritik der paulinischen Briefe.* Berlin: Gustav Hempel, 1852.

Bauer, Bruno, *Philo, Strauß, Renan und das Urchristentum.* Berlin: Gustav Hempel, 1874.

Bauer, Bruno, "Rezension: Das Leben Jesu, kritisch bearbeitet von David Friedrich Strauss." *Jahrbücher für wissenschaftliche Kritik*, December 1835, no. 109, pp. 879–880; no. 111, p. 891; no. 113, pp. 905–912; May 1836, no. 86, pp. 681–688; no. 88, pp. 697–704.

Bauer, Bruno, *Rußland und das Germanenthum*, vols. 1–2. Charlottenburg: Verlag von Egbert Bauer, 1853.

Bauer, Bruno, *Rußland und England*. Charlottenburg: Verlag von Egbert Bauer, 1854.

Bauer, Bruno, "Was ist jetzt der Gegenstand der Kritik?" *Allgemeine Literatur-Zeitung. Monatsschrift*, ed. by Bruno Bauer, 8 (June 1844), 18–26.

Bauer, Bruno, *Zur Orientirung über die Bismarck'sche Ära*. Chemnitz: Ernst Schmeitzner, 1800.

Bauer, Bruno, Edgar Bauer, and Ernst Jungnitz, *Geschichte der französischen Revolution*, vols. 1–3. Leipzig: Voigt and Fernau's Separat-Conto, 1847.

Beauvoir, Simone de, *The Ethics of Ambiguity*, trans. by Bernard Frechtman. New York: Citadel Press, 1948.

Beauvoir, Simone de, *The Second Sex*, trans. by H. M. Parshley. New York: Random House, 1952.

Bekker, Balthasar, *De betoverde Weereld*. Amsterdam: Daniel Van Den Dalen, 1691. (German translation: *Die bezauberte Welt*. Amsterdam: Daniel von Dahlen, 1693.)

Chernyshevsky, Nikolai, *What Is to Be Done?*, trans. by Michal R. Katz. Ithaca and London: Cornell University Press, 1993.

Dostoevsky, Fyodor, *The Brothers Karamazov*, vols. 1–2, trans. by David Magarshack. Harmondsworth: Penguin, 1958.

Dostoevsky, Fyodor, *"Notes from Underground" and "The Double"*, trans. by Jessie Coulson. London: Penguin, 1972.

Dostoevsky, Fyodor, *"Notes from Underground" and "The Grand Inquisitor"*, trans. by Ralph E. Matlaw. Harmondsworth: Penguin, 1991.

Dostoevsky, Fyodor, *Winter Notes on Summer Impressions*, trans. by David Patterson. Evanston: Northwestern University Press, 1988.

[Edelmann, Johann Christian], *Johann Christian Edelmanns Abgenöthigtes jedoch andern nicht wieder auf genöthigtes Glaubens-Bekenntnis*. Neuwied: no publisher given, 1746.

Engels, Friedrich, "Bruno Bauer und das Urchristentum." *Der Sozialdemokrat*, 19–20 (May 4 and 11, 1882) (no page numbers). (Reprint: *Marx-Engels-Gesamtausgabe*, vols. 1–. Berlin: Dietz, 1975ff, vol. 19, pp. 297–305.) (English translation: "Bruno Bauer and Early Christianity," in *Marx/Engels Collected Works*, vols. 1–50. Moscow: Progress Publishers, 1975–2004, vol. 24, pp. 427–435.)

Engels, Friedrich, "Der deutsche Bauernkrieg." *Neue Rheinische Zeitung. Politisch-ökonomische Revue*, 5–6 (1850), 1–99. (Reprint: *Der deutsche Bauernkrieg*. Leipzig: Verlag der Expedition des *Volksstaat*, 1870.) (English translation: *The Peasant War in Germany*, trans. by Moissaye J. Olgin. New York: International Publishers, 1926.)

Engels, Friedrich, *Der Ursprung der Familie, des Privateigenthums und des Staats. Im Anschluss an Lewis H. Morgan's Forschungen.* Hottigen-Zürich: Verlag der Schweizerischen Volksbuchhandlung, 1884. (English translation: *The Origin of the Family, Private Property and the State*, ed. by Tristram Hunt. London: Penguin, 2010.)

Engels, Friedrich, *Die Lage der arbeitenden Klasse in England. Nach eigner Anschauung und authentischen Quellen.* Leipzig: Otto Wigand, 1845. (English translation: *The Condition of the Working Class in England*, ed. by David McLellan. Oxford: Oxford University Press, 1993.)

Engels, Friedrich, "Herrn Eugen Dühring's Umwälzung der Wissenschaft. Philosophie. Politische Oekonomie. Sozialismus." *Vorwärts* (January 3–July 7, 1878). (Reprint: *Herrn Eugen Dühring's Umwälzung der Wissenschaft. Philosophie. Politische Oekonomie. Sozialismus.* Leipzig: Druck und Verlag der Genossenschafts Buchdruckerei, 1878.) (English translation: *Anti-Dühring. Herr Eugen Dühring's Revolution in Science*, trans. by Emile Burns. Moscow: Progress Publishers, 1947.)

Engels, Friedrich, "Ludwig Feuerbach und der Ausgang der klassischen deutschen Philosophie." *Die neue Zeit: Revue des geistigen und öffentlichen Lebens*, 1886, vol. 4, no. 4; pp. 145–157 (Parts I–II); no. 5, pp. 193–209 (Parts III–IV). (Reprint: *Ludwig Feuerbach und der Ausgang der klassischen deutschen Philosophie. Mit Anhang: Karl Marx über Feuerbach vom Jahre 1845.* Stuttgart: J. H. W. Dietz, 1888.) (English translation: *Ludwig Feuerbach and the Outcome of Classical German Philosophy*, ed. by C. P. Dutt. New York: International Publishers, 1941.)

Engels, Friedrich, *Socialisme utopique et socialisme scientifique*, trans. by Paul Lafargue. Paris: Derveaux Libraire-Éditor, 1880. (In German as *Die Entwicklung des Sozialismus von der Utopie zur Wissenschaft.* Hottigen-Zürich: Verlag der Schweizerischen Volksbuchhandlung, 1882.) (English translation: *Socialism Utopian and Scientific*, trans. by Edward Aveling. London: Swan Sonnenschein & Co.; New York: Charles Scribner's Sons, 1892.)

Engels, Friedrich, "Umrisse zu einer Kritik der Nationaloekonomie." *Deutsch-Französische Jahrbücher*, 1–2 (1844), 86–114. (English translation: "Outlines of a Critique of Political Economy," in *Marx/Engels Collected Works*, vols. 1–50. Moscow: Progress Publishers, 1975–2004, vol. 3, pp. 418–443.)

Erdmann, Johann Eduard, *Grundrisse der Geschichte der Philosophie*, vols. 1–2. Berlin: Wilhelm Hertz, 1866 (vol. 1, *Philosophie des Alterthums und Mittelalters*; vol. 2, *Philosophie der Neuzeit*). (English translation: *A History of Philosophy*, vols. 1–3, trans. by Williston S. Hough. London: George Allen & Unwin; New York: Macmillan, 1889.)

*Examen de la religion dont on cherche l'Eclairissement de Bonne Foi.* (No date, place of publication or publisher is listed).

Feuerbach, Ludwig, "Das Wesen der Religion," in Ludwig Feuerbach, *Die Epigonen*, vol. 1. Leipzig: Otto Wigand, 1846, pp. 117–178. (Reprint: *Das*

*Wesen der Religion*, 2nd ed. Leipzig: Otto Wigand, 1849.) (English translation: *The Essence of Religion*, trans. by Alexander Loos. Amherst, NY: Prometheus Books, 2004.)

Feuerbach, Ludwig, *Das Wesen des Christenthums*. Leipzig: Otto Wigand, 1841. (2nd revised ed.: *Das Wesen des Christenthums*. Leipzig: Otto Wigand, 1843.) (English translation: *The Essence of Christianity*, trans. by Marian Evans. New York: Calvin Blanchard, 1855.)

Feuerbach, Ludwig [Ludovico Andrea Feuerbach], *De ratione, una, universali et infinita. Dissertatio inauguralis philosophica.* Erlangen, 1828.

[Feuerbach, Ludwig], *The Fiery Brook: Selected Writings of Ludwig Feuerbach*, trans. by Zawar Hanfi. Garden City, NY: Anchor Books, 1972.

Feuerbach, Ludwig [anonymous], *Gedanken über Tod und Unsterblichkeit aus den Papieren eines Denkers, nebst einem Anhang theologisch-satyrischer Xenien, herausgegeben von einem seiner Freunde.* Nüremburg: Johann Adam Stein, 1830. (English translation: *Thoughts on Death and Immortality. From the Papers of a Thinker, along with an Appendix of Theological-Satirical Epigrams, Edited by One of His Friends*, trans. by James A. Massey. Berkeley: University of California Press, 1980.)

Feuerbach, Ludwig, *Geschichte der neuern Philosophie. Darstellung, Entwicklung und Kritik der Leibnitz'schen Philosophie.* Ansbach: Carl Brügel, 1837.

Feuerbach, Ludwig, *Geschichte der neuern Philosophie von Bacon von Verulam bis Benedict Spinoza.* Ansbach: Carl Brügel, 1833.

Feuerbach, Ludwig, *Grundsätze der Philosophie der Zukunft.* Zürich and Winterthur: Verlag des literarischen Comptoirs, 1843. (English translation: *Principles of Philosophy of the Future*, trans. by Manfred H. Vogel. Indianapolis: Hackett Publishing Company, 1986.)

[Feuerbach, Ludwig], *Ludwig Feuerbach in seinem Briefwechsel und Nachlass sowie in seiner philosophischen Charakterentwicklung*, vols. 1–2, ed. by Karl Grün. Leipzig and Heidelberg: C. F. Winter'sche Verlagshandlung, 1874.

Feuerbach, Ludwig, *Ludwig Feuerbach's sämmtliche Werke*, vols. 1–10. Leipzig: Otto Wigand, 1846–1866.

Feuerbach, Ludwig, *Pierre Bayle, nach seinen für die Geschichte der Philosophie und Menschheit interessantesten Momenten.* Ansbach: Carl Brügel, 1838.

Feuerbach, Ludwig, "Vorläufige Thesen zur Reformation der Philosophie," in Arnold Ruge, ed., *Anekdota zur neuesten deutschen Philosophie und Publicistik.* Zürich and Winterthur: Verlag des Literarischen Comptoirs, 1843, vol. 2, pp. 62–86. (English translation: "Provisional Theses for the Reformation of Philosophy," in Lawrence S. Stepelevich, ed., *The Young Hegelians: An Anthology.* Cambridge: Cambridge University Press, 1983, pp. 156–171.)

Feuerbach, Ludwig, "Zur Kritik der Hegelschen Philosophie." *Hallische Jahrbücher für deutsche Wissenschaft und Kunst*, ed. by Arnold Ruge and Theodor Echtermeyer, 1839, no. 208, pp. 1157–1160; no. 209, pp. 1165–1168; no. 210, pp. 1673–1677; no. 211, pp. 1681–1684; no. 212, pp. 1689–1693; no. 213, pp. 1697–1702, no. 214, pp. 1705–1709; no. 215, pp. 1713–1718; no. 216, pp. 1721–1725. (English translation: "Towards a Critique of Hegel's Philosophy," in Lawrence S. Stepelevich, ed., *The Young Hegelians: An Anthology*. Cambridge: Cambridge University Press, 1983, pp. 95–128.)

Fibiger, Johannes, *Mit Liv og Levned, som jeg selv har forstaaet det*, ed. by Karl Gjellerup. Copenhagen: Gyldendal, 1898.

Fichte, Johann Gottlieb, *Grundlage des Naturrechts nach Principen der Wissenschaftslehre*. Jena and Leipzig: Christian Ernst Gabler, 1796. *Grundlage des Naturrechts nach Principen der Wissenschaftslehre. Zweiter Theil oder Angewandtes Naturrecht*, Jena and Leipzig: Christian Ernst Gabler, 1797. (English translation: *Foundations of Natural Right*, trans. by Michael Baur, ed. by Frederick Neuhouser. Cambridge: Cambridge University Press, 2000.)

Goethe, Johann Wolfgang von, *Faust. Eine Tragödie*, in *Goethe's Werke. Vollständige Ausgabe letzter Hand*, vols. 1–55. Stuttgart and Tübingen: J. G. Cotta'sche Buchhandlung, 1828–1833, vol. 12 (1828). (English translation: *Faust I & II*, trans. by Stuart Atkins. Princeton: Princeton University Press, 1994.)

*Gutachten der Evangelisch-theologischen Facultäten der Königlich Preußischen Universitäten über den Licentiaten Bruno Bauer in Beziehung auf dessen Kritik der evangelischen Geschichte der Synoptiker*. Berlin: Ferdinand Dümmler, 1842.

Habermas, Jürgen, "Struggles for Recognition in the Democratic Constitutional State," in Amy Gutmann, ed., *Multiculturalism: Examining the Politics of Recognition*. Princeton: Princeton University Press, 1994, pp. 107–148.

Habermas, Jürgen, *Theory and Practice*, trans. by John Viertel. Boston: Beacon Press, 1973.

Habermas, Jürgen, *The Theory of Communicative Action*, vol. 2, *Lifeworld and System: A Critique of Functionalist Reason*, trans. by Thomas McCarthy. Boston: Beacon Press, 1987.

Hegel, G. W. F., *Berliner Schriften: 1818–1831*, ed. by Johannes Hoffmeister. Hamburg: Felix Meiner, 1956.

[Hegel, G. W. F.], *Briefe von und an Hegel*, vols. 1–4, ed. by Johannes Hoffmeister (vols. 4.1 and 4.2 ed. by Friedhelm Nicolin), 3rd ed. Hamburg: Felix Meiner, 1961–1981. (Partial English translation: *Hegel: The Letters*, trans. by Clark Butler and Christiane Seiler. Bloomington: Indiana University Press, 1984.)

Hegel, G. W. F., *Encyklopädie der philosophischen Wissenschaften im Grundrisse*. Heidelberg: August Oßwald's Universitätsbuchhandlung, 1817. (English translation: *Encyclopaedia of the Philosophical Sciences in Outline and Critical Writings*, ed. by Ernst Behler. New York: Continuum, 1990.) *Encyclopädie der philosophischen Wissenschaften im Grundrisse*, 2nd ed. Heidelberg: August Oßwald, 1827. *Encyclopädie der philosophischen Wissenschaften im Grundrisse*, 3rd ed. Heidelberg: Verwaltung des Oßwald'schen Verlags (C. F. Winter), 1830. (English translation: *Hegel's Logic: Being Part One of the Encyclopaedia of the Philosophical Sciences*, trans. by William Wallace. Oxford: Clarendon Press, 1975. *Hegel's Philosophy of Nature: Being Part Two of the Encyclopaedia of the Philosophical Sciences*, trans. by A. V. Miller. Oxford: Clarendon Press, 1970. *Hegel's Philosophy of Mind: Being Part Three of the Encyclopaedia of the Philosophical Sciences*, trans. by William Wallace and A. V. Miller. Oxford: Clarendon Press, 1971.)

Hegel, G. W. F., "Fünf Gymnasial-Reden, gehalten zu Nürnberg," in *Vermischte Schriften, I-II*, ed. by Friedrich Förster and Ludwig Boumann, vols. 16–17 (1834–1835), in *Georg Wilhelm Friedrich Hegel's Werke. Vollständige Ausgabe*, vols. 1–18, ed. by Ludwig Boumann, Friedrich Förster, Eduard Gans, Karl Hegel, Leopold von Henning, Heinrich Gustav Hotho, Philipp Marheineke, Karl Ludwig Michelet, Karl Rosenkranz, and Johannes Schulze. Berlin: Duncker und Humblot, 1832–1845, vol. 16, pp. 131–199.

Hegel, G. W. F., *Georg Wilhelm Friedrich Hegel's Werke. Vollständige Ausgabe*, vols. 1–18, ed. by Ludwig Boumann, Friedrich Förster, Eduard Gans, Karl Hegel, Leopold von Henning, Heinrich Gustav Hotho, Philipp Marheineke, Karl Ludwig Michelet, Karl Rosenkranz, and Johannes Schulze. Berlin: Duncker und Humblot, 1832–1845.

Hegel, G. W. F., *Naturrecht und Staatswissenschaft im Grundrisse. Grundlinien der Philosophie des Rechts*. Berlin: Nicolaische Buchhandlung, 1821. (English translation: *Elements of the Philosophy of Right*, trans. by H. B. Nisbet, ed. by Allen Wood. Cambridge and New York: Cambridge University Press, 1991.)

Hegel, G. W. F., *System der Wissenschaft. Erster Theil, die Phänomenologie des Geistes*. Bamberg and Würzburg: Joseph Anton Goebhardt, 1807. (English translation: *Hegel's Phenomenology of Spirit*, trans. by A. V. Miller. Oxford: Clarendon Press, 1977.)

Hegel, G. W. F., *Vorlesungen über die Aesthetik*, Parts I–III, ed. by Heinrich Gustav Hotho, vols. 10.1–3 (1835–1838), in *Georg Wilhelm Friedrich Hegel's Werke. Vollständige Ausgabe*, vols. 1–18, ed. by Ludwig Boumann, Friedrich Förster, Eduard Gans, Karl Hegel, Leopold von Henning, Heinrich Gustav Hotho, Philipp Marheineke, Karl Ludwig Michelet, Karl Rosenkranz, and Johannes Schulze. Berlin: Duncker und Humblot, 1832–1845. (English translation: *Hegel's Aesthetics. Lectures on Fine Art*, vols. 1–2, trans. by T. M. Knox. Oxford: Clarendon Press, 1975, 1998.)

Hegel, G. W. F., *Vorlesungen über die Geschichte der Philosophie*, Parts I–III, ed. by Karl Ludwig Michelet, vols. 13–15 (1833–1836), in *Georg Wilhelm Friedrich Hegel's Werke. Vollständige Ausgabe*, vols. 1–18, ed. by Ludwig Boumann, Friedrich Förster, Eduard Gans, Karl Hegel, Leopold von Henning, Heinrich Gustav Hotho, Philipp Marheineke, Karl Ludwig Michelet, Karl Rosenkranz, and Johannes Schulze. Berlin: Duncker und Humblot, 1832–1845. (English translation: *Lectures on the History of Philosophy*, vols. 1–3, trans. by E. S. Haldane. London: K. Paul, Trench, Trübner, 1892–1896; Lincoln and London: University of Nebraska Press, 1995.)

Hegel, G. W. F., *Vorlesungen über die Philosophie der Geschichte*, ed. by Eduard Gans, vol. 9 (1837) (2nd ed. by Karl Hegel, 1840), in *Georg Wilhelm Friedrich Hegel's Werke. Vollständige Ausgabe*, vols. 1–18, ed. by Ludwig Boumann, Friedrich Förster, Eduard Gans, Karl Hegel, Leopold von Henning, Heinrich Gustav Hotho, Philipp Marheineke, Karl Ludwig Michelet, Karl Rosenkranz, and Johannes Schulze. Berlin: Duncker und Humblot, 1832–1845. (English translation: *The Philosophy of History*, trans. by J. Sibree. New York: Willey Book Co., 1944.)

Hegel, G. W. F., *Vorlesungen über die Philosophie der Religion*, Parts I–II, ed. by Philipp Marheineke, vols. 11–12 (1832) (2nd ed., 1840), in *Georg Wilhelm Friedrich Hegel's Werke. Vollständige Ausgabe*, vols. 1–18, ed. by Ludwig Boumann, Friedrich Förster, Eduard Gans, Karl Hegel, Leopold von Henning, Heinrich Gustav Hotho, Philipp Marheineke, Karl Ludwig Michelet, Karl Rosenkranz, and Johannes Schulze. Berlin: Duncker und Humblot, 1832–1845. (English translation: *Lectures on the Philosophy of Religion*, vols. 1–3, trans. by E. B. Speirs and J. Burdon Sanderson. London: Routledge and Kegan Paul; New York: Humanities Press, 1962, 1968, 1972.)

Hegel, G. W. F., *Vorlesungen über die Philosophie der Religion*, Parts I–III, ed. by Walter Jaeschke. Hamburg: Felix Meiner, 1983–1985, 1993–1995, vols. 3–5 of G. W. F. Hegel, *Vorlesungen. Ausgewählte Nachschriften und Manuskripte*, vols. 1–17. Hamburg: Felix Meiner, 1983–2008. (Part I, *Einleitung. Der Begriff der Religion* = vol. 3. Part II, *Die Bestimmte Religion. a: Text* = vol. 4a. Part II, *Die Bestimmte Religion. b: Anhang* = vol. 4b. Part III, *Die vollendete Religion* = vol. 5.) (English translation: *Lectures on the Philosophy of Religion*, vols. 1–3, ed. by Peter C. Hodgson, trans. by Robert F. Brown, P. C. Hodgson, and J. M. Stewart with the assistance of H. S. Harris, Berkeley: University of California Press, 1984–1987.)

Hegel, G. W. F., *Vorlesungen über die Philosophie der Weltgeschichte: Berlin 1822–1823*, ed. by Karl Heinz Ilting, Karl Brehmer, and Hoo Nam Seelmann. Hamburg: Felix Meiner, 1996, vol. 12 of G. W. F. Hegel, *Vorlesungen. Ausgewählte Nachschriften und Manuskripte*, vols. 1–17. Hamburg: Felix Meiner, 1983–2008. (English translation: *The Philosophy of World History*, vol. 1, *Manuscripts of the Introduction and the Lectures of 1822-3*, trans. by Robert F. Brown and Peter C. Hodgson with the assistance of William G. Geuss. Oxford: Oxford University Press, 2011.)

Hegel, G. W. F., *Wissenschaft der Logik*, vols. 1–3. Nürnberg: Johann Leonard Schrag, 1812–1816. (English translation: *The Science of Logic*, trans. by George di Giovanni. Cambridge: Cambridge University Press, 2010.)

Heiberg, Johan Ludvig, *Fata Morgana, Eventyr-Comedie*. Copenhagen: Schubothe, 1838.

Heiberg, Johan Ludvig, *Heiberg's Introductory Lecture to the Logic Course and Other Texts*, ed. and trans. by Jon Stewart. Copenhagen: C. A. Reitzel, 2007 (*Texts from Golden Age Denmark*, vol. 3).

Heiberg, Johan Ludvig, *Nye Digte*. Copenhagen: C. A. Reitzel, 1841.

Heiberg, Johan Ludvig, *Om Philosophiens Betydning for den nuværende Tid. Et Indbydelses-Skrift til en Række af philosophiske Forelæsninger*. Copenhagen: C. A. Reitzel, 1833. (English translation: *On the Significance of Philosophy for the Present Age*, in *Heiberg's On the Significance of Philosophy for the Present Age and Other Texts*, ed. and trans. by Jon Stewart. Copenhagen: C. A. Reitzel, 2005 [*Texts from Golden Age Denmark*, vol. 1], pp. 85–119).

Heiberg, Johan Ludvig, *A Soul After Death*, trans. by Henry Meyer. Seattle: Mermaid Press, 1991.

Heine, Heinrich [Henri Heine], "De L'Allemagne depuis Luther." *Revue des deux Mondes* (1834), "Première Partie," Tome 1, 473–505; "Deuxième Partie," Tome 4, 373–408; "Troisième Partie," Tome 4, 633–678. (In German as *Zur Geschichte der Religion und Philosophie in Deutschland* in Heine, *Der Salon*, vols. 1–2. Hamburg: Hoffmann und Campe, 1834, vol. 2, pp. 1–284.) (English translation: *On the History of Religion and Philosophy in Germany and Other Writings*, ed. by Terry Pinkard, trans. by Howard Pollack-Milgate. Cambridge: Cambridge University Press, 2007.)

Heine, Heinrich, "Die armen Weber." *Vorwärts! Pariser deutsche Zeitschrift*, 55 (July 10, 1844).

Heine, Heinrich, "Die schlesischen Weber," in *Album. Originalpoesien*, ed. by Hermann Püttmann. Borna [sc. Bremen/Brussels]: Albert Reiche, 1847, pp. 145–146.

Heine, Heinrich, *Neue Gedichte, Zeitgedichte*. Hamburg: Hoffmann und Campe; Paris, J. J. Dubochet & Cie., 1844.

Heine, Heinrich, *The Poetry of Heinrich Heine*, ed. by Frederic Ewen. Secaucus, NJ: Citadel Press, 1969.

Heine, Heinrich, *Vermischte Schriften*, vols. 1–3. Hamburg: Hoffmann und Campe, 1854.

d'Holbach, Baron, Paul-Henri Thiry [Boulanger], *Le Christianisme dévoilé, ou Examen des principes et des effets de la religion chrétienne*. Nancy, Switzerland: de L'Imprim. Philosophique, 1761. (English translation: *Christianity Unveiled, Being an Examination of the Principles and Effects of the Christian Religion*, trans. by W. M. Johnson. New York: [no publisher given], 1835.)

d'Holbach, Baron, Paul-Henri Thiry [Jean-Baptiste de Mirabaud], *Système de la Nature ou Des Loix du Monde Physique et du Monde Moral*, vols. 1–2. London [Amsterdam]: [no publisher given], 1770.

Kierkegaard, Søren, *Concluding Unscientific Postscript*, vols. 1–2, trans. by Howard V. Hong and Edna H. Hong. Princeton: Princeton University Press, 1992.

Kierkegaard, Søren, *Either/Or, Part 1*, trans. by Howard V. Hong and Edna H. Hong. Princeton: Princeton University Press, 1987.

Kierkegaard, Søren, *Johannes Climacus, or De omnibus dubitandum est*, trans. by Howard V. Hong and Edna H. Hong. Princeton: Princeton University Press, 1985.

Kierkegaard, Søren, *Kierkegaard's Journals and Notebooks*, vols. 1–11, ed. by Niels Jørgen Cappelørn, Alastair Hannay, David Kangas, Bruce H. Kirmmse, George Pattison, Vanessa Rumble, and K. Brian Söderquist. Princeton and Oxford: Princeton University Press, 2007–2020.

Kierkegaard, Søren, *Papers and Journals: A Selection*, trans. with introductions and notes by Alastair Hannay. London and New York: Penguin, 1996.

Kierkegaard, Søren, *The Sickness unto Death*, trans. by Howard V. Hong and Edna H. Hong. Princeton: Princeton University Press, 1980.

Kierkegaard, Søren, *Søren Kierkegaard's Journals and Papers*, vols. 1–6, ed. and trans. by Howard V. Hong and Edna H. Hong. Bloomington and London: Indiana University Press, 1967–1978.

Kierkegaard, Søren, *Søren Kierkegaards Papirer*, vols. I to XI–3, ed. by Peter Andreas Heiberg, Victor Kuhr, and Einer Torsting. Copenhagen: Gyldendalske Boghandel, Nordisk Forlag, 1909–1948.

Kierkegaard, Søren, *Søren Kierkegaards Skrifter*, vols. 1–28, K1–K28, ed. by Niels Jørgen Cappelørn, Joakim Garff, Jette Knudsen, Johnny Kondrup, and Alastair McKinnon. Copenhagen: Gad Publishers, 1997–2012.

Kierkegaard, Søren, *Two Ages: The Age of Revolution and the Present Age, A Literary Review*, trans. by Howard V. Hong and Edna H. Hong. Princeton: Princeton University Press, 1978.

Marx, Karl, *Karl Marx. Ökonomisch-Philosophische Manuskripte. Kommentar von Michael Quante*. Frankfurt am Main: Suhrkamp, 2009.

Marx, Karl, "Konspekt von Bakunins Buch *Staatlichkeit und Anarchie*," in *Marx-Engels-Werke*, vols. 1–46, ed. by the Institut für Marxismus-Leninismus. Berlin: Dietz, 1956–2018, vol. 18, pp. 597–642. (English translation: "Notes on Bakunin's Book *Statehood and Anarchy*," in *Marx/Engels Collected Works*, vols. 1–50. Moscow: Progress Publishers, 1975–2004, vol. 24, pp. 485–526.)

Marx, Karl, "Ökonomisch-philosophische Manuskripte aus dem Jahre 1844," in *Marx-Engels-Werke*, vols. 1–46, ed. by the Institut für Marxismus-Leninismus. Berlin: Dietz, 1956–2018, vol. 40, pp. 465–588. (Partial English translation: "Economic and Philosophic Manuscripts of 1844," in *The Marx-Engels Reader*, ed. by Robert C. Tucker. New York and London: W. W. Norton & Company, 1978, pp. 66–125.)

[Marx, Karl], *Marx-Engels-Gesamtausgabe*, vols. 1–. Berlin: Dietz, 1975ff. (commonly abbreviated as *MEGA*). (English translation: *Marx/Engels Collected Works*, vols. 1–50. Moscow: Progress Publishers, 1975–2004 [commonly abbreviated as *MECW*].)

Marx, Karl, *The Marx-Engels Reader*, ed. by Robert C. Tucker. New York and London: W. W. Norton & Company, 1978.

[Marx, Karl], *Marx-Engels-Werke*, vols. 1–46, ed. by the Institut für Marxismus-Leninismus. Berlin: Dietz, 1956–2018.

Marx, Karl, "Thesen über Feuerbach," in *Marx-Engels-Werke*, vols. 1–46, ed. by the Institut für Marxismus-Leninismus. Berlin: Dietz, 1956–2018, vol. 3, pp. 5–7. (English translation: "Theses on Feuerbach," in *The Marx-Engels Reader*, ed. by

Robert C. Tucker. New York and London: W. W. Norton & Company, 1978, pp. 143–145.)

Marx, Karl, "Zur Kritik der Hegelschen Rechtsphilosophie," in *Marx-Engels-Werke*, vols. 1–46, ed. by the Institut für Marxismus-Leninismus. Berlin: Dietz, 1956–2018, vol. 1, pp. 201–333. (English translation: *Critique of Hegel's "Philosophy of Right,"* trans. by Annette Jolin and Joseph O'Malley. Cambridge: Cambridge University Press, 1970.)

Marx, Karl, "Zur Kritik der Hegel'schen Rechts-Philosophie. Einleitung." *Deutsch-Französische Jahrbücher*, 1–2 (1844), 71–85. (English translation: "Contribution to the Critique of Hegel's *Philosophy of Right*: Introduction," in *The Marx-Engels Reader*, ed. by Robert C. Tucker. New York and London: W. W. Norton & Company, 1978, pp. 53–65.)

Marx, Karl and Friedrich Engels, *Die deutsche Ideologie. Kritik der neuesten deutschen Philosophie in ihren Repräsentaten Feuerbach, B. Bauer und Stirner, und des deutschen Sozialismus in seinen verschiedenen Propheten*, in *Marx-Engels-Werke*, vols. 1–46, ed. by the Institut für Marxismus-Leninismus. Berlin: Dietz, 1956–2018, vol. 3, pp. 9–530. (English translation: *The German Ideology*. London: Lawrence & Wishart, 1965; Moscow: Progress Publishers, 1964.)

Marx, Karl and Friedrich Engels, *Die heilige Familie, oder Kritik der kritischen Kritik. Gegen Bruno Bauer & Consorten*. Frankfurt am Main: Literarische Anstalt, 1845. (English translation: *The Holy Family or Critique of Critical Critique*, trans. by Richard Dixon. Moscow: Foreign Languages Publishing House, 1956. *The Holy Family*, trans. by Richard Dixon and Clemens Dutt, in *Marx/Engels Collected Works*, vols. 1–50. Moscow: Progress Publishers, 1975–2004, vol. 4, pp. 5–211.)

Merleau-Ponty, Maurice, *Sense and Non-Sense*, trans. by Hubert Dreyfus and Patricia Allen Dreyfus. Evanston: Northwestern University Press, 1964.

Nietzsche, Friedrich, *Der Antichrist. Versuch einer Kritik des Christenthums*, in *Nietzsche's Werke*, vols. 1–20. Leipzig: C. G. Naumann, 1895–1904, vol. 8 (1895). (Reprint: *Der Antichrist*, in *Kritische Studienausgabe*, vols. 1–15, 2nd ed., ed. by Giorgio Colli and Mazzino Montinari. Berlin and New York: De Gruyter, 1988, vol. 6, pp. 165–254.) (English translation: *The Anti-Christ*, in *Twilight of the Idols/ The Anti-Christ*, trans. by R. J. Hollingdale. Harmondsworth: Penguin, 1968, pp. 113–199.)

Nietzsche, Friedrich, *Götzen-Dämmerung oder Wie man mit dem Hammer philosophirt*, in *Nietzsche's Werke*. Leipzig: C. G. Naumann, 1889. (English translation: *Twilight of the Idols or How to Philosophize with a Hammer*, in *Twilight of the Idols/The Anti-Christ*, trans. by R. J. Hollingdale. Harmondsworth: Penguin, 1968, pp. 19–112.)

Ricoeur, Paul, *The Course of Recognition*, trans. by David Pellauer. Cambridge, MA: Harvard University Press, 2005.

Rorty, Richard, *Consequences of Pragmatism*. Minneapolis: University of Minnesota Press, 1982.

Rosenkranz, Karl, *Georg Wilhelm Friedrich Hegel's Leben.* Berlin: Duncker und Humblot, 1844.

Sartre, Jean-Paul, *Being and Nothingness: An Essay on Phenomenological Ontology,* trans. by Hazel E. Barnes. New York: Philosophical Library, 1956.

Schelling, F. W. J., *Philosophie der Offenbarung 1841–42,* ed. by Manfred Frank. Frankfurt am Main: Suhrkamp, 1977 (3rd revised ed., 1993).

Sophocles, *Oedipus the King,* trans. by David Grene, in *Sophocles I.* Chicago and London: University of Chicago Press, 1954.

Stael Holstein, La Baronne de, *De l'Allemagne,* vols. 1–3. Paris: M. Nicolle; London: John Murray, 1813.

Strauss, David Friedrich, *Der alte und der neue Glaube. Ein Bekenntniß.* Leipzig: S. Hirtzel, 1872. (English translation: *The Old Faith and the New,* trans. by Mathilde Blind. Amherst, NY: Prometheus Books, 1997.)

Strauss, David Friedrich, *Streitschriften zur Vertheidigung meiner Schrift über das Leben Jesu und zur Charakteristik der gegenwärtigen Theologie.* Tübingen: Osiander, 1837. (English translation: *In Defense of My Life of Jesus against the Hegelians,* trans. by Marilyn Chapin Massey. Hamden, CN: Archon Books, 1983.)

Voltaire, *Dieu et les hommes, oeuvre théologique, mais raisonnable.* Berlin: Christian de Vos, 1769. (English translation: *God and Human Beings,* trans. by Michael Shreve. Amherst, NY: Prometheus Books, 2010.)

Zychlinski, Franz Zychlin von [Szeliga], "Die Kritik." *Allgemeine Literatur-Zeitung. Monatsschrift,* ed. by Bruno Bauer, 11–12 (October 1844), 25–46.

## Secondary Literature

Adelman, Howard, "Of Human Bondage: Labor, Bondage and Freedom in the *Phenomenology,*" in Donald Phillip Verene, ed., *Hegel's Social and Political Thought.* Atlantic Highlands: Humanities Press, 1980, pp. 119–135.

Althaus, Horst, *Hegel: An Intellectual Biography,* trans. by Michael Tarsh. Cambridge: Polity Press, 2000.

Althusser, Louis, *For Marx,* trans. by Ben Brewster. New York: Vintage, 1970.

Altmeyer, Martin, *Im Spiegel des Anderen. Anwendungen einer relationalen Psychoanalyse.* Gießen: Vandenhoeck & Ruprecht, 2003.

Altmeyer, Martin, "Narzissmus, Intersubjektivität und Anerkennung." *Psyche,* 54 (2) (2000), 143–171.

Altmeyer, Martin, *Narzissmus und Objekt. Ein intersubjektives Verständnis der Selbstbezogenheit.* Gießen: Vandenhoeck & Ruprecht, 2000.

Anderson, Sybol S. C., *Hegel's Theory of Recognition: From Oppression to Ethical Liberal Modernity.* New York and London: Continuum, 2011.

Ansell-Pearson, Keith, *How to Read Nietzsche.* New York: W. W. Norton, 2005.

Aris, Reinhold, *History of Political Thought in Germany from 1789 to 1815,* 2nd ed. London: Frank Cass, 1965.

Avineri, Shlomo, *The Social and Political Thought of Karl Marx*. Cambridge: Cambridge University Press, 1968.

Baugh, Bruce, "Hegel in Modern French Philosophy: The Unhappy Consciousness." *Laval théologique et philosophique*, 49(3) (1993), 423–438.

Baumgarten, Michael and Wilfried Schulz, "Topoi Hegelscher Philosophie der Kunst in Heines *Romantischer Schule*." *Heine Jahrbuch*, 17 (1978), 55–94.

Bautz, Timo, *Hegels Lehre von der Weltgeschichte. Zur logischen und systematischen Grundlegung der Hegelschen Geschichtsphilosophie*. Munich: Wilhelm Fink Verlag, 1988.

Becker, Werner, *Idealistische und materialistische Dialektik. Das Verhältnis von Herrschaft und Knechtschaft bei Hegel und Marx*. Stuttgart: Kohlhammer, 1970.

Beiser, Frederick C., *After Hegel: German Philosophy 1840–1900*. Princeton and Oxford: Princeton University Press, 2014.

Beiser, Frederick C., ed., *The Cambridge Companion to Hegel and Nineteenth Century Philosophy*. Cambridge: Cambridge University Press, 2008.

Beiser, Frederick C., *Enlightenment, Revolution, and Romanticism: The Genesis of Modern German Political Thought 1790–1800*. Cambridge, MA and London: Harvard University Press, 1992.

Beiser, Frederick C., *Late German Idealism: Trendelenburg and Lotze*. Oxford: Oxford University Press, 2013.

Benhabib, Seyla, *Situating the Self: Gender, Community, and Postmodernism in Contemporary Ethics*. New York: Routledge, 1992.

Benjamin, Jessica, *Beyond Doer and Done To: Recognition Theory, Intersubjectivity and the Third*. New York and London: Routledge, 2018.

Benjamin, Jessica, *The Bonds of Love: Psychoanalysis, Feminism, and the Problem of Domination*. New York: Pantheon, 1988.

Benjamin, Jessica, *Like Subjects, Love Objects: Essays on Recognition and Sexual Difference*. New Haven: Yale University Press, 1995.

Benjamin, Jessica, *Shadow of the Other: Intersubjectivity and Gender in Psychoanalysis*. New York and London: Routledge, 1998.

Benz, Ernst, *Nietzsches Ideen zur Geschichte des Christentums und der Kirche*. Leiden: E. J. Brill, 1956.

Berlin, Isaiah, *Karl Marx: His Life and Environment*. New York: Oxford University Press, 1959.

Bernstein, J. M., "From Self-Consciousness to Community: Act and Recognition in the Master-Slave Relationship," in Z. A. Pelczynski, ed., *The State and Civil Society: Studies in Hegel's Political Philosophy*. Cambridge: Cambridge University Press, 1984, pp. 14–39.

Betts, C. J., *Early Deism in France: From the So-Called "déistes" of Lyon (1564) to Voltaire's "Lettres philosophiques" (1734)*. The Hague: Martinus Nijhoff, 1984.

Bier, William C., *Alienation: Plight of Modern Man?* New York: Fordham University Press, 1972.

Bloom, Harold, *The Anxiety of Influence: A Theory of Poetry*. New York: Oxford University Press, 1973.

Bockmühl, Klaus, *Leiblichkeit und Gesellschaft. Studien zur Religionskritik und Anthropologie im Frühwerk von Ludwig Feuerbach und Karl Marx*. Göttingen: Vandenhoeck & Ruprecht, 1961.

Boey, Conrad, *L'aliénation dans la Phénoménologie de l'esprit de G. W. F. Hegel*. Paris and Bruges: Desclée, De Brouwer, 1970.

Brauer, Oscar Daniel, *Dialektik der Zeit. Untersuchungen zu Hegels Metaphysik der Weltgeschichte*. Stuttgart and Bad Cannstatt: Frommann-Holzboog, 1982.

Brazill, William J., *The Young Hegelians*. New Haven: Yale University Press, 1970.

Breazeale, Daniel and Tom Rockmore, eds., *Fichte, German Idealism, and Early Romanticism*. Amsterdam and New York: Rodopi, 2010 (*Fichte-Studien-Supplementa*, vol. 24).

Breckman, Warren, *Marx, the Young Hegelians, and the Origins of Radical Social Theory*. Cambridge: Cambridge University Press, 1999.

Bremes, Hans E., ed., *140 Jahre Weberaufstand in Schlesien. Industriearbeit und Technik – gestern und heute. Ein Beitrag zur politischen Kulturarbeit*. Münster: Verlag Westfälisches Dampfboot, 1985.

Brown, Edward J., *Stankevich and His Moscow Circle, 1830–1840*. Stanford: Stanford University Press, 1966.

Brownlee, Timothy L., "Alienation and Recognition in Hegel's *Phenomenology of Spirit*." *Philosophical Forum*, 46(4) (2015), 377–396.

Burbidge, John W., *Hegel on Logic and Religion: The Reasonableness of Christianity*. Albany: State University of New York Press, 1992.

Burbidge, John W., "'Unhappy Consciousness' in Hegel: An Analysis of Medieval Catholicism?," *Mosaic*, 11 (1978), 67–80.

Burrow, J. W., *The Crisis of Reason: European Thought, 1848–1914*. New Haven and London: Yale University Press, 2000.

Butler, Judith, *The Psychic Life of Power: Theories in Subjection*. Stanford: Stanford University Press, 1997.

Butler, Judith P., *Subjects of Desire: Hegelian Reflections in Twentieth-Century France*. New York: Columbia University Press, 1987.

Camponigri, A. Robert, *Philosophy from the Romantic Age to the Age of Positivism*. Notre Dame and London: University of Notre Dame Press, 1971 (*A History of Western Philosophy*, vol. 4).

Carr, Edward H., *Michael Bakunin*. London: Macmillan, 1937.

Carver, Terrell, *Friedrich Engels: His Life and Thought*. London: Macmillan, 1989.

Clarke, James Alexander, "Fichte and Hegel on Recognition." *British Journal for the History of Philosophy*, 17(2) (2009), 365–385.

Clarkson, Kathleen L. and David J. Hawkin, "Marx on Religion: The Influence of Bruno Bauer and Ludwig Feuerbach on His Thought and Its Implications for the Christian-Marxist Dialogue." *Scottish Journal of Theology*, 31 (1978), 533–555.

Cobben, Paul, *The Nature of the Self: Recognition in the Form of Right and Morality*. Berlin and New York: De Gruyter, 2009.

Cobben, Paul, *The Paradigm of Recognition: Freedom as Overcoming the Fear of Death*. Leiden and Boston: Brill, 2012.

Colletti, Lucio, *Marxism and Hegel*, trans. by Lawrence Garner. London: New Left Books, 1973.

Comstock, W. Richard, "Hegel, Kierkegaard, Marx on 'The Unhappy Consciousness.'" *Internationales Jahrbuch für Wissens- und Religionssoziologie*, 11 (1978), 91–119.

Conway, Daniel W., "Modest Expectations: Kierkegaard's Reflections on the Present Age." *Kierkegaard Studies Yearbook* (1999), 21–49.

Conway, Daniel W., *Nietzsche's Dangerous Game: Philosophy in the Twilight of the Idols*. Cambridge: Cambridge University Press, 1997.

Conway, Daniel W. and K. E. Gover, eds., *Social and Political Philosophy: Kierkegaard and the "Present Age."* London and New York: Routledge, 2002 (*Søren Kierkegaard: Critical Assessments of Leading Philosophers*, vol. 4).

Cook, Roger F., ed., *A Companion to the Works of Heinrich Heine*. Rochester, NY: Camden House, 2002.

Copleston, Frederick, *A History of Philosophy, vol. 7, Modern Philosophy, Part 1: Fichte to Hegel, Part II: Schopenhauer to Nietzsche*. Garden City, NY: Image Books, 1965.

Cyzevskyj, Dmitrij, "Hegel in Rußland," in Dmitrij Cyzevskyj, ed., *Hegel bei den Slaven*. Bad Homburg vor der Höhe: Gentner, 1954, pp. 145–396.

Dale, Eric Michael, *Hegel, the End of History, and the Future*. Cambridge: Cambridge University Press, 2014.

Del Giudice, Martine, "Bakunin's Preface to Hegel's Gymnasial Lectures: The Problem of Alienation and the Reconciliation with Reality." *Canadian-American Slavic Studies*, 16(2) (1982), 161–189.

Del Giudice, Martine, *The Young Bakunin and Left Hegelianism: Origins of Russian Radicalism and the Theory of Praxis, 1814–1842*, PhD thesis. McGill University (1981).

De Nys, Martin J., *Hegel and Theology*. London and New York: T. & T. Clark, 2009.

Desmond, William, *Hegel's God: A Counterfeit Double?* Aldershot: Ashgate, 2003.

D'Hondt, Jacques, *Hegel in his Time*, trans. by John Burbidge. New York: Broadview Press, 1988.

Douzinas, Costas, "Identity, Recognition, Rights or What Can Hegel Teach Us about Human Rights?" *Journal of Law and Society*, 29(3) (2002), 379–405.

Dudley, Will, ed., *Hegel and History*. Albany: State University of New York Press, 2009.

Dunning, Stephen N., "Love Is Not Enough: A Kierkegaardian Phenomenology of Religious Experience." *Faith and Philosophy*, 12 (1995), 22–39.

Dupré, Louis, *The Philosophical Foundations of Marxism*. New York: Harcourt Brace Jovanovich, 1966.

Duquette, Daniel, "The Political Significance of Hegel's Concept of Recognition in the *Phenomenology*." *Bulletin of the Hegel Society of Great Britain*, 29 (1994), 38–54.

Edgar, Matthew, "Deer Park or the Monastery? Kierkegaard and Hegel on Unhappy Consciousness, Renunciation, and Worldliness." *Philosophy Today*, 46 (2002), 284–299.

Evanow, Serge N., *N. V. Stankevich and His Circle: The Idealistic Movement of the 1830's*. Berkeley: University of California Press, 1953.

Fackenheim, Emil L., *God's Presence in History*. New York: New York University Press, 1970.

Fackenheim, Emil L., "On the Actuality of the Rational and the Rationality of the Actual," in Jon Stewart, ed., *The Hegel Myths and Legends*. Evanston: Northwestern University Press, 1996, pp. 52–49.

Fackenheim, Emil L., *The Religious Dimension in Hegel's Thought*. Bloomington: Indiana University Press, 1967.

Feuerlicht, Igance, *Alienation from the Past to the Future*. Westport, CN and London: Greenwood Press, 1978.

Fiala, Andrew G., *The Philosopher's Voice: Philosophy, Politics, and Language in the Nineteenth Century*. Albany: State University of New York Press, 2002.

Fischer, Kuno, *Hegels Leben, Werke und Lehre*. Heidelberg: C. Winter, 1901.

Fischer, Kuno, *Schellings Leben, Werke und Lehre*. Heidelberg: C. Winter, 1899.

Frank, Joseph, *Dostoevsky: The Seeds of Revolt, 1821–1849*. Princeton: Princeton University Press, 1976.

Frank, Joseph, *Dostoevsky: The Years of Ordeal, 1850–1859*. Princeton: Princeton University Press, 1983.

Frank, Joseph, *Dostoevsky: The Stir of Liberation, 1860–1865*. Princeton: Princeton University Press, 1986.

Frank, Joseph, *Dostoevsky: The Miraculous Years, 1865–1871*. Princeton: Princeton University Press, 1995.

Frank, Joseph, *Dostoevsky: The Mantle of the Prophet, 1871–1881*. Princeton: Princeton University Press, 2002.

Frank, Joseph, *Dostoevsky: A Writer in His Time*. Princeton: Princeton University Press, 2009.

Fraser, Nancy, "Social Justice in the Age of Identity Politics: Redistribution, Recognition, and Participation," in Nancy Fraser and Axel Honneth, *Redistribution or Recognition? A Political-Philosophical Exchange*. New York: Verso, 2003, pp. 7–109.

Fridlender, Georgi Michailowitsch, "Heinrich Heine und die Äsethetik Hegels," in Karl Wolfgang Becker, Helmut Brandt, and Siegfried Scheib, eds., *Heinrich Heine. Streitbarer Humanist und volksverbundener Dichter. Internationale wissenschaftliche Konferenz aus Anlaß des 175. Geburtstages von Heinrich Heine, Weimar 1972*. Weimar: Nationale Forschungs- und Gedenkstätten, 1973, pp. 35–48.

Fromm, Erich, *Marx's Concept of Man*. New York: Frederick Ungar Publishing, 1961.

Gadamer, Hans-Georg, *Hegel's Dialectic: Five Hermeneutical Essays*, trans. by P. Christopher Smith. New Haven: Yale University Press, 1976, pp. 54–74.

Gallert, Eberhard, *Heinrich Heine*, 4th ed. Stuttgart: J. B. Metzler, 1976.

Gardiner, Patrick L., ed., *Nineteenth-Century Philosophy*. New York: The Free Press; London: Collier-Macmillan, 1969.

Gargano, Antonio, *Bruno Bauer*. Naples: Città del Sole, 2003.

Gebhardt, Jürgen, "Karl Marx und Bruno Bauer," in Alois Dempf, Hannah Arendt, and Friedrich Engel-Janosi, eds., *Politische Ordnung und menschliche Existenz. Festgabe für Eric Voegelin zum 60. Geburtstag*. Munich: C. H. Beck, 1962, pp. 202–243.

Gebhardt, Jürgen, *Politik und Eschatologie. Studien zur Geschichte der hegelschen Schule in den Jahren 1830–1840*. Munich: C. H. Beck, 1963 (*Münchener Studien zur Politik*, vol. 1).

Girard, René, *Resurrection from the Underground: Feodor Dostoevsky*, trans. by James G. Williams. East Lansing: Michigan State University Press, 2012.

Glöckner, Dorothea, "'The Unhappiest One' – Merely an Inscription? On the Relationship between Immediacy and Language in the Work of Kierkegaard," in Paul Cruysberghs, Johan Taels, and Karl Verstrynge, eds., *Immediacy and Reflection in Kierkegaard's Thought*. Leuven: Leuven University Press, 2003 (*Louvain Philosophical Studies*, vol. 17), pp. 41–53.

Gloy, Karen, "Bemerkungen zum Kapitel 'Herrschaft und Knechtschaft' in Hegels *Phänomenologie des Geistes*." *Zeitschrift für Philosophische Forschung*, 39 (1985), 187–213.

Gottlieb, Gabriel, "A Family Quarrel: Fichte's Deduction of Right and Recognition," in *Kant and His German Contemporaries*, vol. 2, *Aesthetics, History, Politics, and Religion*, ed. by Daniel Dahlstrom. Cambridge: Cambridge University Press, 2018, pp. 170–192.

Gottlieb, Gabriel, ed., *Fichte's Foundations of Natural Right: A Critical Guide*. Cambridge: Cambridge University Press, 2016.

Gouldner, Alvin, *Against Fragmentation: The Origins of Marxism and the Sociology of Intellectuals*. Oxford: Oxford University Press, 1985.

Grawtiz, Madeleine, *Bakounine: biographie*. Paris: Plon, 1990.

Grebing, Helga, *History of the German Labour Movement: A Survey*, trans. by Edith Körner. Leamington Spa: Berg Publishers, 1985.

Green, John, *A Revolutionary Life: Biography of Friedrich Engels*. London: Artery Publications, 2008.

Green, Ronald M., *Kierkegaard and Kant: The Hidden Debt*. Albany: State University of New York Press, 1992.

Greene, Murray, "Hegel's 'Unhappy Consciousness' and Nietzsche's 'Slave Morality'," in Darrel E. Christensen, ed., *Hegel and the Philosophy of Religion*. The Hague: Martinus Nijhoff, 1970, pp. 125–141.

Grimsley, Ronald, *Søren Kierkegaard: A Biographical Introduction*. London: Studio Vista, 1973 (*Leaders of Modern Thought*).

Gumppenberg, Rudolf, "Bewußtsein und Arbeit. Zu G. W. F. Hegels *Phänomenologie des Geistes*." *Zeitschrift für Philosophische Forschung*, 26 (1972), 372–388.

Gutman, Amy, ed., *Multiculturalism: Examining the Politics of Recognition*. Princeton: Princeton University Press, 1994.

Hannay, Alastair, *Kierkegaard: A Biography*. Cambridge: Cambridge University Press, 2001.

Hanson, Jeffrey, ed., *Kierkegaard as Phenomenologist: An Experiment*. Evanston: Northwestern University Press, 2010.

Hare, John E., "The Unhappiest One and the Structure of Kierkegaard's *Either/Or*," in Robert L. Perkins, ed., *Either/Or, Part I*. Macon, GA: Mercer University Press, 1995 (*International Kierkegaard Commentary*, vol. 3), pp. 91–108.

Harries, Karsten, *Between Nihilism and Faith: A Commentary on "Either/Or"*. Berlin and New York: De Gruyter, 2010 (*Kierkegaard Studies Monograph Series*, vol. 21).

Harris, H. S., *Hegel's Ladder*, vol. 1: *The Pilgrimage of Reason*, vol. 2: *The Odyssey of Spirit*. Indianapolis: Hackett, 1997.

Harvey, Van A., *Feuerbach and the Interpretation of Religion*. Cambridge: Cambridge University Press, 1997.

Hayman, Ronald, *Nietzsche: A Critical Life*. Oxford: Oxford University Press, 1980.

Heise, Wolfgang, *Realistik und Utopie. Aufsätze zur deutschen Literatur zwischen Lessing und Heine*. Berlin: Akademie-Verlag, 1982.

Hellman, Robert J., *Berlin – The Red Room and White Beer: The "Free" Hegelian Radicals in the 1840s*. Washington, DC: Three Continents Press, 1990.

Henderson, W. O., *The Life of Friedrich Engels*, vols. 1–2. London: Frank Cass, 1976.

Hengst, Heinz, *Idee und Ideologieverdacht, Revolutionäre Implikationen des deutschen Idealismus im Kontext der zeitkritischen Prosa Heinrich Heines*. Munich: Wilhelm Fink, 1973.

Hodenberg, Christina von, *Aufstand der Weber. Die Revolte von 1844 und ihr Aufstieg zum Mythos*. Bonn: Dietz, 1997.

Hodgson, Peter C., *Hegel and Christian Theology: A Reading of the Lectures on the Philosophy of Religion*. Oxford: Oxford University Press, 2005.

Hodgson, Peter C., *Shapes of Freedom: Hegel's Philosophy of World History in a Theological Perspective*. Oxford: Oxford University Press, 2012.

Hohler, Thomas P., *Imagination and Reflection: Intersubjectivity. Fichte's Grundlage of 1794*. The Hague: Martinus Nijhoff, 1982.

Honneth, Axel, *Anerkennung: Eine europäische Ideengeschichte*. Frankfurt am Main: Suhrkamp, 2018.

Honneth, Axel, *The I in We: Studies in the Theory of Recognition*, trans. by Joseph Ganahl. Cambridge, UK and Malden, MA: Polity Press, 2012.

Honneth, Axel, *The Pathologies of Individual Freedom: Hegel's Social Theory*, trans. by L. Löb. Princeton and Oxford: Princeton University Press, 2001.

Honneth, Axel, *The Struggle for Recognition: The Moral Grammar of Social Conflicts*, trans. by Joel Anderson. Cambridge: Polity Press, 1995

Hook, Sidney, *From Hegel to Marx: Studies in the Intellectual Development of Karl Marx*. New York: Humanities Press, 1958.

Hosfeld, Rolf, *Heinrich Heine: Die Erfindung des europäischen Intellektuellen – Biographie*. Munich: Seidler Verlag, 2014.

Hunt, Tristram, *The Frock-Coated Communist: The Revolutionary Life of Friedrich Engels*. London: Penguin, 2009. (Published in the USA as *Marx's General: The Revolutionary Life of Friedrich Engels*. New York: Henry Holt, 2009.)

Hyppolite, Jean, *Genesis and Structure of Hegel's Phenomenology of Spirit*, trans. by Samuel Cherniak and John Heckman. Evanston: Northwestern University Press, 1974.

Hyppolite, Jean, *Introduction to Hegel's Philosophy of History*, trans. by Bond Harris and Jacqueline Bouchard Spurlock. Gainesville: University Press of Florida, 1996.

Hyppolite, Jean, "La *Phénoménologie* de Hegel et la pensée française contemporaine," in *Figures de la pensée philosophique. Écrits (1931–1968)*, vol. 1. Paris: Presses Universitaires de France, 1971, pp. 231–241.

Ikäheimo, Heikki and Arto Laitinen, eds., *Recognition and Social Ontology*. Leiden and Boston: Brill, 2011 (*Social and Critical Theory*, vol. 11).

Jackson, M. W., "Hegel: The Real and the Rational," in Jon Stewart, ed., *The Hegel Myths and Legends*. Evanston: Northwestern University Press, 1996, pp. 19–25.

Jaeggi, Rahel, *Alienation*, trans. by Frederick Neuhouser and Alan E. Smith. New York: Columbia University Press, 2014.

Jaeschke, Walter, *Die Religionsphilosophie Hegels*. Darmstadt: Wissenschaftliche Buchgesellschaft, 1983.

Jaeschke, Walter, *Die Vernunft in der Religion: Studien zur Grundlegung der Religionsphilosophie Hegels*. Stuttgart-Bad Cannstatt: Frommann-Holzboog, 1986. (English translation: *Reason in Religion: The Foundations of Hegel's Philosophy of Religion*, trans. by J. Michael Stewart and Peter C. Hodgson. Berkeley and Los Angeles: University of California Press, 1990.)

Jakowenko, Boris, ed., *Geschichte des Hegelianismus in Rußland. Erster Band*. Prague: Josef Bartel, 1934.

Jakowenko, Boris, ed., *Zweiter Beitrag zur Geschichte des Hegelianismus in Rußland. Hegel und die Anfänge des Slawophilentums (1839–1849)*. Prague: Josef Bartel, 1935.

Janeff, Janko, "Zur Geschichte des russischen Hegelianismus." *Deutsche Vierteljahrsschrift für Literaturwissenschaft und Geistesgeschichte*, 10 (1932), 45–73.

Janke, Wolfgang, "Anerkennung. Fichtes Grundlegung des Rechtsgrundes." *Kant-Studien*, 82(2) (1991), 197–218.

Jarczyk, Gwendoline and Pierre-Jean Labarrière, *Le malheur de la conscience ou l'accès à la raison. Liberté de l'autoconscience: stoïcisme, scepticisme et la conscience malheureuse. Texte et commentaire*. Paris: Aubier, 1989.

Jarczyk, Gwendoline and Pierre-Jean Labarrière, *Les premiers combats de la reconnaissance. Maîtrise et servitude dans la Phénoménologie de l'esprit de Hegel*. Paris: Aubier, 1987.

Johnson, Frank, ed., *Alienation: Concept, Term, and Meanings*. New York and London: Seminar Press, 1973.

Jurist, Eliot, "Hegel's Concept of Recognition." *The Owl of Minerva*, 19 (1987), 5–22.

Jurist, Eliot, "Recognition and Self-Knowledge." *Hegel-Studien*, 21 (1986), 143–150.

Kainz, Howard P., *Hegel's Phenomenology, Part 1: Analysis and Commentary.* Alabama: University of Alabama Press, 1976; Athens, OH: Ohio University Press, 1988; *Part 2: The Evolution of Ethical and Religious Consciousness to the Absolute Standpoint.* Athens, OH: Ohio University Press, 1983.

Kamenka, Eugene, *The Philosophy of Ludwig Feuerbach.* London: Routledge & Kegan Paul, 1970.

Kaufmann, Walter, "The Inevitability of Alienation," introductory essay in Richard Schacht, *Alienation.* London: George Allen & Unwin, 1971.

Kegel, Martin, *Bruno Bauer und seine Theorien über die Entstehung des Christentums.* Leipzig: Quelle & Meyer, 1908.

Kelly, Aileen, *Mikhail Bakunin: A Study in the Psychology and Politics of Utopianism.* New York: Clarendon Press, 1982.

Kelly, George A., "Notes on Hegel's Lordship and Bondage." *Review of Metaphysics*, 19 (1965), 780–802.

Kenafick, K. J., *Michael Bakunin and Karl Marx.* Melbourne: A. Mailer, 1948.

Kliem, Manfred, ed., *Friedrich Engels: Dokumente seines Lebens.* Frankfurt am Main: Röderberg-Verlag, 1977.

Kodalle, Klaus-M. and Tilman Reitz, eds., *Bruno Bauer (1809–1882): Ein "Partisan des Weltgeistes"?* Würzburg: Königshausen & Neumann, 2010.

Kohut, Adolph, *Ludwig Feuerbach. Sein Leben und seine Werke.* Leipzig: F. Eckardt, 1909.

Kojève, Alexandre, *Introduction à la lecture de Hegel. Leçons sur la Phénoménologie de l'esprit professées de 1933 à 1939 à l'École des Hautes Études*, ed. by Raymond Queneau. Paris: Gallimard, 1947. (English translation: *Introduction to the Reading of Hegel: Lectures on the Phenomenology of Spirit*, trans. by Allan Bloom. Ithaca: Cornell University Press, 1980.)

Kossoff, Philip, *Valiant Heart: A Biography of Heinrich Heine.* New York: Cornwall Books, 1983.

Koyré, Alexandre, *Études sur l'historie de la pensée philosophique en Russie.* Paris: Librairie philosophique J. Vrin, 1950.

Krijnen, Christian, ed., *Recognition: German Idealism as an Ongoing Challenge.* Leiden and Boston: Brill, 2013.

Kroneberg, Lutz and Rolf Schloesser, *Weber-Revolte 1844. Der schlesische Weberaufstand im Spiegel der zeitgenössischen Publizistik und Literatur.* Cologne: C. W. Leske, 1979.

Krüger, Eduard, *Heine und Hegel. Dichtung, Philosophie und Politik bei Heinrich Heine.* Kronberg: Scriptor-Verlag, 1977.

Kupisch, Karl, *Vom Pietismus zum Kommunismus.* Berlin: Lettner-Verlag, 1953.

Lämke, Ortwin, *Heines Begriff der Geschichte. Der Journalist Heinrich Heine und die Julimonarchie.* Stuttgart and Weimar: J. B. Metzler, 1997.

Landry, Stan M., "From Orthodoxy to Atheism: The Apostasy of Bruno Bauer: 1835–1843." *Journal of Religion and Society*, 13 (2011), 1–20.

Lefebvre, Jean Pierre, *Der gute Trommler. Heines Beziehung zu Hegel*, trans. by Peter Schöttler. Hamburg: Hoffmann und Campe, 1986.

Leier, Mark, *Bakunin: The Creative Passion: A Biography*. New York: Thomas Dunne Books, 2006.

Lenz, Max, *Geschichte der Königlichen Friedrich-Wilhelms-Universität zu Berlin*, vols. 1–2.2. Halle: Verlag der Buchhandlung des Waisenhauses, 1910–1918.

Leopold, David, "The Hegelian Antisemitism of Bruno Bauer." *History of European Ideas*, 25 (1999), 179–206.

Levine, Norman, *Divergent Paths: The Hegelian Foundations of Marx's Method*. Lanham and Oxford: Lexington Books, 2006.

Liedtke, Christian, *Heinrich Heine*. Reinbek bei Hamburg: Rowohlt Verlag, 1997 (2006).

Löwith, Karl, *From Hegel to Nietzsche: The Revolution in Nineteenth-Century Thought*, trans. by David E. Green. London: Constable and Co., 1965.

Lowrie, Walter, *Kierkegaard*. London: Oxford University Press, 1938.

Lowrie, Walter, *A Short Life of Kierkegaard*. Princeton: Princeton University Press, 1942.

MacLaughlin, Paul, *Mikhail Bakunin: The Philosophical Basis of His Anarchism*. New York: Algora Publishing, 2002.

Mandelbaum, Maurice, *History, Man, and Reason: A Study of Nineteenth-Century Thought*. Baltimore and London: Johns Hopkins University Press, 1971.

Marcus, Steven, *Engels, Manchester and the Working Class*. New York: Random House, 1974.

Marcuse, Herbert, *Collected Papers of Herbert Marcuse*, vols. 1–6, ed. by Douglas Kellner and Clayton Pierce. London and New York: Routledge, 2017.

Marcuse, Herbert, *Heideggerian Marxism*, ed. by Richard Wolin and John Abromeit. Lincoln and London: University of Nebraska Press, 2005.

Marcuse, Herbert, *One-Dimensional Man: Studies in the Ideology of Advanced Industrial Society*. London and New York: Routledge, 2002.

Marcuse, Herbert, *Reason and Revolution: Hegel and the Rise of Social Theory*. Boston: Beacon, 1960.

Marx, Werner, *Das Selbstbewußtsein in Hegels Phänomenologie des Geistes*. Frankfurt am Main: Klosterman, 1986.

Mayer, Gustav, *Friedrich Engels: A Biography*, trans. by Gilbert Highet and Helen Highet, ed. by Richard Howard Stafford Crossman. London: Chapman & Hall, 1936.

Mayer, Gustav, *Friedrich Engels. Eine Biographie*, vol. 1, *Friedrich Engels in seiner Frühzeit 1820 bis 1851*. Berlin and Heidelberg: Springer, 1920. (The second volume of Mayer's biography only appeared in 1934, when it was printed along with a revised edition of the first volume: *Friedrich Engels. Eine Biographie*, vol. 1,

*Friedrich Engels in seiner Frühzeit 1820 bis 1851*, and vol. 2, *Engels und der Aufstieg der Arbeiterbewegung in Europa*, 2nd ed. The Hague: Martinus Nijhoff, 1934.)

McCarney, Joseph, *Hegel on History*. London and New York: Routledge, 2000.

McCarthy, Vincent A., *The Phenomenology of Moods in Kierkegaard*. The Hague and Boston: Martinus Nijhoff, 1978.

McLellan, David, *Engels*. Glasgow: Fontana/Collins, 1977.

McLellan, David, *The Young Hegelians and Karl Marx*. New York: F. A. Praeger, 1969.

Mehring, Franz, *Karl Marx: The Story of His Life*, trans. by Edward Fitzgerald. Ann Arbor: University of Michigan Press, 1962.

Mendel, Arthur P., *Michael Bakunin: Roots of Apocalypse*. New York: Praeger Publishers, 1981.

Merklinger, Philip M., *Philosophy, Theology, and Hegel's Berlin Philosophy of Religion, 1821–1827*. Albany: State University of New York Press, 1993.

Mertz, John Theodore, *History of European Thought in the Nineteenth Century*, vols. 1–4. Edinburgh: W. Blackwood, 1896–1912.

Meszaros, Istvan, *Marx's Theory of Alienation*. New York: Harper & Row, 1972.

Miles, Thomas P., "The Ethics of Resistance: Camus' Encounter with German Idealism," in Jon Stewart, ed., *The Palgrave Handbook of German Idealism and Existentialism*. Basingstoke and New York: Palgrave Macmillan, 2020, pp. 439–472.

Moggach, Douglas, "Fichte's Theories of Intersubjectivity." *The European Legacy*, 1 (6) (1996), 1934–1948.

Moggach, Douglas, ed., *The New Hegelians: Politics and Philosophy in the Hegelian School*. Cambridge: Cambridge University Press, 2006.

Moggach, Douglas, *The Philosophy and Politics of Bruno Bauer*. Cambridge: Cambridge University Press, 2003.

Moggach, Douglas, ed., *Politics, Religion, and Art: Hegelian Debates*. Evanston: Northwestern University Press, 2011.

Moggach, Douglas, "Post-Kantian Perfectionism," in Douglas Moggach, ed., *Politics, Religion, and Art: Hegelian Debates*. Evanston: Northwestern University Press, 2011, pp. 179–200.

Moggach, Douglas, "Republican Rigorism and Emancipation in Bruno Bauer," in Douglas Moggach, ed., *The New Hegelians: Politics and Philosophy in the Hegelian School*. Cambridge: Cambridge University Press, 2006, pp. 114–135.

Morris, Brian, *Bakunin: The Philosophy of Freedom*. Montreal: Black Rose Books, 1993.

Morris, Warren Frederick, *Escaping Alienation: A Philosophy of Alienation and De-alienation*. Lanham, MD: University Press of America, 2002.

Moyar, Dean, "Fichte's Organic Unification: Recognition and the Self-Overcoming of Social Contract Theory," in Gabriel Gottlieb, ed., *Fichte's Foundations of Natural Right: A Critical Guide*. Cambridge: Cambridge University Press, 2016, pp. 218–238

Moyar, Dean, ed., *The Routledge Companion of Nineteenth-Century Philosophy*. London and New York: Routledge, 2010.

Neuhouser, Frederick, "Deducing Desire and Recognition in the *Phenomenology of Spirit*." *Journal of the History of Philosophy*, 24 (1986), 243–262.

Neuhouser, Frederick, *Foundations of Hegel's Social Theory: Actualizing Freedom*. Cambridge, MA: Harvard University Press, 2003.

Nicolaevsky, Boris and Otto Mänchen-Helfen, *Karl Marx: Man and Fighter*. London: Methuen, 1936.

Nicolaus, Helmut, *Hegels Theorie der Entfremdung*. Heidelberg: Manutius, 1995.

Nicolin, Günter, ed., *Hegel in Berichten seiner Zeitgenossen*. Hamburg: Felix Meiner, 1970.

Ollman, Bertell, *Alienation: Marx's Conception of Man in Capitalist Society*. London and New York: Cambridge University Press, 1971.

O'Neill, John, ed., *Hegel's Dialectic of Desire and Recognition: Texts and Commentary*. Albany: State University of New York Press, 1996.

Oppy, Graham and N. N. Trakakis, eds., *Nineteenth-Century Philosophy of Religion*. London and New York: Routledge, 2014 (*The History of Western Philosophy of Religion*, vol. 4).

O'Regan, Cyril, *The Heterodox Hegel*. Albany: State University of New York Press, 1994.

Ottmann, Henning, "Herr und Knecht bei Hegel: Bemerkungen zu einer misverstandenen Dialektik." *Zeitschrift für Philosophische Forschung*, 35 (1981), 365–384.

Paris, Bernard J., *Dostoevsky's Greatest Characters*. New York: Palgrave Macmillan, 2008.

Pattison, George, "The Present Age: The Age of the City." *Kierkegaard Studies Yearbook* (1999), 1–20.

Peled, Yoav, "From Theology to Sociology: Bruno Bauer and Karl Marx on the Question of Jewish Emancipation." *History of Political Thought*, 13(3) (1992), 463–485.

Perkins, Robert L., ed., *History and System: Hegel's Philosophy of History*. Albany: State University of New York Press, 1984.

Perkins, Robert L., ed., *The Sickness unto Death*. Macon, GA: Mercer University Press, 1987 (*International Kierkegaard Commentary*, vol. 19).

Petkanič, Milan, "Passion and Age: Kierkegaard's Diagnosis of the Present Age." *Human Affairs: A Postdisciplinary Journal for Humanities and Social Sciences*, 14(2) (2004), 165–182.

Phelan, Anthony, *Reading Heinrich Heine*. Cambridge: Cambridge University Press, 2006.

Pinkard, Terry, *German Philosophy 1760–1860: The Legacy of Idealism*. Cambridge: Cambridge University Press, 2002.

Pinkard, Terry, *Hegel: A Biography*. Cambridge: Cambridge University Press, 2000.

Pinkard, Terry, *Hegel's Phenomenology: The Sociality of Reason*. Cambridge: Cambridge University Press, 1994.

Pippin, Robert B., *Hegel on Self-Consciousness: Desire and Death in the Phenomenology of Spirit*. Princeton and Oxford: Princeton University Press, 2011.

Pippin, Robert B., *Hegel's Practical Philosophy: Rational Agency as Ethical Life.* Cambridge: Cambridge University Press, 2008.

Planty-Bonjour, Guy, *Hegel et la pensée philosophique en Russie 1830–1917.* The Hague: Martinus Nijhoff, 1974.

Pöggeler, Otto, *Hegels Idee einer Phänomenologie des Geistes.* Freiburg and Munich: Karl Alber, 1973.

Pölcher, Helmut, "Schellings Auftreten in Berlin (1841) nach Hörerberichten." *Zeitschrift für Religions- und Geistesgeschichte,* 6(3) (1954), 193–215.

Popitz, Heinrich, *Der entfremdete Mensch: Zeitkritik und Geschichtsphilosophie des jungen Marx.* Basel: Verlag für Recht und Gesellschaft, 1953.

Pyziur, Eugene, *The Doctrine of Anarchism of Michael A. Bakunin.* Milwaukee: Marquette University Press, 1955.

Quante, Michael and Amir Mohseni, eds., *Die linken Hegelianer Studien zum Verhältnis von Religion und Politik im Vormärz.* Paderborn: Wilhelm Fink, 2015.

Quante, Michael and David P. Schweikard, eds., *Marx Handbuch: Leben, Werke, Wirkung.* Stuttgart: J. B. Metzler, 2016.

Rae, Gavin, "Hegel, Alienation, and the Phenomenological Development of Consciousness." *International Journal of Philosophical Studies,* 20(1) (2012), 23–42.

Rae, Gavin, *Realizing Freedom: Hegel, Sartre, and the Alienation of Human Being.* London: Palgrave MacMillan, 2011.

Randolph, John, *The House in the Garden: The Bakunin Family and the Romance of Russian Idealism.* Ithaca: Cornell University Press, 2007.

Rauch, Leo, "Desire, An Elemental Passion in Hegel's *Phenomenology.*" *Analecta Husserliana,* 28 (1990), 193–207.

Régnier, Marcel, "Hegel in France." *Bulletin of the Hegel Society of Great Britain,* 8 (1983), 10–20.

Rockmore, Tom, *Marx after Marxism: The Philosophy of Karl Marx.* Oxford: Blackwell, 2002.

Rosen, Zvi, *Bruno Bauer and Karl Marx: The Influence of Bruno Bauer on Marx's Thought.* The Hague: Martinus Nijhoff, 1977.

Rosen, Zvi, "The Influence of Bruno Bauer on Marx's Concept of Alienation." *Social Theory and Practice,* 1 (1970), 50–68.

Rotenstreich, Nathan, *Alienation: The Concept and Its Reception.* Leiden: E. J. Brill, 1989.

Rubel, Maximilien and Margaret Manale, *Marx without Myth: A Chronological Study of His Life and Work.* New York: Harper & Row, 1975.

Rühle, Otto, *Karl Marx: His Life and Work.* London: George Allen & Unwin Ltd., 1929.

Sammons, Jeffery L., *Heinrich Heine: A Modern Biography.* Manchester: Carcanet New Press, 1979.

Samyn, Liesbet, "How to Cure Despair: On Irony and the Unhappy Consciousness." *Kierkegaard Studies Yearbook* (2009), 317–351.

Samyn, Liesbet, "Yearning for the Grave: The Unhappy Consciousness in Hegel's *Phenomenology of Spirit* and in Kierkegaard's *Either/Or*," in Andreas Arndt, ed., *Geist? Zweiter Teil.* Berlin: Akademie Verlag, 2011, pp. 255–261.

Sarkar, Husain, *The Toils of Understanding: An Essay on "The Present Age".* Macon, GA: Mercer University Press, 2000.

Sayers, Sean, *Marx and Alienation: Essays on Hegelian Themes.* Basingstoke and New York: Palgrave Macmillan, 2013.

Scanlan, James P., *Dostoevsky the Thinker.* Ithaca and London: Cornell University Press, 2002.

Schacht, Richard, *Alienation.* London: George Allen & Unwin, 1971.

Schacht, Richard, *The Future of Alienation.* Urbana: University of Illinois Press, 1994.

Schacht, Richard, *Nietzsche.* London: Routledge, 1983.

Schlitt, Dale M., *Divine Subjectivity: Understanding Hegel's Philosophy of Religion.* London and Toronto: Associated University Presses, 1990.

Schmidt am Busch, Hans-Christoph and Christopher F. Zurn, *The Philosophy of Recognition: Historical and Contemporary Perspectives.* Lanham: Lexington Books, 2010.

Schnädelbach, Herbert, *Philosophy in Germany 1831–1933*, trans. by Eric Matthews. Cambridge: Cambridge University Press, 1984.

Schuffenhauer, Werner, *Feuerbach und der junge Marx. Zur Entstehungsgeschichte der marxistischen Weltanschauung*, 2nd revised ed. Berlin: VEB Deutscher Verlag der Wissenschaften, 1972.

Schulz, Heiko, "Marheineke: The Volatilization of Christian Doctrine," in Jon Stewart, ed., *Kierkegaard and His German Contemporaries*, Tome II, *Theology*. Aldershot and Burlington: Ashgate, 2007 (*Kierkegaard Research: Sources, Reception and Resources*, vol. 6), pp. 117–142.

Schwarzschild, Leopold, *The Red Prussian.* New York: Charles Scribners, 1947.

Schweitzer, Albert, *The Quest of the Historical Jesus: A Critical Study from Reimarus to Wrede*, with an Introduction by James M. Robinson. New York: MacMillan, 1961.

Schweitzer, David R. and R. Felix Geyer, eds., *Alienation Theories and De-alienation Strategies: Comparative Perspectives in Philosophy and the Social Sciences.* Northwood: Sciences Reviews Ltd., 1989.

Schweitzer, David R. and R. Felix Geyer, eds., *Theories of Alienation: Critical Perspectives in Philosophy and the Social Sciences.* Leiden: Martinus Nijhoff, 1976.

Seeger, Reinhart, *Friedrich Engels. Die religiöse Entwicklung eines Spätpietisten und Frühsozialisten.* Halle: Akademischer Verlag, 1935.

Siebert, Rudolf J., *Hegel's Philosophy of History: Theological, Humanistic and Scientific Elements.* Washington, DC: University Press of America, 1979.

Siep, Ludwig, *Anerkennung als Prinzip der praktischen Philosophie. Untersuchungen zu Hegels Jenaer Philosophie des Geistes.* Freiburg: Karl Alber, 1979.

Siep, Ludwig, "Der Kampf um Anerkennung zu Hegels Auseinandersetzung mit Hobbes in den Jenaer Schriften." *Hegel-Studien*, 9 (1974), 155–207.

Smith, Steven B., "Hegel on Slavery and Domination." *Review of Metaphysics*, 46 (1992), 197–124.

Solomon, Robert C., *In the Spirit of Hegel: A Study of G. W. F. Hegel's Phenomenology of Spirit*. New York and Oxford: Oxford University Press, 1983.

Sorensen, Michael Kuur, *Young Hegelians Before and After 1848: When Theory Meets Reality*. Frankfurt am Main: Peter Lang, 2011.

Speight, Allen, *Hegel, Literature and the Problem of Agency*. Cambridge: Cambridge University Press, 2004.

Speight, Allen, *The Philosophy of Hegel*. Stocksfield: Acumen, 2008.

Starcke, C. N., *Ludwig Feuerbach*. Stuttgart: Ferdinand Enke, 1885.

Stepanova, Evgeniia Akimovna, *Engels: A Short Biography*. Moscow: Progress Publishers, 1988.

Stepelevich, Lawrence S., "Hegelian Nihilism: Karl Werder and the Class of 1841." *Philosophical Forum*, 46(3) (2015), 249–273.

Stewart, Jon, "The Architectonic of Hegel's *Phenomenology of Spirit*." *Philosophy and Phenomenological Research*, 55(4) (1995), 747–776.

Stewart, Jon, *The Cultural Crisis of the Danish Golden Age: Heiberg, Martensen and Kierkegaard*. Copenhagen: Museum Tusculanum Press, 2015 (*Danish Golden Age Studies*, vol. 9).

Stewart, Jon, "Die Rolle des unglücklichen Bewußtseins in Hegels *Phänomenologie des Geistes*." *Deutsche Zeitschrift für Philosophie*, 39 (1991), 12–21.

Stewart, Jon, "El oficio de la filosofía. La dialéctica de la teoría y la práctica," in Hans Hiram Pacheco García and Victor Hugo Robledo Martínez, eds., *Las preguntas de la Esfinge 5. Psicoanálisis y figuras de la interpretación*. Zacatecas: Taberna Libraria Editores, 2020, pp. 169–192.

Stewart, Jon, "Hegel: Kierkegaard's Reading and Use of Hegel's Primary Texts," in Jon Stewart, ed., *Kierkegaard and His German Contemporaries*, Tome I, *Philosophy*. Aldershot and Burlington: Ashgate, 2007 (*Kierkegaard Research: Sources, Reception and Resources*, vol. 6), pp. 97–165.

Stewart, Jon, "Hegel's Historical Methodology in *The Concept of Irony*." *Kierkegaard Studies Yearbook* (2011), 81–100.

Stewart, Jon, *Hegel's Interpretation of the Religions of the World: The Logic of the Gods*. Oxford: Oxford University Press, 2018.

Stewart, Jon, "Hegel's *Phenomenology* as a Systematic Fragment," in Frederick C. Beiser, ed., *The Cambridge Companion to Hegel and Nineteenth-Century Philosophy*. Cambridge and New York: Cambridge University Press, 2008, pp. 74–93.

Stewart, Jon, "Hegel's Theory of the Emergence of Subjectivity and the Conditions for the Development of Human Rights." *Filozofia*, 74(6) (2019), 456–471.

Stewart, Jon, "Heiberg's Conception of Speculative Drama and the Crisis of the Age: Martensen's Analysis of *Fata Morgana*," in Jon Stewart, ed., *The Heibergs and the Theater: Between Vaudeville, Romantic Comedy and National Drama*.

Copenhagen: Museum Tusculanum Press, 2012 (*Danish Golden Age Studies*, vol. 7), pp. 139–160.

Stewart, Jon, *A History of Hegelianism in Golden Age Denmark*, Tome I, *The Heiberg Period: 1824–1836*, Tome II, *The Martensen Period: 1837–1842*. Copenhagen: C. A. Reitzel, 2007 (*Danish Golden Age Studies*, vol. 3).

Stewart, Jon, *Idealism and Existentialism: Hegel and Nineteenth- and Twentieth-Century European Philosophy*. New York and London: Continuum International Publishing, 2010.

Stewart, Jon, "Kierkegaard's Phenomenology of Despair in *The Sickness unto Death*." *Kierkegaard Studies Yearbook* (1997), 117–143.

Stewart, Jon, *Kierkegaard's Relations to Hegel Reconsidered*. New York: Cambridge University Press, 2003.

Stewart, Jon, "La 'nota discordante' de Hegel: La crisis cultural y la inspiración detrás de *Sobre la importancia de la filosofía para la época presente* de Heiberg." *Estudios Kierkegaardianos. Revista de filosofía*, 4 (2018), 25–44.

Stewart, Jon, ed., *The Palgrave Handbook of German Idealism and Existentialism*. Basingstoke and New York: Palgrave Macmillan, 2020.

Stewart, Jon, "Schopenhauer's Charge and Modern Academic Philosophy: Some Problems Facing Philosophical Pedagogy." *Metaphilosophy*, 26(3) (1995), 270–278.

Stewart, Jon, *Søren Kierkegaard: Subjectivity, Irony and the Crisis of Modernity*. Oxford: Oxford University Press, 2015.

Stewart, Jon, *The Unity of Content and Form in Philosophical Writing: The Perils of Conformity*. London, New Delhi, New York and Sydney: Bloomsbury, 2013.

Stewart, Jon, *The Unity of Hegel's Phenomenology of Spirit: A Systematic Interpretation*. Evanston: Northwestern University Press, 2000.

Stewart, Jon, "Werder: The Influence of Werder's Lectures and *Logik* on Kierkegaard's Thought," in Jon Stewart, ed., *Kierkegaard and His German Contemporaries*, Tome I, *Philosophy*. Aldershot and Burlington: Ashgate, 2007 (*Kierkegaard Research: Sources, Reception and Resources*, vol. 6), pp. 335–371.

Stone, Alison, ed., *The Edinburgh Critical History of Nineteenth-Century Philosophy*. Edinburgh: Edinburgh University Press, 2011.

Stuke, Horst, *Philosophie der Tat. Studien zur Verwirklichung der Philosophie bei den Junghegelianern*. Stuttgart: Ernst Klett, 1963.

Taylor, Charles, "The Politics of Recognition," in Amy Gutman, ed., *Multiculturalism: Examining the Politics of Recognition*. Princeton: Princeton University Press, 1994, pp. 25–73.

Ten, C. L., ed., *The Nineteenth Century*. London and New York: Routledge, 1994 (*Routledge History of Philosophy*, vol. 7).

Testa, Italo and Luigi Ruggiu, eds., *"I That Is We, We That Is I." Perspectives on Contemporary Hegel Social Ontology, Recognition, Naturalism, and the Critique of Kantian Constructivism*. Leiden and Boston: Brill, 2016.

Thomas, Paul, *Karl Marx and the Anarchists*. London and Boston: Routledge & Kegan Paul, 1980.

Thulstrup, Niels, *Kierkegaard's Relation to Hegel*, trans. by George L. Stengren. Princeton: Princeton University Press, 1980.

Tilliette, Xavier, ed., *Schelling im Spiegel seiner Zeitgenossen*. Turin: Bottega d'Erasmo, 1974.

Toews, John Edward, *Hegelianism: The Path toward Dialectical Humanism, 1805–1841*. Cambridge: Cambridge University Press, 1980.

Tomba, Massimiliano, "Exclusiveness and Political Universalism in Bruno Bauer," in Douglas Moggach, ed., *The New Hegelians: Politics and Philosophy in the Hegelian School*. Cambridge: Cambridge University Press, 2006, pp. 91–113.

Tomba, Massimiliano, *Krise und Kritik bei Bruno Bauer. Kategorien des Politischen im nachhegelschen Denken*. Frankfurt am Main: Peter Lang, 2005.

Tomba, Massimiliano, *Marx's Temporalities*, trans. by Peter D. Thomas and Sara R. Farris. Leiden and Boston: Brill, 2013 (*Historical Materialism*, vol. 44).

Tucker, Robert C., *Philosophy and Myth in Karl Marx*. Cambridge: Cambridge University Press, 1972.

Ullrich, Horst, *Der junge Engels*, vols. 1–2. Berlin: Deutscher Verlag der Wissenschaften, 1961–1966.

Verene, Donald P., *Hegel's Recollection: A Study of Images in the Phenomenology of Spirit*. Albany: State University of New York Press, 1985.

Wahl, Jean, *La conscience malheureuse*. Paris: Denoël et Steele, 1936.

Walicki, Andrzej, *A History of Russian Thought from the Enlightenment to Marxism*, trans. by Hilda Andrews-Rusiecka. Stanford: Stanford University Press, 1979.

Walker, John, *History, Spirit and Experience: Hegel's Conception of the Historical Task of Philosophy in His Age*. Frankfurt am Main and New York: Peter Lang, 1995.

Wartofsky, Marx W., *Feuerbach*. Cambridge: Cambridge University Press, 1982.

Waser, Ruedi, *Autonomie des Selbstbewußtseins. Eine Untersuchung zum Verhältnis von Bruno Bauer und Karl Marx (1835–1843)*. Tübingen: Francke Verlag, 1994.

Welz, Claudia, "Kierkegaard and Phenomenology," in John Lippitt and George Pattison, eds., *The Oxford Handbook of Kierkegaard*. Oxford: Oxford University Press, 2012, pp. 432–455.

Westphal, Merold, *History and Truth in Hegel's Phenomenology*. Atlantic Highlands: Humanities Press, 1979.

Widmann, Franz, *Hegel: An Illustrated Biography*, trans. by Joachim Neugroschel. New York: Pegasus, 1968.

Wildt, Andreas, "'Recognition' in Psychoanalysis," in Hans-Christoph Schmidt am Busch and Christopher F. Zurn, eds., *The Philosophy of Recognition: Historical and Contemporary Perspectives*. Lanham: Rowman and Littlefield, 2010, pp. 189–209.

Wilkins, Burleigh Taylor, *Hegel's Philosophy of History*. Ithaca: Cornell University Press, 1974.

Williams, Robert R., *Hegel's Ethics of Recognition*. Berkeley: University of California Press, 1997.

Williams, Robert R., *Recognition: Fichte and Hegel on the Other*. Albany: State University New York Press, 1992.

Wilson, John R., "'Signs of the Times' and 'The Present Age': Essays of Crisis." *Western Humanities Review*, 26 (1972), 369–374.

Wind, H. C., *Anerkendelse. Et tema i Hegels og moderne filosofi*. Aarhus: Aarhus Universitetsforlag, 1998.

Windfuhr, Manfred, "Heine und Hegel. Rezeption und Produktion," in Manfred Windfuhr, ed., *Internationaler Heine-Kongreß 1972*. Hamburg: Hoffmann und Campe, 1973, pp. 261–280.

Winiger, Josef, *Ludwig Feuerbach, Denker der Menschlichkeit*. Darmstadt: Lambert Schneider Verlag, 2011.

Winnicott, D. W., *Playing and Reality*. London and New York: Routledge, 2005.

Wood, Allen W., *Hegel's Ethical Thought*. Cambridge: Cambridge University Press, 1990.

Wood, Allen W., *Karl Marx*. London: Routledge & Kegan Paul, 1981.

Wood, Allen W. and Songsuk Susan Hahn, eds., *The Cambridge History of Philosophy in the Nineteenth Century (1790–1870)*. Cambridge: Cambridge University Press, 2012.

Yovel, Yirmiahu, "Hegel's Dictum that the Rational is Actual and the Actual is Rational: Its Ontological Content and Its Function in Discourse," in Jon Stewart, ed., *The Hegel Myths and Legends*. Evanston: Northwestern University Press, 1996, pp. 26–41.

Zinke, Jochen, "Heine und Hegel. Stationen der Forschung." *Hegel-Studien*, 14 (1979), 295–312.

# INDEX OF NAMES

# SUBJECT INDEX